HOMOSEXUALITY

HOMOSEXUALITY
Social, Psychological, and Biological Issues

Edited by

William Paul, *Ed. D., Co-Editor*

James D. Weinrich, *Ph.D., Co-Editor & Managing Editor*

John C. Gonsiorek, *Ph.D., Associate Editor*

Mary E. Hotvedt, *Ph.D., Associate Editor*

Final Report of the SPSSI Task Force on Sexual Orientation

Published in cooperation with the
Society for the Psychological Study of Social Issues

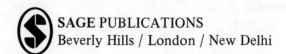

SAGE PUBLICATIONS
Beverly Hills / London / New Delhi

For information address:

SAGE Publications, Inc.
275 South Beverly Drive
Beverly Hills, California 90212

SAGE Publications India Pvt. Ltd.
C-236 Defence Colony
New Delhi 110 024, India

SAGE Publications Ltd
28 Banner Street
London EC1Y 8QE, England

Printed in the United States of America

Library of Congress Cataloging in Publication Data

Main entry under title:

Homosexuality.

  Bibliography: p.

  Includes index.
    1. Homosexuality—Addresses, essays, lectures.
I. Paul, William, 1939-   . II. Society for the
Psychological Study of Social Issues.
HQ76.25.H6735   306.7'66   82-5653
ISBN 0-8039-1825-9   AACR2

FIRST PRINTING

Dedicated to
Clara Mayo
1931-1981
President of
The Society for the Psychological Study of Social Issues
1981-1982,
who fought against the poison of labels,
and for the individuality of all people.

CONTENTS

FOREWORD

You are about to read a unique and extraordinary book: unique in its broadly multidisciplinary flavor; extraordinary in the richness and depth of its analysis. This book is neither a dry, clinical appraisal of homosexuality nor a "how to" manual. Rather, it is a scholarly analysis that is unusually well-written, thorough, thoughtful, and provocative. You may find portions of this book controversial, disturbing, even disagreeable—but you will surely find the book very much worth your while.

Since its inception nearly 50 years ago, SPSSI (The Society for the Psychological Study of Social Issues) has been committed to the application of social scientific knowledge, to a clearer understanding of social issues. SPSSI has also long been committed to the view that although collectively engineered projects are notoriously painful to produce, the resulting collaboration and quality more than justify any time, trouble, or inconvenience. The present project is a prototypical illustration of this SPSSI philosophy. The book's 31 chapters are the culmination of four years of hard work and struggle by the project's four editors, numerous contributing authors, and a bevy of advisors. It has been my privilege to serve as liaison between SPSSI and the key individuals involved in this project. I have read every chapter and countless newsletters and written exchanges. It is with enormous pleasure that I have watched the transformation of this project from a grandly ambitious idea into a genuinely important contribution.

We in SPSSI were pleased to authorize the formation of a task force on sexual orientation. We are proud and delighted to sponsor this, the outgrowth of its labors.

Jeffrey Z. Rubin

PREFACE

Until very recently, the study of homosexuality was entirely the concern of researchers in psychology, psychiatry, and biology. Their goal was usually an attempt to discover the origins of or the treatment for conduct widely viewed as perverse, abnormal, unnatural, or—most kindly—deviant. Many scientists in the recent past, even those with impeccable liberal credentials, pursued research which emphasized solely questions of etiology, which narrowly focused on differences between "homosexuals" and "heterosexuals" or which reduced all aspects of life to an appendage of a same-sex erotic choice.

The renaming of the study of homosexuality as the study of the lives of gay men and lesbians signals a basic shift away from these traditions. The recognition that gay people have a sociology, history, culture, and political economy represents a break with the past—and is not only important in and of itself but has helped to free psychologists, psychiatrists, and biologists from becoming obsessive about moral or mental health concerns. However, perhaps of more importance is that the focus of attention of these disciplines as they approach questions of gay male and lesbian life has largely abandoned lines of inquiry which existed simply to stigmatize the objects of their attention. While these negative research concerns retain some adherents, more and more our attention is engaged by a different range of problems.

An understanding of lives of gay men and lesbians has to begin with the largely hostile character of the society in which they acquire and maintain their same-gender erotic, affectional, intellectual, and cultural preferences. As an invisible minority, people with these desires and preferences cultivate them in secret, often in the face of angry and uncomprehending parents, brothers, sisters, peers, teachers, doctors, ministers—nearly everyone from whom they want love and kindness. The problem of intolerance toward those with same-gender erotic and affectional preferences must be recognized as a problem for the society similar to intolerance toward religious, ethnic, or racial groups. Once this is understood as the basic context, we may then be able to formulate appropriate research questions.

11

Whatever levels of unhappiness or dis-ease that might exist among gay men and lesbians have to be understood in terms of this social context. If the mundane activities of child care, church attendance, job security, meeting friends, falling in love are all undertaken with a sense of risk and danger from a potentially lethal environment, then clearly there can be no neutral study of mental health. The important issue, as psychologist Charles Silverstein has pointed out, is there can be no circumstance in which those with same-gender preferences can be compared with those with opposite-gender preferences using the latter as a control group. What could we possibly be "controlling" for?

There are many new and promising ways of thinking about gay men and lesbians. The view that they constitute a minority group, that the lesbian mother often shares the lifestyle of any single parent, that the gay couple goes through cycles of closeness and detachment similar to all couples, that there is nothing in modern evolutionary biology that places a same-gender preference outside of nature—in short, that gay people's lives must be understood as all lives are understood, using the skills of a humane human science—these are all commonalities that seem strange and odd to those still committed to studying the etiology and psychopathology of the individual homosexual.

One of the great advances in our understanding has been with the inclusion of gay male and lesbian scientists among those who can legitimately ask questions and supply the answers. Homosexuals were to be silent in our scientific inquiries, speaking only when asked a question. After all (it was argued), wouldn't scientists who were "homosexual" be biased? No one asked whether "heterosexual" scientists might not be prejudiced or might ask the wrong questions or mismanage the analysis. Heterosexuality, after all, was normal, and a lack of interest in a same-gender erotic partner was mistaken as scientific disinterest. A major force in the change to more adequate standards of research has been the activities of both scientists and nonscientists in gay male and lesbian communities who have resisted the oppressive consequences of what appeared to be objective research.

This volume, too, represents a new set of voices that need to be heard about the lives of gay people. As with all scientific enterprises, the findings are tentative, the methods public, and the answers subject to further testing. They are part of the beginning of a new inquiry—one long overdue.

John Gagnon

· I ·

Introduction

Edited by
William Paul and
James D. Weinrich

· 1 ·

A Short History of the Task Force on Sexual Orientation

John P. De Cecco

This book is the published report of the Task Force on Sexual Orientation to the Society for the Psychological Study of Social Issues (SPSSI), a division of the American Psychological Association. In April 1978, SPSSI President Lawrence Wrightsman authorized William Paul to establish in the society's name a task force "for the purpose of developing educational materials regarding the nature of homosexuality." Paul, who was then a doctoral student in education at Harvard University, as early as 1977 had spearheaded the effort to obtain sponsorship of a task force. His original intention was to compile a report of 100 pages or less which would be an accurate summary of current knowledge of homosexuality and could be made available to the media to counteract the misinformation and unfortunate stereotypes that were often disseminated.

Since the literature on homosexuality has been accumulating over the past century and increasing at a staggering rate, the plans for a short report soon were expanded into a book. Acting on the advice of the society, Paul obtained the assistance of three individuals who had wide knowledge of the field. In 1978, James Weinrich was a Junior Fellow in the Society of Fellows at Harvard. He joined the Task Force in what eventually became a triple capacity: general project coordinator (i.e., co-editor, along with Paul), editor of the Biology section of this book, and managing editor of the final publication. Weinrich had completed a dissertation on human sexuality and sociobiology at Harvard. John Gonsiorek, who completed his doctoral training in clinical psychology during the life of the Task Force, provided editorial leadership for the chapters on mental health: clinical conceptions, diagnoses, and treatment of homosexuality. Mary Hotvedt, who was then a doctoral student at the State University of New York at Stony Brook, took on the important editorial task of obtaining contributions dealing with interpersonal relations and parenting.

Each of the editors had been engaged in research on homosexuality: Weinrich, as mentioned, on sociobiology, Paul on preconceptions of homosexuality in the media and academic research, Gonsiorek on the psychological assessment of adjustment in homosexual men and women, and Hotvedt on lesbian mothers and their children. Their own active participation in research on homosexuality gave them ready access to a network of scholars on which to draw for contributions.

In launching the work of the Task Force the editors relied on an advisory committee of three members: John Gagnon, Evelyn Hooker, and myself. Our major function was to provide names of potential contributors and to critique successive drafts of the chapters on the basis of our own knowledge and research experience. On a rotational basis each of us chaired the advisory committee. We assisted Paul and Weinrich in planning presentations at the annual meetings of the American Psychological Association and presided over meetings of the task force itself, which were held annually in conjunction with the meetings of the association—first in Toronto (1978) and then in New York (1979), Montreal (1980), and finally in Los Angeles (1981). I believe I speak for all three members of the advisory committee in declaring that the editors and, through them, the authors were warmly receptive to our critiques and suggestions.

The initial task of the editors was to identify general areas and topics within areas to be covered by the report. The second was to find knowledgeable, qualified, and willing authors. In the search for authors, both the Women's Division of the American Psychological Association and the Association of Gay Psychologists were notably helpful. In selecting chapters, several issues were considered. It was, of course, necessary to find authors who were sympathetic to the goal of describing the incubus under which homosexuality labors but who would not sacrifice systematic inquiry to political advocacy. Contributors had to be able and willing to prepare pieces that would be faithful to knowledge in the field and yet comprehensible and stimulating for the educated lay reader. It was also essential to include authors of both sexes and all sexual orientations—since to do otherwise would be to practice social intolerance on one front while exposing it on another.

Not every contribution solicited or promised was delivered; not every article delivered was published; and no contribution escaped the awesome pruning that was the inevitable result of examination by layers of reviewers.

The final surgery and sewing-up were performed by Weinrich, who, as managing editor, was reminded by the publisher that short books often are read while long ones are ignored. Separate publication of the Mental Health section (see *American Behavioral Scientist,* March 1982, Volume 25, Number 4) permitted some extra pruning to be done in that section for this volume. Reports of some major studies germane to the book, like the one Michael Shively and I have conducted at the Center for Research and Education in Sexuality at San Francisco State University, could not be included, since final reports of our work had not been prepared as the manuscripts neared completion. Other potential contributors were fully occupied preparing their books and articles for publication.

No project involving so many participants and groups could escape its moments of confusion and even despair. All of the editors, who were in the process of establishing academic and professional careers, experienced major dislocations during the life of the project, which involved moving to new positions and often settling in new regions of the country. By publishing the Task Force newsletters, by corresponding voluminously, and by maintaining close telephone contact, the editors and the authors finally brought the project to completion.

SPSSI was solid in its support of the work of the Task Force. It provided the initial funding, which was supplemented in 1979 by the Mark De Wolfe Howe Fund at Harvard. Two of the society's presidents, Lawrence Wrightsman and June Tapp, showed great interest in the progress of the work. Three of SPSSI's members acted as intermediaries and expeditors: Lois Biener of Wellesley College, Marilynn Brewer of the University of California at Santa Barbara, and Jeffrey Rubin of Tufts University. After critiquing and obtaining SPSSI's review of the manuscript, they went on to facilitate its publication.

I view the volume as taking its honored place in the vast scholarly effort to detoxify homosexuality that began with Karl Heinrich Ulrichs in the nineteenth century and has continued with the work of Havelock Ellis, Magnus Hirschfeld, Alfred Kinsey and his colleagues and successors at Indiana University, and Evelyn Hooker. The volume, however, also stands as a unique enterprise in that the contributors are (for the most part) young men and women who, in the first bloom of their academic and professional careers, have matched fearlessness with scholarly competence in taking on homosexuality as a social issue.

• 2 •

Introduction

*William Paul
James D. Weinrich*

To most Americans, homosexual activities and people are mysterious. Recent controversies concerning sexual orientation have generated a considerable amount of emotional public debate, and in some cases this controversy has led to serious social conflicts. The authors of this volume are scholars who believe that factual information would be beneficial to this debate. Accordingly, we have compiled this collection of research on homosexual and bisexual behavior.

Our objectives have been

(1) to provide essays that can serve as a factual educational resource;
(2) to combine information from the social and biological sciences in order to apply it to social issues and questions of public policy;
(3) to elicit both positive and critical response from educational institutions, scientific organizations, and individuals or groups concerned with such social policy issues; and
(4) to translate these data into clear language that invites a wide audience to discuss this social issue.

These objectives reflect the essential goal of SPSSI itself: to apply scientific knowledge to social issues and public concerns.

But this volume is not a comprehensive study of homosexual behavior; the subject is far too complex. What we do provide, however, are *new* approaches from scholars in a *variety* of disciplines and comprehensible texts with the references scholars need to follow up the points we have made. Even so, there are very real limitations in applying social research to social policy—a question addressed in several of the chapters to follow.

Science is not a court of law whose results can either award or deny civil rights. In democratic nations, individual liberties are inherent, and individuals are presumed innocent of general prejudgments.

In the past, social science has been limited by moral and social doctrines about the ways humans ought to behave. The existence of any kind of doctrine tends to inhibit open scientific investigation by providing ready-made answers, and especially by limiting the kinds of questions that can be asked. Such quasi-official doctrines influence who gets tenure, whose research is funded, and whose work is cited by other workers. These powerful doctrines, seldom questioned in public debate, have serious consequences when people try to understand homosexuality. Indeed, a process of selective attention in the study of homosexuality has been documented by Gonsiorek (1977), Morin (1977), and others.

Part of the problem stems from an exaggerated concern for public sensibility. Homosexuality is often considered too hot to handle; supposedly the public would prefer to know nothing about it. But recently several public controversies have shown that substantial numbers of sincere people *are* seriously concerned about alleged dangers homosexuality might pose for young people and for society at large.

This book is designed to begin the process of providing better answers. It is divided into six sections, including Introduction and Conclusion, with each of the four topic areas edited by a different scholar. Since (arguably) the most common perception nowadays is that homosexuals are mentally ill, Section II covers mental health. Here we ask what kinds of psychotherapy are needed in the gay community, whether being homosexual in and of itself constitutes psychopathology, and so on. Probably the next most common feeling among lay persons is that there is something unnatural about homosexuality—homosexual acts do not result in reproduction, and many people do not detect homosexual feelings in themselves. Thus, section III is on biology. In the fourth section, on life adaptations, we see gay people as unsurprising members of the greater community—sometimes in terms an outsider would use, and sometimes the way homosexuals themselves would. Next, the social and cultural issues section addresses how societies as a whole relate to homosexuality—in legal matters and in the question of minority status accorded or denied to homosexuals.

In each chapter, we have asked the authors to end with a statement of conclusions, giving what they believe to be the consequences of their academic findings for society at large. The section editors have summarized these in their own summary and conclusions sections, which includes the final chapter summarizing the findings of the book as a whole.

In this multilayered process, there is of course no presumption that individual authors agree with each other or even with the final set of recommendations. But it is hoped that each conclusion would be endorsed by a majority of the authors—perhaps a different majority in each case.

· 3 ·

Whom and What We Study
Definition and Scope of
Sexual Orientation

William Paul
James D. Weinrich

The question of precisely who is and who is not a homosexual is a controversial issue in itself. Various kinds of behaviors and individual lifestyles have been confused with sexual orientation. Shively and De Cecco (1977) distinguished among social sex role (the way society expects you to act according to your sex), gender identity (whether you consider yourself female or male), and gender role (whether you act so as to be taken as male or female). Each of these has been confused with homosexuality. Variations in these parameters (e.g., cross-dressing) and in certain others (e.g., sado-masochism and fetishism) are not discussed in this volume because they occur among both heterosexuals and homosexuals.

"Gay" is a popular term for people who define themselves as homosexual, in contrast to the term "straight" originally used by gay people to describe heterosexuals, but also used widely by heterosexuals in other contexts. "Gay" is not a word recently adopted or stolen by homosexuals. Indeed, Boswell (1980) has shown that "gay" is a very old term that predates the word "homosexual," although its precise meaning has varied and is difficult to establish in some eras.

A person's sexual activity can be exclusively homosexual, but that person may not be gay according to that person's own point of view. Some authors (Morin & Garfinkle, 1978) have proposed that "gay" should refer only to those homosexuals who are publicly self-identified. Unfortunately, linguistic points cannot be made by prescription, and this helpful suggestion does not reflect actual use among either homosexual or heterosexual people. Likewise, the large number of complaints lodged by usage panels and in popular linguistics columns against the word "gay" are futile and wrong-headed (Bonnell, 1978).

The process of "coming out" and defining oneself as gay, together with the additional act of coming out publicly as gay, can create profound and dramatic events in the lives of homosexuals living in a hostile society. It is perhaps because of this that the term "sexual preference" is now popular. Yet we employ the term "sexual orientation" because most research findings indicate that homosexual feelings are a basic part of the individual's psyche, rather than something that is consciously chosen. The term "lifestyle" describes certain forms of gay social and cultural expression and does not describe the more fundamental sexual orientation, even though those expressions are undoubtedly chosen.

Bisexual experience is common, both historically and currently. A cross-cultural study of male homosexuals in America, Holland, and Denmark (Weinberg & Williams, 1974) found that 36 to 59 percent (depending on the country) of the most homosexual individuals studied had had heterosexual intercourse. Yet these men thought of themselves as gay and were drawn from gay communities. The sexual experience of lesbians is at least as diverse, and probably more so (Bell & Weinberg, 1978). In accord with the common practice in modern sex research, our use of the term "homosexual" includes those who may have had heterosexual experiences. "Bisexual" is used only when we want to indicate specifically someone whose attractions are not confined primarily to one sex. For further discussion of this question, see the introduction to the Mental Health section in this volume.

SEXUAL ACTIVITY

This aspect of sexual orientation seems to be especially fascinating to the public at large. But an examination of sexual activities alone conveys a narrow view of the people involved. Sharp divisions between homosexual and heterosexual activities have not been common in the histories of most societies (see Churchill, 1967; Ford & Beach, 1951). The studies by Kinsey and his associates (1948, 1953), based on in-depth interviews with over 15,000 subjects, indicated an amount of homosexual activity vaster than previously suspected. The original findings have recently been updated (Gebhard, 1972; Gebhard & Johnson, 1979), as Table 3.1 shows.

These figures cannot be used uncritically; they relate to a particular sample population at a particular time. Most of the statistics report behavior, as opposed to inner orientation or fantasy. This fact alone should recommend

TABLE 3.1   American Homosexuality According to Kinsey

	% Responding*	
	Men	Women
Had homosexual activity before puberty	47-57	30-43
Had more than "a little" homosexual fantasy during masturbation recently**	8-11	5-6
Had 5 or more partners or 21 or more orgasms from homosexual relations	10-17	3-5
Said he or she will probably have homosexual relations in the future	6-12	2-4
During most recent time period, had homosexual relations to orgasm and was		
never married	10-49	2-11
currently married	0-5	0-2
separated, widowed, or divorced	0-18	0-8

SOURCE: Gebhard and Johnson (1979). The authors warn that these figures underrepresent respondents with little education.
NOTE: Each range of percentages represents the second highest and second lowest figure for the various education/race/age breakdowns provided for that category.
*Respondents were of various races, educations, and ages over 16.
**Includes "present, but frequency unknown" category, the most common response.

caution to those who would conclude, for example, that *many* more men than women *today* are homosexual in *orientation*.

What effects have the Kinsey studies had on popular debate? At first, many found these figures hard to accept. The traditional image of homosexuals had been one of a tiny minority of mysterious individuals leading hidden lives in a few urban centers. Public beliefs apparently are changing, however, with popular estimates of the incidence of homosexuality becoming embarrassingly large. In a recent series of Gallup polls on homosexuality (1977), only 10 percent of those surveyed believed that less than 10 percent of males are homosexual (see Table 3.2). Over one-quarter believed that homosexuals represented 20 percent or more of the population—the latter proportion also holding true for the public's beliefs about lesbians. Whether these opinions simply indicate increased media coverage of homosexuality or are derived from personal experience, disclosure by friends, fantasy, or increased direct awareness remains a mystery.

Other surveys (ably summarized by Gebhard, 1972) have tended to yield figures for exclusive homosexuals in the United States of about 2 to 5 percent. A major problem facing such studies is the risk involved in self-disclosure, especially where the studies fail to ensure complete anonymity. It is possible—indeed, it seems quite likely—that these recurrent 2-5 percent figures represent those people who live gay lifestyles within tolerant or cosmopolitan communities.

These figures, taken together, amount to perhaps 25 million Americans

TABLE 3.2   American Homosexuality According to the Public*

| | % Responding | |
Estimated % of Homosexuality in Population	Male Homosexuals	Female Homosexuals
less than 10	20	22
10 to 19	19	17
20 or more	27	26
don't know	34	35

SOURCE: Gallup Poll, July 1977.
*"Just your best guess, what percentage of the wo/men in the United States do you think are homosexual?"

with varying degrees of homosexual orientation (some proportion being children who will grow up to experience homosexual orientations). While self-defined gay people are fewer, they certainly number several millions of persons. According to which definition of "homosexual" one uses, homosexuals represent the first, second, or third most common minority in the United States today.

THE SOCIAL PROFILE OF THE HOMOSEXUAL POPULATION

The kinds of questions so commonly asked about sexual orientation tend to focus our attention on intensely personal aspects such as sexual activity, psychological conditions, and self-identification. This rather limited view can be expanded by examining some of the social characteristics of homosexuals. We have found three to be especially important:

Social Invisibility: The great majority of homosexuals, including openly gay and lesbian people, are not easily identifiable.
Social Diversity: There are as many kinds of homosexuals as there are kinds of heterosexuals.
Social and Personal Differentiation: The ways in which people adapt to having a homosexual orientation vary according to the relative tolerance or hostility of the social environment.

Social invisibility creates an obstacle to study and understanding. Researchers commonly have difficulty in finding a representative sample of homosexuals. Even Kinsey, after studying so many homosexuals for so long, estimated that he could have accurately guessed homosexual orientation in advance in only 15 percent of those he interviewed.

Social diversity has been extremely well documented in the recent studies (Bell & Weinberg, 1978; Bell, Weinberg, & Hammersmith, 1981) conducted for the Kinsey Institute with research funds from the National Institute of Mental Health. Even these researchers encountered problems in trying to assemble the most representative group of respondents. Data from these people, collected in 1969, may have missed growing cultural developments in the gay younger generation of the late 1960s and early 1970s. Yet this study of homosexuality is the largest conducted specifically on the subject. Other investigations, too, have consistently found diversity.

Social invisibility makes it possible for people to be ignorant of social diversity. As a result, wildly inaccurate stereotypes of homosexuals have been perpetuated. At best, heterosexuals often tend to imagine a very limited collection of gay "types." Yet even some of the most cherished stereotypes may be wrong. Consider, for example, the assumed (and thus scarcely discussed) connection between male heterosexuality and varsity sports in college. A modest but intriguing study by Garner and Smith (1977) surveyed sexual activities among athletes on varsity teams of one sport at five southwestern universities. Athletes in this sport reported significantly higher rates of homosexual activity than had been found in previous studies of other populations. Similarly, when professional football player David Kopay publicly announced his homosexuality and asserted that three of the starting quarterbacks in the pro football leagues were known to be homosexual, his statements did get modest coverage in the news pages, but discussion on the sports pages was deafeningly absent.

While social invisibility is now commonly understood and social diversity is rapidly becoming so, the question of social and personal differentiation is a matter of some controversy. Some gay liberation activists describe a sharp social division, as if homosexuals constitute a nationality or a different race, while many of their opponents believe that they are so alien and bizarre as to be totally separate from the majority. Yet the evidence indicates that the supposedly sharply polarized divisions between gay and straight are not as real as some would claim, and that human beings do not fit into sexual jackets quite so easily. Sexual orientation and social identity are not identical—except, perhaps, when labels are externally imposed.

There may well be some interesting *average* differences between gay and straight populations. Yet, as will be shown in the Life Adaptations section of this volume, similarities between gays and the majority population are far greater than the differences. There is no contradiction in believing both of the latter two sentences; what is misleading is to stress one at the utter expense of the other. We hope that after finishing with this volume, readers will no longer be able to do so.

CONCLUSIONS

(1) Homosexual orientation is frequently confused with social sex role, gender identity, gender role, and other variations.

(2) There is much homosexual activity in the general population, and several million citizens have a predominantly homosexual orientation.

(3) The homosexual population is characterized by social invisibility, social diversity, and social and personal differentiation.

(4) Because of social invisibility, untrue stereotypes are widespread.

(5) Because of social diversity, drawing conclusions about individuals on the basis of their sexual orientation is likely to lead to error.

(6) Attaching importance to homosexual orientation causes social and personal differentiation of homosexuals from heterosexuals, to a mild but not clear-cut degree.

4

Social Issues and Homosexual Behavior
A Taxonomy of Categories and Themes in Anti-Gay Argument

William Paul

"God puts homosexuals in the same category as murderers" (Bryant, 1977).

The purpose of this chapter is to identify, define, and examine some major elements of the way in which homosexual orientation becomes a social issue, by examining arguments which oppose full social equality for Gay men and Lesbians.[1] The nature and content of these arguments has elicited very little inquiry, even though they exert great influence on the way the issues are defined in the first place.

The main focus in this chapter is a textual analysis of 81 printed materials, which are supported by cross-checking with brief interviews with 39 people publicly opposing full social equality for Gay people. The results from these two analyses are applied to current mass media portrayals of the Gay rights issue. The social and educational contexts of these ideas and debates are then examined—especially limitations on academic freedom in the study of these issues, for this ultimately affects the availability of factual information to the public. The data suggest that quasi-official academic controls may have imposed misinformation on a confused public that crucially influences the quality of arguments in this historic social controversy. Thus, the content of these positions is investigated, not merely in their logical senses, but also in their propagandistic and thematic manifestations, some of which are quite subtle.

Author's Note: This research was supported, in part, by grants from SPSSI, the Human Rights Foundation, and the Mark De Wolfe Howe Fund at Harvard University.

To analyze ideologies it is sometimes necessary to isolate underlying themes and to dissect out of catalogued beliefs the generalizations and assumptions that lend them unity and coherence, because frequently it is these underlying premises that are appealing [Toch, 1965, p. 23].

TEXTUAL ANALYSIS OF PRINTED MATERIALS

Many researchers have shown that myth, taboo, and the power of symbols contribute to the distorted views of homosexuality seen as facts by so many people in Western societies (especially in England and America). Historians (Taylor, 1965; Crompton, 1978; Boswell, 1980), anthropologists (Westermarck, 1908; Carrier, 1980), and psychiatrists (Szasz, 1970; Marmor, 1980b) all agree that homosexuality has—without basis in fact—been interpreted and mystified to symbolize or amount to something other than it really is.

There is no reason to expect that these misconceptions have magically disappeared even though new arguments have appeared. Therefore, I want to look past the particular arguments used in public controversy concerning gay rights—arguments which are so often deployed like troops in battle, with camouflage, strategies, and covert aims. The hypothesis is that certain arguments are actually manifestations of a more powerful but less explicit theme; when the arguments are demolished, the theme nevertheless rises again in modified form, while retaining the nonrational thematic force. Smith (1949) and Dollard (1957) have shown, for example, that themes of sexual threat have permeated the racist feelings of Whites toward Blacks—yet this real issue often remained unstated in debate or education (see Chapter 29).

Accordingly, over the past few years I have undertaken a thematic analysis of categories and themes used in anti-Gay arguments. The methodology I used is described in the next section; the results follow. Readers uninterested in the scholarly details should skip to the results section.

Definitions

An *argument* is (according to the *Oxford English Dictionary*) "a connected series of statements or reasons intended to establish a position; a process of reasoning." An argument *category* is (according to Drever, 1964) "a class, usually based on essential or fundamental considerations," of arguments which share closely related premises or corollary assumptions and are often based on related kinds of evidence. Usually an argument category is made up of several arguments which all evaluate evidence by a similar criterion—for example, "homosexuality is unnatural" is the criterion used in the Natural Law category. As I began my inquiry, I postulated four major categories of antihomosexual argument: Natural Law, Personal Disorder,

Social Pathology, and Moral-Religious Values. To these I have found it necessary to add a fifth: Social Utility. Examples of these categories will be given below.

The definition of *theme* is more problematic. In social science, the term is defined in ways that vary and are occasionally ambiguous (Daugherty & Janowitz, 1958). Loosely speaking, a theme is a topic of discourse. More precisely, the *Oxford English Dictionary* defines it as "a subject treated by action . . . ; hence, that which is the cause *of* or *for* specified action, circumstance or feeling." Themes can be loaded and can, in turn, "load" an argument.

Themes have been studied and utilized in propaganda and other forms of psychological warfare (Daugherty & Janowitz, 1958; Lerner, 1971).[2] Thematic strategies have been employed to evoke existing feelings, fears, and motivations and to stimulate new ones. Emotionally laden terms and topics are effective, as are those loaded with added meanings. As will be seen, themes can appear covertly, as hidden messages within explicit arguments, sometimes as insinuations, and often as evocative visual images appealing to raw fear.

One of my objectives in studying the current barrage of anti-Gay propaganda has been to identify and understand any evidence of systematic psychological warfare appearing in public debate and mass media, as distinct from simple expressions of traditional beliefs about homosexuality. This necessarily includes an analysis of both rational arguments and themes, with some understanding of how they combine and interact. To some extent, this is a phenomenological inquiry, in that I have relied on informed impressions of propaganda samples as experienced by myself and others who contributed their independent impressions and insights. This is appropriate to a pilot study where a major task is discovery. Qualitative methods using subjective impressions continue to play an important role in propaganda, advertising, and other forms of mass persuasion. Stephens advises that propaganda analysis is an art—not yet a science (1955), but able to generate factual data.

With limitations acknowledged, this study provides some service to important tasks of social science: exploration, description, classification, and explanation. Some important objectives of this investigation are to identify essential ingredients of anti-Gay rationale and locate these in the current context while using earlier propaganda analysis designs as applicable guides.

Methods

Between 1977 and 1981 I collected about 250 items of printed material pertaining to homosexuality. From these I rejected items supporting Gay rights and those not relating to social issues. The final sample contained 81 items. (A few items not in the sample due to their being published before 1977 will nevertheless be quoted as illustrations.)

This is a formulative study (Stellitz, Jahoda, Deutsch, & Cook, 1959) designed to undertake some basic tasks of scientific inquiry in finding, identifying, and providing initial classification for what is studied—in this case, arguments. There are, of course, serious limitations to this sampling procedure, since it was necessarily an unsystematic matter of opportunity yielding a very mixed sample of arguments appearing in varied media and formats. Therefore, no statistical analysis was conducted. This is no great impediment to a formulative inquiry at this stage of qualitative investigation and classification, since only one example of a particular kind of combination of argument and theme is required to know that one exists. Actually, the themes listed here each appeared in the materials at least two times, and usually much more often, while the argument categories account for 94 percent of the sample.[3]

As methodological guides I found McCall and Simmons (1969) quite helpful. Barton and Lazarsfeld (1969) provided especially useful taxonomic procedures for descriptive systems which clearly influence the taxonomy presented here.[4]

The current taxonomy of themes (which I will refine further in the future) is presented in the lefthand column of Figure 4.1. The two-dimensional nature of the chart, with the five categories of argument across the top, permits any given argument to be classified into its appropriate argument category and its theme(s).

This taxonomy is proposed both as a means of understanding anti-Gay argument and a basis for further research by myself and others. I was the principal judge in classifying arguments and themes. However, as the study proceeded, I conducted three kinds of cross-checking. I asked 4 colleagues and 16 college students (graduate and undergraduate students at Harvard, San Francisco State, and Wellesley) to assess my judgments. First they were asked to classify the items themselves, using earlier versions of the scheme in Figure 4.1, and setting aside items that did not seem to fit for further classification. Second they were given a set of already classified items and asked for a critical assessment. A third kind of cross-checking involved consultation with informants, seven people actively involved or familiar with Gay rights controversies on a national level.[5]

There are, of course, some limitations and ambiguities in this current taxonomy. Certain argument categories, for example, can also operate as themes. In addition, the two-dimensional design of the taxonomy probably does not account for all the possible interactions. Quite simply, it is likely that more complex and subtle factors are involved than are indicated by these descriptive findings, many of which must rely on subjective impressions.

Finally, the description of results in this article is quite limited by space constraints. Ideally, at least one example of each interaction should be described with the source cited.[6]

Selected Examples of Interactions Between Themes and Argument Categories

Figure 4.1 shows how particular antihomosexual arguments were classified according to both category and theme. For example, consider the following quotation from Cameron (1978):

> Biologically absurd behavior like homosexuality cannot be condoned or accepted as normal without endangering normal development of our young toward their own duty to reproduce.

This argument falls into the Natural Law category, because its reference to biology implies that there is a natural order and that this order is upset by homosexual people. There is a less obvious, secondary Social Pathology argument present, in that "duty to reproduce" implies a social order being disrupted. Thematically, however, this brief position has a number of potential persuasive subtexts: Contagion and Danger to the Young are suggested, since *it* may spread if "condoned," Gender Role Violation is present in the "duty" of reproduction, and finally a general but explicit Abnormality theme (which also equates acceptance of homosexuality with danger) exists. "Biologically absurd" was among the phrases associated with homosexuality by Nazi propagandists as quoted by Bleuel (1973, p. 118), as was "duty to reproduce."

Now consider the conclusion reached by Hatterer (1970) and Bergler (1958), among others, that homosexuals tend to be neurotic, unhappy, unstable individuals leading disordered lives. This is an example of the Personal Disorder category, since it presumes that the criterion used to evaluate homosexuality is that of mental health. The themes expressed are Pollution, Abnormality, and Victim Blaming.

A mass mailing from the Moral Majority of Santa Clara (California) distributed in 1980 argued that homosexuals are morally decadent, exerting a generally bad influence on society—in particular, promoting hedonism. Here the argument categories are Moral-Religious Values and Social Pathology, but the themes are Contagion and Pollution.

Anthropologists Marshall and Suggs (1971, p. 236) wrote that "social approval of active homosexuality is tantamount to declaring that society has no interest in, or obligation to make well, the sociopsychologically deviant so as to prevent a disturbing behavior pattern from spreading in its midst—or that the society is not concerned with its own survival!" The main category here is Social Pathology (with perhaps a minor in Personal Disorder); the

	CATEGORIES OF ARGUMENT: (common lines of reasoning, premise, or proof, etc.)				
THEMATIC ELEMENTS: (general concerns, feelings, assumptions or reactions: latent or manifest)	NATURAL LAW	PERSONAL DISORDER	MORAL AND RELIGIOUS VALUES	SOCIAL PATHOLOGY	SOCIAL UTILITY
CONTAGION: (general)					
Contagion to the Young					
Contagion to Groups					
POLLUTION: (general)					
Pollution As Inflicted					
Pollution As Revulsion					
GENDER ROLE VIOLATION:					
ABNORMALITY:					
MYSTERY AND POWER: (general)					
Conspiracy & Secrecy					
Power					
Uncertainty					
AVOIDANCE: (general)					
Avoidance As Propriety					
Visibility As Flaunting					

DANGER: (general threat)
Danger to the Young
Danger to the Family
Physical Threat & Violence

EVIL: (general immorality)
Malice
Aggression (militant evil)

VICTIM BLAMING:

GENERALIZATION:

From B. Paul, *Categories & Themes Article.*

FIGURE 4.1   Taxonomy of Arguments and Thematic Content in Anti-Gay Positions

35

themes are Danger and Contagion. Elsewhere (p. 234), the same authors warn that "although little known or publicized, the military . . . has been plagued periodically by the formation of 'homintern' (homosexual rings)." Here the theme of Mystery and Power (subcategory Conspiracy and Secrecy) is paramount.[7]

The final argument is Social Utility, exemplified by the positions of Van den Haag (1974) and Hechinger and Hechinger (1978): Even though there may be nothing intrinsically bad about homosexual preferences, the predominant reaction is so emotional and volatile that bringing up the issue could be disruptive to larger common concerns. Here the themes are Victim Blaming and Avoidance.

These examples should be sufficient to give an impression of the classification process. There is unfortunately not enough space to give full definitions of the various themes and categories. Some are self-explanatory and become clear in subsequent examples.

Results

(1) *Social utility* was found as a necessary descriptive category for arguments sharing such common elements as *denial, avoidance,* or *neutralization* of Gay and Lesbian civil rights issues. Moderation was common, but also victim blaming.

(2) *Thematic interactions with arguments* were found, as expected. Likely theme properties were suggested: Uncertainty, Latency, Action, Transience, and Feeling.

(3) *New themes and subthemes* were found, as listed in Figure 4.1.

(4) *Arguments and themes in selected academic materials* were found to share common essentials with those found in explicit antihomosexual materials.

(5) *Systematic techniques of propaganda and psychological warfare* were identified in many materials. Examples of psychological warfare included incitements to violence and intergroup hatred or fear, vilification, and false information.

(6) *Other Target Groups* were attacked with anti-Gay rhetoric and themes. Feminists and the women's movement in general (including heterosexuals) were the most common targets. These examples also included psychological warfare techniques.

These findings can be viewed as only preliminary results of a pilot study designed to identify essential ingredients of antihomosexual arguments and some of their origins. Further study is required, with sufficient funding to provide for large-scale, systematic sampling procedures and statistical analysis.[8]

In addition to the particular categories they fall into, other properties of themes were found. First, the themes display *transience:* the capacity to cut across boundaries of the argument categories. That is, a given theme does indeed show up being supported by, in many cases, each of the five argument categories, even though each category uses a different standard of evidence and criterion for what is good or bad. Thus, for example, the theme of homosexual contagion shows up as contaminating moral-religious values, infecting the capacity of the young to reproduce, spreading a mental disorder, and emanating secretive forces that are socially pathological, or at least socially inconvenient or divisive. Like other themes, Contagion is flexible and mobile. The display of transience is not just a tautological consequence of the classificatory scheme; empirically, it could have turned out that as the argument categories changed, the themes would have, too.

In particular, Contagion, Danger to Children, and Mystery-Power are pervasive combinations appearing profusely within all categories of argument, but especially in Social Pathology (commonly expressed as "threat to the family") and in Moral-Religious Values (e.g., Robison, 1980; Noebel, 1978; Cameron, 1978). And in a two-page mass mailing by Anita Bryant (May 1977), Contagion and Danger to Children combined appear no less than 11 times. The title, for example, is *Save Our Children*.

Arendt (1951) describes Nazi propaganda as designed to evoke the deepest intimate feelings (home, mother, children, etc.). Parsons prescribes propaganda themes that "confer personal meanings," while Riley and Cottrell describe messages that arouse feelings and elicit action. Both are among numerous similar citations Daugherty and Janowitz provide in their huge casebook of applied psychological warfare (1958) describing thematic techniques also found here.[9]

Second, many of the themes are latent—not plainly expressed, but present nevertheless. I suspect that such latent themes achieve greater emotional power precisely because they are not overt. Falwell (1980, p. 3), for example, wrote: "This is why I fear for our nation today! For homosexuality tears at the very foundation of the home—God's sacred family unit—and the cornerstone of our American family unit." Falwell did not say directly that homosexuality "attacks" the things he holds dear, but the message is there; homosexuality not only "tears at," it "eats," "devours," "attacks," "strangles," "consumes," "poisons," "strikes at," "dismembers," and so on. Such terms of aggressive attack are profuse in the literature of the New Right. This is discussed further shortly.

Some themes appear to come out of traditional homosexual stereotypes which persist in popular imagination as providing current propagandists with responsive audiences already predisposed and vulnerable to thematic messages. Heiden calls propaganda "the art of drawing an opinion *from* the masses" (1944, in Arendt, 1951). Also, Lingle et al. (1979) find that impressions about others and their recall from memory are heavily influenced by *superordinate themes,* which tend to organize impressions by reducing them to judgmental simplicities then stored in memory. When recalled, these superordinate themes tend to be trusted more than other, more complex information. Judgmental perceived traits are then recalled as "facts." As seen in Gonsiorek's social psychology article (Chapter 10), stigma and prejudice can exert powerful influences on both memory and perception.

Research on racism has found a number of examples that are quite comparable to antihomosexual response. Anthropologist Ian MacCrone made a relevant discovery in prewar White South African society. This provides a point of comparison, drawn from racism, of how existing belief and taboo can generate interactions of argument with underlying themes.

> When a white woman marries a negro, some people become ill and vomit. In South Africa natives are considered savages and are often assumed to be like wild animals. Sexual intercourse between natives and Europeans therefore appears to be a form of perversion, and a sense of revulsion is elicited because such acts are defined as "unnatural" as well as "immoral" [MacCrone, 1937, p. 301].

So the rationale is a combination of Natural Law, Disorder, and Moral-Religious categories; but the overwhelming theme, the action property and the emotion (revulsion and vomiting), is Pollution, together with general abnormality.

Racist taboo reactions of this kind have occurred among some Americans and thereby served as a source of argument and potential propaganda against racial equality. Social Utility positions, for example, have been utilized against integration on the grounds that such intense majority reaction is so widespread that any mingling of the races would be so volatile and divisive as to be simply unworkable. The similarity to antihomosexual reactions is illuminating, and also the use of such reactions as a basis for Social Utility arguments, some of which are recently developed.

Third, some of the arguments used and the themes expressed changed over time. Above, I indicated how I added the Social Utility category after the other four argument categories failed to cover the full range of arguments. Indeed, Social Utility arguments accounted for an increasing share of public positions taken against the Gay rights movement. There was an increasing emphasis on denial of any need for the debate, or that any civil rights or minority issues were involved. Opponents increasingly proclaimed their conditional support for "equal civil rights." Social Utility arguments thus created the impression that their advocates were taking a higher road, with less overt hostility toward Gays. However, the use of volatile themes, indirectly expressed, persisted. One recent outcome, apparently, is the creation of entirely new stereotypes—the stereotype of Gays (Gay men especially, but Lesbians also) as exemplifying Aggression or Physical Threat and Violence[10] (along with successful careers, prestige, wealth, and privilege—with similarities to anti-Semitic notions).

In their successful campaign to repeal a Gay rights ordinance, Moral Majority of Santa Clara mailings (1980) relied heavily on Danger to Children and Contagion themes but escalated the rhetoric to include inaccurate claims that the largest mass murders in America were committed by "gays" on "young boys."

Discussion

> Reality . . . is fragile and adjudicated—a thing to be debated, compromised and legislated. Those who succeed in this world are those who are most persuasive and effective in having their interpretations ratified as true reality [McCall & Simmons, 1969, p. 42].

The mass media are the "big leagues" of propaganda, especially in their capacity to bear explicit thematic messages along with more covert subtexts. The visual mass media, during the course of this study, broadcast images with striking similarities to the printed materials collected. Mixed messages in all of these productions combined seemingly moderate Social Utility arguments with powerful negative subthemes—especially the themes of Danger, Mystery, Contagion, and Pollution.

The 1979 film *Cruising* took a rather moderate and tolerant line—at least concerning overt attitudes. But the imagery was of Danger, Pollution, Mystery, some Gender Role Violation (e.g., transvestites), Mental Abnormality, and Contagion (New York Times, July 28, 1979). Russo's definitive analysis of homosexuality in film (1981) finds numerous portrayals of themes described here, especially as subtext.

The 1979 film *Windows* presented a similar array of threatening and mysterious imagery focused on Lesbians. Some of these themes were new, like the above, reflecting an increased attention to Lesbians in anti-Gay productions.

The 1980 television documentary on CBS, "Gay Power, Gay Politics," served as an example of a classic propaganda effort directed against Gay people and their civil rights movement. The producers presented many factual distortions, yet took a relatively moderate, Social Utility line of argument. But the imagery was much more negative. San Francisco Gay men were portrayed as affluent and a politically powerful elite. The existence of discrimination was denied, and the Gay rights movement was defined primarily as an effort to obtain unlimited opportunities for public sexual activity and other hedonistic recreations. Sexual activity was a major focus of attention, together with the assertion that enormous Gay political power was wielded merely to protect sexual activity in public. But the program's imagery portrayed threats to children and promoted the new image connecting the Gay community with physical threats and violence. Following an extensive investigation by journalist and sociologist Randy Alfred into the events portrayed by CBS, the network was censured by the National News Council (1981).[11]

The print media, too, have done their share. *Time* journalist John Leo's arguments are fairly representative of the Social Utility category:

> Polls show resistance to homosexuals as schoolteachers, and to laws that seem to enshrine homosexuals as a specially protected minority. . . . For most heterosexuals, the issue is not tolerance but social approval. . . . Systematic or massive discrimination . . . is clearly not the case with homosexuals, who unlike blacks and women, are already well integrated into the economy.
>
> Americans are questioning their own gut feeling that homosexuality is wrong. Many are downright ashamed or guilty about this aversion. Is their feeling merely instinct and prejudice? Or are there valid, respectable reasons for distaste for homosexuality and its public claims? [*Time,* January 8, 1979, p. 47].

Note how "*its* public claims" are defined as the issue. The notion that an *it*, rather than people, forms a civil rights movement and makes public claims subtly transforms people into objects. The issues, and the people involved, are dehumanized. As a proven propaganda technique, *it* was employed by Goebbels to describe "the Jewish menace" and "Jewification" (Bleuel, 1973). Literature distributed by the Moral Majority in 1980, opposing a Gay civil rights ordinance in Santa Clara County, read: "Don't let IT spread!" "IT" was rendered in purple.

Such extreme renderings, like the New Right's use of terms connoting aggressive threat when describing Gay people, are often interpreted as simply the linguistic fire and brimstone of traditional belief systems. This certainly accounts for much of the wrath. Traditional beliefs are translated into social discourse and political life as a spontaneous reaction to a challenge by new belief systems. But apparently more moderate versions, such as Leo's article and the CBS documentary, have been widely cited as authoritative sources in anti-Gay propaganda campaigns. One consistent theme in this propaganda is the Contagion/Avoidance/Power complex represented in the notion that everything visibly Gay is somehow emanating the power of sexuality. Even a mundane expression of Gay social identity is perceived as a form of provocative sexual display or "flaunting." Gagnon and Simon (1967, p. 137) were indeed right when they wrote:

> We have allowed the homosexual's sexual object choice to dominate and control our imagery of him. We have let this single aspect of his total life experience appear to determine all his products, concerns and activities. The

mere presence of unconventional sexuality seems to give the sexual content of his life an overwhelming significance. [Yet] homosexuals . . . vary profoundly in the degree to which their homosexual commitment and its facilitation becomes the organizing principle of their lives.

Another important theme in antihomosexual writings is Mystification. Many convey a general sense of homosexuality as an alien, threatening influence with unpredictable consequences, yet which is known to be destructive to individual character, morality, stability, and vital social institutions including the family and religion. Homosexuality—"it"—is viewed as a threat that is so general, and so similar to other conditions such as drug abuse or prostitution, that "it" becomes a moral metaphor for evil of many kinds. "It" amounts to a translation of sin into the terms of social policy.

Beyond particular arguments and issues, the Gay rights controversy itself tends to be mystified, especially in the widespread perception that anti-Gay public hostility is unfathomable and impervious to change. It is not surprising that these perceptions of invincibility are widely promoted by groups which have successfully used the "Gay issue" as a kind of political blunt instrument. In politics, a shared perception of power *is* power—a fact these groups seem especially aware of in their self-portrayal as an overwhelming force.[12]

Only rarely, of course, does this process of mystification become conscious. In a recent debate within the Presbyterian Church General Assembly, those favoring ordination of Gay people presented an array of factual data in support of their position. Those opposing ordination of Gay people, who nevertheless supported their full civil rights, responded with a statement of remarkable candor: "It is not so much what homosexuality *is* that is important, but rather what we *believe* about it" (Presbyterian Blue Book, Note 1).

Other Christian folk, less charitably inclined perhaps than the Presbyterians, play hardball with some of the propaganda seen here, in thematic anti-Gay attacks ranging from role modeling to mass murder. Mystery and Power are conspicuous as subtle background themes, as seen in implicit assumptions that homoerotic attraction is delicious and perhaps addictive, a force of unknown powers.

Uncertainty is a common property of themes as they operate in anti-Gay argument. Thematic subtext often conveys the sense of uncertain (and uncontrollable) evil consequences of homosexuality in a given area of concern. Danger to the Young is irrefutable in particulars, since the danger can be interpreted as an open-ended range of bad possibilities. It can mean anything from role-modeling and immoral social environment to seduction, child molestation, and violent rape of the young. Like a psychiatric projective test, a theme can invite internal fears:

Can you imagine the influence a practicing homosexual teacher has over a young impressionable child? .... and there will be nothing you or I can do about it then to protect our innocent children [Falwell, 1980, p. 3].

We do not know to what extent large segments of public opinion are influenced by such appeals. Some people are highly susceptible. Increased anti-Gay violence has been reported following several propaganda barrages (see Chapter 29).

One must not make the mistake of equating this analysis of anti-Gay ideas or literature with a public opinion survey. In fact, the latter kind of survey has tended to show considerable ambivalence on the subject in the public at large. For example, the General Social Survey (Sherrill, 1974) found that while 70 percent of respondents believed homosexuality to be "wrong," they supported civil rights for Gay people on two of three items. (Sherrill's data were collected in 1973 by the National Opinion Research Center in Chicago.) Plummer (1975) found a similar tendency in a 1963 survey by the British Market Research Bureau:

Many people's views of homosexuality were found to be vague and fluid, not to mention inconsistent. Few had thought out their ideas at all—most reacted largely in terms of feelings mixed with (often contradictory) "okay" opinions probably borrowed from reading matter. It is thus likely that opinions are likely to be extremely vulnerable to propaganda—in either direction, and especially if the propaganda has some authoritative backing.

It is likely that vague, fluid, and inconsistent views are related to a lack of information available to the public. In the absence of facts, "authorities" can emerge with explanations of complex issues. During the initial phase of this study in 1977, preliminary assessments led to some tentative predictions as to how the national antihomosexual campaign would develop. Several were confirmed as more sophisticated propaganda appeared in 1978 (e.g., Cameron, 1978), and by 1980 included professional and very slick instruments of mass persuasion using techniques of marketing and expensive visual media (see Robison, 1980; Moral Majority of Santa Clara Mass Mailing, 1980).

As predicted, discredited sickness theories (Disorder) tended to be relinquished in favor of mass appeals more nebulous (and less refutable)—social threats such as Danger to the Family. The "pro-family" campaign was initiated by a number of groups with a nationwide spontaneity (1978-1980) that strongly suggested strategic coordination, and certainly ample national funding sources.

In contrast to the early, relatively crude argumentation of Anita Bryant, later more articulate anti-Gay publications provided material that filled up the cells in Figure 4.1 with many examples of predicted thematic interactions that until then were simply postulates (e.g., Cameron, 1978; DuMas, 1980).[13]

The Lesbian as Feminist as Threat to Family Equation: Heterosexual Targets Included

Del Martin, the pioneer Lesbian leader, has observed that homophobia is used as a weapon to enforce conformity to conventional gender roles—and that this threat has crucially affected heterosexual women (Martin & Lyon, 1972). Her insight is consistent with what appears in the materials studied here; Anti-Lesbian and anti-Feminist arguments tend to be fused in themes of Gender Role Violation (e.g., Lesbians/Feminists as enemies of motherhood) and Danger to Family and Children (e.g., Feminists/Lesbians as enemies of Mom and the kids). But Gender Role Violation is portrayed as attacking the natural order, the cosmic glue that holds everything together. The interchangeability of Lesbians and Feminists in these arguments calls attention to the fact that these anti-homosexual rhetorical armaments can be aimed quite readily at heterosexual people in selected target groups. Hence the Equal Rights Amendment can be defined by Schlafly as "lesbian privileges," on national television. Literature promoting the Family Protection Act in various formats consistently imparts suggestions that homosexuals act in concert with feminists, and that one will incur the other's label. Robison, of the Religious Roundtable, is typical (1980).

Although analyses of authoritarianism and homophobia empirically demonstrate the strong relationship between sex role rigidity and homophobia (Morin & Garfinkle, 1978), as does the history of fascism (Bleuel, 1973), the materials studied here paradoxically reveal the integral nature of equal rights for women and for Gay people.[14] Ultimately, the anti-Gay arguments reveal far more than intended.

While an examination of anti-Feminist argument was quite beyond the scope of this investigation, so many examples appeared together or interwoven with antihomosexual ideas that comparisons were routinely presented. A clear impression emerged that a category/thematic analysis of anti-Feminist rhetoric by someone more familiar with the field would be likely to improve our understanding of propaganda directed against equal rights for women.

Bleuel's account of Nazi attacks on equality for women is a rich resource in this regard. He provides an array of well-referenced examples of Nazi propaganda and practice, in which clear relationships appear between their antihomosexual and anti-Feminist ideologies. Most of the argument categories and themes shown in this study are applied to both target groups. Further study comparing Nazi ideology and propaganda to some of the current anti-Feminist rhetoric produced by certain elements of the New

Right might illuminate current events with uncomfortable clarity (see Chapter 29 for anti-Gay examples).

CROSS-CHECKING BY FIELD INTERVIEWS

In order to refine and expand the results obtained from the printed materials study, I conducted concurrent interviews with men and women who publicly advocated some limitation of full social equality for Gay people. This study is necessarily more impressionistic, but useful as a point of comparison.[15]

Methods

I conducted brief field interviews with 39 people, as described above. Sites included hearings on antidiscrimination bills in the Massachusetts State Legislature during 1977 and 1978, anti-Gay public demonstrations in Washington D.C. during 1979, and similar demonstrations in California (San Francisco, 1980-1981; Sacramento, 1980; San Jose, 1980). I approached respondents at public events and identified myself as "a social scientist studying intergroup conflict and public policy," and explained that the homosexual rights controversy is an important part of debates on public policy today. After proper introductions, agreement to participate, and assurances of confidentiality, the brief interviews proceeded with my asking questions, approximately as follows:

(1) What do *you* personally think is the main issue?
(2) What is the next most important major issue?
(3) Yes, I can understand that, but what if someone couldn't agree? What else would you say?

There are of course many difficulties with such a procedure. Hence, these interviews should be seen as a comparative vantage point, rather than a formal independent investigation. In several ways, respondents were self-selected, and hence to an unknown degree a biased sample. Many refused to participate, referred me to a group representative, or broke off the interview after the first few questions. Groups of devout religious conservatives were heavily represented, indicating a biased sample but also posing a question as to the sources of ideas. Interview conditions varied greatly. There was a wide variation in the number of onlookers, in whether people or groups were arguing (and if so, with what degree of vehemence), and in my own nonverbal self-presentation (in clothing, etc.). After the interview, I recorded notes on content and impressions.[16]

Results and Discussion

Many respondents expressed suspicion or skepticism of my motives (e.g., "Are you a reporter?", or "Are you with that Gay rights bunch?"). A number seemed motivated to save my soul, and a few began argumentative attacks. But for the most part, participants turned out to be friendlier and much less hostile than I had anticipated.

The arguments expressed by the respondents seemed thin in comparison to the printed materials. This is not surprising, given the nature of the encounters. Religious sentiments were much more prominent in these responses than in the printed material sample—but not more so, it seems, than in printed materials of the religious right. Especially in these cases, there seemed to be a tendency, whatever the initial response, for later responses to revert to religious expressions, as if this was the *real* basic position (e.g., "Homosexuality violates *God's law!*" or "The *Bible* condemns homosexuality!").

Nevertheless, as with the printed materials, arguments often jumped across categories of rationale in chains of reasoning that tended to be circular and self-supporting. For example, basic assumptions about what is sexually natural were used to conclude that Gays must be sick. Sick people, in turn, cannot safely be allowed to "flaunt" their deviant lifestyles without injuring the social or moral order, which was defined as an attack on the family—which, in turn, is the natural biological unit ensuring the survival of humanity. And so on. At the end of these circular chains, there was often a return to a moral/religious premise grounded in an essentially religious conception of natural law. As expected, within these chains of reasoning, certain themes or combinations of themes would often appear: "the family," "it's spreading," "protect the young," or simply, "it's disgusting." Many felt *their* rights violated by "Gay influence." A majority felt generally imposed upon by "the Gays" (and other modernities).

Changes over time appeared as the study progressed. During 1978, certain new arguments appeared—Social Utility arguments in particular became more frequent. Gays were seen as demanding "special privileges" and a special "protected status." Civil rights were not seen as threatened, nor was this the "real" demand being made by Gays; rather, Gays were seen as demanding public validation or approval of homosexuality or a Gay lifestyle.

Social Utility rationale has some interesting characteristics, whether in print or personal responses. Avoidance appears as an important theme in these "moderate" positions, with denial as a common variation. These are common psychological defense mechanisms which appear quite prominently in clinical literature, a possible connection that merits further study. Anthropological data on taboo are also pertinent, since avoidance appears to be the most common reaction in many cultures, especially to pollution as danger (Douglas, 1966).

After 1979, many more "authorities" were cited supporting Social Utility ideas. Some Social Utility positions can take a less moderate turn, however, as in common tendencies to blame Lesbians and Gay men, or homosexuality in general, for oppression inflicted by others ("they bring it on themselves"). Rupp, for instance, with a career in conducting autopsies as a forensic pathologist, concludes that homocides inflicted on homosexuals are symptomatic of their disorder. The good doctor is not at all concerned with the prospect that higher victimization rates might be related to hatreds influencing the murderers, or perhaps unequal protection by the law (Rupp, 1980). Rupp is an example of the "scientific authorities" referred to by people I interviewed. Lack of basic information about the topic was typical of most responses.

THE SOCIAL CONTEXT OF
DEBATE AND INFORMATION

Feelings are clearly an important source of many of the popular attitudes expressed in social discourse. To a great extent, the themes found in this study can be viewed at least partially as feelings that find expression by way of arguments. The arguments are often actually rather secondary and interchangeable. The gut-level emotion is the primary concern, made manifest in the more general themes. The publicity tapping these feelings is probably designed for susceptible target audiences already so inclined, as suggested earlier.

But if feelings are one root of the issue, then they are subject to change. And change they have. Two surveys conducted around 1970 establish a baseline. Simmons (1969) asked 180 respondents to rate homosexuals by a list of traits, thereby revealing stereotypes remarkably close to those which emerged from this category/theme study. Homosexuals were called sexually abnormal (72 percent), perverted (52 percent), mentally ill (40 percent), repulsive (14 percent), dangerous (10 percent), and sinful (10 percent). Gorer (1971) found that his British sample rated "revulsion and disgust" as the most common reaction (23-25 percent). Notice, however, that these extreme emotional reactions were expressed only by minorities of the respondents. Levitt and Klassen (1974) found the same in a 1970 U.S. national probability sample.

More recent surveys—those taken around 1980—appear to show increasingly positive attitudes (Harris, 1977; Gallup, 1977; California Poll, 1977)—especially in terms of civil rights questions and acceptance of Gay *people,* as distinct from the general *issue* of homosexuality. Judgments of remote concepts may differ considerably from those imposed on real people. White Protestants, for example, might respond that "Roman Catholocism" is "always wrong" (just as majorities respond that homosexuality is "always wrong") yet do not necessarily transfer this attitude to Catholic people.

This conclusion, from a ten-year baseline, must be interpreted with caution, for the surveys did not aim at precisely the same target population. However, even a one-year baseline can show significant changes. The NBC exit polling of voters taken in 1980 and 1981 (Note 2) showed an increase in voters who state their support for civil rights laws protecting Gay citizens from discrimination: from 44 percent (1980) to 48 percent (1981). Opposition declined from 41 percent to 38 percent.[17]

The importance of people, as opposed to inanimate concepts, is further illustrated by the study by Staats (1978). A group of Arizona college students was asked to select traits supposedly typical of homosexuals. The most frequently selected trait was "sensitive" (48 percent), followed by "individualistic." Others were "intelligent," "honest," "imaginative," "neat," and "cowardly"—this last endorsed by only 16 percent. The contrast with earlier studies is enormous and may not be due entirely to the passage of time. College students are usually reported to be more liberal than the population at large, and in particular are likely to have actually met Gay people—or at least to be more directly aware of them due to the existence of Gay students' groups on campuses, for example. This emphasizes the point made above: Understanding homosexuals as *people* is a key to reducing stigma against them—as it is for any group. After all, the ten-year period spanned by the various studies has also seen a vast increase in publicly visible Gay people everywhere—not just on college campuses, although the change there has been impressive. This increase in visibility appears to have had a positive effect, both on the arguments expressed in public and on people's gut-level feelings.

The California Poll in 1977, during a statewide public controversy on Gay civil rights, showed an interesting finding. If a person was simply acquainted with a Lesbian or Gay man, not necessarily on a basis of friendship, the probability of support for equal rights increased enormously.

THE SPREAD OF MISINFORMATION AND THE ACADEMIC RESPONSIBILITY

In "The Social Functions of Ignorance," Moore and Tumin (1964) present examples of how social systems enforce a lack of information, and misinformation, in the service of popularly shared "official" realities. Examples of approved public ignorance include "reinforcement of group mandates" (p. 522), "preservation of stereotypes" (p. 523), and a social isolation in defense of traditional values, a process that includes inhibition of open inquiry (p. 521). They see enforcement of sexual taboo as a particular focus in the suppression of knowledge about the nature and extent of the violation of norms. The widespread hostility to Kinsey's historic findings is explained as a particular reaction to the incidence of sexually taboo behavior Kinsey revealed among Americans.

Moore and Tumin contend that *imposed ignorance* is the basis of taboo enforcement. Access to knowledge that such activities are quite common is perceived, at worst, as tacit encouragement of them and, at best, as defiance of polite fictions supporting taboo. Recall the Presbyterians who stated that it was not the truth but the beliefs about homosexuality that mattered.

Who, then, has imposed this ignorance? Responsibility can clearly be widely shared. But this section addresses the academic responsibility to provide public access to accurate information, as an alternative to popular myth and propaganda.

Social scientists and clinicians deemed expert on the subject have, until the recent increase in Gay and Lesbian visibility, been in a unique position to speak with authority about a secretive and largely invisible Gay population. Although there have been exceptions, generally the universities, academics, and clinicians have not fulfilled their responsibility to transmit accurate information. There is not space, of course, for a comprehensive account; but examples in this chapter and throughout this volume (for example, the Mental Health section) indicate that scholars are not immune to prejudice and taboo. The purpose here is to understand arguments, not refute them, but some specific examples of the problem are in order.

Gadpaille, a psychiatrist and author of works on homosexuality, displays a common tendency found in this literature to present inaccurate or selective information as scientific opinion, but which actually expresses traditional belief:

> Any form of sexuality that would threaten the survival of the species can be tolerated only so long as it remains a minority expression. Were it to become the behavioral norm, it would automatically be destructive and therefore, on the biological level, must be classified as abnormal. Only through the great predominance of normal sexual behavior can any species, mankind included, afford its variants [1975, p. 6].

The Biology section in this volume reveals these assertions as inaccurate. Here, it is sufficient to suggest that an educational textbook would include accurate information, or at least not obscure polemics in the cloak of science.

In Gadpaille's view, celibacy would also threaten survival of the species. Or would it? In the social insects (ants, bees, and wasps) only a tiny minority of individuals have a capacity to reproduce (queens and drones). In any case, the biological data in this book show that homosexual behavior is far from "abnormal" in the natural world. Among humans homosexual behavior of various kinds has been found to be normal, even idealized, in quite a few societies which continued to flourish (see Chapter 25). And finally, humanity is hardly endangered by a low birthrate, but rather the opposite. Contagion and Danger themes can be detected as subtext here, in the odd notion that there is any conceivable prospect of homosexuality becoming a majority norm.

Assertions by other academics range from the openly hostile—psychoanalyst Bergler describing homosexuals as "essentially disagreeable persons" (1958, p. 47)—to stereotyped gossip: "Homosexual jealousy is notorious" (Katchadourian & Lunde, 1975, p. 325). Research has shown this sort of bias, distortion, and opinion appearing widely in educational materials—for example, in health science texts (Newton, 1979) and introductory psychology texts (McDonald, 1981).

It is common to find academic authors either avoiding the topic or stating unsupported positions that are essentially similar to the propaganda described here. Many such views fall well below ordinary standards of scholarship. Not surprisingly, then, academic and medical sources have been employed in anti-Gay propaganda. Moreover, conditions in clinics and universities are such that the development and dissemination of accurate findings about homosexuality have been inhibited. These conditions encourage the persistence of unproven beliefs about homosexuality in academic disciplines. Such quasi-official doctrines have some influence on the public debate, in that they often dominate sources of information (Morin, 1977).

Evidence of bias and thought control exists. Several academic associations of social scientists have passed resolutions calling for encouragement of research into homosexuality and for an end to discrimination against Gay scholars and clinicians. (See, for example, the resolution of the American Anthropological Association: Taylor, 1980.) Widespread discrimination and intimidation persist, however. In a report for the Board of Social and Ethical Responsibilities of Psychology of the American Psychological Association (BSERP, 1979) a task force on the status of Lesbians and Gay men in psychology found bias and discrimination against openly Gay and Lesbian psychologists, and especially graduate students. They also described conditions which seriously inhibit free and open research on the topic, ranging from restrictions on funding to the discouragement of research projects and simple avoidance of the subject. Similar conditions were found in a 1981 report by a task force of the American Sociological Association (Note 3). A similar situation prevails in anthropology (Taylor, 1980; Read, 1980) and in the mental health disciplines (see the Mental Health section of this volume). The personal consequences for the careers of scholars who pursue sexual orientation research include stigmatization (Henslin, 1972; Weinberg & Williams, 1972; Humphreys, 1975; Warren, 1977) and job discrimination, not to mention avoidance by funding agencies (Warren, 1977).

Taboo enforcement restricts sources of factual information, and this can have serious consequences for public misunderstanding. The scarcity of research on Lesbians is but one example. A reading of the evidence gathered by a number of independent investigators cited in this section shows that a number of conclusions are warranted:

(1) Widespread institutional avoidance and outright discrimination seriously inhibit open research and education about homosexuality, and Lesbians and Gay men as people.
(2) There is powerful support and enforcement in educational institutions for implicitly approved sets of ideas that amount to quasi-official doctrines on homosexuality.
(3) These conditions comprise a form of thought control that inhibits the free flow of ideas and information, thus restricting and censoring free public access to accurate knowledge on these issues and thereby distorting public understanding and communication about the issues.

On the other hand, there are signs that times are changing. There are encouraging recent expansions of research on sexual orientation. Yet, for the most part, internationally respected researchers (such as Kinsey) have been attacked and their projects nearly suppressed by powerful forces that have sometimes included government agencies (Pomeroy, 1972; Tripp, 1975). In contrast, a number of researchers with openly anti-Gay sentiments and allegiance to officially approved theories on homosexuality have benefited from advantages in private and government support. Some of these scholars have attacked researchers and projects that might generate findings with favorable implications for Gay civil rights issues. Dr. Harold Voth, for example, chose the *National Enquirer* as his forum to attack the Center for Homosexual Education, Evaluation, and Research (CHEER) at San Francisco State University:[18]

Of course homosexuals are discriminated against. They are discriminated against because they are not normal people. And it's stupid to spend money [as CHEER does] finding out what social problems they have [National Enquirer, April 3, 1979, p. 4].

CONCLUSIONS

Quasi-official doctrine on the topic of homosexuality can be promulgated and enforced in many ways. Sometimes the doctrine is imposed officially and openly; sometimes, unofficially and covertly.

An example of the former route was provided recently by the Texas Department of Education, which recently rejected a text on sexual hygiene's quite moderate statement that many psychiatrists no longer believe that homosexuality is a mental illness. This is a blatant restriction of free access to information. It is a form of thought control no different in principle from methods employed by totalitarian systems. Some anti-Gay social forces are in fact totalitarian on the Gay issue, since for them only one view is allowable—any other views are considered dangerous, if not contagious. Texas students have been prevented from discovering that there *is* a debatable issue when it comes to homosexuality and mental health.

An example of unofficial and covert enforcement begins with a linguistic insight. Educational psychologist John De Cecco (1968) discussed how themes can be used in instruction. Since persuasion is an aspect of learning, his point is important. De Cecco described "thematic prompts" (after Taber) as transmitting cues which elicit desired interpretations or completions of ideas or sentences.

> The thematic prompt depends on the student's previous associations of a word or phrase since they derive from the denotations and connotations of the words which compose them [De Cecco, 1968, p. 508].

Think, for example, of the following sentence completion task:

> Renowned for animal loyalty and affection, man's best friend is surely a _____.

Anyone raised in American culture knows that this sentence is completed with the word "dog." Outsiders to the culture, however, might have an entirely different set of denotations and connotations associated with the various phrases like "loyalty and affection" or "man's best friend." Such outsiders might more quickly notice the sexism involved, might be amused that the correct answer was not deemed to be "woman," and so on.

Now consider the following incomplete sentence:

> The reason I don't want any _____s as teachers is that they flaunt their lifestyle in class.

Anyone raised in American culture "knows" that heterosexuals never flaunt their lifestyle in class—only homosexuals do. The word "flaunt" is a code word or euphemism, with hidden meanings. Consider the comparable anti-Semitic usage of the word "pushy" as a euphemism for "Jewish."

De Cecco elaborated more sophisticated thematic meanings in *inductive prompts,* which involve arrangements of stimuli or context that allow a person to *induce* relationships not explicitly described. In arguments, these might translate to thematic innuendo or implication. Consider, for example, the endlessly repeated notion that *"Homosexuals do not reproduce. They recruit"* (Bryant, 1977; emphasis in original). The implication, clear to any-one raised in American culture, is that recruitment is bad. But this implica-tion falls apart—just as do the sentence-completion examples cited above—as soon as one is able to get outside the culture. Many fundamen-talists, for example, not only reproduce—and exploit the innocence of their own children to indoctrinate them with official church doctrine—but also recruit.

Openly Gay people are often described in the media with the adjective "admitted" or "self-confessed." For example, when an Eagle Scout was dismissed from Scouting for Gay civil rights activities, the press described him as "an admitted homosexual" (San Francisco Chronicle, May 1, 1981). But he had not "admitted" anything, nor had he described himself as "ho-mosexual;" rather, he had affirmed his identity, which he defined as Gay. Linking "admitted" or "confessed" with "Gay" implies guilt or shame. It is insinuated in a way that makes this guilt or shame appear self-evident.

One cannot come away from such considerations without the strong impression that in regard to homosexuality, bigotry is still respectable. Oth-erwise informed people in positions of responsibility, including mass media and education, have tended to avoid Gay-related issues or Gay people in anything but a negative context. The justification commonly given—respect for beliefs of the majority—recalls the rationale once given for excluding Black people from the media.

Knowledge is an ultimate enemy of prejudice. The restriction of knowl-edge, therefore—whether consciously so intended or not—is an agent of prejudice.

Many academics and policymakers believe the taboo against homosexu-ality is so deeply ingrained in the masses that no real change is possible. This overlooks the evidence that public attitudes have changed in positive ways for Gay people, although such change is painful and slow. The educational task before us requires not only that we respond to the issues with factual information, but also that we undertake educational strategies of demystifi-cation which use imagery and empathic appeals—approaches that may be informed by a developing thematic analysis. Our focus should be on the reduction of social distance between Gays and straights by approaches which humanize the issues: from homosexuality as "it" to Gay men and Lesbians as *people.*

NOTES

1. "Gay" and "Lesbian" are used here as forms of social, cultural, and personal identity or expression, in addition to sexual orientation as distinct from "homosexual" and "bisexual," which are scientific and clinical terms properly referring specifically to sexuality. As proper nouns in this sense, both Lesbian and Gay are capitalized. It should be emphasized that "Gay" does not belong or refer only to homosexually oriented males, although this is a common misconception. For clarity, it is useful to refer to both Lesbians and Gay men. For brevity, terms like Gay people used here refer to both women and men.

2. Some of the great names in American social science (and universities) were active in this work during World War II and the Cold War: Parsons, Becker, Cottrell, Riley, Lazarfield, Allport, Lasswell, Scott, Lerner, among others.

3. In the highly pragmatic world of propaganda analysis, subjective assessments of materials remain a necessary option in dealing with matters of meaning, nuance, intensity, and, most of all, social context. These authors and a number of other major investigators in this field concur that informed impressions are essential in slippery areas like thematic propaganda.

4. Taxonomies in Daugherty and Janowitz (1958) served as helpful early guides. Useful qualitative insights were also provided by Dr. Damien Martin (NYU) in his unpublished analysis of anti-Gay rhetoric (presented, in part, as a paper at the American Psychiatric Association Annual Convention, San Francisco, 1980).

5. I am grateful for the suggestions, assessments, and critical contributions of the following scholars: James Weinrich, John De Cecco, and John Gagnon (SPSSI Task Force); Robert Rosenthal and Marcia Gutentag (Harvard); John Adair and Wayne Lankamp (San Francisco State); John Newmeyer (Haight-Ashbury Free Clinic); and Robert W. Smith (C.I.A., Retired). Knowledgeable informants who contributed data on anti-Gay and anti-Feminist propaganda include Phyllis Lyon, Del Martin, Bruce Voeller, Toby Marotta, Randy Alfred, Jean O'Leary, and Ron Gold.

6. This is an abbreviated version of a 63-page research report. The complexity of the thematic interactions described here, with adequate examples, will require several future articles which focus on specifics. One account, with factual response to arguments and themes, can be seen in Paul and Lyon (1982).

7. Such unsupported assertions appear to be a vestige of the McCarthy era. "Much fear and alarm was incited by allegations that 'homosexual conspiracies' and 'infiltration' were somehow linked to communist subversion. Ensuing investigations (i.e., witchhunts) led to numerous firings of government employees who were accused or suspected of 'perversion'" (Tripp, 1975). Note how *Homintern* resembles *Comintern* (the Communist International). Insinuations and blanket accusations of the sort made by Marshall and Suggs (1971) present informative examples of psychological warfare techniques disguised as social science. The aim is group vilification and incitement of fear and hatred. Tactics include "black" propaganda (erroneous "facts" from unknown sources). These authors give no supporting evidence or sources.

8. Sophisticated methods are currently used in anti-Gay and anti-Feminist campaigns, including marketing research to identify target audiences who are susceptible to certain appeals (e.g., danger to children or family).

9. Notions that homosexuals are somehow necessarily hostile to heterosexuals recall the predispositions found in authoritarian personalities to impute maliciousness in others (Adorno et al., 1950). Totalitarian ideologies of both the Left and Right have been especially prone to see homosexuality as a threat, and homosexual people as enemies (Churchill, 1967). Related incitements of public fear have had violent consequences, as seen in Chapter 29, and other recent evidence (Paul, 1981).

10. This physically violent label is a rather abrupt change from the historically popular stereotype of Gay men as weaklings and cowards (see data by Simmons, 1969; Gorer, 1971; and Levitt & Klassen, 1974). Likewise, the new-found stereotype of affluence contrasts with certain previously shadowy figures, living marginal lives in disgrace, having sacrificed career, respect, and so on (see Russo, 1981, on Gays in film).

11. Alfred's seven-month investigation gathered documentation and statements by independent observers thoroughly contradicting the CBS version of events portrayed. Alfred's

evidence indicated deliberate intent by producers George Crile and Grace Diekhouse to distort and misrepresent the Gay community. Censure of CBS by the National News Council was widely interpreted as an important precedent won by the Gay movement on behalf of all minorities.

12. A primary task of psychological warfare, according to Lerner (1971), is demoralization of the enemy by neutralizing the will to resist. A primary means is to generate an image of irresistible power.

13. In each succeeding Gay rights referendum, increasing amounts of funding and professional expertise have flowed into local community groups opposing Gay civil rights. Examples of mass mail voter campaigns reveal sophisticated propaganda materials, skillful strategies of dissemination—and money.

14. There are important integral relationships between the Lesbian and women's movements, with corresponding hostile reactions from the New Right. Important Lesbian perspectives on conventional gender role ideology include Ponse (1978), Martin and Lyon (1972), and Ettore (1980).

15. It is important to remember that these brief field interviews were conducted primarily as a cross-check for the textual analysis. As a cross-check, this was useful but limited, since the sample was disproportionately religious. Furthermore, a majority of people interviewed were questioned on site with an organized group—hence a "party-line" was often expressed.

16. Aside from cross-checking and comparison here, parts of the interviews will be published separately in a brief account with a somewhat different focus.

17. These two polls were conducted before and after the 1980 presidential campaigns, during which a huge anti-Gay barrage was directed at liberals by the New Right, especially in the South and Midwest. This media blitz utilized many of the rhetorical and imagery combinations described here. The outcomes, in terms of these polling data, suggest that Gay people *gained* in public opinion.

18. With the advent of the Reagan administration, and considerable ideological control over grants by members of the New Right, funding for education and research on sexual orientation has been almost totally halted—especially any studies that might relate in a positive way to the Gay and Lesbian communities. CHEER is one of the agencies denied funding. Of course, huge cutbacks have been inflicted on all social science funding.

REFERENCE NOTES

1. Presbyterian Blue Book I & II. Report on the church and homosexuality. 1978. Available from 1201 Interchurch Center, 475 Riverside Drive, New York, NY 10027.
2. NBC Exit Poll, August 1980 and May 1981. Reported in the *San Francisco Sentinel,* July 24, 1981.
3. *Report of the American Sociological Association's Task Group on Homosexuality.* Available from Joan Huber, Department of Sociology, University of Illinois, Urbana, IL 61801.

· II ·

Mental Health

Edited by
John C. Gonsiorek

• 5 •

Introduction

John C. Gonsiorek

This section of this volume is devoted to mental health concerns. The chapters collected here provide a broad overview of this topic, approaching a variety of issues from a number of different perspectives. This introduction is intended to provide the reader with some basic concepts preparatory for an understanding of this area, and then introduce the component chapters.

One of the initial and major problems in the scientific study of homosexuality is the definition of who is homosexual. This issue remains highly problematic, and perhaps the best course is to outline briefly considerations and concepts bearing on the definition of homosexuality.

Much of the theorizing of the nineteenth century viewed homosexuality as either willful sin or a biologically determined sickness, with the common explanation being that homosexuals were another sex, different from male or female, and more akin to hermaphrodites and other individuals with genetic or structural anomalies. This confusion, along with a merging of gender identity or transgender phenomena with sexual orientation variation, continues to haunt and confuse the study of sexual behavior—about which more will be said later.

Freud (1905 [1953]) suggested a genuinely new idea—namely, that a basic bisexuality is inherent in all persons. Early learned experiences and the ensuing personality characteristics then determine which individuals as adults were homosexual, heterosexual, or bisexual. Specifically, Freud suggested that the manner in which a child handled the Oedipal conflict was a primary determinant of later sexual orientation (Freud, 1920 [1971]). However, many psychoanalytic thinkers, especially in the United States, have rejected the concept of inherent bisexuality (although this idea is defended by some: see Thompson, 1963), while retaining the idea of the Oedipal conflict as central in the determination of sexual orientation.

Therefore, despite Freud's reconceptualization that the potential for all varieties of sexual expression was inherent in all individuals, in the mid-twentieth century the prevailing opinion held that sexual orientation was essentially a dichotomous phenomenon, with most individuals being hete-rosexual and a few homosexual. This led, however, to difficulties in catego-rizing individuals who did not fit neatly into those categories. Vague and intangible concepts such as "latent homosexuality" and "pseudo-homo-sexuality" emerged in an attempt to postulate that individuals who were not one or the other were actually one or the other. The concept of latent homosexuality can be tricky conceptually, as Salzman (1965) has noted, because it may refer either to a potential of homosexuality in anyone (akin to Freud's notion of inherent bisexuality) or a dormancy only in those who are truly homosexual but not behaviorally or consciously so.

Rado (1963) attempted a critical evaluation of the concept of bisexual-ity, but his analysis was not illuminating because he foundered on that other difficult point: confusing genetic or structural anomalies (such as hermaphroditism), with gender identity problems and sexual orientation. Bieber et al. (1962) proposed another variation on this theme. They suggested that latent homosexuality did not exist, but that homosexuals were latent heterosexuals—that is, heterosexuals were completely hete-rosexual with no homosexual component, and homosexuals are potential heterosexuals.

One final variation on this theme is the work of Ovesey (1963, 1965), who differentiated three needs which could result in homosexual behavior: needs for homosexual activity, power, and dependence. While he did not conceptualize these needs as mutually exclusive, Ovesey termed those individuals who were motivated predominantly by the latter two needs *pseudohomosexual*. While this concept has at times been viewed as important and useful, it is little more than a restatement of the observation, commonplace to the point of being trite, that individuals can use sex to meet other nonsexual needs. While there is no harm (and probably some validity) to this idea, it is confusing and deceptive to imply that individuals engaging in homosexual behavior can be better understood or differen-tiated than any other group of individuals by using this idea. There are no data to support a conclusion that homosexual or bisexual individuals use sexual expression to meet other nonsexual needs any more than does humanity in general.

While theorizing about allegedly covert forms of homosexuality was proceeding at a frantic and increasingly complex pace, Kinsey et al. (1948, 1953) had completed and published their work. The Kinsey group concep-tualized sexual behavior as falling on a seven-point continuum, from exclusively heterosexual (score of 0) to exclusively homosexual (score of 6). A person in the middle of the scale (score of 3) would be more or less equally bisexual, for example. Both behavior and fantasies were used to assign ratings. For a summary of the Kinsey data, see Chapter 3.

Two aspects of the Kinsey work are noteworthy in this context. First, the frequency and distribution of homosexual behavior had never before been so carefully studied, and it was not believed to be so frequent and widespread until the Kinsey studies. Second, the notion of a heterosexual-homosexual continuum revolutionized theorizing about sexuality and challenged the dichotomous, either-or view of sexual orientation. The concept remains controversial in some quarters to this day, but it has gained general acceptance over the years.

Recently, Shively and De Cecco (1977) expanded the Kinseyan continuum concept, taking their cues from Bem's (1974) revisions of the concept of masculinity-femininity. Shively and De Cecco have proposed that a single continuous scale—like Kinsey's—is insufficient to explain sexual behavior and orientation. They have suggested that sexual orientation can be conceptualized better with two continuous scales, one perpendicular to the other. Separate ratings for homosexual and heterosexual behavior can then be made. In their system, for example, an individual with a high rating on homosexual orientation could simultaneously have a high or low rating, or any in between, on heterosexual orientation. Their proposed scheme would eliminate a limiting and restrictive implication in the Kinsey scale—namely, that the bisexual positions are watered-down mixtures of the two extreme components, and that one form of sexual expression is at the expense of the other.

Another important aspect of the model proposed by Shively and De Cecco is a breakdown of sexual identity into four components: biological sex, gender identity, social sex role, and sexual orientation. Biological sex refers to genetic and morphological features; gender identity refers to the psychological sense of being male or female; social sex role refers to culturally conditioned behaviors and attitudes that differ by sex; and sexual orientation refers to sexual and affectional interest in the same or opposite sex. While Shively and De Cecco's division into four components and, in particular, their conceptualization of the sexual orientation component are at this point theoretical paradigms requiring empirical support, their model does represent one of the most complex, yet clarifying frameworks for understanding homosexuality.

There are a number of other considerations in a definition of homosexuality. The original Kinsey continuum ratings used composite scores of sexual behaviors and fantasies to arrive at the ratings. Some researchers have suggested that a third aspect is important: affectional, as opposed to sexual, preference. This aspect refers to the sex with whom an individual prefers to relate on an affectional or intimacy, as opposed to sexual behavior or fantasy, level. Further, as these three aspects need not be congruent, it has been suggested that it may be useful to rate individuals *separately* on the three aspects of sexual behavior, sexual fantasy, and affectional preference.

Yet another complication is the possibility of change in sexual orientation over time. All of the rating and categorization schemes described so far are measurements taken at one point in time. At this point, it is unknown how stable sexual orientation remains over time. While it appears to be as stable as traits in the behavioral sciences ever are, there are some suggestions that for some individuals there may be genuine, spontaneous change in sexual orientation over time (as opposed to an acknowledgment of long-suppressed feelings, which often occurs when an individual "comes out of the closet"). Finally, the *meaning* of sexual experience, and perhaps sexual orientation, may also change over time. Some of these changes may be related to aging, change of perspective, personal experiences, and the natural history of the individual. Again, this area is unresearched.

Attempts at defining homosexuality by the use of psychiatric diagnosis have been less than illuminating and, in their current state, border on the ludicrous. In 1973, the American Psychiatric Association removed homosexuality from its list of psychiatric disorders, replaced by the vague and confusing *sexual orientation disturbance* diagnosis. This latter seemingly referred to a situation in which a homosexual individual was disturbed by his or her homosexuality. As can be guessed, this new diagnosis led to a variety of conjectures as to its meaning—which, however, remained elusive.

This situation was rendered completely nonsensical, however, with the publication in 1978 of the new list of psychiatric disorders (DSM-III) which referred to an "ego-dystonic homosexuality." This is defined as "a desire [in a homosexually behaving person] to acquire or increase heterosexual arousal." As Walker notes, this creates a situation where it appears to be a mental illness to desire to acquire or increase heterosexual arousal. Walker eloquently discusses the details and ramifications of this new diagnostic category and also asks: "Since when does the desire to gain a new skill (whether heterosexuality or piano-playing) require a psychiatric diagnosis?" (Walker, in press).

Current psychiatric diagnosis concepts are useless at best and, at worst, a potentially dangerous avenue for justifying continued labelling of homosexuals as ill despite the lack of evidence for that designation.

All of the concepts presented so far relate to the nature or definition of homosexuality. Still another consideration is the question of what measures one uses as evidence of homosexuality. Verbal self-ratings, strictly behavioral measures of sexual activity, ratings of fantasy content, and psychophysiological measures of pupil dilation or genital engorgement or blood supply have all been used as measures of sexual orientation. Despite this diversity of measurement techniques, it is not clearly known how well these different measures correlate, or even if they are measuring the same thing. However, it is reasonable to assume that how one measures a phenomenon will affect the definition and conceptualization of that phenomenon.

This cursory review of the problems in defining and measuring homosexuality can end with no conclusion at this point in time, except perhaps to suggest to the reader that the complexity and lack of hard information and decisive theory be always kept in mind.

The largest single methodological problem in the scientific study of homosexuality can now be addressed: how to define and obtain a representative—or even useful—homosexual sample. As one can guess from the above discussion, this is no easy task. However, samples of homosexual individuals for research have generally lacked even the most rudimentary familiarity with most of the issues outlined above. Without being iconoclastic or extreme, it can safely be said that no research endeavor to date has used a representative homosexual sample.

The problem is as follows: Demographically oriented research has consistently concluded that homosexual behavior cuts across social, economic, educational, ethnic, racial, religious, regional, and other sociological variables (see Gebhard, 1972, for a review of this literature). For a phenomenon that has been so frequently studied, homosexual behavior remains remarkably uncorrelated with most of the major groupings into which social scientists assign their subjects. There has been little to suggest that the homosexual population in general differs from the U.S. adult population in general, except that the homosexual population tends to be disproportionately unmarried and childless. In fact, the knowledge that a given individual is homosexual is a relatively uninformative fact. Yet, every study in this area has sampled from particular, and sometimes unusual, segments of the broadly homosexual population.

In many earlier studies, samples were often drawn from legally or psychiatrically involved homosexuals. These samples are unacceptable for a variety of reasons. Any comparison between homosexual patient groups and heterosexual nonpatient groups is clearly specious: the patient versus nonpatient dimension is overriding, regardless of sexual orientation. Comparisons between homosexual and heterosexual patients in many settings are difficult to untangle. In those cases where there are psychiatric problems in addition to the issue of sexual orientation, one is hard pressed to determine when the psychiatric problem ends and the sexual orientation concern begins. The use of a heterosexual patient control group is inadequate. It may be more stressful to be, for example, a homosexual schizophrenic than a heterosexual schizophrenic and in ways which are not readily discernible.

There is also the influence of social context in many patient settings; there have been and still remain some mental health professionals who are intolerant of homosexuality. If a researcher is aware enough of a patient's homosexuality to include that person in a homosexual sample, the possibility exists that the subject may experience distress merely as a result of that knowledge, contributing further to whatever stresses previously existed.

Some research has been based on individuals who are in psychotherapy for difficulties relating to their sexual orientation. The comparison group usually consists of heterosexual psychotherapy cases who have sought help for a variety of reasons. In these cases, the homosexual sample, by definition, consists of nonadjusted homosexuals. While findings based on such samples may be illuminating in discovering things about nonadjusted homosexuals, it is not clearly known whether these findings are applicable to nonpatient homosexuals.

In fact, one study suggests that these findings are clearly not applicable (Turner, Pielmaier, James, & Orwin, 1974). Male homosexuals who sought aversion therapy treatment for their homosexuality were compared to a sample of male nonpatient homosexuals from homophile organizations who had never sought psychiatric treatment. The Eysenck Personality Inventory (EPI) and the Sixteen Personality Factor Questionnaire (16PF) were given to both groups. The patient group scored significantly higher on measures of neuroticism and were more aggressive, tense, conservative, and group-dependent than the nonpatient group. As the discussion in the article on psychological testing will indicate, these results can be taken as merely suggestive. However, at the very least, there are no good reasons to assume that homosexual patient samples are representative of homosexuals in general and some hints that they may clearly be unrepresentative.

Samples of homosexuals in psychoanalysis present an added complication. Given the requirements of such treatment—that it is intensive, expensive, often upsetting, and of extremely long duration—it is likely that persons who willingly undergo this regime are exceptionally motivated or exceptionally troubled or both. Further, psychoanalytic patients are notoriously atypical in that they are often better educated, more intelligent, and of higher socioeconomic status. Involuntary patient samples have all the shortcomings of psychiatrically involved samples and also some of the difficulties of legally involved samples, described below.

Legally involved samples are inappropriate, as are samples from institutions such as the armed forces. The salient feature about legally involved samples is that their homosexual behavior has come to the attention of law enforcement agencies. Given the adverse consequences of legal involvement and the fact that most homosexuals do not become legally involved on account of homosexual behavior, this sample probably includes a good proportion of homosexuals whose reality testing or behavioral controls are tenuous. Consenting adult sodomy statutes are extremely difficult to enforce. With very few exceptions, homosexuals who are legally involved become so not because of private sexual relations with a consenting adult but because sexual relations are either not in private, not consenting, or not with an adult, or because of other unusual circumstances, such as police entrapment or harassment. Clearly, these samples are unusual and atypical.

Samples of prisoners whose crimes are nonsexual but who are known to prison authorities, and samples from the armed forces or similar institutions, all suffer from the problem of the "known homosexual." Given the inevitably aversive and perhaps dangerous consequences of being known as homosexual in such environments, these individuals are an unusually stressed group. In addition, homosexuality in prison must be viewed with caution, as it probably reflects more about the social hierarchy among prisoners than it does their sexual orientation (see Money, 1972, pp. 73-74).

The unsuitability of psychiatrically and legally involved samples has come to be accepted by most researchers in recent years. More current studies tend to utilize normal or functioning homosexual samples, obtaining subjects through gay and lesbian bars, social and friendship networks, organizations, and clubs. While these samples are interesting in their own right, they do not constitute a representative sample of homosexuals.

Gay or lesbian bar samples heavily tap individuals who use alcohol. Bar samples are probably also skewed toward the urban, the young, the extroverted, and those lacking a consistent sexual partner. Further, sources in the gay and lesbian communities estimate that the percentage of homosexuals who go to gay and lesbian bars with any frequency may be as low as 10 to 25 percent.

Homosexual organizations are likely to be relatively skewed toward persons who are open about being homosexual and probably more politically active or conscious. Any ideas about characteristics of open versus "closeted" homosexuals can only be speculative at this point, but this quality alone places these individuals in a minority and makes them unusual. Samples using friends of the experimenter and derived contacts are likely to be biased in the direction of being like the experimenter: well-educated, middle-class, and so on. Samples from social networks will tend to be homogeneous and contain consistent biases, as friendship networks by their nature contain like individuals. Further, research done in the United States has almost exclusively utilized white, non-Hispanic samples.

Finally, it must be remembered that in many places homosexuals remain potential and even likely targets for embarrassment and harassment. Some homosexuals, particularly those who are successful and established professionally, may realistically be unwilling to take the risks involved in being subjects of research. Furthermore, this may tell us something about those homosexuals who are willing to be researched.

Burdick and Stewart (1974) studied male homosexual undergraduates from a university homosexual organization. In the first part of the study, all subjects were administered the EPI. All were asked to return in a few days to complete the second part of the study, which they were told was a battery of physiological measurements. This second part was a deception; the experimenters simply listed which subjects returned (25 out of 67 did). Those individuals who returned had significantly higher mean scores on both the neuroticism and extroversion scores of the EPI. Burdick and Stewart theorized that there is a tendency for homosexuals who readily volunteer for psychological research to be less well-adjusted than those who do not.

While this conclusion is probably premature, it does raise the issue that homosexual volunteers for research may be an unusual group. The assumption that research volunteers are likely to be representative of homosexuals is not justified or warranted.

Note that our discussion of sampling so far has not referred to the issues and complexities in defining who is homosexual, discussed earlier in this introduction. The reason is that most researchers have not attended to these complexities. The level of sophistication used in most studies consists of an assumption that individuals who are in homosexual organizations, bars, and the like, or who say they are homosexual, are, in fact, homosexual. There is a further assumption that control groups are entirely heterosexual—despite the fact that the Kinsey data would suggest otherwise. More astute researchers asked their heterosexual samples if they were heterosexual, and the most astute have asked both their samples for a self-rated Kinsey score. However, these researchers have varied as to what Kinsey scores constitute a homosexual sample; some have used exclusive homosexuals (Kinsey 6), while others have included a mix of bisexuals and homosexuals, including some predominant heterosexuals (Kinsey 1 through 6), as well as other combinations.

The point should be clear by now that the research on homosexuality has been characterized by poor and biased sampling procedures and vague, erroneous, or simplistic assumptions about the definition of homosexuality. That raises two questions: Can adequate sampling and definition be accomplished? Can the literature tell us anything valid about homosexuals? The answer to both is a cautious and qualified yes.

While it is impossible to obtain a completely representative sample of homosexuals, workable approximations can be achieved. There is nothing to suggest an important relationship between homosexuality and most major demographic variables. Therefore, any homosexual sample should mimic the major demographic characteristics of the locality from which the sample is taken. The other principle is that sampling should be diverse. As any subgroup in the general homosexual population is bound to be skewed in some fashion, homosexual subjects should be drawn from as wide a variety of sources as possible. These sources and the demographic characteristics of the samples should then be described in considerable detail. While these procedures will not eliminate sampling problems, they should reduce them, and a clear and detailed description of procedures will make any biases apparent.

One final sampling suggestion is as follows. It can be argued that homosexual populations, especially in some areas, have a higher general level of stress due to social and political pressures. As recent research developments have indicated, the amount and degree of life stressors is measurable (Paykel, Prusoff, & Uhlenhuth, 1971). It is possible, then, and it may be advisable in some research situations, to have homosexual and heterosexual samples roughly equivalent on measures of life stressors.

As for the second question, it is not possible to make noteworthy statements about homosexuality in general, given the problematic state of the literature. However, that does not mean that certain questions cannot be answered. For example, the question of whether homosexuality per se is or is not pathological and indicative of psychological disturbance is easily answered. As will be discussed in the next chapter on psychological testing, numerous studies on a variety of samples have consistently concluded that there is no difference in psychological adjustment between homosexuals and heterosexuals. Therefore, if other studies find that some homosexuals are disturbed, the proper conclusion is that they are disturbed for reasons other than sexual orientation, or perhaps for reasons in conjunction with sexual orientation; but it cannot be maintained that sexual orientation per se and psychological adjustment are related.

Further, while it is not possible to generalize about homosexuals, it is possible to make some carefully weighed statements about those homosexual samples that have been adequately researched. These samples tend to be white, male, young, middle-class, and educated. This bias plagues much research in the behavioral sciences. Therefore, while generalizations beyond the samples studied must be avoided and conclusions must be reserved and cautious, some things have been learned about some homosexuals.

A number of studies will now be discussed to illustrate some of the problems of sampling, definition, and faulty assumptions. This concern for elucidating underlying theoretical problems and methodological issues permeates many parts of this section, and will surface again elsewhere in this book. This emphasis is a deliberate attempt to educate the reader in a long-range fashion so that as new theories and data develop, a reader can be equipped with conceptual tools to evaluate and understand new ideas. One of the more important purposes is to train the reader to be a skeptical and discerning consumer of the past, current, and future literature on mental health and homosexuality.

Oliver and Mosher (1968) conducted a study using a prison sample, and their work is a good example of the difficulties with legally involved samples. Based on guard reports, they identified three groups which they termed *heterosexual, homosexual insertee,* and *homosexual insertor.* Using the MMPI, they found that the homosexual insertee group had significantly higher scores on a number of scales than the heterosexual group, but that the homosexual insertor group had even greater elevations, and on more of the scales. While this study may be an interesting examination of psychological characteristics of various prisoners, it is difficult to see what bearing this study has on homosexuality. Using prison guard reports is highly suspect; the insertee group is probably best characterized by their role as victims and as a group are likely to be vulnerable and less powerful for a variety of reasons, only one of which might be homosexuality.

Doidge and Holtzman (1960) looked at four groups of Air Force trainees. One group was suspected of homosexual offenses and judged predominantly homosexual; another was suspected of homosexual offenses and judged "accessory." Both groups had been interrogated. A heterosexual group, suspected of other kinds of offenses, had also been interrogated and constituted the third group. A final group consisted of heterosexual normals, neither suspected of offenses nor interrogated. MMPI profiles of the homosexual accessory, heterosexual disciplinary, and heterosexual normal groups were very similar. The homosexual predominant group had a markedly different profile, with extreme elevations on many MMPI scales. Doidge and Holtzman concluded that homosexuality per se was indicative of psychopathology.

This study illustrates a number of severe methodological errors and also illustrates the social context of research. Although Doidge and Holtzman were satisfied with their sampling procedures, their description of the advantages of studying male homosexuals in the Air Force sounds more like a case against such a study:

> The almost complete lack of privacy and the barracks-type of living are likely to stimulate sexual drives in male homosexuals. Prevailing cultural attitudes and stringent military policy heighten the conflict, precipitating contact with the psychiatric clinic. In the Air Force, all homosexual suspects are subjected to exhaustive interrogations by special investigators [1960, p. 9].

Based on the authors' own description, it is apparent that homosexuals in such a setting are subjected to extreme levels of harassment and stress, to the point of "precipitating contact with the psychiatric clinic," and that the control groups they used were inadequate.

Further, the authors provided no clear and replicable explanation of how they determined which persons were accessory or predominant homosexuals. As one group is indistinguishable from normals and the other is severely disturbed, this distinction and the mechanism by which it was made are crucial. Finally, the profile of the predominant homosexual group is so disturbed (from a clinician's standpoint, their group profile looks like an acute schizophrenic reaction) that one wonders if that elusive criterion for selection as predominantly homosexual is disorganization of psychotic proportions. This study, then, is an example of the inadequacy of legally and psychiatrically involved samples, of how certain social contexts are inappropriate for research efforts, and of how research may create the problem it seeks to investigate.

Similar issues are demonstrated in Cattell and Morony's (1962) study of Australian males. One group consisted of prisoners convicted of homosexual acts; another, of prisoners convicted of general nonhomosexual crimes; a third group of unconvicted homosexuals obtained through social worker contacts; and a fourth group of (presumably) heterosexual normals who were employed as clerical workers. Using the 16PF, Cattell and Morony claimed that the profiles of the two homosexual groups were highly similar and could, for all practical purposes, be taken as representing a homosexual-type profile. They stated that this homosexual-type profile was significantly different on many scales from both the Australian general criminal and American normal profiles, using a rather complicated statistical procedure to make this comparison. They concluded that homosexuality, per se, was neurotic and pathological.

It would appear that Cattell and Morony's unconvicted homosexual sample was meant to be a counterpart to the heterosexual normal group in the same way that the homosexual prisoner group was a counterpart to the heterosexual prisoner group. However, it seems that this unconvicted homosexual sample is in some sense psychiatrically involved, or at least somehow involved with agents of society. Their description of this sample is as follows: "Through discreet social worker contacts, and discreet infiltration of the communication channels of homosexuals, it was possible to get measures on 33 uncharged male homosexuals." This poorly described sample does not appear on the surface to be a functioning homosexual group; the reason why these individuals are known to social workers is not explained. Therefore, what Cattell and Morony appear to have obtained are two highly particular samples of homosexuals: one from prisons and the other through social worker contacts.

In addition, their combining of the two homosexual groups into a type is suspect. While there were similarities in scores between the homosexual groups, there were also differences, and combining these groups is more confusing than informative. Further, Cattell and Morony then argued that while there were differences between the American normative, or normal, sample on which the test was standardized and the Australian heterosexual normal group, these were not statistically significant. Based on this argument, they then compared the composite Australian homosexual-type group to the American normative sample. This kind of comparison is invalid. The fact that the American normative and Australian heterosexual normal groups were not statistically significant does not preclude the possibility that those differences biased the data analysis; especially when using a peculiarly derived composite homosexual-type group and also when using, as Cattell and Morony did, an unusual statistical technique (multivariate data analysis) that is very sensitive to chance variation in the data. This technique is best used with larger samples and requires replication before firm conclusions can be drawn. Any comparisons made should have been with Australian samples only, not only for the reasons above but also to avoid an invalidating cross-cultural biasing effect. Finally, Evans (1970) has criticized this study on other grounds, stating that the authors' interpretation of the data was questionable.

The Cattell and Morony study is a good example of how combining samples in inappropriate ways, using improper comparison groups, and using questionable sampling procedures (as well as the more technical problems with statistical analysis and interpretation of data) can work together to make a potentially interesting study misleading and worthless.

One final example, the study by Bieber et al. (1962), will focus more on the social contextual factors—specifically researcher bias—although this study, too, is riddled with major problems in sampling and interpretation of results, as discussed by Gonsiorek (1977, pp. 12-13). This study is noteworthy because it is an excellent example of extreme researcher bias. It compared male heterosexual and homosexual patients in psychoanalysis. This sample, as discussed above, is problematic in its own right. More important, the same group of psychoanalysts developed a theory about homosexuality; developed the questionnaire to test their theory; designed the research study; served as analysts for the patient subjects; served as raters in the research project on their own patients; interpreted the results; and finally concluded that their theory had been verified. There are too many sources of potential researcher bias in this manner of research. In fact, it would be difficult to imagine how to build more potential for research bias into experimental procedures than the Bieber group did.

By now, it is hoped that the reader has gained some perspective on the difficulties in defining homosexuality, sampling from homosexual populations, and the methodological problems of research on mental health and homosexuality. Again, the importance of a skeptical frame of reference in reading scientific literature on homosexuality cannot be emphasized enough.

The chapters prepared for this section can be divided into three parts, each with a different focus. Those by John Gonsiorek and Eli Coleman comprise the first part. Gonsiorek's review of psychological test data is an attempt to synthesize this literature into a clear answer to the question of whether homosexuality per se is related to psychological adjustment or other personality characteristics. Coleman's review of the literature on treatment of homosexuality examines the question of whether homosexuality can be changed to heterosexuality. These chapters conclude that homosexuality is unrelated to psychological adjustment, and that there is no reason to believe homosexuality can be reliably changed into heterosexuality. These two chapters form a basis for abandoning the illness and change-oriented notions about homosexuality, which have neither empirical support nor pragmatic utility. It should be noted, if only in passing, that the above conclusions are maintained despite recent claims by Masters and Johnson (1979) that they can revert or cure homosexuality. While Coleman does mention their work briefly, it has been reviewed in detail (see Gonsiorek, 1981) and found sorely lacking in the basics of scientific methodology, data analysis, and clinical credibility.

The next two chapters discuss the important theoretical, ethical, and social issues that have sharply and often painfully emerged as the illness model of homosexuality has crumbled. Richard Pillard and Gerald Davison outline and discuss many of the enduring and important issues, Pillard focusing on the relationship between the role of mental health disciplines, the treatment of homosexuality, and its social consequences; and Davison presenting a discussion of the ethical concerns involved.

With the outmoded concepts about mental health and homosexuality discarded and the theoretical implications of these changes elucidated, the last set of chapters focuses on the future. While no single model has yet been developed to replace the old disease-oriented model of homosexuality, a number of new and exciting systems of thought have come into focus in recent years. Three chapters, all very different from each other, offer the reader a glimpse of emerging models. Two of these have been extremely shortened for this volume due to space limitations imposed in the final editing; they appear full-length in an earlier Task Force publication (Gonsiorek, 1982b). Readers who are interested in clinical applications are referred to Gonsiorek (1980) for an overview and to Gonsiorek (1982a) for a detailed psychotherapy practitioner's handbook of new models.

Joel Hencken's chapter is an attempt to review a school of thought which has perhaps been the strongest proponent of the disease model of homosexuality—psychoanalysis—and breathes fresh life into some old ideas, demonstrating how some aspects of psychoanalytic thought may be compatible, indeed useful, for a nonillness view of homosexuality.

Coleman's paper (1982) on developmental stage theory attempts to examine the process of coming to terms with one's sexual identity and how it affects behavior, personality, and attitudes. Finally, my chapter (1982c) examines how social psychological forces may act on homosexual individuals, altering behavior and self-concept and perhaps providing an explanatory mechanism for some of the psychological processes observed in homosexual individuals.

In this way, the reader may review the past, mull over present issues, and consider future ideas in the area of mental health and homosexuality.

ACKNOWLEDGMENTS

While the ideas and efforts of many individuals helped shape this section, one individual's contribution stands out: Robert D. Wirt, Director of Clinical Psychology Training at the New School for Social Research, and past Director of the Programs in Health Care Psychology and Clinical Psychology Training at the University of Minnesota, generously reviewed the manuscripts. His meticulous and focused criticisms, gently proffered, helped ensure the high caliber of professional writing. Mark Snyder, Professor of Social Psychology, University of Minnesota, provided a valuable critique of the social psychology article. Nathaniel London, Clinical Professor, University of Minnesota Medical School and Training and Supervising Analyst, Chicago Institute for Psychoanalysis, provided guidance on the psychoanalysis chapter. Their assistance is also deeply appreciated.

· 6 ·

Results of Psychological Testing on Homosexual Populations

John C. Gonsiorek

An examination of psychological test findings with regard to homosexuality may appear to be one of the drier aspects of the scientific study of homosexuality. Scores on scales of various tests may seem removed from the quality of individuals' lives and common-sense notions of mental illness and psychological adjustment. However, in this chapter I intend to demonstrate that a careful examination of psychological test data can not only answer the important question of whether homosexuality per se is a sign of mental illness or psychological disturbance, but also clarify a number of other issues that tend to become confused in the study of homsexuality.

For example, much of the psychoanalytic theorizing about the causes of homosexuality focuses on certain family patterns which are alleged to predispose a child toward homosexuality. Whether or not one believes these theories of causality of homosexuality (and this topic is heatedly debated, with no apparent winner in sight), there is an implication in much of this research that since such a pattern is alleged to be more frequent in families of homosexuals, this is evidence that homosexuality per se is disturbed because such family patterns are indicative of psychological disturbance. On the face of it, this reasoning may sound plausible. In reality, however, such reasoning is circular. The veracity of theories which hold that certain family patterns are pathological are very much in question. When "differences" are found, this is alleged to be evidence in favor of the theory. But the existence of difference does not explain what those differences mean.

Careful examination of an example can help clarify this point. Suppose one divides subjects into two groups on the basis of a variable of interest:

heterosexual versus homosexual (forgetting for a moment the difficulties in determining sexual orientation as discussed in the introduction), low average versus high average IQ, introverted versus extroverted personalities, and so on. One may then study a variety of interesting variables in the two groups to determine if they differ on these variables. Suppose further that one finding is that the two groups differ on a variable which one's favorite theory says is a sign of psychological disturbance. Can one then conclude that the group with more of this variable is more disturbed?

NO. All kinds of errors in research design may have contaminated the results. However, even if the research design is strong, and the results are replicated in other independent research, the problem remains of determining the *meaning* of such findings. Given the immature state of knowledge in the behavioral sciences, it is not sufficient or even reasonable to assert that because one's favorite theory would lead to a conclusion that family pattern x means disturbance, therefore individuals with family pattern x are more disturbed. What would be required for proof of greater disturbance in one group are reliable, valid, and well-established measures of disturbance. Then if the group with the allegedly disturbed family pattern *also* scored in a disturbed range on these measures, there would be strong evidence for both a conclusion of greater disturbance in the group and for one's favorite theory. If the well-established measure of disturbance does not show disturbance in the group then one's favorite theory—or other research design factors—may be at fault. But certainly, a conclusion that the group with family pattern x is more disturbed is completely unwarranted.

Such reliable, valid, and well-established measures of psychological disturbance have been administered in research comparing homosexual and heterosexual populations, and this is the literature on psychological (or psychometric) testing, which will be reviewed below. This explanation was offered to illustrate that psychometric data are of crucial importance because they are the touchstone by which other theories and ideas about homosexuality must be tested. These psychological test data are the most accurate tools the behavioral sciences possess with regard to the question of psychological adjustment or disturbance. Any responsible and serious theory of homosexuality must take this information into account.

Homosexuals and heterosexuals may differ from each other in many ways; indeed, it would be curious if they did not. However, the answer to whether these differences indicate disturbance can be found in the results of the most reliable and well-validated indices of disturbance in the mental health armamentarium: psychological testing. And to anticipate the conclusion of this chapter, these testing results overwhelmingly suggest that if there are consistent, measurable differences between heterosexual and homosexual populations, they are not in the range of scores indicative of greater disturbance in the homosexual groups.

It is important to understand a few other crucial concepts before proceeding. One of these is the notion of normal range differences. Normality, whether defined as day-to-day adjustment in life, scores on various psychological tests, absence or presence of certain signs and symptoms, or any other valid measure, is not a unitary phenomenon. Normal, if it is to have any meaning at all, refers to a *range* of behavior, characteristics, test scores, or whatever, and it is this *normal range* that is the meaningful and workable concept of normality. Because normal is most usefully defined as a range of possibilities, it is possible for two groups of subjects to have different average, or mean, scores and both be normal—that is, within the normal range. For example, individuals or groups of differing heights, different cholesterol levels, or different degrees of social introversion or extraversion can all be in the normal range.

Differences can even be statistically significant and still be in the normal range. In some circumstances, it is possible to create statistical significance by using large samples or repeated independent measures. The existence of statistical significance only indicates that the differences meet certain mathematical criteria for being assigned a probability, or likelihood, of occurrence. Differences which are thus real mathematically may or may not be important or meaningful in a psychological or clinical sense, or in the context of what is known about normal ranges of difference. Finally, the existence of statistical significance provides no necessary justification for the manner in which such differences are interpreted. One of the useful features about a well-constructed psychological test is that the limits of the normal range for different populations are determined by independent research evidence, not by theory alone or by the comparative characteristics of the groups used in a given study.

A final concept is also important: the notion of base rates. Does the statement that homosexuality per se is not a sign of psychological disturbance mean that there are no disturbed homosexuals? Absolutely not. It means that the proportion, or base rate, of disturbed individuals in homosexual and heterosexual populations is roughly equivalent. Using the following figures solely for illustrative purposes, if 5 percent of the general population is seriously disturbed psychologically, 10 percent moderately disturbed, 15 percent slightly disturbed, and 70 percent within the normal range, then the statement that homosexuality is not in itself indicative of disturbance may mean that roughly the same proportions also hold in homosexual populations (that is, that many disturbed homosexuals can be found).

Further, there are some reasons (one being increased levels of external stress) to believe that certain measures of disturbance may be higher in certain homosexual populations. This also can be congruent with a conclusion that homosexuality in itself is not an indicator of psychological disturbance, because if homosexuals as a group are subject to more environmental stress, then a proper comparison group may not be heterosexuals in general, but heterosexuals with roughly equivalent environmental stress. Use of improper comparison groups is confusing and often invalid because one then compares groups with inherently different base rates.

For example, if one is examining the effects of fluoride in drinking water on the height, weight, and general health of Minnesota males, comparing this sample to a group of chronically undernourished Sub-Saharan tribesmen will create a serious base rate problem, whereas a comparison of Northern European males of roughly the same socioeconomic status of the Minnesota group would reduce that problem. Likewise, a given score on a social introversion-extraversion measure may be average if one is a shy but well-adjusted Ph.D. candidate in Eighteenth-Century Philosophy from rural North Dakota and of Scandinavian extraction, or markedly atypical if one is a highly gregarious but well-adjusted salesperson with an eleventh-grade education from Brooklyn and of Sicilian extraction.

By ignoring these concepts of normal range and base rates, a researcher can artificially create disturbed individuals of any category: homosexuals, heterosexuals, Presbyterians, lawyers, persons under six feet tall, and so on.

These issues are the essence of the sampling problems mentioned in the introduction to this section. The vast majority of the studies to be reviewed in this chapter are flawed in that they sample from particular, as opposed to general, segments of homosexual populations, or from extreme or unusual groups, such as prisoners or psychiatric patients. This makes interpreting a general pattern difficult, although not impossible. Enough studies of tolerable research design have been performed on a variety of samples.

Despite all these problems, a clear and consistent pattern emerges from studies on homosexuals using psychological testing: Homosexuality in and of itself is unrelated to psychological disturbance or maladjustment. Homosexuals as a group are not more psychologically disturbed on account of their homosexuality. Differences within the normal range often appear between homosexual and heterosexual groups in these studies. However, considerable differences between different groups of homosexual subjects are also found, making it difficult to ascertain if there are clear differences in personality between homosexuals and heterosexuals. Further, attempts to differentiate homosexuals from heterosexuals on the basis of psychological testing have not been generally successful. The reader who may be interested in a more technical and detailed treatment of these and other issues is referred to two recent comprehensive reviews of this literature (Gonsiorek, 1977; Meredith & Reister, 1980). A review of the more salient research now follows.

One line of psychological test research on homosexual populations has attempted to create special scales, signs, or scoring patterns that could differentiate homosexuals from heterosexuals. Two tests, the Minnesota Multiphasic Personality Inventory (MMPI) and the Rorschach, have attracted virtually all of the attempts to do this. This is not surprising, as these two are probably the most commonly used and widely researched tests for assessing personality.

The original Masculinity-Femininity (MF) scale of the MMPI was an attempt to discriminate homosexuals from heterosexuals. The inability of this scale to do this without an intolerably high inaccuracy rate (particularly in the direction of calling many more people homosexual than actually exist in the groups; this is termed a *false positive rate*) was so striking that early proponents of the MMPI quickly issued caveats about the scale's ineffectiveness at making this differentiation (see Dahlstrom, Welsh, & Dalhstrom, 1973).

A number of other researchers attempted to create and utilize new scales for the MMPI to differentiate homosexuals from heterosexuals. These included attempts with a Homosexuality Scale (HSX) (Friberg, 1967; Manosevitz, 1971; Panton, 1960; Pierce, 1973); a Masculine-Feminine Index (MFI) (Aronson & Grumpelt, 1961; Singer, 1970); a Sexual Deviate (SD) Scale (Hartman, 1967); as well as others. The results of this research activity were disappointing. Panton's (1960) HSX scale may have some utility in differentiating men who engage in homosexual activity while in prison from those who do not, but the remainder of this research was not able to effect the desired differentiation. As the reader will recall from the introduction, prison populations are problematic and at best represent little more than prison populations. Attempts to use other MMPI scales fared no better (see Gonsiorek, 1977, pp. 17-20).

Using the Rorschach, a number of attempts were made to discover signs that could predict homosexuality. Wheeler's (1949) 20 signs for male homosexuality attracted most of the efforts in this area. However, when Goldfried et al. (1971) reviewed the literature on Wheeler's signs, they concluded that only 6 of the 20 could probably discriminate homosexual tendencies. This is a much more vague and less useful concept than homosexual behavior. In addition, these studies depended heavily on patient samples, making them useful for discriminating homosexual psychiatric patients from heterosexual psychiatric patients at best but of little value beyond these samples.

Another kind of study has addressed itself to the question of whether homosexuality per se is pathological. For convenience, these studies will be reviewed by psychological tests used. All of the studies discussed below have some sampling problems to varying degrees, and a handful were so strikingly flawed as to warrant discussion in the introduction as prototypes of poor design. However, some information can be obtained from these works.

Using the MMPI to compare male homosexuals and heterosexuals, a number of researchers found that homosexuals as a group did not score in the disturbed or pathological ranges of the various clinical scales (Braaten & Darling, 1965; Dean & Richardson, 1964; Horstmann, 1972; Manosevitz, 1970, 1971; Panton, 1960; Pierce, 1973).

The Dean and Richardson (1964) study sparked a small debate that is instructive because it illustrates some of the issues outlined earlier in this chapter. In this study, homosexual subjects scored significantly higher than heterosexuals on three clinical scales. However, as the scores of both homosexual and heterosexual groups were both within the normal range, the authors concluded that the homosexual group was not more disturbed than the heterosexual group. However, Zucker and Manosevitz (1966) proposed that Dean and Richardson had "explained away" important differences, emphasized the three scales that were significantly different, and proposed a diagnostic scheme based on these three scales. Dean and Richardson (1966) countered with the points raised earlier—namely, that significant differences may be interesting, but they are not indicative of disturbance unless the scores of one group are in a range which other research validates as pathological. As the scores of both groups in the original study were within the normal range, Dean and Richardson concluded that they should not be used to imply that the homosexual group was more disturbed.

On MMPI studies with homosexual women, both Miller (1963) and Ohlson and Wilson (1974) found no indication of greater disturbance in either homosexual or heterosexual groups. Interestingly enough, there were significant but normal range differences in both these studies, with the heterosexual groups scoring higher on a number of clinical scales. As both groups in each study were within the normal range, the authors correctly concluded as they did. However, at least one writer (Freedman, 1975) has been led astray by such studies and has erroneously concluded on the basis of significant but normal range differences that some homosexual samples may be better adjusted psychologically. This illustrates the same specious and fallacious reasoning that Zucker and Manosevitz, as well as many others, fell victim to, but with the conclusion reversed.

Two other studies (Doidge & Holtzman, 1960; Oliver & Mosher, 1968) were reviewed in the introduction as examples of particularly poor

research design. While these studies did find significant differences suggestive of greater psychological disturbance (that is, in the pathological
range) in their homosexual samples, these findings are by-products of
faulty sampling and poor design.

Other tests that have been frequently utilized in this line of research are
Cattell's 16 Personality Factor Questionnaire (16PF) and Eysenck's Personality Inventory (EPI), as well as different versions and subsections of
these tests. A study by Cattell and Morony (1962) conducted in Australia
and using the 16PF concluded that homosexuality per se was neurotic and
indicative of psychopathology. However, as was discussed in the introduction to this section, this study is so seriously flawed as to be useless. Evans
(1970) also criticized this study on a number of grounds and conducted his
own study on American male homosexuals. While he did find differences
between his homosexual and heterosexual groups, he concluded that
these differences were of sufficiently small magnitude as to support a
conclusion that homosexuality per se was not necessarily an indication of
psychological disturbance.

Siegelman (1972b), using a derivation of the 16PF, studied male homosexuals and heterosexuals. He found some normal range differences and
concluded that there was no difference in psychological adjustment
between his heterosexual and homosexual groups. In addition, Siegelman
added another feature to his research design—a traditional measure of
masculinity-femininity—separated his homosexual sample into high and
low scores on femininity, and ran further comparisons on these subgroups. He found that the high feminine homosexuals scored the most
differently from the heterosexual sample and concluded that while homosexuals in general are no less well adjusted than heterosexuals, a subgroup
of high feminine homosexuals may be maladjusted. Siegelman, however,
was cautious about this last statement and alternately suggested that the
nature of adjustment may be different in male homosexual and heterosexual groups.

A number of studies were conducted comparing homosexual and
heterosexual women, all of them using the EPI, except for Siegelman
(1972a), who used a derivation of the 16PF. The bulk of these studies
(Freedman, 1971; Wilson & Green, 1971; Hopkins, 1969; Siegelman,
1972a) concluded that there is no evidence to support differences in
psychological adjustment between homosexual and heterosexual women.
Two other studies (Eisinger, 1972; Kenyon, 1968) concluded that their
homosexual samples were psychologically disturbed; however, these two
studies have research design problems which make their interpretation
difficult. Eisinger did not compare homosexual and heterosexual groups,
but rather compared scores from a homosexual sample with normative

data for the EPI. As Eisinger gave no information on demographic characteristics of her sample, and little information in general, it is difficult to
determine if this comparison was appropriate. Kenyon used Kinsey ratings
of 0 to define the heterosexual sample and ratings of 1 through 6 to define
the homosexual sample. As the reader will recall from the discussion in the
introduction, this means that some predominantly heterosexual and
bisexual individuals were mixed together in this "homosexual" sample.
Kenyon's data are therefore difficult to interpret unless they can be broken
down by Kinsey ratings in a more meaningful fashion.

A number of researchers utilized an objectively scored test called the
Adjective Check List (ACL). Chang and Block (1960), using this test,
found no differences in general adjustment between homosexual and
heterosexual males. Evans (1971), using the same test, found that male
homosexuals appeared to have more problems with self-acceptance than
heterosexual males, but that only a small minority of the homosexuals
could be considered maladjusted. Thompson et al. (1971) used the ACL to
study psychological adjustment of both male and female homosexuals and
heterosexuals, concluding that sexual orientation was not related to personal adjustment in either sex.

All the studies reviewed so far have utilized objective personality tests,
tests which use an objectively scored, usually true-false format, and with a
considerable. body of empirical research to guide interpretation of the
tests. Projective tests use a more freestyle response format; their scoring,
while structured, often requires some degree of subjective judgment; and
the amount of research about interpretation of these results tends not to
be as voluminous or scientifically rigorous. However, proponents of this
variety of psychological testing have argued that these less-structured
testing formats are more sensitive to the subtleties of certain personality
variables. A number of studies using such tests have focused on
homosexual-heterosexual group comparisons.

Some of the unsuccessful attempts at differentiating homosexuals and
heterosexuals using the Rorschach were discussed earlier in this chapter.
A famous study using projective testing was conducted in the late 1950s by
Evelyn Hooker (1957). This study is also noteworthy because it was an
early, and one of the most serious, challenges to the belief that homosexuality per se was indicative of psychological disturbance. Hooker administered a battery of projective tests [Rorschach, Thematic Apperception
Test (TAT), and Make-A-Picture-Story Test (MAPS)], to 30 homosexual
and 30 heterosexual males, all recruited from community organizations
and none with legal or psychiatric involvement. All the projective test
protocols were then given to a panel of projective test experts. These
raters were given no information on which protocols were from heterosex-

ual or homosexual subjects. The raters were unable to differentiate the homosexual from heterosexual subjects. Hooker concluded that homosexuality as a clinical entity does not exist and that homosexuality per se is not pathological.

This review of the psychometric studies on homosexuality is not complete, but it does include the better-known and better-designed studies in this area. Reviews by Gonsiorek (1977) and Meredith and Reister (1980) can be consulted for greater detail. The general conclusion is clear: These studies overwhelmingly suggest that homosexuality per se is not related to psychopathology or psychological adjustment. The few studies which suggest the contrary are among the weakest methodologically, and some of these are so flawed as to be uninterpretable. However, differences between homosexual and heterosexual groups are typically found, and these tend to be within the normal range. However, the pattern of these differences is not sufficiently consistent to describe a typical homosexual personality or adjustment style. These differences may reflect idiosyncracies in the samples used, or they may reflect the generally increased level of stress experienced by many homosexuals in a society that is generally intolerant of homosexuality. These differences, then, may be varieties of mild stress reactions or perhaps indicate the development in some homosexuals of an increased variety of coping mechanisms to deal with these stresses. Some of the processes theorized to mediate this relationship between homosexuals and a rejecting society are discussed in Chapter 10.

CONCLUSIONS

It is my contention that the issue of whether homosexuality per se is a sign of psychopathology, psychological maladjustment, or disturbance has been answered, and the answer is that it is not. The studies reviewed and the findings in this chapter ought to be the touchstone of further theory and research in the study of homosexuality, because psychological tests are the most carefully designed, reliable, valid, and objective measures of adjustment in the armamentarium of the behavioral sciences. Again, this is not to say that psychologically disturbed homosexuals do not exist; nor does it mean that no homosexuals are disturbed because of their sexuality. Rather, the conclusion is that homosexuality in and of itself bears no necessary relationship to psychological adjustment. This should not be surprising; heterosexuals disturbed because of their sexuality fill many therapists' caseloads. Because sexual expression is one of the most intimate, psychologically rich, and complex of all human interactions, it is not surprising that individuals who are troubled or disturbed will likely manifest problems in their sexual relationships, regardless of sexual orientation.

Finally, until the findings cited here are overturned by psychological test data of equal or better research design, breadth, and numbers, theories contending that the existence of differences between homosexuals and heterosexuals implies maladjustment are irresponsible, uninformed, or both.

· 7 ·

Changing Approaches to the
Treatment of Homosexuality
A Review

Eli Coleman

Today's counselors and therapists are faced with the theoretical, ethical, moral, and practical decisions as to how to treat their clients with same-sex sexual preferences. The traditional approach has been to treat homosexuality as an illness and thus to find ways to cure the homosexual and eliminate same-sex feelings and behavior.

This illness model of treatment has been based on psychoanalytic theories of personality and psychopathology. Many psychoanalysts have believed that homosexuality is a result of disturbed familial relationships. In 1962, Bieber and his associates published their famous study of homosexuality. These psychoanalysts thought that in most cases of homosexuality, the mothers were close-binding, possessive, and overintimate. The mothers seemed to seek the intimacy and closeness with their sons that was lacking in their marital relationships. The fathers in these case studies were invariably described as distant, absent or hostile. The prehomosexual sons developed a fear and hate for their fathers on the one hand and a yearning for their affection on the other. The prehomosexual sons feared retaliation for their sexual desires for their mothers. Bieber and his associates believed that these children grew up and developed a fear of heterosexual intercourse and competition for women as a way of defending against aggressive males. They sought out homosexual contact as a way of gaining sexual gratification and avoiding the anxiety involved with heterosexual activity. It was also a way for them to get the love and acceptance from men they were not able to get from their fathers. Treat-

81

ment based on this understanding of homosexuality has been to uncover these early childhood conflicts and reduce the individual's neurotic fear of heterosexuality.

Psychoanalysts' notion of disturbed familial relationship as the cause of homosexuality has been seriously questioned by other psychologists and personality theorists (see Chapter 6). In fact, many who grow up in environments described by Bieber and his associates do not develop a homosexual orientation and vice versa.

Nevertheless, psychoanalysts who have accepted Bieber's notions have attempted to cure homosexuality through psychoanalysis. The reported results of this form of treatment have been far from encouraging. Bieber et al. (1962) reported that 29 of their 106 male homosexuals (27 percent) showed a significant shift to heterosexuality aftter 150-350 hours of therapy. Most of this improvement occurred for the "bisexuals" in this study. The effects of this amount of therapy on those who were not "cured" by this method were not discussed by the authors. Psychoanalytic therapists Mayerson and Leif (1965) reported that half of their 19 male patients treated had became exclusively heterosexual four years after termination. In the psychoanalytic studies, most of the change has occurred for bisexuals and little or no change has occurred for predominantly or exclusively homosexual patients. Another major problem found in the psychoanalytic studies is that *success* has usually been defined as the elimination of homosexual *behavior*. These researchers have assumed that change in behavior reflects change in orientation or preferences. Behavior may be altered, but one's sexual orientation is probably better reflected in one's attitudes and fantasies.

Learning theorists and behavior therapists, on the other hand, have traditionally seen homosexuality as maladaptive rather than as an illness per se. However, similar to psychoanalysts, behavior therapists have tried to "cure" their homosexual patients. In general, the results have not been much better than those reported by psychoanalysts. Some of their methods have been to modify sexual fantasies. Heterosexual fantasies have been paired with masturbation, while homosexual fantasies have been extinguished (see McGuire, Carlisle, & Young, 1965). The most widely known method of extinguishing arousal to homosexual fantasies has been through the use of electrical shock while viewing slides of same-sex nudes (see Feldman & MacCullough, 1965). An alternative procedure which does not involve the use of shock has been the use of aversive imagery (Cautela, 1966, 1967). The patient is asked to imagine an attractive homosexual scene followed by the suggestion of nausea for equally repulsive thoughts. After sufficient pairings, the patient's reaction to homosexual stimuli is pain, anxiety, or neutral feelings. Theoretically, this leads to the elimination of homosexual behavior. There are a number of single case studies of males who have been "successfully" treated by these techniques.

These techniques have been criticized for a number of reasons. Davison (1977 and Chapter 8 this volume), one of the pioneers in this approach, has called for the abandonment of these procedures on the grounds that they are ethically questionable. He believes that homosexuals who voluntarily seek change do so in an atmosphere of discrimination and condemnation. He advises that therapists should not become a part of this discrimination. Some have questioned the long-term effects of these techniques. Others have noted that the positive results that have been reported are due to the pressure applied to the patient to report change. They would be unlikely to report no change if that meant more shocks or aversive imagery.

Another behavioral approach that has been designed to "cure" homosexuality is systematic desensitization. This approach is based on the assumption that homosexuality is due to anxiety about heterosexuality. Therapy is designed to reduce anxiety toward heterosexual stimuli. Again, successful single case studies have been reported for these methods. The criterion for success in these studies as well as those for other behavioral approaches has been change in behavior and there is no evidence that there has been a long-term shift in orientation, attitude, or fantasy. (For a more complete review of the behavioral and psychoanalytic studies, see Coleman, 1978.)

Masters and Johnson (1979), who have revolutionalized the area of sexual therapy and counseling, recently reported on their attempts to help homosexuals *revert* or *convert* to heterosexuality. They present the most optimistic reports of change to date. Masters and Johnson treated 54 men and 13 women who expressed a desire to move into full heterosexual functioning. Through careful screening, Masters and Johnson eliminated 23 percent of these applicants for treatment because of lack of motivation or because of complicating psychological illnesses. The majority of clients treated had prior heterosexual experience which ranged decreasingly from dominant to considerable (Kinsey ratings 2 to 4). (Kinsey ratings were assigned based on reported sexual history experience. Fantasy patterns or emotional attachments were not considered.) Two-thirds of the clients treated were currently married. These clients who had prior heterosexual experience were defined as *reversion* clients. *Conversion* clients were defined as individuals who had little or no prior homosexual experience (Kinsey ratings 5 or 6). There were only 9 male and 3 female conversion clients.

Treatment involved the rapid-treatment techniques (two weeks' duration) which were developed by Masters and Johnson for the treatment of heterosexual inadequacies. This treatment is mainly designed to give accurate sex information, improve sexual communication, and to focus on sexual pleasuring rather than on performance. Treatment always included the presence and support in therapy of a committed or casual partner of the opposite sex. Masters and Johnson continued to utilize their male-female dual-team approach to sex therapy.

Successful treatment was never defined by Masters and Johnson. They have concluded that their results can only be reported in terms of incidence of failure. However, even such failure was never clearly defined. At one point, Masters and Johnson reported that they "felt more secure" in accepting men and women into treatment when, the clients "freely expressed their reservations about making the complete change in role preference or openly stated their desire to function in both roles." However, Masters and Johnson never reported whether their "non-failure" clients made the complete change in role preference or not. Although unclear, failure seems to have been defined as a failure to *perform* or *behave* as a heterosexual. Again, as psychoanalytic and behavioral therapists, Masters and Johnson simply look at reported changes in behavior and assume a change in sexual preference or orientation. Since many people have behaved and will continue to behave in a way that is inconsistent with their preferences (usually because of societal pressures), this assumption cannot be made.

Given their definitions of failure, Masters and Johnson report an overall 27 percent failure rate for males and 31 percent for females. These results suggest that Masters and Johnson's treatment approach might be the most successful known for changing *behavior*. These results become even more dramatic given the fact that they accomplished these results in a two-week treatment format. In addition, the changes, for the most part, seem to have lasted over a five-year follow-up period. Masters and Johnson's follow-up statistics must be viewed cautiously, in that 28 percent of the clients were lost in the follow-up procedures. The authors theorize that the overall failure rate is probably closer to 33 percent and not more than 45 percent. They think that with improved acceptance and follow-up procedures the overall failure rates might be reduced significantly.

A NEW MODEL OF TREATMENT

The illness model of homosexuality is being overshadowed today by a new model of treatment. There has been a flood of literature which has put to rest the notion that homosexuality is an illness in the first place. As early as 1957, Evelyn Hooker took a radical departure in the study of homosexuality. Instead of looking at patient populations to develop notions and theoretical frameworks, she studied nonpatient male homosexuals and compared them with nonpatient heterosexuals. The two groups were similar in terms of age, intelligence, and schooling. Both groups were given a battery of psychological tests. She then asked trained professionals to separate the homosexuals from the heterosexuals based on the results of the tests. The two groups could not be distinguisehd. Although a certain percentage of each group showed considerable maladjustment, the percentages were essentially the same for both heterosexuals and homosexuals.

There have been a number of other significant studies concluding that there is no psychopathology associated with homosexuality itself. The only difference found for homosexual populations in comparison to heterosexual populations is their choice of sexual interest and gratification. (For a detailed review of the literature, see Gonsiorek, 1977.)

During the 1970s, more emphasis was given to studying the lifestyle and adjustment of individuals with same-sex preferences. Researchers such as Freedman (1971) and Bell and Weinberg (1978) found that homosexuals who have been able to "come out" (to acknowledge their homosexuality) seem to be the healthiest psychologically in terms of more positive self-esteem, fewer anxiety symptoms, and less depression.

Treatment based on this new understanding of homosexuality has been to enhance homosexual functioning rather than to try to eliminate it. One of the first reports of such treatment came in 1970 by Johnsgard and Schumacher. These authors used a group therapy approach for male homosexuals which emphasized trust, openness, expression of feelings, and intimacy. Their main objective was to help these individuals function more fully as human beings.

In 1975, Pendergrass described the use of marriage counseling techniques to improve the psychological functioning of a lesbian couple. The thought of using such procedures probably did not occur to most therapists 10 years previously. In 1976, Duehn and Mayadas described using assertiveness training to help a male homosexual with social and interpersonal problems associated with his decision to come out. They were able to demonstrate that through a program of behavioral rehearsals their patient was able to acquire assertive skills which improved his interpersonal functioning.

Most recently, Masters and Johnson (1979) have reported results of an extensive study of treatment of male and female homosexuals with specific sexual dysfunctions. They treated 57 men and 27 women with complaints such as secondary impotence and primary anorgasmia. These clients were treated with basically the same treatment methods Masters and Johnson applied to heterosexual sexual dysfunctions. The overall failure rate for the clients was approximately 12 percent. The corresponding heterosexual statistic published in 1970 *(Human Sexual Inadequacy)* was approximately 20 percent. These results are impressive, in that they were accomplished in Masters and Johnson's two-week treatment format and were sustained in a five-year follow-up. Masters and Johnson have made a significant contribution to health care professionals by demonstrating the effectiveness of methods designed to increase or improve homosexual functioning.

It would be helpful, however, if Masters and Johnson or others would look more carefully at the sexual dysfunctions that might be related to anal intercourse such as premature ejaculation, impotence related to inability to penetrate, and "analismus" or the inability to be penetrated because of muscular spasm or pain during anal intercourse. These dysfunctions were neglected because among Masters and Johnson's subjects not many engaged in anal intercourse. There is evidence in the general male homosexual population that anal intercourse is performed more frequently than Masters and Johnson suggest (for example, Bell & Weinberg, 1978).

In addition, Masters and Johnson seem to be preoccupied with the notion that homosexuals engage in almost exclusive "my turn-your turn" type of sexual activity. This, they say, contributes to the fact that homosexuals are less performance oriented and do not suffer the kinds of dysfunctions associated with simultaneous sexual activity such as heterosexual coitus. For some reason, Masters and Johnson have not recognized that simultaneous pleasuring occurs for homosexuals even though coitus is not possible for them. This fact has been reported by Bell and Weinberg (1978) in their extensive study of homosexual functioning. There are other ways for simultaneous pleasuring to occur other than coitus. Homosexuals possibly do not engage in simultaneous pleasuring to the degree heterosexuals do; however, it is not absent, as Masters and Johnson seem to imply.

In effect, however, Masters and Johnson and others reflect the growing trend to facilitate homosexual functioning rather than to eliminate it. This new model of treatment has yet to demonstrate its effectiveness sufficiently through research methodology; only a few studies have been completed which have demonstrated its effectiveness. Preliminary results have been promising; however, more research is needed to understand the impact of these therapeutic procedures.

DECIDING ON A TREATMENT PLAN

Prior to the civil rights and gay rights movements, individuals who sought psychiatric or psychological help and had a homosexual orientation were encouraged to change their sexual orientation. Very few individuals came to therapists asking that their sexual orientation be left intact. These decisions were made by the therapist and their clients based more on cultural and societal pressure than on scientific knowledge. As a result, individuals underwent treatment to eliminate homosexual behavior and to adopt heterosexual functioning. Few were successful, but there was no alternative treatment approach.

The gay liberation movement changed things rapidly. Existing treatments designed to "cure" homosexuality were questioned from ethical, moral, theoretical, and practical standpoints. It is ironic that these questions were raised by some therapists who once boasted of success in treating their homosexual clients. Most notably, Davison, in his presidential address to the Association for Advancement of Behavior Therapy in 1974, argued that for ethical reasons therapists should stop offering therapy to "cure" and instead offer help in improving homosexual functioning. He stated that homosexuals who come for change in their sexual orientation do so in an atmosphere of discrimination and condemnation. He stated that this was hardly a free-will choice. He encouraged therapists to stop offering a cure for something which could no longer be considered an illness.

Other therapists, such as Begelman (1977) and Silverstein (1977), have argued that "as moral agents of society" therapists should not participate in society's persecution of homosexuals by offering "cures." Instead, therapists should enlist the aid of clients to combat the social system that has been responsible for unjustifiably creating their negative self-image.

It is unethical and morally questionable to offer a "cure" to homosexuals who request a change in their sexual orientation. While there have been reports that changes in behavior have occurred for individuals seeking treatment (see Masters and Johnson, 1979), it is questionable whether it is beneficial to change their behavior to something that is incongruent with their sexual orientation.

There is the problem of clients who simply will not accept treatment that is based on improving homosexual functioning. Therapists such as Freund (1977) have thought that for these clients counseling toward heterosexual adjustment is acceptable as a "second-best choice." There are more therapists today who will work with these individuals with the goal of heterosexual adjustment if the clients recognize that treatment is designed to change behavior and that they should not expect that all thoughts, fantasies, attitudes, or even behavior of same sex would be eliminated. This treatment approach should be offered cautiously. Clients must explore their reasons for wanting such goals. They must understand the meaning and signficance of their decision to act in a way that is incongruent with their sexual orientation. They must understand the external forces that affect their decisions to do so. The danger with this approach is that in helping clients increase their sexual repertoire to include heterosexual activity this may lead to the feeling that their basic sexual orientation is not acceptable or tolerated. This would lead to the same sense of failure that is generated by attempts to "cure" individuals of their homosexuality. Masters and Johnson try to avoid this result by reassuring clients that there is nothing inherently wrong with homosexual functioning. Yet Masters and Johnson's willingness to help their clients change their basic sexual orientation says something different, and the negative message seems clearly implied. Masters and Johnson and other therapists who might offer treatment to change sexual orientation should include in their treatment goals encouraging greater acceptance and understanding of clients' homosexual identity. As part of the goal of increasing heterosexual functioning there must also be work on helping clients recognize and accept their homosexual identity and value this identity in a predominantly heterosexual society.

CONCLUSION

The illness model of homosexuality is slowly being put to rest. Research that has been conducted on nonpatient populations of homosexuals has proved that fact. We are simply left with the fact that homosexuality is a normal variation in sexual expression and that the main difference between homosexuals and heterosexuals is their choice of sexual and affectional preference. This may explain why attempts to treat homosexuals based on an illness model have not been successful.

In contrast, there is growing evidence that therapists can have a positive impact in facilitating homosexual functioning. Research is still needed to evaluate treatment approaches with this aim. For example, we need to know more about the effects of coming-out groups on self-esteem, psychological adjustment, and interpersonal skills. Other treatment approaches that have been initiated need to be evaluated carefully.

In the meantime, therapists and counselors are still faced with the ethical, moral, theoretical, and practical decisions of determining treatment goals. Masters and Johnson and others believe we should leave that decision completely up to our clients and remain value-free. It is naive to think that we are, can, or should be value-free agents. We cannot continue to participate in society's unfair discrimination against homosexuality. There has been and should continue to be more emphasis in treatment of homosexuals on assisting them to recognize and accept their sexual identity, to improve interpersonal and intersocietal functioning, and to help them value this identity in a predominantly heterosexual society.

· 8 ·

Politics, Ethics, and
Therapy for Homosexuality

Gerald C. Davison

Imagine for a moment that you are an anxious person and that being anxious is against the law. You must try to hide your fears from others. Your own home may be a safe place to feel anxious, but a public display of apprehension can lead to arrest or at least to social ostracism. At work one day an associate looks at you suspiciously and says, "That's funny. For a crazy moment there I thought you were anxious." "Heck no," you exclaim a bit too loudly, "not me!" You begin to wonder if your fellow worker will report his suspicions to your boss. If he does, your boss may inform the police, or will at least change your job to one that requires less contact with customers, especially with those who have children.

There are many parallels between the way an anxious person is treated in this seemingly improbable fantasy and the current plight of homosexuals. In the United States alone it is estimated that at least four million people are predominantly homosexual. If each such individual has an average of two contacts per week, nearly a quarter of a billion homosexual acts are engaged in each year in this country. Millions of other people who are bisexual are involved in homosexual activity from time to time (Gebhard, 1972; Chapter 3 this volume).

Author's Note: *Some of the material in this article is drawn from previous publications: G. C. Davison and J. M. Neale,* Abnormal Psychology: An Experimental Clinical Approach *(2nd ed.), New York: John Wiley, 1978, by permission; G. C. Davison, "Homosexuality: The Ethical Challenge,"* Journal of Consulting and Clinical Psychology, *1976, Vol. 44, pp. 157-162, and G. C. Davison, "Not Can But Ought: The Treatment of Homosexuality,"* Journal of Consulting and Clinical Psychology, *1978, Vol. 46, pp. 170-172, copyright by the American Psychological Association, portions reprinted by permission.*

Sexual attraction among members of the same sex has been amply documented throughout recorded history in many different cultures. In many societies homosexual practices have been suppressed by harsh laws; indeed, in most states of contemporary America laws exist by which homosexuals can be arrested and imprisoned, although not all these statutes are rigidly enforced. Never have societal sanctions eliminated homosexuality, nor does it seem likely that they could. The widespread prevalence of homosexuality, even though such practices are often threatened by punishment, has led some workers to believe that this aspect of sexuality is, in some important way, part of human nature.

Recent years have seen a growing liberalization of laws regulating adult human sexual conduct. Several professional groups, including the American Psychological Association and the American Psychiatric Association, have moved away from an illness view of homosexuality. One of the earliest progressive statements was issued in 1974 by the Association for Advancement of Behavior Therapy while I was president of that group:

> The AABT believes that homosexuality is in itself not a sign of behavioral pathology. The Association urges all mental health professionals to take the lead in removing the stigma of mental illness that has long been attributed to these patterns of emotion and behavior. While we recognize that this long-standing prejudice will not be easily changed, there is no justification for a delay in formally according these people the basic civil and human rights that other citizens enjoy.

As encouraging as these developments have been to those committed to removing the stigma of homosexuality, a less obvious but perhaps even more important political and ethical issue must be addressed —namely, the continuing availability of therapeutic regimens for altering sexual orientation from same-sexed to opposite-sexed partners. The following may illustrate this predicament:

> API (Apocryphal Press International). The Governor recently signed into law a bill prohibiting discrimination in housing and job opportunities on the basis of membership in a Protestant Church. This new law is the result of efforts by militant Protestants, who have lobbied extensively during the past ten years for relief from institutionalized discrimination. In an unusual statement accompanying the signing of the bill, the Governor expressed the hope that this legislation would contribute to greater social acceptance of Protestantism as a legitimate, albeit unconventional, religion.

> At the same time, the Governor authorized funding in the amount of two million dollars for the coming fiscal year to be used to set up within existing mental health centers special units devoted to research into the most effective and humane procedures for helping Protestants convert to Catholicism or Judaism. The Governor was quick to point out, however, that these efforts, and the therapy services that will

accompany and derive from them, are not to be imposed on Protestants, rather are only to be made available to those who express the voluntary wish to change. "We are not in the business of forcing anything on these people. We want only to help," he said.

THE MYTH OF THERAPEUTIC NEUTRALITY

My basic premise is, to paraphrase Halleck (1971), that therapists never make ethically or politically neutral decisions.

Any type of psychiatric intervention, even when treating a voluntary patient, will have an impact upon the distribution of power within the various social systems in which the patient moves. The radical therapists are absolutely right when they insist that psychiatric neutrality is a myth [1971: 13].

The very naturalness of what therapists agree to do with particular kinds of cases tends to blind them to their prejudices and biases. Surely no ethical issues are worth discussing when one helps the severely disturbed child to stop banging his head against the wall. But this is an extreme case, and I suggest that most of what therapists deal with falls into that important gray area in which biases play a role in what is done. This seems to be particularly the case in the approach to those people who complain of being troubled by their homosexual behavior or feelings. I believe that any comprehensive perusal of the clinical and experimental literature in all therapies will confirm the assertion that most therapists by and large regard homosexual behavior and attitudes to be undesirable, sometimes pathological, and at any rate generally in need of change toward a hetero-sexual orientation.

SOME RELEVANT AND IRRELEVANT ISSUES
SURROUNDING HOMOSEXUALITY

Allow me to mention briefly some exclusions that I hope will be obvious. I am not talking about homosexual behavior that is part of a psychotic pattern of existence. For example, the male who has the delusion that he is Marie Antoinette out to seduce every available twentieth-century man would be exhibiting a pattern of sexual behavior that is best viewed as part of an unfortunate psychotic aberration. I would similarly not want to conclude that heterosexuality is sick because there are male psychotics who chase female nurses and try to fornicate with them in hospital dayrooms.

There is something else implicit in what I will be saying, so let me make it explicit at this juncture. Though I will often be referring to "homosexuals,"

I am in agreement with investigators such as Kinsey, Pomeroy, and Martin (1948) and Churchill (1967), who urge that we construe sexual preference as a continuum on which people can be placed according to the relative frequencies of their homosexual-heterosexual fantasies, feelings, and behavior. Clearly the available survey data strongly indicate that a significant number of human beings lie between the extremes of exclusive homosexuality and exclusive heterosexuality.

In any discussion of homosexuals in therapy, the question of the normality of homosexual preference has often been raised. Many studies have failed to find differences in "mental health" between heterosexuals and homosexuals (see Evans, 1970; Gagnon & Simon, 1973; Chapters 5 and 6 this volume). However, some point to Bieber et al.'s (1962) data and to a conceptual replication by Evans (1969) as evidence supporting a pathology view of homosexuality. There are a number of serious flaws in the Bieber study, not the least of which is the fact that the male homosexuals were all in therapy. However, there is also a major *logical* error in reasoning— namely, that one has demonstrated pathology of homosexuality by showing that male homosexuals have child-rearing experiences that are *different* from those of male heterosexuals. One cannot attach a pathogenic label to a pattern of child rearing unless one a priori labels the adult behavior pattern as pathological. For example, Bieber et al. found that what they called a "close-binding intimate mother" was present much more often in the life histories of the analytic male homosexual patients than among the heterosexual controls. But what is wrong with such a mother unless you happen to find her in the background of people whose current behavior you judge *beforehand* to be pathological? Moreover, even when an emotional disorder is identified in a homosexual, it could be argued that the problem is due to the extreme duress under which the person has to live in a society that asserts that homosexuals are "queer" and that actively oppresses them.

There is another issue that is worth discussing. Many people point to brutality in homosexual relationships, prompting the conclusion that homosexuality could not possibly be normal. To such objections I would reply that homosexuals who engage in destructive activities and who suffer in poor relationships do not have a monopoly on stormy interpersonal functioning. Simply because there is so much marital discord in this country, one seldom hears people concluding that heterosexuality is inherently bad. What I am suggesting is that clinicians might perhaps pay more attention to the *quality of human relationships,* to the way people deal with each other rather than to the particular gender of the adult partners. If one follows this further, we might consider a shift in focus in therapy with homosexuals that pays little attention to the fact that the partners are the same sex and more attention to the kind of relationship a person might be in and how that relationship might be improved (see Chapter 7). Naturally, when therapeutic efforts are aimed in this direction, I believe one inevitably ends up having to deal with the tremendous legal and social oppression of these groups of people.

NO CURE WITHOUT A DISEASE

I believe that clinicians spend time developing and analyzing procedures only if they are concerned about a problem. It seems very much the case with homosexuality. And yet, consider the rhetoric that typically speaks of social labeling of behavior rather than viewing a given behavior as intrinsically normal or abnormal. Consider also the huge literature on helping homosexuals (at least males) change their sexual preference and the paucity of literature aimed at helping the labelers change their prejudicial biases and encouraging the homosexual to develop as a person without changing. How can therapists honestly speak of nonprejudice when they participate in therapy regimens that by their very existence—and regardless of their efficacy—would seem to condone the current societal prejudice and perhaps also impede social change?

This point has been enunciated independently by Begelman (1975) in a critique of behavior therapy, but his argument applies to any intervention:

> [The efforts of behavior therapists to reorient homosexuals to heterosexuality] *by their very existence constitute a significant causal element in reinforcing the social doctrine that homosexuality is bad.* Indeed, the point of the activist protest is that behavior therapists contribute significantly to preventing the exercise of any *real* option in decision-making about sexual identity, by further strengthening the prejudice that homosexuality is a "problem behavior," since treatment may be offered for it. As a consequence of this therapeutic stance, as well as a wider system of social and attitudinal pressures, homosexuals tend to seek treatment *for being homosexuals.* Heterosexuals, on the other hand, can scarcely be expected to seek voluntary treatment for being "heterosexual," especially since all the social forces arrayed— including the unavailability of behavior therapy for heterosexuality—attest to the acknowledgement of the idea that whatever "problems" heterosexuals experience are not due to their sexual orientation. The upshot of this is that contrary to the disclaimer that behavioral therapy is "not a system of ethics" (Bandura, 1969, p. 87), the very act of providing therapeutic services for homosexual "problems" indicates otherwise [p. 180].

I further suggest that the availability of a technique encourages its use. For example, many behavior therapists who have good clinical success with systematic desensitization and who are also persuaded by the experimental literature that it is useful for reducing anxiety try to conceptualize client problems in terms of this technique. Thus, a depression might be viewed as a consequence of unnecessary sensitivities that themselves could be translated into an anxiety hierarchy. By the same token, I would suggest that the extensive clinical and experimental work in aversion therapy (for example, Feldman & MacCulloch, 1971), or "Playboy therapy" (see Davison, 1968), or heterosocial-heterosexual skills training channel the assessment and problem-solving activities of behavioral clinicians into working to change sexual orientation and to persuade homosexual clients that this is a worthwhile goal. Why else would they be spending so much time working on the techniques?

A PROPOSAL ON
THERAPY WITH HOMOSEXUALS

Consistent with much of the thoughtful gay literature (see Silverstein, 1977), I suggest that therapists stop engaging in voluntary therapy programs aimed at altering the choice of adult partners to whom clients are attracted. As Silverstein (Note 1) put it at the 1972 Association for Advancement of Behavior Therapy convention in a discussion of male homosexuality:

> To suggest that a person comes voluntarily to change his sexual orientation is to ignore the powerful environmental stress, oppression if you will, that has been telling him for years that he should change. To grow up in a family where the word "homosexual" was whispered, to play in a playground and hear the words "faggot" and "queer," to go to church and hear of "sin" and then to college and hear of "illness," and finally to the counseling center that promises to "cure," is hardly to create an environment of freedom and voluntary choice. The homosexual is expected to want to be changed and his application for treatment is implicitly praised as the first step toward "normal" behavior.
>
> What brings them into the counseling center is guilt, shame, and the loneliness that comes from their secret. If you really wish to help them freely choose, I suggest you first densensitize them to their guilt. Allow them to dissolve the shame about their desires and actions and to feel comfortable with their sexuality. After that, let them choose, but not before. I don't know any more than you what would happen, but I think their choice would be more voluntary and free than it is at present [p. 4].

In other words, Silverstein suggests that therapists inquire into the determinants of the client asserting that he or she wants to change. He proposes that these determinants may be based on prejudice and ignorance and therefore *should not* be catered to or even strengthened by an establishment of therapists who offer their services to those clients who "express the wish to change."

But what would be the consequences of this? Does this not limit the choices available to the person troubled by his sexual orientation? Who is the behavior therapist or psychotherapist to decide for potential clients which options should be available in therapy? To my mind the most frank answer—but one that seems unpalatable to many—has been elaborated by Halleck (1971): Therapists already have made these decisions, perhaps not fully aware of their larger implications. By working so diligently on change techniques, is not the mental health establishment affirming that the prejudices and laws against certain sexual acts are in fact well founded? What are therapists really saying to clients when, on the one hand, they assure them that they are not abnormal and, on the other hand, present them with an array of techniques, some of them painful, which are aimed at eliminating that set of feelings and behavior that have just been pronounced normal? What is the real range of "free choice" available to homosexually oriented people who are racked with guilt, self-hate, and embarrassment and who must endure the burden of societal prejudice and discrimination? What of the anxieties arising from this discrimination— how have therapists helped them with *these* problems?

London (1969) has suggested that an unappreciated danger in behavior control technology is our increasing ability to engineer what we have regarded as free will. Thus therapists seem to be capable of making people want what is available and what they feel clients should want. Moreover, just because therapists can assert that they are not doing something against the will of their clients does not free them from the responsibility of examining those factors that determine what is considered free expression of intent and desire on the part of our clients.

In a related vein—and this should be familiar not only to therapists but to those who have been clients themselves—Halleck (1971) says:

> At first glance, a model of psychiatric practice based on the contention that people should just be helped to learn to do the things they want to do seems uncomplicated and desirable. But it is an unobtainable model. Unlike a technician, a psychiatrist cannot avoid communicating and at times imposing his own values upon his patients. The patient usually has considerable difficulty in finding the way in which he would wish to change his behavior, but as he talks to the psychiatrist his wants and needs become clearer. In the very process of defining his needs in the presence of a figure who is viewed as wise and authoritarian, the patient is profoundly influenced. He ends up wanting some of the things the psychiatrist thinks he should want [p. 19].

Though Halleck, as a psychiatrist, is addressing himself to a medical audience, his questions are obviously relevant to all the helping professions.

But is it not harsh and unfeeling to propose that therapists deny a particular client the possibility of loosing himself or herself from his or her homosexual attraction and turning him or her on to the other half of the adult population? What about the homosexual client who could conceivably want to switch, not out of societal pressures but out of a sincere desire for those things that in our culture are usually part of the heterosexual package—a spouse and children? Why deny such a person—rare though he or she may be—the opportunity to fulfill such desires? Is not the scheme I am proposing a kind of "coercive liberalism," to use London's phrase? Coercive liberalism goes something like this: I will help you be happier, freer, more fulfilled, etc.—and you will have no choice but to be so according to my standards. By proposing that preference-change programs with homosexuals be terminated, I am obviously running this risk. One solution would be simply to accept the risk; that, I believe, is consistent with the feelings of Halleck. But another way out of this dilemma is to propose that a concerted program of clinical research be encouraged for the development of maximally effective procedures to help heterosexually oriented people become homosexually oriented if it can somehow be determined that they *really want to*. That is, therapists might consider the possibility that many heterosexuals may with to change, or at least *expand*, their sexual activities, as some homosexuals may wish to do. Are mental health professionals prepared to devote themselves to this kind of sexual enhancement enterprise?

NOT CAN BUT OUGHT

When trying to garner support for my proposal that we should stop trying to change homosexual orientations, I was interested for some time in documenting the failure of various behavior change regimens in eliminating homosexual inclinations. Of particular interest was the question of whether aversion therapy of various kinds had proved effective in stamping out homosexual behavior and inclinations. And indeed, I tend to believe the evidence is still lacking for a suppression of homosexual behavior or ideation via aversive procedures. Nonetheless, even if one were to demonstrate that a particular sexual preference could be modified by a negative learning experience, there remains the question of how relevant these data are to the ethical question of whether one *should* engage in such behavior change regimens. The simple truth is that data on efficacy are quite irrelevant. Even if we could effect certain changes, there is still the more important question of whether we *should*. I believe we should not.

POLITICS AND MORALITY

The arguments put forth here should be viewed at what Rappaport (1977) calls the institutional level, not the level of the individual. An institutional analysis of human problems is concerned with those values and ideologies that guide the basic decision-making of a particular society. This is the domain of workers who typically identify themselves as community psychologists or psychiatrists. In contrast, most therapists are accustomed to focusing on the individual, assuming that society is basically benign and that psychological suffering can best be alleviated by helping the client adjust to prevailing values and conditions. My underlying assumption is that issues surrounding therapy for homosexuality should be addressed at an institutional level.

The thrust of this article, then, is sociopolitical and ethical. While it may be interesting to present data suggesting that sexual preferences *can* be altered (for example, Sturgis & Adams, 1978), such efforts are irrelevant and, worse, misleading. It seems preferable to acknowledge candidly that therapists are purveyors of ethics, that they are contemporary society's secular priests (London, 1964), and that this heavy moral responsibility is inherent to the conduct of psychotherapy.

It has recently been suggested that therapists have some kind of abstract responsibility to satisfy a client's expressed needs (Sturgis & Adams, 1978). Would that it were so simple. Therapists constrain themselves in many ways when clients ask for assistance, and clients make certain requests of some therapists and will not do so with others. Requests alone have never been a sufficient criterion for providing a particular form of therapy.

Finally, there is nothing in the above that advocates not dealing with homosexuals in therapy. It is one thing to say that one should not treat homosexuality; it is quite another to suggest that one should not treat homosexuals. Indeed, what I am suggesting is that therapists finally consider the problems in living experienced by homosexuals. Such problems are perhaps especially severe, given the prejudice against their sexual orientation. It would be nice if an alcoholic homosexual, for example, could be helped to reduce his or her drinking without having his or her sexual orientation questioned. It would be nice if a homosexual fearful of interpersonal relationships, or incompetent in them, could be helped without the therapist assuming that homosexuality lies at the root of the problem. It would be nice if a nonorgasmic or impotent homosexual could be helped as a heterosexual would be rather than guiding his or her wishes to change-of-orientation regimens. Implicit in this article is the hope that therapists will concentrate their efforts on such *human* problems rather than focusing on the most obvious "maladjustment"—loving members of one's own sex.

CONCLUSIONS

Change of orientation therapy programs should be eliminated. Their availability only confirms professional and societal biases against homosexuality, despite seemingly progressive rhetoric about its normality. Forsaking the reorientation option will encourage therapists to examine the life problems of some homosexuals, rather than focusing on the so-called problem of homosexuality. Viewing therapists as contemporary society's secular priests rather than as value-neutral technicians will sensitize professionals and laypeople alike to large-scale social, political, and moral influences in human behavior.

REFERENCE NOTE

1. Silverstein, C. *Behavior modification and the gay community.* Paper presented at the annual convention of the Association for Advancement of Behavior Therapy, New York City, October 1972.

· 9 ·

Psychotherapeutic Treatment for the Invisible Minority

Richard C. Pillard

I. PSYCHOTHERAPY AND THE INSTITUTIONALIZATION OF PREJUDICE

Homosexuals are profoundly stigmatized within our society. This stigma is expressed at every level, from decisions of the Supreme Court to children's curse words: "faggot" and "queer." Most homosexuals have at some time suffered tangibly as a result of their sexual orientation: rejected by parents and friends, discriminated against by employers, condemned by the clergy, trivialized by the media. Every day, homosexuals, for no other reason, are abused, jailed, beaten and even killed.[1] Some homosexuals try to mitigate their persecution by concealing their sexual preference and may do so with remarkable skill. They become an invisible minority. But then they must accept the burden of living a double life like a spy in enemy territory. In any event, there is no escape from the intangible consequences of society's hatred which is incorporated, in various forms, as self-hatred.

It would be reasonable to expect that mental health professionals should be the first to recognize this situation; their sensitivity to human suffering should make them the homosexual's natural ally. Furthermore, the institution of medicine has enormous influence. There are times when these assets have been used in ways that are beneficial to gay people, but it will be the purpose of this article to show, for the most part, that the opposite is the case.

Aversion to homosexuality is deeply rooted in the traditions of Western society. Szasz says, "For centuries, no penalogical distinction was made between religious unorthodoxy and sexual misbehavior, especially homo-sexuality. . . . Heretics were accused of unnatural vice [homosexuality] as a matter of course" (Szasz, 1970, p. 164). The reasons for the especially degraded position of homosexuality, even as compared with other minori-ties, are complex. They include the threat it poses to the heterosexual's sexual identity and rejection of the (until recently) desirable quality of maximum reproductive capacity. Homosexuality stimulates envy toward those who may be seen as enjoying sex without the responsibility of marriage and family commitments. Also of importance is the observation that overt homosexuality may disrupt authority patterns among members of the same sex which depend to some extent on covert or noneroticized homosexual feelings (Wickler, 1972; Rangell, 1963).

Weinberg (1972) has suggested the term "homophobia" for the dread of homosexuality. As the word suggests, the fear of the homosexual is not a rational response to a real threat but, as with phobias in general, an exaggerated anxiety focused on specific persons or situations which can be avoided so that other areas of the personality may remain anxiety-free. The projection of undesirable characteristics onto minority groups is a common social strategy, as the study of racism and anti-Semitism teaches (Allport, 1954; Chapter 29 this volume).

A further important point about minority group prejudice is that it tends to become institutionalized—that is, a structured part of the social milieu. This means that hatred of a minority group tends to evolve into customs and laws which eventually isolate that minority, forcing it to adopt charac-teristics that are then judged as different and inferior. As this process occurs, it becomes less necessary for individual members of the majority culture to undertake the psychologically costly task of hating the minority or of acting in ways hostile to it. This work is done automatically because of the inferior position assigned by society.

An example of this process, an instance of racism, was described by Hastings and Kunnes (1967). Medical students were sent to various phar-macies to fill a standard prescription for digoxin. Some of the students were white and well dressed, others were black and poorly dressed. The students did not identify themselves, but simply presented their prescrip-tion and noted the price charged by the pharmacist. The authors found that the poorly dressed black students were charged significantly more for their prescription than were the well-dressed white students. The differen-tial was greatest in predominantly black neighborhoods.

This experiment is an illustration of the institutionalization of prejudice. The inferior economic status of black people is in part maintained by the fact that they must pay more than whites. Prejudice of this kind may be subtle and difficult to identify. While the study does not specifically deal with this issue, it is likely that the pharmacists were not aware that they were systematically charging more to blacks. The pricing policy would likely be backed by some rationalization. Indeed, this was illustrated in a subsequent letter to the editor from a pharmacist who attributed different prices to the fact that some people must buy on credit or require a lengthy explanation of how to take their medicine. Racism disappears! Blacks are charged more, not because anyone dislikes them, but because it costs more to service people who are perceived as poor and stupid.

Such demonstrations make us aware that prejudice need not consist of conscious feelings. On the contrary, the aspect that is most corrosive is built into our culture and, therefore, need never be consciously experienced. All of us are involved in this racism, as we cannot help but be, by the nature of our participation in a society that has institutionalized minority oppression.

These comments on institutionalized racism have been presented in some detail to make the point that the mental health professional may not experience discomfort with or dislike of lesbians or gay men, but this is no guarantee that behavior toward them is not oppressive and harmful. A survey of physicians' attitudes revealed that most nonpsychiatrists experienced discomfort when treating male homosexuals. By contrast, 100% of the psychiatrists in the sample reported "often" or "always" feeling comfortable in such a situation. They also reported that their attitudes "seldom" or "never" adversely affected their treatment of homosexual patients (Fort, Steiner, & Conrad, 1971).

But homosexuals have a very different perception. A spokesperson for the gay community addressed these comments to the American Psychiatric Association:

> In recent years, an adversary situation has developed between the psychiatric profession and the homosexual community. While much of psychiatry seems unaware of this, it is felt with growing resentment and bitterness by the homosexual community, who increasingly see psychiatry as THE major enemy in a battle against deeply rooted societal prejudice, and see psychiatrists as singularly insensitive and obtuse to the destruction which they are wreaking upon homosexuals. . . . The homosexual community looks upon efforts to change homosexuals to heterosexuality, or to mold younger, supposedly malleable homosexuals into heterosexuality . . . as an assault upon our people comparable in its way to genocide [Gittings, Note 1].

Gittings's comment is supported by Saghir and Robins (1973) who surveyed the attitudes of lesbians and gay men toward psychotherapy: "A significant proportion of [homosexual men] felt negatively about their psychotherapeutic experience. They believed that it was of no value or that it even made things worse *due to lack of understanding by the therapist or to his personal prejudice against homosexuality"* (italics added). Clearly, the psychiatrist's perception of his attitudes is in many cases quite at odds with the patient's.

II. EDUCATION AND
THE ROOTS OF PREJUDICE

The quotation from Saghir and Robins illustrates a frequent criticism from gay people—that psychiatrists lack knowledge and understanding of their sexual practices and lifestyle. This criticism is reinforced as one reviews the writings of psychiatrists and the contents of residency training programs.

Here are quotes from Redlich and Freedman's textbook, *The Theory and Practice of Psychiatry* (1966): "There is often a rather aggressive element in homosexual practice; hostile fantasies play a large role in homosexual relationships. . . . In contrast to normal heterosexual relationships, aggression may not be dissipated by homosexual behavior" (p. 386).

Aggressive elements are a part of all sexual relationships, and my own impression is that they are expressed and "dissipated" to about the same extent in both homosexual and heterosexual activity—although no one can more than guess because of the imprecision of the concepts and because the issue has not been systematically studied.

> In big cities, homosexuals form their own society with its own roles, rules and lingo. In these societies homosexuals also try to justify their neurotic sexual choice and to protect themselves against what they consider unfair, discriminatory and punitive practices by the heterosexual population. With an inverted pride, many homosexuals cite . . . the number of gifted artists, writers and actors among them [Redlich & Freedman, 1966, p. 387].

In this passage, Redlich and Freedman seem to confuse the defense of one's civil rights with justification of a neurotic object choice. The fact that gay people are as capable as anyone of hard work and creative achievement is not regarded as a positive attribute but as "inverted pride," whatever that may be.[2]

A SIECUS handbook for sex counselors says, "In anal intercourse, of course, there is rear entrance and the recipient is turned away and lying face down. These drawbacks . . . make it a less favored sexual activity" (Moore, 1969). In fact, homosexuals often have intercourse face to face. They make love like everyone else. Why is it that in these, as in most writings on the subject, information is presented inaccurately or with such an undertone of disgust that true understanding is impossible?

Not only in books, but also in training programs, there is no adequate attempt to equip the therapist-in-training with an understanding of lesbians and gay men as members of a subculture. Such an attempt requires more than an occasional seminar. An effort must be made to understand and undo the acculturation process to which the young therapist has been exposed so that learning can take place unobstructed by anxiety.

Observe what happens when homophobia is not dealt with. A psychiatry resident presented a homosexual patient at a group conference. After he gave the patient's history in some detail, the supervising psychiatrist asked about the patient's sexual habits. The resident had not inquired about them. The supervisor asked, "Do you know what homosexuals do in bed?" The resident, blushing and sweating, said that he did not. Not one of some 20 professionals present would admit having any knowledge about specific homosexual practices.

Information about how gays make love is available through one's own sexual experiments or fantasies or simply by asking someone who knows. Nevertheless, most people are at pains to deny their knowledge. To admit knowing how "they" make love opens the possibility that one will be found to have a homosexual component and will be, therefore, tainted. Being as ignorant as possible is a common strategy to prove that one has not been infected by unorthodox and dangerous knowledge.

All of the examples in this section demonstrate a regular and essential feature of minority group stigmatization: the vulnerability to being psychologically (and often physically) ghettoized. Psychological ghettoization is accomplished by avoiding contact with minority members so that feelings of empathy, of shared humanity, are not formed and so that pejorative characteristics can be more easily ascribed. Information about the minority, which is often misinformation, is derived from "experts" who have little genuine relationship with the minority members themselves. The latter are often prevented from speaking in their own behalf, except those sufficiently indentified with the expert view to endorse it.[3]

Good teaching can frequently modify defensive reactions and might begin with Allport's advice given 25 years ago.

> Prejudice . . . may be reduced by equal status contact between the majority and minority groups in pursuit of common goals. The effect is greatly enhanced if this contact is sanctioned by institutional supports . . . and provided that it is of a sort that leads to perception of common interests and common humanity between members of the two groups [1954, p. 281].

When I discuss this topic with medical students, I recruit gay men and lesbians to act as resource persons for small group meetings. Most students react with enthusiasm to this experience. "They are okay; they are just like us" are frequent comments and revealing of the psychology of this particular learning experience. The perception of gays as inhuman aliens is being undone. Guilt about the student's own homosexual feelings is relieved. Anxiety, as well as relief, may be part of the experience, but the group setting is designed to keep distress within tolerable limits. (Anxiety and warding off are more frequently observed among the faculty. They often express concern that students will be unable to handle these encounters constructively and that they might receive "the wrong kind of information.")

Meaningful relations with homosexuals are an enriching, not a demeaning, experience for mental health professionals; we must become able to seek more opportunities for them to occur.

III. PSYCHIATRY AS AN AGENT OF THE CULTURE

Above, I suggested that homosexuals are often misunderstood in the writings and teachings of psychiatrists because fear and anxiety (largely outside awareness) prompt them to avoid the subject or to deal with it in biased or stereotyped ways. This section examines the behavior of social institutions toward the homosexual and the role the mental health establishment plays in supporting this behavior.

Gender identity is a personality attribute that emerges in the first years of life and is reinforced by practically every human interaction. The first words spoken about a newborn infant are to announce its sex. We continually train the child in appropriate gender behavior and how to direct sexual impulses in socially approved ways. There are, nevertheless, a certain number of individuals who, for reasons not well understood, do not identify with their biological gender or do not choose a heterosexual object, or both.[4]

Some societies deal with these individuals by accepting the homosexual role during certain phases of development or as a lifetime role for certain individuals. But in our own there is no support whatever for this orientation (Money & Ehrhardt, 1972). Homosexual youngsters have the alternative of concealing their preferences and, if they will not or cannot, they are usually driven out, most often into an anonymous urban social milieu.

Parents know how much support must be given their adolescent children as they establish patterns of dating, begin to exchange affection, court, and marry. These supports are needed to negotiate a period of development during which biological drives frequently exceed the child's capacity to control them. Our knowledge of personality development should lead us to expect that the homosexual adolescent, without the benefit of parental and cultural sanctions, would have great difficulty achieving a mature love relationship—that is, one that is both sexually fulfilling and accompanied by enough nonsexual intimacy and permanence to provide a suitable environment for personal growth and for the rearing of children. Such adolescents would experience a high level of guilt, would engage in impulsive and transient relationships, and would have difficulty using their love to enrich the nonsexual areas of life. Observation of many gay adolescents shows that this is frequently the case.

Mental health workers might reflect on the harm done to personal development by the absence of an acceptable social role for homosexuals. They might take steps to reinforce or even create situations in which such a role would be possible. That they have not done so partly reflects the nature of our training, which does not emphasize intervention in social processes. But I believe there is a more important reason why so little attention is being paid to the effect of social influences during adolescence and young adulthood. Professionals, by reason of their selection and training, tend to be heavily committed to prevailing social values and to supporting the institutions that nurture those values. It might be said that the mental health profession is being co-opted by schools, colleges, industry, the Army, the church, and the courts. The bigger and more powerful the institution, the more eager professionals seem to join it.[5] Psychotherapy is important to these institutions because it may make individuals more tractable—increase their sensitivity to the forces of socialization—but especially because the therapist becomes a party to the private thinking of social dissidents. Psychotherapists, even if they do not reveal specific case material, are able to give the institution's leadership some idea of what the troublemakers are up up to; and, as we shall see, they may help to legitimize actions that are not in the patient's interest.

Here are two examples to illustrate the use of the mental health professional in this way. At a large university, the members of a gay student organization decided to have a dance. They brought their proposal before the student council, which voted to support the dance. However, the dean opposed it and turned for advice to several psychiatrists employed by the university. The psychiatrists decided that permission for the dance should be refused, giving as their reason that it would be too stressful for those heterosexual students who were struggling with their sexual identity. The gay dance, they argued, might precipitate homosexual panic or at least create serious anxiety among the more sexually immature students.

In this instance, the psychiatrists decided that the interests of the institution, as defined by its dean, came first. This decision was arrived at contrary to the wishes of the students, as expressed by the student council, and without consulting officials at other universities where gay dances had already been held to see whether homosexual panic had in fact occurred. Needless to say, they did not talk to the gay students and apparently did not consider whatever stress they may have incurred to be worthy of thought.

In planning the dance, the gay students were trying to establish for themselves the same opportunity for companionship everyone else enjoys. Without this opportunity, they would be forced to go to bars and cruising areas where the emphasis is on furtive and impersonal sexual relationships. These would define what it is like to be a homosexual. Many gay adolescents, after experiencing the life of bars and midnight streets, come to a therapist frightened and depressed, filled with self-hate because of the extremity to which their loneliness has driven them. The therapist sees a patient like this as a confirmation of his textbook view of "ego defects" and "immature object relationships."

A second example has a similar theme: Two young men had lived together for several years. Both were active members of their church and were interested in having their relationship recognized by the congregation. They discussed with their minister the possibility of having a marriage ceremony. He agreed, in view of their commitment to each other and to the church, that it would be an appropriate action. The ceremony was approved by the governing board of the congregation and was performed, attended by several hundred of the couple's friends. As news of the marriage became public, others outside the congregation brought pressure on the church hierarchy to do something about this maverick minister who had conducted a "gay marriage." The bishop consulted several psychiatrists, who advised him that the minister was paranoid. The psychiatrists made this "diagnosis" without bothering to examine the "patient." Because of it, the minister was recommended for a medical leave of absence and, when he refused to take one, was forced out of his parish.

In both of these examples, gay people were attempting to gain social support to establish productive and lasting relationships, the lack of which is constantly cited as a typical homosexual trait. Their attempts were opposed by institutional administrators who saw it as their duty to support existing cultural values. The administrators were faced with a decision which they feared would be seen for what it was: opposition to homosexuality. They sought advice from mental health professionals in their employ in an attempt to turn an administrative decision into a medical decision, opposition to which is more difficult because of the great prestige medical decision-making enjoys. The psychiatrists sold their support to an institution. There was not even a pro forma examination of the "patient"— an indication that the rights of homosexuals can be more easily disregarded than those of criminals and psychotics.

The feature of these examples which cannot be too strongly emphasized is that the participating psychiatrists believe they are practicing medicine by diagnosing illness and making recommendations for its containment. In fact, they are defining illness and helping to ensure that the subsequent behavior of the "patients" conforms to their definition. Homosexuals are deprived of social support and then stigmatized when their behavior reflects that deprivation.

IV. THERAPISTS AND THEIR RESPONSIBILITY TO THEIR PATIENTS

We have discussed the difficulty lesbians and gay men encounter in a society that ostracizes them and have pointed out several ways in which the mental health worker reinforces, though often unknowingly, this outsider status. We now consider more specifically the psychotherapist's role in the diagnosis and treatment of homosexuality as a mental disorder.

In the early 1970s it was the position of the American Psychiatric Association that homosexuality was an illness. It appeared in the *Diagnostic and Statistical Manual* as "Sociopathic Personality Disturbance, sexual deviation, homosexuality," with this explanation: "Individuals to be placed in this category are ill primarily in terms of society and of conformity with the prevailing cultural milieu, and not only in terms of personal discomfort and relations with other individuals" (American Psychiatric Association, 1965). (This definition, of course, has implications for all forms of nonconforming behavior.) There was considerable debate about whether an illness label for homosexuality was justified. Szasz (1970) believed that it was not, on the grounds that mental illness is not "illness" in the medical sense. Green (1972) and Marmor (1965) took a narrower view that there are mental illnesses but the evidence is not sufficient to include homosexuality among them. Others believed that while it might not be a mental disorder, most homosexuality could not be considered the outcome of normal personality development. Still others continued to view it as a classical mental disorder.

In the winter of 1973, the APA trustees voted to replace the "sociopathic" label with the term "sexual orientation disturbance . . . for individuals whose sexual interests are directed primarily toward people of the same sex and who are either disturbed by, in conflict with, or wish to change their sexual orientation." Further changes evolved in more recent drafts of the *Diagnostic and Statistical Manual,* none of them satisfactory to everyone. Here I will not even summarize the issues in this debate[6] except to point out that there is a responsible body of professional opinion which opposes any diagnosis at all, a fact of which both therapists and prospective patients should be aware.

In some medical centers, renewed attention is being given to patients' rights. New patients may be furnished with a document, a Bill of Rights, which guarantees them access to information about their illness and the right to make informed decisions about treatment. This trend recognizes that medical decision-making has become so complex that special measures are necessary to protect the patient's status within the doctor-patient relationship. The same is true for patients with mental disorders. Though psychotherapists may be convinced they know the causes and proper treatment of homosexuality, and though some patients may share that conviction, there is still an obligation to recognize that psychotherapists' views are sometimes wrong and that patients must undertake the responsibility for deciding what is in their own best interest.

Specifically, therapists should disclose whatever information the patients want and need to understand their condition and to make an intelligent decision about therapy. This includes information about various legitimate treatments—their cost, length, and the benefits and hazards reasonably to be expected from each. Neither examination nor treatment should be coerced, and patients' confidences must be protected. These standards would be observed for patients with a medical complaint, and there is no reason to treat a gay patient differently—if the therapist is serious about regarding the condition as a form of illness. It is my contention that some therapists do not follow these standards. They discourage patients from learning about homosexual life, exaggerate the benefits of treatment, and coerce patients to accept the desirability of heterosexual life. Therapy becomes something more like religious conversion than medical treatment.

One important issue in the approach to gay patients is whether sexual orientation can be altered by present treatment methods and, if so, with what probability and at what cost. There are two major treatment modalities which claim efficacy in this respect: psychoanalytically oriented psychotherapy (individual and group) and behavior or aversion therapy. (I omit consideration of psychosurgery and hormone therapy, as those treatments are documented by only a few case reports.) The proponents of these treatments have no doubt about their benefits.

Bieber et al. (1962), authors of the largest reported sample of psychoanalytically treated cases, say: "The shift from homosexuality to exclusive heterosexuality for 27 percent of the [homosexual] patients is of outstanding importance since these are the most optimistic and promising results thus far reported" (p. 276).

An article in the *New York Times* (Feb. 28, 1971) headlined "More Homosexuals Aided to Become Heterosexual." The article quoted the opinions of leading psychoanalysts to the effect that 25-50% of homosexuals, regardless of age or adjustment, can be helped to become heterosexual. "As the ranks of former homosexuals grow [one psychiatrist] envisions the development of a Homosexuals Anonymous, a self-help approach that could do for homosexuals what Alcoholics Anonymous has done for alcoholics."

Psychoanalyst Harold Voth (1971) says:

> Homosexuality becomes treatable when the physician is clear about classifying the condition as an illness . . . and is not himself burdened by similar unconscious forces. . . . The mental health professions should take a strong stand against homosexuality . . . and encourage these sick people to recognize their illness and try to rid themselves of it.

Frank (1972) in a brief review of treatment methods and outcomes suggests:

> It would be desirable . . . to combat the sense of hopelessness and inevitability so prevalent among homosexuals by widely publicizing the fact that current treatment methods enable about one-fifth of exclusive homosexuals to achieve some heterosexual interests and competence if they really wish to do so.

Redlich and Freedman (1966) say:

> Homosexuals can be treated only if they sincerely and strongly want treatment. . . . Often, the patient and therapist have to be satisfied with a better general adjustment . . . [and] a lessening of the self-destructive neurotic tendencies. The well-adjusted homosexual who has accepted his deviant sex role is in fact virtually untreatable.

These comments all suggest that homosexuality is a disease that should be stamped out and can be, if only those afflicted will "recognize their illness." Those who won't, who are "well adjusted," are nevertheless not healthy but "untreatable." The emphasis of these and many similar evaluations of treatment tends to wander from a critical look at the shortcomings of the treatment and to focus on the shortcomings of patients whose motivation must be bolstered by a strong stand from mental health professionals. If homosexuality is not disappearing, it is not the treatment but patients who are worthless. They refuse to want what the doctor thinks is good for them and therefore cannot be "helped." While the quotations were taken from practitioners of analytic psychotherapy, the point of view is shared by some behavior modification therapists as well. They are equally optimistic, if not more so, about the results of their treatment.

My own evaluation of these estimates of the possibility of changing sexual orientation is that they constitute consumer fraud. As Coleman shows in Chapter 7, there is scant evidence that *any* treatment can shift sexual orientation in a significant number of people over more than a brief period of time.

The conviction of therapists that treatment causes a change in sexual orientation sometimes comes not from studies of *outcome* but from the intimate participation in *process*—that is, the observation that a shift in patient dynamics followed some technical maneuver or the recovery of a repressed memory or the overcoming of a resistance. But the attribution of causes is tricky business. We should remember that healers since the beginning of time have been convinced, most often wrongly, that favorable changes were their own doing. Unfavorable changes are forgotten or ignored. It would be interesting to know, for example, how many patients with heterosexual histories began homosexual behavior during psycho therapy. This number is not zero, but I have never seen it reported, no doubt because such a development would be considered a reflection on the competence of the therapist.

Let me qualify these criticisms by pointing out that anyone who has done psychotherapy research knows its extraordinary difficulties. The shortcomings of current studies more often may be the result of tactical problems than of the researcher's bias. Nor is my objection to psychotherapy or behavior therapy themselves, which I regard as generally of value in helping people to attain their life goals. I object to advertising the expected outcome of a treatment on the basis of evidence that cannot be regarded as adequate. This diminishes the value of what the therapist has to offer.

While the above comments apply equally to analytic and behavior therapy, another objection has been raised more specifically about the behavior or aversive therapies. These treatments, used to change the patient's sexual orientation, depend on associating punishment, such as an emetic drug or electric shock,[7] with homosexual stimuli and a reward or cessation of punishment with heterosexual stimuli. Gradually homosexual impulses are supposed to be extinguished and heterosexual ones to be reinforced. Homosexuals have felt particularly oppressed by behavior therapy. The idea of shock seems an unacceptably painful and humiliating way of changing the sexual response.

Behavior therapists reply that many forms of treatment are painful yet do not raise an ethical objection. The cost of a pretty nose is the pain of rhinoplasty. Moreover, shock is not a necessary feature of aversion therapies. Some techniques depend on the development of mental images of nauseating situations and avoid external aversive stimuli altogether. Behavior therapists' most important argument, however, is that they treat only those who want treatment; those who consider the pain and humiliation too high a price are free to refuse. This brings us to the issue of informed consent to treatment, which is a matter of concern for all forms of therapy.

An example of the complexity of the informed consent issue comes from a panel discussion at a meeting of the American Psychiatric Association. Dr. Charles Socarides, as reported by *Psychiatric News* (Sept. 5, 1973), gave this advice to employers who are concerned about a homosexual employee: "Don't dismiss him—have him examined." No doubt this statement was intended to show good will toward gay people. Just being examined is preferable to being forcibly hospitalized, shocked, or drugged. But it is still a coercive use of psychotherapy. What if the employees do not want to be examined or if the examination reveals facts about them which are adverse? Why should examinations be a matter of policy for homosexuals? If employees are doing their job, why should they not be let alone? The examination may seem voluntary, but it is coerced by the threat of loss of one's job.

A Michigan Circuit Court ruled that an involuntary mental patient was not competent to give consent to a psychosurgery procedure designed to reduce his aggressive tendencies (*Psychiatric News,* June 2, 1972). The court said:

> The institutionalization of the mental patient tends to strip him of his sense of self-worth and physical and mental integrity, and he . . . clearly has diminished capacity for making a decision about irreversible experimental psychosurgery. . . . It is impossible for an involuntarily detained mental patient to be free of ulterior forms of restraint or coercion.

Ulterior forms of restraint and coercion are not features of involuntary hospitalization alone. They are ubiquitous in the laws, customs, taboos, habits, and ethical principles that to some extent necessarily restrain any who wish to live in a community. The problem for the individual is how to deal with these restraints—which ones to endorse, which to oppose and how—so as to maximize one's freedom of choice. The problem for us as therapists is that as the mental health professions increase their alliance with powerful institutions, they develop similar interests in preserving the very coercions which, as the court says, tend to strip persons of their self-worth and make it impossible for them to be free. The homosexual is coerced into treatment because it is socially undesirable to be homosexual, a situation the pronouncements of the mental health professions tend to reinforce. The gay person has the choice of "voluntarily" accepting examination and its sequelae or choosing to remain a sick, degraded "untreatable."

As Frank observes,

> It seems probable that both the personal suffering of homosexuals and the social problems they present could be more effectively combatted by devoting the same resources (i.e., those which might be used to improve therapeutic methods) to efforts to reduce the social stigmatization and abolish the legal sanctions to which they are now subjected [1972, p. 67].

When the social oppression of gay people is over they will be able to make truly voluntary decisions to keep or to change their sexual orientation and to judge what such a change is worth in money and suffering. Chapter 8 further elaborates on these issues.

V. SUMMARY AND CONCLUSIONS

Lesbians and gay men, like racial minorities, are frequently the objects of social oppression. This homophobia is structural—that is, it is more often built into the cultural fabric and less often consciously perceived by the participants. In the training of psychotherapists, information is given which is often denigrating, expressive of hostile feelings, or simply wrong. The role of institutions in maintaining oppression of homosexuals has been examined and illustrated. Proponents of various therapies for homosexuality often fail to evaluate their treatments critically and do not fairly represent them to potential patients. Therapy can thus constitute a covert and coercive form of behavior control.

During the past two or three years, homosexual men and women have become far more willing to give up their invisible minority status and confront psychiatrists and others who are seen as blocking their chance for an open and healthy life. While there is a long way to go on this issue, most members of the mental health professions have shown a commendable willingness at least to engage in the dialogue which is a first step toward effecting change. The American Psychiatric Association for the past several years has sponsored panels at which gay speakers could present their views and recently established a task force to study gay issues. A spirit is emerging in which learning by both sides can take place. Confrontation is necessary and good. Human rights, if they are to have any meaning for character growth, must be fought for, exercised, and guarded. The freedom lesbians and gay men are winning for themselves in the long run will be liberating for everyone.

REFERENCE NOTE

1. Gittings, B. *Gay, proud, and healthy,* 1973. Available from Gay Activists Alliance of Philadelphia, P.O. Box 15786, Middle City Station, Philadelphia, PA 19103.

NOTES

1. As this was written, the Boston papers reported that two gay men were picked up by six youths, driven to a remote place, beaten, stabbed, and thrown into a sewer. One died. Some may feel that the two men exercised poor judgment in allowing themselves to be picked

up on a lonely street late at night. This argument is heard whenever trouble occurs. The victim, like rape victims, is blamed for his misfortune. See Chapter 29 on minority status.

2. The authors' feelings about the subject are further suggested by the sentence which begins their following section. "Next to homosexuality, the most frequent perversion is sexual intercourse with domestic animals."

3. Several years ago, a local television station ran a news segment under the title "Homosexuals Speak for Themselves." It consisted of an elderly psychiatrist reporting the loneliness and adolescent fixations he observed in gay patients. The psychiatrist was not gay himself, nor had he extensive experience with those who were. A request for time to let gay people really speak for themselves was denied by the station.

4. The former are transsexuals (Gender Dysphoria Syndrome); the latter are homosexuals. These are sometimes overlapping but frequently quite separate situations. Some Gender Dysphoric persons are heterosexual, and most homosexuals show appropriate gender role behavior.

5. Frank Snepp, author and former CIA agent, said, "When you join the [CIA], from beginning to end, you confront psychiatry all the way. To get in you undergo a psychiatric test. . . . If you seem relatively stable and normal sexually—and that's very important from the agency's standpoint—then you're home free" (Psychiatric News, Jan. 19, 1979).

6. The interested reader should see Green's article and comments of the discussants which follow it. Also see "A Symposium: Should Homosexuality be in the APA Nomenclature?" (1973).

7. Electric shock applied to an arm or leg as an aversive stimulus in behavior modification should not be confused with electroconvulsive therapy or ECT. The latter treatment is not considered here.

· 10 ·

Social Psychological Concepts in the Understanding of Homosexuality

John C. Gonsiorek

The purpose of the full-length version of this chapter (published in *American Behavioral Scientist*) is to examine a few alternative methods of conceptualizing some aspects of homosexual behavior, using theories and ideas from social psychology. This chapter is a portion of that longer version, and examines how social psychological theories of stereotyping illuminate the processes of applying a stereotype to a person and having one applied to oneself.

In stereotyping, the audience

(a) categorizes other individuals, usually on the basis of highly visible characteristics, such as race or sex, (b) attributes a set of characteristics to all members of that category, and (c) attributes that set of characteristics to any individual member of that category. Stereotypes are usually simple, overgeneralized and widely accepted [Snyder, 1980, p. 2].

One of the functions of stereotypes is to make the world more predictable and hence manageable, even though the true effects are distortions about certain persons.

Theories about stereotyping suggest that a number of processes occur which create and maintain stereotypes: (a) Stereotyped beliefs influence the individual's attempts to remember and interpret previously learned information about the stereotyped individual(s), and (b) stereotyped beliefs influence and alter the dynamics and outcomes of subsequent social interactions between the audience and the stereotyped individuals.

In other words, an individual, having adopted stereotyped beliefs about a target, will (a) selectively remember and reinterpret past events in the target's life history in ways that confirm these current stereotyped beliefs and (b) will act on these current stereotyped beliefs in ways that cause the actual behavior of the target to validate the individual's stereotyped beliefs about the target.

The process of retrospective interpretation—in which the past may be used as a source of evidence with which to bolster, rationalize, and justify current stereotyped beliefs—has been well-researched on a number of stereotyped groups (for a review of this literature, see Schur, 1971). Memory researchers have long emphasized the role of active constructive processes in remembering (see Snyder, 1980, p. 5). .The reconstructive processes may take at least two forms: (1) preferential remembering of information that is consistent with stereotyped beliefs about the target and/or (2) selective reinterpretation of past events to give them meaning congruent with current stereotyped beliefs about the target.

Descriptions of some empirical research can exemplify these concepts. In an experiment by Snyder and Uranowitz (1978), three groups of participants read the identical narrative about the life history of a woman named Betty K. This narrative was very detailed, providing information that could be construed as consistent with a variety of different conclusions about Betty K. One week later, the three groups of participants learned further information about Betty K to test the hypothesis of selective reconstruction: One group was told that Betty K was lesbian; another group was told she was heterosexual, and the third learned no new information about her. All three groups were then given a multiple-choice test about factual information in the initial narrative.

The subject's new knowledge about Betty K's sexual lifestyle exerted a strong influence on their answers to factual questions about the real events of Betty K's life. Participants who learned Betty K was lesbian reconstructed the events of her life in a manner reflecting stereotyped beliefs about lesbians (e.g., Betty K had an abusive father, never dated men, was unattractive) while participants who learned Betty K was heterosexual reconstructed her life in a manner consistent with stereotyped ideas about heterosexuals (e.g., Betty K had a tranquil childhood, dated men often, was attractive). Detailed analyses of these results showed that participants were better able to identify accurately those facts about Betty K which confirmed their stereotyped beliefs about her sexuality. Moreover, when they erred, their errors reflected distortions consistent with these stereotyped beliefs.

Other research suggests that similar processes have powerful effects on those persons who are stereotyped. Farina, Allen, and Saul (1968) led college students to believe that they had revealed to another that they were stigmatized (a history of either mental illness or homosexual behavior). In fact, the other subject always received the same neutral information. However, merely believing that another person viewed them as stigmatized influenced their behaviors and caused them to act in such a manner as to be rejected by the other person. Stigmatized individuals seem to expect to be viewed negatively by others and rejected by them. Therefore, they accept and play the very role that leads to this rejection. Another experiment supporting this conclusion is reported by Snyder, Tanke, and Berscheid (1977).

Readers interested in more detailed information about stereotyping are referred to Snyder's article (1980). The literature on stereotyping demonstrates that stereotyped beliefs alter the recollection of material and also cause an additional distortion of introducing new material into a recollection, both of these processes in the direction of altering perceptions to fit and accommodate stereotyped beliefs. This then changes the behavior of the perceivers, causing them to act in ways that tend to confirm their stereotyped beliefs by eliciting behavior in the targets that is in accord with the stereotyped beliefs. The targets then come to believe those stereotyped beliefs about themselves, and shape their behavior accordingly. The closed circle of stereotyping and prejudice is then complete, trapping both the perceivers and targets into distortion and rigidity. When it comes to stereotyped conceptions of other people, all individuals involved may construct for themselves a world in which beliefs create reality.

From a somewhat different perspective, Allport (1954) examined the nature and effects of stereotyping and prejudice. He theorized about the personality characteristics that develop in individuals who are targets of prejudice and described these characteristics as coping mechanisms which people may develop in response to prejudice but which may then become relatively stable personality traits. Allport termed these *traits due to victimization* and believed they were common in most persecuted groups. These traits include excessive concern and preoccupation with minority or deviant group membership, feelings of insecurity, denial of membership in the group, withdrawal and passivity, self-derision, strong in-group ties coupled with prejudice against out-groups, slyness and cunning, self-hate, aggression against one's own group, militancy, enhanced striving, neuroticism, and acting out self-fulfilling prophecies about one's own inferiority.

What is perhaps most interesting about Allport's ideas is that he developed them by observing the effects of prejudice against blacks and Jews. His analysis did not include homosexuals. Yet, the personality traits and coping mechanisms he describes parallel closely descriptions of personality characteristics which certain psychoanalytic writers (Bergler, 1956; Bieber et al., 1962; Hatterer, 1970; Socarides, 1968) describe as inherent and pathological features of homosexuals, and "evidence" that homosexuality per se is a neurotic illness. This is a clear example of a situation where the same phenomena are viewed as intrapsychic and intrinsic to the individuals by one school of thought and as products of a social situation and not intrinsic to the individuals by a social psychological approach. As reviewed in an earlier chapter in this section, the data clearly do *not* support the belief that homosexuality per se is an illness, thereby lending credence to the social psychological explanations. Allport's work is different from the more recent literature on stereotyping described above, in that he places greater emphasis on how social situations shape and alter personality characteristics of stereotyped individuals, while the recent literature places greater emphasis on how the processes of stereotyping affect target individuals' behavior in given situations. It can be seen, then, that there is diversity within social psychological perspectives, as well as the groundwork for complementarity with newer intrapsychic explanations, such as Coleman's and Hencken's.

Weinberg and Williams (1974) completed a major cross-cultural study of homosexuality. One of the situations they examined was those factors which facilitate general life adjustment to homosexuality. They found that those individuals who were well adjusted as homosexuals had rejected the idea that homosexuality was an illness, had close and supportive associations with other homosexuals, and were not interested in changing their homosexuality. In this light it is interesting to note that a variety of writers who advocate that homosexuality is an illness and attempt to "cure" homosexuals say many things in common. These theorists (Bergler, 1956; Bieber et al., 1962; Caprio, 1954; Hatterer, 1970; Socarides, 1968) all agree that in order to "cure" a homosexual, he or she must be convinced that such behavior is sick, be motivated to change, avoid homosexual relationships, and avoid social contacts with other homosexuals. Over and above the major problems Coleman points out in the earlier chapter in this section regarding these attempts to "cure" homosexuals, it is clear that these are precisely the attitudes that Weinberg and Williams (1974) found to be related to poor psychological adjustment in homosexuals. The question then arises whether such theorists who advocate "curing" homosexuals are creating or exacerbating maladjustment in their homosexual patients.

In sum, these social psychological theories suggest that there is, for some homosexual individuals, some truth to the data gathered about them concerning personality traits due to victimization, but that there need not be any truth in seeing these traits as intrinsic to the individuals. They also explain, to some extent, why stereotypes take hold in the first place, how they are maintained even in the face of contradictory evidence, and how they encourage confirmatory behavior in those individuals they are directed against. Finally, they strongly suggest that only by maintaining a balance between understanding the internal characteristics of homosexual individuals as well as the social forces that act on and shape them can a useful and complete psychology of homosexuality emerge.

· 11 ·

Homosexuality and Psychoanalysis
Toward a Mutual Understanding

Joel D. Hencken

My music is not difficult to understand,
it is just badly played.

—Arnold Schönberg

Upon this age, that never speaks its mind,
This furtive age, this age endowed with power
To wake the moon with footsteps, fit an oar
Into the rowlocks of the wind, and find
What swims before his prow, what swirls behind—
Upon this gifted age, in its dark hour,
Rains from the sky a meteoric shower
Of facts . . . they lie unquestioned, uncombined.
Wisdom enough to leech us of our ill
Is daily spun; but there exists no loom
To weave it into fabric; undefiled
Proceeds pure Science, and has her say; but still
Upon this world from the collective womb
Is spewed all day the red triumphant child.

—Edna St. Vincent Millay

Author's Note: *This article is based on "Psychoanalysis and Homosexuality: Invitation to a Dialogue" (unpublished manuscript, Homophile Community Health Service, 1980), which constitutes an extended and more technical treatment of the issues. The author would like to express deep appreciation to Messrs. Robert Burnham, Allan Curran, Thomas Hess, and Ronald Wozniak, to Drs. Betty Berzon, John De Cecco, Ellen Gross, William O'Dowd, Richard Pillard, and Robert Wirt, and especially to Dr. John Gonsiorek, for their careful readings of the manuscript and for their very helpful comments and suggestions on matters of both style and substance.*

This chapter argues for the value of a psychoanalytic, interpretive, developmental approach to the study of the lives of gay people in their psychosocial context. It describes the historical antipathy between pro-gay scholars and spokespersons, and those of a psychoanalytic orientation. This lack of mutual understanding is placed in the context of several historical controversies surrounding psychoanalysis more generally. It is argued that psychoanalysis has emerged as a straw figure in gay politics, where the objectionable views of certain analysts are often erroneously taken as representative of some agreed-upon, monolithic psychoanalytic theory of homosexuality. The political aspects of all social science, including psychoanalysis, are discussed, along with the legitimate criticisms which have been directed against psychoanalysis. I attempt to explicate some of the misunderstandings of psychoanalysis by pro-gay writers, emphasizing the need for rigorous conceptual thinking and an understanding of the theoretical and social context in which particular psychoanalytic formulations are made. This is followed by an exposition of fundamental aspects of a modern psychoanalytic approach to human behavior and development, and how these can be of use in understanding gay people. The discussion emphasizes emerging psychoanalytic models which are alternatives to traditional, causal, natural science, and pathology-oriented ways of understanding human experience and behavior. It is suggested that, by a reanalysis of certain psychoanalytic notions in light of the feminist and gay liberation movements, psychoanalysis—far from being socially reactionary—can serve to illuminate the *psychological processes of the internalization of oppression.* A highly controversial psychoanalytic procedure, the developmental interpretation of sexual behavior, is discussed in some detail as an illustration of the position: that, properly understood and used, the psychoanalytic approach can enrich our understanding of the complex interrelationships among gender, sexuality, sex roles, sexual orientation, and identity.

THE PROBLEM

The relationship between psychoanalysis and homosexuality has been a long and ambivalent one. From its beginnings, psychoanalysis has interested itself in all forms of sexuality. As long as homosexuals shared the cultural assumption that something was wrong with them, psychoanalysis seemed a way of understanding their condition and possibly even remedying it. As regards moral and legal issues, many psychoanalysts, like other psychotherapists, have long held liberal attitudes and have taken the position that homosexuality is not a matter of moral turpitude and that the civil rights of homosexuals should be protected (e.g., Freud, 1935 [1951]).

But with the rise in recent years of the gay liberation movement, an increasing antipathy toward psychoanalysis has developed. The position of gay activism is that the problem is not the existence of homosexuals, but rather the hostility and ignorance of society—that cultural attitudes toward homosexuals are exactly similar to attitudes which, when directed at women or at ethnic minorities, would be called biased and prejudiced. From this vantage point, the once-liberal attitude of many analysts appears reactionary. To gay people who see no good reason to be apologetic or secretive about their sexual orientation, the view of some analysts that homosexuality is a variety of developmental disturbance is experienced as condescending at best—in short, as just another form of bias. This is made all the worse by the fact that psychoanalysis proclaims itself to be in the service of human liberation from ignorance and prejudice, so gay activists are inclined to view analysts as not only obstructive but hypocritical as well. The hostility has escalated as evidence from other kinds of psychological studies (see Chapter 6), which are not typically given much credence by analysts, shows rather consistently that unless homosexuality is *defined* as a pathology, there is no reason for regarding it as one. As if this were not bad enough, when, as often happens, ministers, politicians, attorneys, jurists, and other laypersons use psychoanalytic writings to justify their anti-gay attitudes, gay people's resentment turns to rage, and psychoanalysis is viewed as dangerous and destructive. It should be mentioned here that this antipathy also exists with respect to other mental health disciplines, but the high visibility of psychoanalysis and the influence of its theories on other therapists make psychoanalysis a primary target. The reader who is familiar with the feminist literature will note many similarities to the frequent antagonism toward psychoanalysis by many of the activists in the women's movement.

For their part, analysts seem to have reacted to this situation in two ways. Some have become vocal spokespersons for the pathological view of homosexuality and have interpreted the gay movement as itself a manifestation of the pathology of the individuals involved. This, of course, has added fuel to the fire. A great many other analysts, however, have found themselves in an awkward position and have tended to be rather quiet on the gay issue. Their professional identities are as helpers, yet here they are, cast in the role of oppressors. Their theory and, in the United States, their tradition have been rather apolitical, and the majority of analysts seem better equipped to spot the neurotic features of the personalities of people who fight for social change than to lead the way.

Freud (1930 [1961]) was not an optimist about the possibility of fundamental cultural change. He believed that a certain amount of neurosis was the price of civilization, a price humanity had no choice but to pay. He observed that people at odds with their culture were unhappy. The solution seemed to be to make the best of a bad lot. Psychoanalytic theory has thus, for the most part, concerned itself with the variety of adaptations within a given cultural situation. It has had rather little to say about how people are to deal with cases where it is the culture, so to speak, that should be on the couch. The result, over the past decade or so, is that the battle lines have been drawn—people who take it upon themselves to represent psychoanalysis on the one side, gays and pro-gay authors on the other—and the two groups avoid engaging in any meaningful dialogue with one another, a sorry situation indeed.

The present essay is an attempt to open a dialogue between these factions. Psychoanalysis has addressed many other social issues. The problem is that it tends to leave the designation of particular phenomena as social issues to the culture. But this state of affairs is not unique to psychoanalysis. It is only in recent years that any of the social sciences has come to view homosexuality as other than a clinical or, somewhat more rarely, a social deviance issue. That it is currently impossible to provide a summary of the psychoanalytic literature or theory of homosexuality as a social issue (which would be desirable in the present volume) might be regarded by some as in itself reprehensible; they might even aver that such a literature is inimical to psychoanalysis. The position taken here is that while the first claim may well be true, the second is false.

This chapter makes the fundamental assumption that homosexuality is an intrinsic part of the broad range of human sexual expression, and the question of pathology will not be argued here (however, see Chapter 6, this volume; Hencken, 1977; S. Mitchell, 1978). In what follows, I shall take a new look at psychoanalysis from the point of view of this assumption about gay people and shall try to show that a psychoanalytic perspective on homosexuality can supplement and enhance our understanding of the personal and social fabric of gay people's lives.

This book is representative of the continuing development of a dialogue among social scientists on the subject of homosexuality. To the perhaps understandable question "Why include psychoanalysis at all?" it can only be said at this point that psychoanalysis is probably the only psychological system of thought that can fairly claim to constitute a significant cultural and intellectual force and tradition in the twentieth century in the Western world (Barratt, 1976; Malcolm, 1978). To exclude it would constitute a major lacuna in a volume that aspires to reasonable comprehensiveness and would, in my view, greatly impoverish the developing dialogue (see Klein, 1976).

PSYCHOANALYSIS:
CRITICISMS AND REBUTTALS

Throughout its nearly hundred-year history, psychoanalysis has provoked controversy and criticism. It offended Victorian society's moral sensibilities, behavioral psychology's criteria of science (see Skinner, 1956; but also Barratt, 1976; Feigl & Scriven, 1956; Habermas, 1973; Hook, 1959; Koch, 1964), humanistic psychology's optimism about human nature and freedom (see Klein, 1976), and community psychology's emphasis on social conditions in so-called mental illness. It has been accused of "blaming the victim" and as serving the sociopolitical status quo (Szasz, 1961). More recently, feminist and gay political writers have taken umbrage at its formulations of female sexuality and development and of homosexuality, and have seen it as impeding the progress of the feminist and gay liberation movements by promoting biased and false notions about women and homosexuals which are then used by the establishment as rationalizations for keeping them in an oppressed state (e.g., Millett, 1969). There is merit in many of these criticisms, but, as will be elaborated, this is not justification for the wholesale dismissal of psychoanalysis as a means of understanding human behavior.[1]

For their part, analysts have responded to this series of criticisms in a number of ways. Their claims include: (1) A great majority of the most vocal critics have not bothered to familiarize themselves in any sophisticated fashion with the details of either the theory or the practice they are attacking. (2) The content of psychoanalytic findings, obtained as they are only in the intimate quarters of an intense and protected therapeutic relationship, and against the pressure of many psychological barriers (defenses and resistances), are bound to arouse anxiety and, therefore, intense emotional resistance against their acceptance. (3) The largest part of the formulations of psychoanalysis concerns the operation and content of unconscious processes; therefore, they cannot be tested by whether, say, a person consciously remembers the fantasies attributed to a particular period of childhood. (4) The confidentiality of the therapeutic contract has restricted access by nonanalysts to the data on which psychoanalytic formulations are based; thus, the critics are often ignorant of the relevant facts and cannot be in a position to judge the theories. (5) Of the large number of experimental studies of analytic concepts and theories, most pluck the concepts out of their appropriate contexts and subject them to peculiar and often clearly inappropriate kinds of "tests"; even so, a number of empirical studies provide support for some of the basic analytic propositions (Fisher & Greenberg, 1978; Kline, 1972). (6) The *Zeitgeist* has shifted from individual to group behavior, from internal-psychological to external-social; this may make analysis seem irrelevant to modern concerns but does not demonstrate its propositions concerning intrapsychic processes to be invalid. (7) Psychoanalysis was severely oversold as therapy by its enthusiasts, and much of the disenchantment with it is due to its therapeutic limitations, but this does not necessarily invalidate its methods or theories as a science of human behavior. (8) The proliferation of therapies which appeal to the wish for "quick cures" and to the preference, especially in the United States, for pragmatism and technology over painful introspection and insight makes analysis less salable but not less valid. (9) There is still no serious theoretical alternative; with the highly questionable exception of learning theory (behavior modification), the only serious challenge to psychoanalysis, in terms of scope and sophistication, has been the relatively recent advent of family systems theory (Malcolm, 1978), which, it turns out, is regarded by a number of analysts as a complement to, rather than a replacement for, psychoanalysis (see Peterfreund, 1971; Sander, 1979).

Nevertheless, at least in the United States, psychoanalysis is clearly out of favor in many quarters. In the past decade, even the analytic journals are replete with articles complaining of the lack of creativity and new ideas in the field, the problems of attracting high-quality students to analytic institutes, the isolation from other social sciences, and the feeling that the clinical-psychoanalytic method of investigation has reached the point of diminishing returns (Greenson, 1969).

Furthermore, despite the merits of some of the analysts' arguments, a significant number of serious scholars, even those initially sympathetic and interested in psychoanalysis, have been alienated by analysts who analyze the critic's character instead of addressing the substantive issues; by the apparent use of the confidentiality issue to protect the analyst rather than the client—that is, to keep the data from scrutiny; by the rarity of analysts using other methods so as to interface with other disciplines[2] and permit data from other disciplines to modify analytic theories; and by the perceived smugness of many analysts about what is known in the field, when it is clear that, as it were, all the social sciences have a lot to be modest about. Finally, the rather arcane nature of much psychoanalytic jargon seems frequently to obscure more than it reveals, and this is often interpreted, as with the confidentiality issue, as an unnecessary mystification process (Leites, 1971), a way to maintain a kind of private club while asking the public to accept the pronouncements of the membership.

THE NEED FOR CONCEPTUAL CLARITY

It should be clear by now that understanding psychoanalysis, much less properly evaluating and improving it, is an enormously complicated affair. The foregoing discussion has been an attempt to describe only a part of the constellation of issues that have been raised in this regard, and the issues come from virtually every scholarly discipline and vantage point. There is some truth in all the objections and in all the rebuttals. Yet nearly three-quarters of a century of intense debate has not settled matters. Issues continue to get confused, levels of discourse get mixed, and people hold strong opinions, often without any serious understanding of this fascinating but frequently irritating field.

What is crucial at this point is the recognition that psychoanalysis is many things. It is a group of theories, at various levels of abstraction, about a wide variety of psychological, interpersonal, and social phenomena (Fromm, 1970; Hartmann, 1964; Klein, 1976; Waelder, 1960). It is a group of hypotheses about particular varieties of human development and psychopathology and clinical methods for dealing with them. It is a group of observational procedures and of methods for making sense of observations. It is a group of practitioners, their professional organizations, their special interests, and their training institutes. It is a powerful current in twentieth-century intellectual thought, especially in Western Europe, which influences not only psychology and psychiatry but also other social sciences, the arts, and the humanities (see Barratt, 1976; Brown, 1966; Fromm, 1970; Lacan, 1966; Marcuse, 1955; Ricoeur, 1970).

Finally, psychoanalysis has come to serve as a reference point—a *symbol*—for many individuals and groups. Those who approve of it may describe it as the bastion against behaviorism, the parent of all psychotherapy, or the true core of psychology. Those who disapprove may call it the enemy of women and gay people, the albatross of psychology, or the too-available rationale for prejudice against all unusual behavior.

The intensity of emotional reactions to psychoanalysis is worthy of a social psychological study in its own right. Suffice it to say here that under these circumstances, any rational discussion requires all the participants to specify which aspect or aspects of psychoanalysis are being referred to at any given point in a discussion. This is almost never done in lay or political discussions, and even scholars rarely fare much better. Philosophers seem to do best, but then these kinds of distinctions and specifications are their specialty. In what follows, an attempt will be made to address (a) some of the typical confusions regarding various aspects of psychoanalysis, (b) some of the aspects of psychoanalytic practice and theory which are especially relevant to gay-related issues, and (c) some of the new directions in psychoanalysis which seem to hold special promise.

HOMOPHOBIA, GAY POLITICS, AND PSYCHOANALYSIS

In 1972, in his book *Society and the Healthy Homosexual*, George Weinberg introduced the term *homophobia*, which has since achieved wide currency among gay political activists and theorists and a number of social scientists as well (e.g., Lumby, 1976; Millham et al., 1976; Smith, 1971). It refers, in general, to negative attitudes toward homosexuals or homosexuality based either entirely on prejudice or on experience which is strongly colored by prejudice. An example of the latter case would be a counselor who, based on work with gay couples, concluded that gay relationships are invariably disturbed. Here the prejudice is not direct— the conclusion may not literally be prejudged—for there has been experience with gay couples. The homophobia lies in the failure to realize that the same kind of conclusion would not be drawn about the viability of nongay relationships based on a sample of couples whose relationship disturbance was their reason for entering treatment to begin with.

There is an interesting problem with the way homophobia is currently being used as a concept. It is actually two concepts. The first is observational—prejudice. The second is explanatory—fear. It is ironic that this compound concept is implicitly based on the psychoanalytic notion that phobic or paranoid fears stem from the projection of forbidden wishes (see Fenichel, 1945). That is, homophobia is typically used to explain people's aversion to homosexuality on the basis of their presumed fear of their own homosexuality. While this is almost certainly true in a large number of cases, I think it problematic that we use a term to refer to anti-gay prejudices which implies that there is a single explanation for a wide variety of negative and prejudicial attitudes; these may appear as conscious fear, hate, disdain, condescension, pity, and many others—even apparently positive and liberal attitudes such as "some of my best friends are gay." Surely so varied a range of human reactions has many sources and meanings. I think it important that pro-gay writers not prejudge people with anti-gay prejudices; that is prejudice, too. Oppressed groups are always in danger of adopting the tactics of their oppressors—what Anna Freud (1936 [1953]) called identification with the aggressor.

In this chapter, I will use the term homophobia because it is the term in common use. But it will be used only to designate, not to explain, the various manifestations of anti-gay prejudice. This usage makes homophobia strictly analogous to racism, sexism, anti-Semitism, and the like. Two types of homophobia often receive special labels. *Institutional homophobia* occurs when the negative impact on gay people is a by-product of social institutions and is not directed specifically at gays. For example, a tax benefit reserved for married couples will exclude *all* gay couples, but it will also exclude all unmarried straight couples. *Internalized homophobia* refers to homophobic attitudes held by gay people themselves. With the definition of homophobia, we may proceed to a more detailed discussion of psychoanalysis and gay politics.

Opposition to psychoanalysis has been one of the rallying points in gay politics for several years. Even gays who are unfamiliar with psychology are likely to know the names of Bieber (et al., 1962) and Socarides (1978), two analysts who have done the largest amount of publishing and lecturing on homosexuality as a form of psychopathology. Among politically active gays, they are usually viewed with enormous hostility and contempt, and their writings are widely—and erroneously—assumed to represent *the* psychoanalytic theory of homosexuality. Moreover, all analysts and analytically influenced therapists are frequently assumed to hold the same views. One sometimes gets the impression that many gay people believe that were it not for psychoanalysis, the entire mental health field, and perhaps the entire culture, would be more favorably disposed toward them.

The distinction which must be observed here is the difference between psychoanalysis and the views of certain particular analysts. Even a superficial familiarity with the analytic literature makes clear that, as in the other social sciences, controversy on virtually every major issue is the rule rather than the exception. Bieber and Socarides are the most vocal and prolific analysts on the subject of homosexuality, but they are also the most extreme. Other analytic writers have more moderate and politically insightful views (see, e.g., Marmor, 1980; Ruitenbeek, 1973a, 1973c; Stoller, 1975; also Freud, 1935 [1951]). It should be remembered, for example, that it was Freud (e.g., 1905 [1953b]) who, at the turn of the century in Victorian Europe, enunciated the notion that some degree of homosexuality exists normally in everyone—a concept of innate bisexuality which has brought cheers from few quarters.[3]

Analysts' attitudes toward gay people, as opposed to either homosexuals who seek conversion or who do not act on their homosexuality, have tended to follow changes in the culture at large, although perhaps more slowly than they should. In this context, however, it bears looking at the early works of other authors who are now among the popular theorists of the newer therapies: Ellis (1955) of Rational-Emotive therapy; Lowen (1965) of Bioenergetic therapy; Wolpe (1969) of systematic desensitization, and other behaviorists who devised such techniques as aversion therapy and Playboy therapy for changing sexual orientation. All of these authors, in one way or another, have relegated homosexuality to inferior status, if not downright pathology or maladaptiveness, usually by conceptualizing it as an avoidance of the opposite sex rather than a preference for the same sex (Hencken, 1977). Just as, in the general population, younger people are more inclined to hold liberal attitudes toward homosexuality, so it is among analysts and other therapists. It seems reasonably likely that as analysts socialized under the newer cultural attitudes, including openly gay analysts, take up homosexuality as their area of special professional and theoretical interest, an increasing number of changes in theoretical formulations may be expected.

Nevertheless, the current state of affairs is far from satisfactory, and acknowledgment must be made of some of the specific problems that have generated anti-psychoanalytic attitudes among gay people and pro-gay writers. For example, it is still not uncommon for analysts to undertake treatment with the specific goal of changing sexual orientation, despite evidence that it cannot be done (Chapter 7), and good psychological and ethical arguments that it should not be done (Davison, 1976 and Chapter 8 this volume). It is common for analysts and other therapists to give gay clients confusing mixed messages, where the therapist professes to be utterly neutral about homosexuality, but shows greater interest and enthusiasm about the clients' heterosexual potentials or interests, and is strangely silent when homosexual matters are raised. Surely therapists should be able to recognize mixed messages, for these are precisely the focus of the work when therapists discuss the problems their clients had as children in dealing with parental communications.

On the collective level, to date the American Psychoanalytic Association has failed to adopt a position on homosexuality analogous to those of the American Psychiatric Association and American Psychological Association, which, in 1973 and 1975, respectively, removed homosexuality from their lists of mental disorders and committed themselves to working toward removing the stigma traditionally attached to being homosexual. This appears to be a kind of institutional homophobia, because the organization does not take *any* positions it regards as political. As with institutional racism, it is something that is difficult to get people to acknowledge, much less eradicate. The solution, however, is not necessarily to eliminate the institution itself. It remains to be demonstrated that the objectionable behavior of some analysts is caused by their adherence to psychoanalytic method or theory. Indeed, it is the theme of this essay that psychoanalysis, properly understood and used, can be helpful to gay people.

I believe that what has happened in gay politics partly is that psychoanalysis has been turned into an object of irrational prejudice. The process is much like that of other forms of prejudice (see Allport, 1954). It starts with a kernel of truth—that some analysts are homophobic and some people do use selected portions of psychoanalytic theory to justify their homophobia. But around this truthful kernel are wound many other beliefs, and this stems from having a convenient object on which to focus one's anger and frustration. While this may be psychologically understandable, it has no place in a reasoned, scholarly discussion.

In sum, psychoanalysis has been used and misused in ways injurious to gay people, but it has also become a straw figure in debates about homosexuality; and insofar as anything useful is to be learned, it is necessary to distinguish the aspects of psychoanalysis that are relevant to the discussion at hand. In particular, the political and culturally conditioned behavior of some analysts should not be equated with psychoanalysis.

FUNDAMENTALS OF
THE PSYCHOANALYTIC APPROACH

Another important distinction, analogous to the one between the views of particular analysts and psychoanalysis, is the distinction between psychoanalysis as a set of theories and as an approach to understanding human behavior. The core of the psychoanalytic approach is to place any phenomenon of interest in the context of the individual's life history and to determine its idiosyncratic psychological meaning for that person.

A simple illustration would be a bright, talented college student who comes for career counseling because she is dissatisfied with her choice of a career in nursing. Aptitude and interest tests might be of use in helping her to evaluate her career choice and to determine a new one. But it would be essential to understand the personal historical meaning of *any* career choice for this person. A critical piece of information, which may not be volunteered spontaneously by the client, might be that both her father and older brother are physicians. This means that going into a health field is to be like father and brother—what analysts would call an identification. This would not be the case for someone whose family members were blue-collar workers. However, the identification might result in a psychological conflict; that is, the person might have mixed feelings about the competitive implications of going into father's and brother's field, probably more so because they are males. The original choice of nursing, as opposed to medicine, might represent a flight from the potential aggressive and so-called unfeminine aspects of this competition. It may surprise the psychologically minded reader to know that such a student is quite likely to have no conscious idea that the fundamental issue for her is not one of interests or aptitudes, but one of conflicts over competition with family members and with her concept of femininity. Dealing with these conflicts might well be far more efficient and to the point than assessing aptitudes and interests. At minimum, it would be an important supplement in dealing with the career questions she brings to the counselor. And imagine the additional conflicts if this student were a lesbian and had absorbed some of the cultural stereotypes that lesbians are aggressive, dominant, competitive, and therefore unfeminine, perhaps even unfemale. Then the client would also have to deal with her internalized homophobia, as well as the other issues.

In addition to the emphasis on life-historical meaning in general, psychoanalysis makes two more fundamental assumptions: (1) Many important, especially motivational, aspects of behavior are neither conscious to the person nor obvious to the observer. In the case of the nursing student, she does not demonstrate explicitly in her presenting description that she is motivated to be like her father and brother, nor that she is anxious about competing with them. (2) Making these aspects of behavior visible requires a kind of inference which analysts call *interpretation*. By asking the client certain questions about her life history and current feelings and attitudes, information emerges which renders her career perplexities more meaningful to the observer. When these meanings are communicated (interpreted) to the client, she is better able to see not so much how to change her behavior as what her behavior *is*. What began as an implicit meaning, motive, or conflict becomes explicit. This is what analysts call making the unconscious conscious.

The case of this nursing student, from a psychoanalytic point of view, is being analyzed here very superficially. With a great deal more information about her, together with several specific psychoanalytic hypotheses about the nature of psychological development, one could say a good deal more about the psychological meaning of this woman's career choice and the historical events and unconscious fantasies involved. My purpose is to illustrate the value and utility of the basic psychoanalytic approach to behavior. What Schafer (1976) has called the current received version of psychoanalytic theory contains a great many hypotheses that are, or should be, subject to future modification. The point is that it is not necessary to accept the whole theoretical structure of traditional psychoanalytic theory to recognize the important difference between manifest (explicit) and latent (implicit) levels of behavior.

Psychoanalysis is the only elaborated body of thought that accords the life-historical meaning of behavior and the need for interpretation a central place. At this stage in the evolution of psychology, the excommunication of psychoanalysis would mean the exclusion of these critical aspects of human life from psychology's list of top priorities.

POLITICS AND SCIENCE

While it is not as common as it used to be, one still hears some scientific scholars claim that their work is, or should be, entirely apolitical. It is even more common for the lay public to look to science for objective, unbiased answers to important questions. And it is certainly the great strength of the scientific enterprise that it gathers data which subject beliefs and theories to test and allow them to be modified by evidence. Nevertheless, it is important to recognize that science, even a so-called hard science like physics, is not uninfluenced by culture and personality. Scientists do a great many things besides "pure" science. They design their studies, interpret their results, apply for grants, create theories, report results to various media, testify before governmental committees, run for office in

Homosexuality and Psychoanalysis • 133

their professional organizations, and try to obtain tenure and promotion. Their visions, interests, perceptions, compromises, intrigues, and choices of research topics are the behaviors of human beings, not the products of logic machines. Although these behaviors are significantly disciplined by the canons of logic and scientific method, they are also affected by the full range of influences to which all human behavior is subject, from personal historical events, to cultural and historical attitudes and assumptions, to the practicalities of what kinds of research are currently being funded.

This is even more important in the social sciences, for in social science there is less agreement about what the appropriate canons of scientific practice should be. As Kuhn (1970), a historian of science, has pointed out, the vast majority of scientists—whom he calls normal scientists—do their jobs within some particular framework or paradigm without testing the paradigm itself. Chemists, for example, make use of the notion that matter is made up of molecules to interpret their results far more often than they subject the notion itself to test. It is only when a significant number of results cannot be explained that a new paradigm is called for, and, even more important, according to Kuhn, it is only when a better theory is created that the old one passes away.

In the social sciences our basic notions are far less well established than in physical science. Thus, when psychoanalysts have worked with gay clients, they usually have not challenged their assumptions either that their method can find the cause of homosexuality or that homosexuality is pathological. In consequence, they are likely to fit any data they come across into their preexisting beliefs. What gay political writers are calling attention to is that many of these working assumptions are not well-founded theories, but beliefs about homosexuality that are derived from the culture. Since the culture is fundamentally homophobic, these presuppositions are likely to distort the interpretations of the data. Politics, so-called, therefore intrudes on the scholarly enterprise not only at the level of theory but, more important, at the level of implicit assumptions, which dictate the way we ask questions about the phenomena at hand. Scholars must be very careful to avoid asking questions of the form "Have you stopped beating your wife?"

The present volume is thus an outgrowth of both a scholarly and a political process. Times have changed and with them the questions scholars ask. It is to be hoped that our questions are becoming increasingly useful and less prejudicial as we explore matters of fundamental social concern. It is not enough that we social scientists simply refine our statistical and other technical methods for analyzing data derived from our studies. It is also necessary to examine the bases from which we derive our questions.

CAUSES, MEANINGS, AND
THE DEVELOPMENTAL APPROACH

An aspect of psychoanalysis of special importance to gay people is the developmental or "genetic" point of view. As is well known, it was Freud who first emphasized the significance of early childhood in the development of adult character and psychopathology. He originally believed he was collecting data which could provide a picture of the childhood causes of adult behavior. Following this tradition, the past three or four decades have witnessed an increasing interest by analysts in the direct observation of children and in data from other developmental studies, such as those by the eminent child psychologist Jean Piaget (e.g., 1952; see Wolff, 1960; Greenspan, 1979).

But there is another way to view the information about a person's childhood one acquires in the psychoanalytic situation. This approach emphasizes not the search for causes in the past, but rather understanding of the ways in which people make psychological use of their childhood experiences in the current way they see their lives (see Barratt, 1976; Habermas, 1971, 1973; Lacan, 1966; Ricoeur, 1970; also Schafer, 1976, 1978). In short, the emphasis in this approach is on psychological significance or meaning, rather than on causes.

A number of contemporary writers at the forefront of psychoanalytic thinking have moved in this direction. Instead of having psychoanalysis try to emulate the methods and theories of physical science, these writers have suggested that psychoanalysis avoid its traditional, highly abstract mechanical theories (metapsychology) and organize its data at a level closer to the human dialogue which is the core of the psychoanalytic process (see Barratt, 1976; Gedo, 1979; Gill & Holzman, 1976; Klein, 1976; Schafer, 1976, 1978; Wachtel, 1976, 1977). This approach—or, rather, this group of approaches, for there is great diversity among these writers—offers tremendous opportunity for creative thinking and coordination with other ways of studying human lives, especially with the humanities, which the social sciences have generally avoided (Koch, 1964).

It is difficult to provide a brief summary of the meaning approach. It requires not merely some new definitions and concepts, but a quite different way of thinking than we are accustomed to in the social sciences in the United States, and to a considerable extent it is only understandable by practicing it. But the case of the nursing student described above may begin to suggest the flavor and some of the implications of this enterprise. The emphasis is on exploring people's histories to illuminate exactly what they are doing, at a deeper psychological level than their everyday thinking, and what it means to them that they do it. In terms of nonclinical research, an example of a meaning paradigm for psychological research is the work of Levinson et al. (1978) at Yale, who used extended, unstructured interviews in a multiple case study of adult development, with *biography* rather than causal science as the model for the report of the data.

As a historical note, it is interesting that most people find Freud's case histories more like novellas than scientific reports. In addition, Freud was not enthusiastic about direct observation of children in building his theories, even though those theories so centrally concerned childhood. It is likely that this humanities approach, which many contemporary analytic writers now believe is required by the nature of psychoanalytic data, would have been Freud's preference had he not first been trained as a neurologist (see Klein, 1976). So it may be that this "new" emphasis on personal meanings rather than impersonal causes is more a rediscovery than a discovery (see Gill & Holzman, 1976).

GAY PEOPLE AND
THE DEVELOPMENTAL APPROACH

The developmental emphasis of psychoanalysis has been of grave concern to gay people because, given the homophobic attitudes which pervade our culture, scientists are encouraged to study not how gay people develop, but rather what causes homosexuality (Hencken & O'Dowd, 1977). The clear purpose is to find a method for eliminating homosexuality, either by prevention or by cure. Historically, psychoanalysis has studied various behavior patterns considered pathological by the culture in order to determine clinical etiology and to effect therapeutic change. Thus, there has been a confluence of psychoanalytic method and cultural attitude, and this has led to alarm and anger among gay people. It is not as far-fetched an analogy as it might at first seem to say that many gay people quite appropriately feel about etiology and treatment research the way Jews might have felt about the sincere efforts of the Spanish Inquisition to find out how it might be possible to undo the spiritual damage of growing up in a household that produces Jewishness (see Chapter 29 on minority status).

The study of development as applied to gay people has always meant the search for etiology, and this guilt by association has caused pro-gay people frequently to become anti-developmental. This may be historically understandable, but I would like to suggest three reasons why I believe it is no longer necessary.

First, there is no reason why a modern psychoanalytic look at development, even adopting the natural sciences as its model, need employ the same a priori assumptions as Freud did a century ago (see Holt, 1965). In particular, the basic model of human development was *linear*—everyone was assumed to go through the same stages in the same order. Moreover, the model presupposed that there was only one form of mature, adult personality—the heterosexual "genital character." Such a person had allegedly integrated all the earlier stages of development so seamlessly that they were virtually invisible in his or her adult personality, and had subordinated all the sexual possibilities to heterosexual coitus. Such a person, in psychoanalytic terms, has achieved *genital primacy*.

This model was based on a particular belief about the evolutionary significance of sexual behavior. Heterosexual coitus was considered the acme of sexual behavior, and all others were seen as preparation for, auxiliary to, or a result of coitus; the great variety of noncoital sexual behaviors was explained in terms of falling back to earlier modes of behavior (regression), getting stuck at early levels of development (fixation), and so on (see Fenichel, 1945). Deviations from genital primacy were signs of abnormality or pathology. Reproduction was the only outcome of sexual behavior considered biologically adaptive and thus subject to favorable natural selection. The reader may have noted the striking similarity of this turn-of-the-century biology to traditional Western religious views of sexuality.

In Freud's time, there was no field of population genetics, which emphasizes the desirability of diversity in the gene pool. Neither was there a field of sociobiology, which is currently witnessing the development of models to account for the existence of homosexuality as biologically adaptive, for it is a counterreproductive trait which has far too high an incidence rate—even if it were less than the current estimate of 10%—to exist without some adaptive advantage (see Weinrich, 1976, 1979; Chapter 16 by Kirsch and Rodman).

But now there is an opportunity for great change. A combination of more diverse culturally acceptable sexual lifestyles, together with developments in evolutionary biology, can allow psychoanalytic theory to break out of the confines of the linear genital primacy model and to do theoretical justice to what analysts, of all people, have always known in practice—that the complexity of human experience and behavior is far too great to be explained by any of our current developmental models. At best, our models can shed light on some aspects of behavior worth noticing (see Erikson, 1963, chap. 2), but that is nothing to be despised, given how easy it is to become completely overwhelmed with unintegrated information when looking at human behavior.

Second, psychoanalysis has increasingly become interpersonal in its emphasis. Harry Stack Sullivan in the United States, the British "object relations" theorists starting with Melanie Klein (see Fairbairn, 1954; Guntrip, 1971; Winnicott, 1958), and now the self-theorists (Gedo, 1979;

Kernberg, 1976; Kohut in Ornstein, 1978) are emphasizing the *quality* of human relationships throughout development, with a relative deemphasis on sex of the object, particular sexual practices, and the like. This shift in emphasis brings psychoanalysis closer to the basic values of both humanistic psychology and the various liberation movements and makes cross-fertilization of ideas more likely. In addition, careful psychoanalytic attention to qualitative factors in relationships can provide potentially valuable clues to the kinds of new social settings, community and support systems, and alternative categories of relationships that are being developed in our changing culture. For instance, it can potentially be informative about questions one hears in conversations among gay people such as: What kinds of alternative social settings can be devised in which gay people can meet one another? What sort of community services and settings can enable gay people better to withstand negative social attitudes and to grow as persons? What kinds of relationship patterns besides traditional categories of spouse, friend, and lover might be devised which will satisfy people's varied needs for human interaction?

Third, the approach to life history in terms of meaning allows a truly person-oriented psychology to emerge. It inclines itself to a study of what it means to be gay over the whole course of a person's life and to focus research on issues of interest to the subjects, rather than imposing questions on them. The study of personal meanings is, at its very core, the study of the interaction between individuals and society. An individual's system of personal meanings makes him or her a potential informant on the culture. For example, Rosenwald (1978) offers as a prototype the question: Who should one ask about the meaning of children in our society? People with large families? New parents? Grandparents? Obviously all these people could say something about children. But what about people who go to fertility clinics because they desperately want children but are unable to have them? Rosenwald suggests that this population is uniquely equipped to provide a special perspective on the cultural meaning of children. They will display the conscious desire for children, wherein they describe all of the desirable features of having them. But at the same time they will let slip the many reasons why unconsciously they do not want children: the financial drain, the interference with one's own life, and so on. In their conscious desperation to show how much they want children, they will "blow the cover" on the real but denied attitudes toward children in our culture. Similarly, gay people could function as domestic anthropologists for the study of heterosexuality, for they are exposed to it every day, but as psychological outsiders. Like members of other minority groups, their unique perspective could be enlightening to everyone. What is especially desirable about studying personal-cultural interaction in the meaning mode is that it preserves the uniquely psychological dimension.

An application of such an approach of particular relevance to gay people would be to study the development of the psychological processes which occur when people are subjected to persistent negative attitudes toward central aspects of who they are as persons. Such studies could fruitfully be carried out with respect to gay people, women, the poor, and ethnic minorities. Cross-subcultural comparisons could be very enlightening in a thorough study of the psychological processes in the internalization of oppression.[4] We know a good deal about the external conditions of oppression and about some of its consequences, but between the causes and the effects live individual human beings. Sociological and political theories are not always much help in understanding psychological processes, but psychoanalysis is, *par excellence,* a source of the appropriate kinds of concepts.

A CLINICAL ILLUSTRATION

The importance of understanding the detailed psychodynamics of oppression, as opposed to knowing only about its external causes, can be illustrated with a short clinical vignette. Some time ago, I saw a young gay man briefly before referring him to a coming-out group. He was a bright, attractive fellow with an excellent academic record and social skills. He was anxious, guilty, depressed, and, although he denied it, he was in a kind of chronic, frozen rage about being gay. He felt isolated, alienated, and utterly helpless. While I am not usually inclined to recommend readings to my clients, I did consider doing so in this case, because his homophobic stereotyping and ignorance about gay people seemed so extensive. I was about to make a recommendation when he spotted a book on my shelf (Clark, 1977) and said, "Oh, I've read *that*—for all the good it did me." He went on to explain that he had read at least a dozen books of the type I would have been inclined to recommend. I remembered how I had wished that, when I was his age, such books had been available; all I had been able to find was Bieber et al. (1962), which left me even more upset and depressed than I had already been. I was somewhat taken aback at the lack of beneficial impact of these triumphs of gay liberation. "So much for progress," I thought, and began to explore with the client just how it was that the reading seemed to have had no effect on him.

What turned up, of course, was that what was at one level a reason for self-hatred was at another level a facile explanatory screen behind which other guilt and self-esteem issues lay hidden. As much as he suffered the pain of self-hatred for being gay—and he suffered greatly—there was also a *defensive investment* in keeping his homophobic attitudes, because they served to explain to himself why he hated himself and protected him from having to pursue the question further and risk coming upon other conflicts and issues. In other words, his homosexuality had come to serve as a *symbol* for his self-hatred, as well as being a cause of it. Or, as another client, who had been in therapy for about a year, put it: "I finally realized that I would have been neurotic even if I were straight."

I hope I have not given the impression that I view this client's suffering on account of internalized and external homophobia as superficial. Nothing could be further from the truth. My point is that psychoanalytic concepts about unconscious processes (defenses, fantasies, etc.) permit us to understand two important clinical findings: (a) how it is that substantial improvement in people's current life situation does not necessarily make them feel better, and (b) how it is that adults apparently looking for reassuring information can act, when they obtain it, like children who refuse to believe the "facts of life" and prefer their own fantasy explanations, even ones which cause them great distress. A close look at psychodynamics can spare us from being taken by surprise when the efforts of social reformers are successful, and yet the particular human misery which the social reforms were designed to remedy hangs on much longer than expected.

THE INTERPRETATION OF SEXUAL BEHAVIOR

The last topic I would like to address is the interpretation of sexual behavior. Psychoanalysts are inclined to view sexual behavior and fantasy as a kind of symbolic drama in which frequently nonsexual needs are enacted (see Ovesey, 1969; Stoller, 1975). Before proceeding to a discussion of some particular problems and advantages of this view of sexuality, it is necessary to introduce some information about the nature and source of psychoanalytic notions of the relationship between adult unconscious thinking and child development.

Infantile Sexuality

Psychoanalytic theory was the first systematic psychology to propound the notion that sexuality exists prior to puberty. Even today, there are still a great many people who find this idea either puzzling or offensive. But it is hardly the product of subtle inference or nasty-mindedness. Infantile penile erections and masturbatory stimulation, for example, hardly require scientific studies to establish as facts, but until Freud no adult actually talked about the subject. That adults frequently do not remember, or at any rate do not talk about, sexual feelings in early childhood is at least partly a matter of how their families and culture treat the matter of sexuality in childhood. Psychoanalysis is sometimes accused of "adultomorphizing" children, but it is closer to the truth to say that it recognizes that children are little *people* rather than automated dolls. Their feelings are as deep and as real as those of adults, although they must express them differently because they are biologically and psychologically less mature. In essence, psychoanalytic theories describe how children—in our culture, at any rate—are taught to be less sexual until puberty. The implication is that it is not mysterious that childhood needs appear in adult sexuality: They were always part and parcel of the person's sexuality. For that reason, the terms sexual and nonsexual are somewhat misleading. When they appear in the following discussion, they mean *genital* and *nongenital,* for Freud used the term sexual in a broad sense, including a wide variety of sensual gratifications (Klein, 1976).

Unconscious Thinking

Psychoanalytic theory distinguishes two forms of thinking. The first, *primary process* thinking, occurs developmentally earlier. It is the thinking of the very young child—prelogical, concretistic, egocentric—and it appears in adults who are dreaming, entertaining fantasies, or in "regressed" psychotic states (Freud, 1900 [1953a]). It is also the stuff of which art and metaphor are made. The second, *secondary process* thinking, is developed only gradually over the course of childhood. It is logical, reality-oriented, and more verbal in nature. It is the thinking people engage in when they are focusing their attention on a task. Psychoanalytic theory contends that the secondary process never completely supplants the primary process in the course of adult development, although when a person is reality-focused and in a rather structured situation there is little evidence of the earlier modes of thinking (Klein, 1970). But the primary process is said to persist unconsciously. In other words, we are always thinking, feeling, and so on on at least two levels, and these levels employ different modes (see Beck, 1970, a cognitive theorist who argues for the value of these concepts). The only clue that there is more going on than one is aware of may be the existence of momentary emotional reactions that are not sensible to the person experiencing them. For example, an adult may have had a childhood fear, long forgotten, of going down the bathtub drain. Yet, on a particular day, the person may experience a momentary flash of anxiety while washing his or her hands at the sink. It is as if the child is still there, still fearful, after all those years, but most of the time is quiet about it. Similarly, the secondary process is largely inoperative during dreaming, and most adults who remember their dreams can rather easily recognize that there are childhood elements present.

The other important piece of theory is that unconscious thinking, like the thinking of children, is body-centered. Infants and young children are very interested in their bodies and tend to relate events to themselves in a physical way. As children grow up, body parts come to be used more unconsciously to represent important aspects of their world and experience. Myth, literature, art, and figures of speech are full of allusions to body parts as symbols. Long before Freud, swords were phallic symbols (the Latin root of the word vagina means sheath), the bounty of nature was symbolized by the breast, and so forth. Similarly, if a man feels inadequate, he may concretize the feeling by thinking his penis is too small or he is too short, and this is not necessarily particularly unconscious. The French school of psychoanalysis, following Lacan (1966), makes much of the point that such uses of body parts to represent other things do not mean that the person mainly wants, say, a bigger penis; what he wants is what he *unconsciously fantasizes it means* to have a large penis. In this connection, some time ago I was discussing the now-infamous concept of penis envy in women with a woman colleague. She quipped that Freud's mistake was in calling it penis envy. She said he should have called it "penis greed," which would explain why men can have it, too, and why "one is not enough."[5] Listening to men talk in bars (straight or gay), or talking to women about their male lovers, makes it very clear that men do not "grow out" of boyish preoccupation with phallic concerns, which can manifest themselves as worry about size or potency, a failure to recognize the sexual potential of nongenital body parts, and the like. While the most obvious body parts which can serve as symbols are the penis, vagina, and breasts, psychoanalytic observation reveals that all parts of the body which are capable of producing sensual gratification can be so used, and each is capable of representing a variety of so-called nonsexual needs as well.

We now return to the interpretation of sexual behavior, and the problems of applying this psychoanalytic procedure to gay people. I shall argue that this can be a useful way of looking at sex in the context of a person's life. First, however, it must be said that the particular interpretations made are critically influenced by (a) the interpreter's attitudes toward the behavior, and (b) the concepts and a priori assumptions brought to the inquiry.

An example of the impact of attitudes—a quite subtle one—is a conversation that occurred recently between two friends of my acquaintance. While it is not an example of the interpretation of sexual behavior per se, its relevance will become obvious as the discussion proceeds.[6] The two friends were engaged in a very intense conversation, a significant part of which consisted of analyzing or "processing" the conversation itself. This is a common event when therapists or therapy-oriented people get together, and can be a great source of enlightenment as well as entertainment. At a certain moment in the conversation, they both became consciously aware of the enormous pleasure of each other's company and commented on it. They began to talk about how much attention and care both of them, separately and together, give to language and to thinking in words. Then, as it were, came the time for each of them to deliver an interpretation. The more obsessive-compulsive of the two said, "You know, this is what analysts call the hypercathexis of language—perhaps even the eroticization of language." The English-to-English translation of this statement would be that the person has a strong interest and emotional investment in language, and in a subtle way it has a sensual pleasure for him. The other one said, "It's rather like a way of making love with you."

Note the striking difference in the emotional tone of the two interpretations, the difference in conciseness, and the fact that although they denote exactly the same thing, most people would feel put down by the first interpretation and complimented by the second. Psychoanalysts as writers almost invariable sound like the first person; fortunately, as therapists, they often sound like the second. The difference between the phrasings of the interpretations is highly significant and greatly neglected in the psychoanalytic literature, where it tends to get lost by being subsumed under the notion of tact. It is important—for nonanalysts, but for analysts, too—to be aware that everyone sounds terribly pathological when described psychoanalytically in writing—men, women, gays, straights, even psychoanalysts! The new emphasis on meaning in psychoanalytic writing (e.g., Schafer, 1976) has also, happily, produced a positive change in tone and a deemphasis on pathology.

Regarding the concepts and assumptions brought to the interpretation of sexual behaviors in particular, analysts have tended to interpret all sexual behaviors other than heterosexual coitus as substitutes brought about by psychological conflicts and fixations. This has been cause for great resentment among gay people. Authors like Bieber et al. (1962) and Socarides (1978) take such a reductionistic approach that the reader often concludes that gay sexual behavior is not even sex at all. Furthermore, the implicit fantasies and gratifications in gay sexual activities are frequently viewed as evidence of why the person is gay—that is, as etiological data. This goes back to the earlier distinction between studying causes and studying meanings and reflects a confusion between the two on the part of some analysts (see Gill & Holzman, 1976; Klein, 1976; Ricoeur, 1970; Schafer, 1976, 1978). In what follows, I shall give some specific examples drawn from my experience with gay male clients in analytically oriented therapy.

To begin with, take a male client whose associations to *penis* involve prominent power themes and who reports feeling powerful when performing fellatio. Here one may infer that the taking of the penis (a symbol of power) into the mouth is psychologically similar to the tribal rite of obtaining courage by eating the heart of a lion (a symbol of courage). In analytic terms, people performing fellatio may be magically incorporating the fantasied power of the partner and making it their own, with a resulting increase in their sense of power, substance, competence, security, and so forth. It still remains to be demonstrated that the wish for power *causes* the behavior, especially when it occurs in a complex interpersonal context. Frequently, as most analysts will agree, fantasies get attached to behaviors after the fact. In this case, the power themes do not explain the fellatio, much less the homosexuality; what they show is that the behavior, once present for whatever reasons, is capable of *representing a certain meaning* for that person.

Two of the traditional problems in applying a psychoanalytic approach to the study of gay people's sexual behavior have been (a) the gross oversimplification of the variety of sexual patterns within and across gay persons, and (b) the automatic assumption that each behavior has a more or less particular meaning or set of meanings which can be represented by equations like penis = breast or lover = mother.

One of the most striking things one notices when talking intimately with large numbers of gay people, both clients and nonclients, is that the stereotypic notions involving highly specific sexual and role preferences do not hold up to empirical test. It is extremely common for people to engage in a variety of sexual behaviors without having a marked, rigid preference—the decision having to do with circumstance, partner, and various transient intrapsychic variables—and for people who do have a decided preference (e.g., a gay male's preference for anal sex as the insertor) to experience variations in preference over the course of time. In other words, most gay people cannot be typed in any very useful way as insertors, insertees, passive, active, oral, anal, and so forth without doing violence to the variety of their sexual expression.

In addition, the whole question of sexual symbolism and meaning is further complicated by the fact that there is often a difference in both content and variability between people's sexual behaviors and their fantasies. For example, a person may have a highly stereotyped masturbation fantasy with respect to partner or activity but be very eclectic in his or her choice of interpersonal sexual behaviors. Or it may be the other way around. Fantasy is much more than inhibited action, and action is much more than enacted fantasy. Thus, it is possible for a person's homosexual fantasy to be a symptom—that is, mainly a symbolic communication— while his or her homosexual behavior may be "just" a sexual orientation, like heterosexuality. Or vice versa. A great deal of research is necessary to elucidate the interrelationships between fantasy and behavior.

One of the criticisms of psychoanalysis is that it tends to employ an equation of concepts that may once have been an accurate one but is no longer—for example, female = passive = nurturant = receptive = masochistic = castrated. The equation may be true for some people in terms of unconscious fantasy, but it is important that we not mix levels of discourse by casting our theories in primary process thinking, turning a client's unconscious fantasy directly into a theoretical statement (Schafer, 1976). We must not, for example, say that to be in the sexually receptive position *is* to be masochistic, except as shorthand—and misleading shorthand at that—for saying that this person equates the two in conscious or unconscious fantasy. Moreover, it is important that the data be watched closely for signs that the equations are changing as the culture changes; this is especially important as sex roles evolve. The failure to keep the cultural inputs to unconscious processes at the forefront of its theoretical thinking is a frequent criticism of psychoanalysis. Fromm (1970), himself an analyst, emphasizes that the original formulations of psychoanalysis were made in a specific cultural setting and historical period and have not been sufficiently modified to account for phenomena relating to people of more varied social class, situation, and historical era.

When the unconscious equations of received psychoanalytic theory are *imposed* on sexual behaviors under observation, they can seriously distort the behavioral and experiential facts. For instance, it is typically said that the person receiving the penis in fellatio is the passive partner. This may or may not be the case. It rather depends on what both parties are doing. Slang expressions capture some of the differences quite clearly—for example, compare the expressions "sucking someone off" with "having one's face fucked." A similar case is anal intercourse, where the insertee may well be the more active partner.

One of the most serious problems in this area, however, because of its confluence with cultural stereotypes and with people's self-deprecating and anxiety-arousing fantasies, and because it tends to confound various kinds of sexual variations (e.g., transvestism, transsexualism, homosexuality), is the attribution of *gender* to various sexual activities. For example, it is frequently said that the male insertee is in the feminine role. This may indeed be so for some people at some times, in terms of their conscious or unconscious fantasies. But to make the statement in unqualified form is to *define* anyone who is sexually penetrated by a man as a woman, at least psychologically. A more startling example of homophobia finding its way into scholarship would be hard to find. Such a definition precludes the possibility of actually discovering something about what such sexual acts mean to real individuals. It may make some theorists more comfortable to keep reducing human experience to oversimplified, traditional categories, but it hardly aids in the pursuit of further understanding.

Actually, there is nothing in the basic psychoanalytic approach that requires one to adopt any particular typology of sexual behavioral preferences, or to oversimplify the facts of people's sexual lives and the many symbolic meanings that can be expressed through them. If anything, the psychoanalytic method is a very careful one which attends to the detail of each individual's system of meanings. The multiple-case summaries that appear as general psychoanalytic formulations can be very useful, as long as the data of each client are respected as having priority over theoretical expectations. Stoller (1975) has made an interesting start in the implementation of this point of view.

It can be extremely useful, not only in clinical practice but in general attempts to understand aspects of human sexuality, to look at sexual behaviors and fantasies from the point of view of psychosexual development, as long as the experiences are described in sufficient detail. When dealing with the behavior and experience of, say, performing fellatio, it may be compelling to look at the oral-dependent aspects, the so-called penis= breast equation (Fenichel, 1945). That is, people performing fellatio may experience being nurtured as well as sexually aroused and satisfied. But there is a problem only if people believe their dependency needs are constantly unmet and compulsively perform fellatio in a doomed symbolic attempt to meet those nonsexual needs, or if they want to be able to perform fellatio but are inhibited from doing so because of an inability to allow themselves to be nurtured, together with the unconscious fantasy that, say, semen = milk. As long as there is flexibility, mutuality, pleasure, and satisfaction in the sexual behavior, then by object-relational (interpersonal) standards it is healthy, even if it does not fit a traditional, genital-primacy, heterosexualist model of psychosexual development. The great utility of looking interpretively at sexual behavior, if it is done sensitively and without grinding the axes of various cultural prejudices, is that it can be used to help people decode the messages they are sending to themselves. This can help them to be clearer about what is important to them, what needs are being filled in certain relationships and by certain activities, and what, if anything, they want to change about their lives in order better to fulfill them. There is nothing intrinsically anti-gay about the psychoanalytic approach to psychology. I hope that this essay has at least made it plausible that there is a great potential contribution which psychoanalytic thinking can make to psychology in general and to a positive psychology of gay people in particular, if we take the time and trouble to study it.

Psychoanalytic ideas are not the property of any particular group; they are in the public domain. It is how we make use of them that matters. I should hope that psychoanalysts would take a new look at their discipline and theories in light of the gay and women's movements, and that gay and pro-gay scholars would familiarize themselves more thoroughly with the subtleties of the psychoanalytic approach, so that sophisticated, psycho-analytically informed life-historical research can be undertaken with gay people. I firmly believe such an undertaking would be worthwhile. If this belief seems a more reasonable one than it did when the reader began this essay, I have accomplished my purpose.

SUMMARY

This essay has attempted to elucidate some of the historical, theoretical, and political factors that impinge upon the social scientific study of the lives of gay people. The particular emphasis was on the problems and potentials of a psychoanalytic approach to such a study. It was acknowledged that there are a number of currently unresolved problems in some psychoanalytic formulations and their applications. Several of these are of legitimate concern to gay people and to scholars who find no good evidence for a pathological interpretation of homosexuality.

Nevertheless, these problems arise in part from the erroneous equation of the opinions of certain psychoanalysts with some in fact nonexistent widely accepted, coherent psychoanalytic theory of sexual orientation. Moreover, these problems do not justify the dismissal of psychoanalysis altogether, for this would entail the loss of a valuable approach to the understanding of human experience and behavior. In particular, psychology would lose an eloquent theoretical spokesperson for (a) the complexity and interlocking quality of people's meaning systems as they develop over the life course, (b) the importance of implicit (unconscious) meaning or motivational significance of behavior, and (c) the need for interpretation as a human act of the observer of behavior in order to comprehend its meaning.

Three recent shifts of emphasis in psychoanalytic thinking were noted: (1) emphasis on the quality of interpersonal relationships as opposed to gender of partner or particular sexual behaviors, (2) theorizing at a level closer to clinical observation and psychological experience, as opposed to mechanistic and neurology-like theories of "metapsychology," and (3) increasing adoption of the model for psychoanalysis being the study of human meanings, as opposed to the causal, natural science approach. These shifts can open the way for a nonpathology oriented psychoanalytic study of the lives of gay people which would benefit our understanding of the gay experience, and they can help to elucidate the psychological processes involved in the internalization of oppression in a society hostile to a group to which an individual belongs.

A psychoanalytic procedure found particularly offensive by gay political writers—the interpretation of adult sexual behaviors in terms of psychosexual development—was discussed in some detail. This enterprise has been construed and misused in ways detrimental to gay people. However,

(a) the linear genital-primacy model of psychosexual development on which traditional interpretations were based is partly an artifact of turn-of-the-century biology and can be altered to accommodate more modern biological and social psychological developments, and (b) these interpretations, made in the light of the women's and gay movements, can aid in the study of individuals' meaning systems, which would facilitate our understanding of the nature and impact of negative social pressures. Finally, unlike many political and sociological approaches, psychoanalysis offers a unique source of heuristic *psychological* concepts which, properly used, can be of great value in the investigation of the complex interrelationships among gender, sexuality, sex roles, sexual orientation, and personal identity.

NOTES

1. For interesting discussions which are informed by both the women's and gay movements and by psychoanalysis, see Miller (1973), J. Mitchell (1974), and S. Mitchell (1978).

2. Important exceptions include works published in *Psychological Issues,* a monographic series published since 1959 and currently consisting of over 50 titles; *Psychoanalysis and Contemporary Science,* an annual published in five volumes from 1972 to 1976, and the successor to the annual, *Psychoanalysis and Contemporary Thought,* a quarterly journal. (All are published in New York by International Universities Press.)

3. See Rado (1940) for an example of a passionate argument against the notion of innate bisexuality which, unfortunately, seriously confounds the biological and psychological realms of discourse and adds to the already considerable confusion surrounding the topic. Interestingly, Ruitenbeek (1973b), despite a quite different, accepting attitude toward homosexuals, attacks the idea that true bisexuals even exist, based on the rather odd implicit notion that the existence of any significant homosexual responsivity makes a person a homosexual, despite concurrent heterosexual responsivity.

4. Some interesting precursors to this way of using psychoanalysis are found in the works of Brown (e.g,, 1966), Marcuse (e.g., 1955), and Reich (e.g., 1932). Also, see Sartre (1948). Each of these authors has made important contributions; unfortunately, all of them have either stylistic, political, or theoretical postures which have limited their audiences.

5. I am grateful to my friend and schoolmate, Ellen G. Gross, Ph.D., of Ann Arbor, Michigan, for this concept.

6. I am grateful to my friend, Sanford Reder, M.D., of Boston, Massachusetts, for this example.

· 12 ·

Developmental Stages of the Coming-Out Process

Eli Coleman

Homosexuality, although somewhat more tolerated in contemporary American society than in the past, still remains stigmatized. This societal view has caused many people who have same-sex sexual interests to develop negative conceptions of themselves as "deviant," "sick," or "immoral." Many people who have identified themselves as gay or lesbian, despite the pressure by society to view themselves in this negative manner, develop into mentally healthy individuals with positive self-concepts (e.g., Hooker, 1957; Freedman, 1971). Therefore, friends, family members, ministers, teachers, and counselors can be instrumental in facilitating the growth and development of individuals with same-sex interests beyond negative conceptions of themselves to a more positive and healthy view. For example, therapists who challenge their clients' conceptions of homosexuality, exposing myths and stereotypes of homosexuality and providing information of a more healthy viewpoint, can help their clients develop more positive conceptions of homosexuality.

In order to further the understanding of people who have contact with homosexuals, a proposed conceptual framework and five stages of development of individuals with same-sex interests will be presented in this chapter (as published in their full length in the *American Behavioral Scientist*). Elsewhere (Coleman, 1978), I proposed a new model of treatment of homosexuality which assists individuals with same-sex interests to recognize, accept, and value their identity and to help them adjust to their identity in a predominantly heterosexual society. The new model employs developmental concepts rather than the concepts of illness or maladaption utilized by some psychoanalytic and behavioral psychotherapists.

FIVE STAGES OF SAME-SEX
SEXUAL IDENTITY DEVELOPMENT

Five stages describe the life patterns seen in many homosexual individuals: "pre-coming out," "coming out," "exploration," "first relationships," and "integration." This framework is useful in understanding individuals and helpful in facilitating them through the stages to a healthier and more mature outlook, although individuals vary in their progress through stages (see Coleman, 1982).

Pre-Coming Out

The awareness of same-sex interests and feelings is usually a slow and painful process. Individuals who become aware of these feelings are most likely to reject, dismiss, or repress them. Pre-coming out refers to the process of preconscious awareness of a same-sex identity. The most obvious consequence of this growing awareness is the negative impact on self-concept.

These individuals frequently develop negative conceptions of themselves because of the negative societal attitudes toward homosexuality and conceive of themselves in the same way society does—different, sick, confused, immoral, and depressed. Individuals feel indirect rejection when they hear peers, religious leaders, or family make negative statements about homosexuals and homosexuality. This indirect rejection is usually felt very deeply; thus, it keeps them from revealing this aspect of themselves to anyone. Consequently, many individuals at this stage are often depressed because they are not being accepted as themselves.

Fisher (1972) states:

every time a homosexual denies the validity of his feelings or restrains himself from expressing, he does a small hurt to himself. He turns his energies inward and suppresses his own vitality. The effect may be scarcely noticeable: joy may be a little less keen, happiness slightly subdued, he may simply feel a little rundown, a little less tall. Over the years, these tiny denials have cumulative effect [p. 249].

Most individuals in this stage would never reveal themselves to anyone, including their therapists. It is not that they are *actively* concealing this information because their own awareness of their same-sex identity is carefully protected by such defenses as denial, suppression, and repression. Some might enter therapy complaining of generalized problems such as depression, poor self-concept, lack of direction in life, and/or poor interpersonal relationships. Some simply have a sense of not fitting in with others.

The following case is descriptive of a person in a pre-coming out stage.

> Mark came to me for counseling because he didn't know what he was doing with his life. He had just taken a leave of absence from medical school after one year's successful work. He didn't think he wanted to be a doctor although he couldn't really articulate why. No other career alternatives seemed appealing. He was extremely depressed and suicidal. He had become quite withdrawn. He said that his friends seemed to be deserting him. I suspected some sexual identity concerns because of his lack of intimate relationships and his great difficulty looking directly at me when talking about himself. After many sessions of trust building, my suspicions were confirmed when Mark, finally, but still with great hesitation, told me, "I think I might be queer." This was the first time Mark had admitted this fact to anyone, including himself.

The conflict of this stage is resolved in several ways. Some individuals decide to commit suicide. Others hide their true sexual identity from themselves and others and continue to suffer from chronic low-grade depression. The only healthy resolution to the developmental tasks of this stage is for these people to acknowledge their same-sex feelings and interests to themselves. This acknowledgment is important for individuals with exclusive same-sex interests as well as for individuals with mixed same-sex and opposite-sex interests. Fortunately, Mark was able to accomplish this very important developmental task and come out to himself and acknowledge his own same-sex interests. In telling me, his therapist, he had already begun some of the developmental tasks of the second stage of the coming-out process—coming out.

Coming Out

In the pre-coming-out stage, individuals with same-sex interests have some notions of their sexual identity but have repeatedly dismissed these notions. They certainly do not identify themselves as gay or lesbian. However, at this point, they stop fighting with themselves and begin a period of reconciliation, or making peace with their sexuality. Self-admission is the first developmental task of the coming-out stage. Once these feelings are identified and acknowledged, the next developmental task is to tell others. The person told is usually a friend, minister, or therapist.

Acceptance or rejection at this point is critical. Acceptance can have a powerfully positive effect on these individuals. For the first time, they can perceive acceptance for who they are. As a result, positive conceptions of themselves are built and self-esteem increases. This usually leads to telling more people and a further building of the self-concept. (Empirical support comes from Hammersmith & Weinberg, 1973; Dank, 1973; Weinberg & Williams, 1974.)

Rejection during the coming-out stage, on the other hand, can be powerfully negative and do further damage to the self-concept, and some may return to the pre-coming-out stage. These individuals usually experience a chronic low-grade depression.

Because of the vulnerability of the self-concept during this stage, it is important that positive responses be gained during it. Individuals with same-sex interests should choose carefully those people and/or counselors they want to know about their sexual identity. Although there is never complete certainty, individuals can usually predict how friends, family, or counselors will respond. It is very important that those first people be ones who will respond positively. Once these individuals build a number of positive responses to their sexual identity, it makes it much easier to withstand a negative response or even the indirect negative responses from society.

Here is an example of a man who had been aware of his true sexual identity and began working on the developmental tasks of the coming-out stage.

> Richard was a 26-year-old senior in college majoring in business administration. He came in for counseling on the recommendation of one of his friends. He had known for quite some time that he had "homosexual tendencies" but wished he could be rid of "those tendencies." I told him that I could not get rid of those thoughts for him but that we could examine why they were troubling him. Many of his concerns about his feelings toward other men revolved around what other people would think of him. Richard was very concerned about status and social standing. If he ever acted out his feelings, he would be doomed. To him "all queers" were the "scum of the earth." Although he tried to separate himself from other gay people, inside he felt like scum himself. Plaguing him was the fact that Richard was in love with his roommate but was terrified in admitting that fact. I spent a number of sessions educating him what gay life was all about. I then referred him to a gay social group for him to meet and talk with some gay people. He became more comfortable with his feelings and about himself. My acceptance of him was a significant element in his own acceptance of himself. Using our relationship as a paradigm, I explained the value of being more open with his friends. After much trepidation, he told his best friend that he was gay. He received some very positive support. At this point, Richard became involved in a "coming-out group" which I was facilitating at the time. This group focused on problems and concerns related to coming-out issues. The group provided support and feedback for Richard and helped him accept, acknowledge, and value himself as a gay person.

The perceived status of the person being told greatly affects the probability of self-concept change. For example, a positive response from a close friend (like Richard's best friend) will obviously mean more to someone than a stranger's response.

Obviously, the more significant the other, the more powerful the effect a positive or negative response could be. Parents and family members can have a profound effect. In working with parents and family members of gay men and lesbians, I have become increasingly aware of the similarity of the coming-out process for them and their family members.

Gay men and women often forget how long it took to recognize and accept their sexual identity enough to be able to tell another person openly. Once the parent or family member is made aware that their son, daughter, brother, sister, husband, or wife is gay or lesbian, it takes a long time before she/he can acknowledge and accept this fact. Just as the gay man or lesbian may have once felt a negative response from themselves at the prospect of a gay or lesbian identity (pre-coming-out stage), it is not surprising that the parent or family member would have the same response. For most gay men and lesbians today, the chances of an immediate positive parental or familial response is not large. This does not mean that they should not be told. Each situation must be examined individually. It seems that gay men and lesbians might tell their parents and family members when they have built up enough positive responses from significant others that they could withstand a negative response. It can be important for gay men and lesbians to persevere with their parents and family members through their grief process. These family members grieve the loss of image of their son or daughter as married and having their grandchildren. However, gay men and lesbians can be encouraged by the fact that while it took them a long time to fully accept themselves, that prospect exists for their parents and family members, too. Somehow, the gay men and lesbians and their relatives eventually discover that the worth of their being or relationships has nothing to do with their sexual identity.

Exploration

Exploration refers to the stage of experimenting with a new sexual identity. It is in this stage that gay men and lesbians make contact with the gay and lesbian community. They explore ways of meeting others and learning new interpersonal skills.

Exploration is a period of sexual as well as social exploration. When gay men and lesbians finally give themselves permission to become sexual with members of their own sex, there is naturally a surge of interest and intrigue. This can be a period of making up for a lost adolescence.

This stage is often misunderstood by the individuals themselves as well as outsiders. This natural and essential social and sexual experimentation can be viewed as promiscuous behavior. But gay men and lesbians must retrace some developmental steps of adolescence as they come to know and understand their true sexual identity. As an adolescent stage, this is characterized by awkwardness, intensity, and confusion.

American society tends to sexualize the homosexual; not surprisingly, individuals can get locked into seeing themselves as sexual beings with their self-esteem tied to sexual conquests. From a more positive standpoint, during this stage individuals develop a sense of personal attractiveness and social and sexual skills needed for a more integrated adult lifestyle.

The following case illustrates how a gay man can get stuck in this developmental stage:

> David was a 20-year-old college student who came in for counseling because he was "depressed." He told me that he had been "out of the closet" for two years. Since then, he had become very involved in the gay activist movement on campus. He spent every weekend in the gay bars and baths. Most of his contacts with other gays were sexual in nature. As he put it, "I've slept around." At first, he told me that sleeping with many sexual partners was exciting and "ego-building." He had never thought of himself as a sexually attractive person until he came out. Now all his sexual encounters were quite flattering. Recently, however, he had been quite depressed. He began to doubt whether anyone was interested in him other than for sex. He realized that he didn't really have any friends or close relationships. David was already worrying about old age and what that would bring. He said that he wasn't interested in any romantic relationship with another man because "these things never work out anyhow." David was extremely frustrated and depressed about his situation.

David entered the experimentation stage after successfully completing the developmental tasks of coming out. During this period, he actively explored and experimented with his developing sexual identity. He began to develop interpersonal skills in the gay community and developed a sense of personal attractiveness and competence—to work on developmental tasks at the next stage. However, instead of feeling accomplishment, he felt shame. He cognitively construed his behavior as being immature and sinful. It was important for me to help him reconstrue his behavior as a healthy and important step in his growth and development. I helped him understand that his depression was a signal that he was ready to move on, that he now needed more. He was ready to work on new developmental tasks. It has been very important to my clients to give them an understanding of this admittedly chaotic and confusing stage. Clients need to be given permission to enter this stage and to be given time to explore and experiment. I think it is a mistake to push people to form long-term committed relationships at this point. I remember as an adolescent that I was always told to play the field. For most people, that is good sound advice from their elders.

The amount of sexual experimentation might differ between males and females. With changing sex-role stereotypes, however, there is more permission for females to engage in this type of exploratory sexual behavior which was previously licensed to males in our society.

First Relationships

When gay men and lesbians conceive of themselves as capable of loving and being loved, they are ready to enter this next stage of first relationships. The period of exploration has lost its intrigue, and there is a yearning for more stable and committed relationships. They have a sense of personal attractiveness and competence and so now see themselves as eligible for a relationship. Intimacy becomes the primary need to be fulfilled in this stage.

Even with this positive framework, first relations can be disastrous. A number of factors are involved that make these relationships difficult to endure. Because of the newness of these kinds of relationships, individuals entering them may not be completely sure that gay or lesbian relationships can work. In fact, society has long said that gay and lesbian relationships never last very long and are fraught with rejection and hurt. This becomes self-defeating or a self-fulfilling prophecy. On the other hand, because of an intense need for intimacy, gay men or lesbians desperately want relationships to work. Thus, first relationships are often characterized by intensity, possessiveness, and a lack of trust. Gay men or lesbians feel that they have worked through too many things for these relationships to end in disaster. They have reached their goal, and it must work! They want the relationships to be perfect in every way. With these expectations, it doesn't take much to dim hopes and dreams. In the initial stages of the relationship, intense positive responses are extremely helpful to their self-concepts; however, in later stages, responses usually become negative. One of the partners will begin to feel cramped and confined in trying to live up to all the expectations. Their responses will become defensive. They will make attempts to assert independence as a result of feeling confined and obliged. In addition, these feelings can cause a loss of sexual interest in the partner and an increased interest in sexual activity outside the relationship. These relationships can end on a very turbulent note, causing some gay men and lesbians to return to the exploration stage because they become convinced that long-term, intimate relationships never develop. They return to the concept of themselves as a sexual object, sexual deviant adolescent, and ineligible for long-term committed relationships.

The following case will illustrate the problems of first relationships.

Gary was a 35-year-old graduate student who was referred to me by his physician after a serious suicide attempt. The suicide attempt was prompted by the fact that Gary's lover had left him. This had been Gary's first long-term committed relationship to another man. He went through the "bar and bath scene" and finally decided that there had to be something more to being gay than that. He met another young man who felt similarly, and they fell in love. After only a few weeks, they decided to move in together. At first, the relationship was extremely good for both of them. They had never before expressed love to another man with such meaning and intensity. Before this, they had not seen themselves as eligible for any kind of relationship. Gary said that he worked very hard to make the relationship work. But then he found his lover was starting to withdraw. Gary became suspicious that his lover was seeing another man outside of their relationship. He began to distrust his lover. They started to have sexual difficulties, and this convinced him that his lover was "cheating on him." One evening, Gary discovered that his suspicions were true. He took an overdose of sleeping pills and was found unconscious the next day. He was very disappointed that his suicide attempt did not work. He seriously questioned if relationships could ever work or that he could ever be happy being gay.

After the termination of a first relationship, individuals will continue in the same destructive pattern of relationships, or their relationships will evolve into more mature and healthy ones. Evolution can take place when gay men and lesbians begin to realize that the enormous expectations, the possessiveness, the lack of trust, all contributed to the breakup of their relationship. They recognize that mature relationships are based on mutual trust and freedom. Also important in this evolution process is the continued identity formation and the continued building of self-acceptance. In addition, the desire for fulfilling relationships becomes stronger and stronger. Intimacy needs help to overcome the difficulties of this stage.

Integration

Individuals who have achieved integration see themselves as fully functioning persons in their society. They behave in an open, warm, friendly, and caring way. Relationships in this stage are usually more successful because individuals are confident that they are capable of maintaining a long-term, committed relationship. Consequently, there is less possessiveness and jealousy, which mark the demise of many relationships. Gay men and lesbians at this stage are more eligible for successful relationships, as well as psychologically prepared for natural and sometimes inevitable rejections. Rejections are seen in perspective and are handled with normal grief reactions but do not become psychologically crippling events.

Individuals at this stage still face the developmental tasks of adulthood, such as middle and old age. However, with an integrated identity, many individuals at this stage report a greater ease in confronting these tasks than individuals who are still working on earlier developmental stages.

HELPING GAY MEN AND LESBIANS
THROUGH DEVELOPMENTAL STAGES

Before anyone can help a gay man or lesbian through developmental stages, an appreciation of the various stages and an understanding of the movement from stage to stage are helpful. There are a few things for friends, family members, ministers, and health care professionals to keep in mind which can help people move through these stages.

Understanding Your Own Feelings

Before anyone can help a gay man or lesbian, he/she must examine his/her own feelings about same-sex activity and relationships. How comfortable is the individual with the thought of two men or two women engaging in sexual activity? How would an individual feel if he/she found out that a close relative was gay or lesbian? How would the individual react? What about the individual's own same-sex thoughts and fantasies? Can the individual honestly encourage the gay man or lesbian to act on their same-sex feelings? Or, for someone who has not identified themselves as gay or lesbian, can the individual encourage same-sex exploration? It might be helpful if the individual would discuss these issues with a person who is either gay or lesbian.

It would be important for individuals to be more familiar with gay men and lesbians and their lifestyles. If the individual has not had any contact with gay men and lesbians, he/she should take time to become acquainted with individuals who identify themselves as gay or lesbian. Contacting a local gay or lesbian counseling, social, or political agency would be a good place to start.

Acceptance

Acceptance of the gay man or lesbian can have a powerful effect and impact on their self-concepts. Complete understanding is not needed to be accepting. A positive reaction to finding out that a friend, client, family member, or co-worker is gay or lesbian has the potential of challenging any negative self-conceptions the person might have and counteracting society's negative reactions. Individual reactions can have a greater impact than all the direct and indirect reactions of society.

Destroying Myths

A great number of myths support the negative responses members of society dole out. Individuals can counteract those negative responses more effectively if they can help gay men or lesbians see through the myths and stereotypes that exist. In order to do this, the individual can become familiar with these myths and possess accurate information about the realities of same-sex sexual identity. Usually gay men or lesbians who are in the pre-coming-out stage believe these myths implicitly. It is unlikely that they will go through a healthy coming-out process until the myths are destroyed.

Acceptance With Significant Others

The coming-out stage is the most important stage of building self-acceptance. Gay men and lesbians find it very difficult to develop positive self-concepts until they have received positive reactions for their sexual identity. Individuals can encourage gay men and lesbians to take some calculated risks in telling others. This does not mean gay men and lesbians need to tell the world in order to feel better about themselves. However, telling some significant people in their lives can be critical in developing positive self-conceptions. Calculated risks are important because each positive reaction can help the person take greater risks of disclosure and yet negative reactions can inhibit that process.

CONCLUSION

A developmental model of the coming-out process has been presented which can be helpful in understanding the unique identity formation of individuals with same-sex feelings and interests. This model has been extremely helpful to the clients I have worked with in helping them understand what is happening to them. It has also been helpful to others who know or live or work with gay men and lesbians. I hope that this model can help eliminate the view of gay men and lesbians as sick, immoral, and/or deviant. We can look at ways of helping them through the difficult developmental tasks which lead to greater adjustment, satisfaction, acceptance, and happiness.

• 13 •

Summary and Conclusions

John C. Gonsiorek

This section has attempted to provide the reader with an overview of issues pertaining to mental health and homosexuality. In addition to the substantive clinical and empirical material covered in the first few articles, some of the major theoretical political and social issues in this area have also been discussed. Finally, the section concludes with a number of papers illustrating newer theoretical attempts to understand various aspects of homosexuality. And throughout, the authors have attempted to impart methodological and conceptual tools so that the reader can be a more discerning and critical consumer of the literature on this topic—past, present, and future.

It is apparent that homosexuality is a considerably more complex phenomenon than was previously believed. There are a variety of ways of defining and measuring homosexual behavior. While no one approach can be viewed as best or proper, it is clear that any adequate model must take into account a diversity of considerations, as outlined in the introductory chapter. Given these difficulties in the measurement and definition of homosexuality, the most that can be asked of researchers and theoreticians is that they approach these problems in a sophisticated, informed, coherent, and replicable manner.

As I outlined in Chapter 5, the quality of research design in most studies of homosexuality is generally weak, at times appalling so. This is especially true in the area of selection of samples of homosexual subjects. This state of affairs has left much of the research in the area problematic and most of the earlier research worthless. Current research knowledge, if applied well, could markedly improve the quality of future research.

A number of conclusions from the existing works can be drawn. There is no empirical justification for the viewpoint that homosexuality, in and of itself, is a psychiatric illness or related to poor psychological adjustment.

Research on psychological testing does not support an illness model. Further, since objective measures of psychological adjustment are probably the most powerful, reliable, and well-validated techniques for arriving at judgments about psychological adjustment, any theoretical position which postulates homosexuality as an illness is seriously shaken, if not refuted, by these results. If it is an illness, then homosexuals as a group should reliably score in a range which points to a pathological level of psychological functioning. They generally do not, and therefore such illness models are untenable on empirical grounds. In this light, researchers or practitioners who continue to advocate illness models are ignorant or irresponsible or both.

Differences falling generally within the normal range are a common finding of this line of research. However, these differences are not consistent and appear to reflect minor differences in the samples used.

Given the difficulties in defining and measuring homosexuality and the lack of evidence for an inherent pathology of homosexuality, it is not surprising that attempts to change homosexuality to heterosexuality are unimpressive in their results and fraught with ethical dilemmas. The research which purports to show that homosexual clients can be made heterosexual suffers from inadequate followup, hazy definitions of success or failure, conceptual confusion, and generally meager results. Change is rare, if it exists at all; and most instances of apparent change usually involve bisexual individuals who increase their preexisting heterosexual repertoires.

Newer models of therapy have been developing over the past decade. These emphasize helping homosexual clients to improve their functioning and develop a positive homosexual identity. While these approaches are new and generally unresearched, they hold promise.

Further, there are considerable ethical dilemmas in attempts to change sexual orientation. While some homosexual clients may express a desire to change sexual orientation, there may frequently be covert coercion operating in this decision, including that of therapists. It is suggested that therapists look beyond client requests to "change" homosexual orientation and examine social and societal pressures as well as realistic life problems homosexual clients may have. The existence of programs to change sexual orientation is not only problematic, in that such programs promise results they cannot produce on a long-term basis, they also may place the therapist in a position of siding with the status quo in victimizing and discriminating against individuals who are homosexual.

Often, in the training of psychotherapists, social oppression of homosexuals is implicitly supported. As a result, mental health practitioners often become agents of social control and not human development, and mental health institutions often perpetuate the stigmatization homosexual individuals experience. Mental health practitioners need not only examine the limitations of their techniques but also understand the social and cultural context in which they operate. Too often, mental health practice becomes an attempt to control and normalize society's minorities. Neither society nor the mental health institutions nor homosexual patients are well served by this state of affairs.

Finally, this section illustrates some emerging viewpoints which seek to reconceptualize ideas about mental health and homosexuality. Social psychological concepts can be especially useful in this regard. Not only do they offer alternative explanations for some of the same processes described in the old illness model, but these theories also explain how labelling, stereotyping, and prejudice can shape and determine the perceptions, memories, and behaviors of homosexual and nonhomosexual individuals, locking both into severely constrained behavior patterns, rigid and distorted understandings of each other and themselves, and creating self-fulfilling prophecies which produce the reality they seek to explain. In addition, social psychological explanations may be helpful in providing a social context against which the study of homosexuality may assume a more balanced perspective, and in explaining how social forces may shape the development of certain personality characteristics. In general, social psychological concepts may provide complementary additions or challenging alternatives to more intrapsychic explanations of homosexuality.

While psychoanalytic thought has been traditionally associated with illness models of homosexuality, this is more the result of historical accident and mutual misunderstanding rather than theoretical imperatives. Psychoanalytic thinkers and their pro-homosexual critics have seriously misunderstood each other and thereby blocked meaningful dialogue. There is nothing intrinsically anti-homosexual about psychoanalysis, and more thoughtful applications of this viewpoint may serve to create an interpretive developmental approach to the lives of homosexual individuals. In particular, this approach can illuminate the psychosocial processes of the internalization of oppression, as well as other aspects of homosexuality.

New models of the coming-out process can serve to elucidate the identity formation of homosexual individuals. In the process of coming to terms with same-sex feelings and interests, many individuals go through a variety of developmental processes which can be mistaken for psychological problems if a developmental life history perspective is lost. By examining changes over time as individuals develop identities, a more clinically useful and theoretically powerful model can emerge.

This mental health section can best be viewed as an introduction to the study of mental health issues and homosexuality. This topic is in a period of rapid change, and if this section serves as a useful heuristic for appraising new information, then it has met a goal as important as summarizing the current state of knowledge.

· III ·

Biology

Edited by
James D. Weinrich

· 14 ·

Introduction

James D. Weinrich

The nature-nurture controversy is dead. So why does it continue to occupy so much of our attention? The question is not whether genes (nature) or environment (nurture) have more important effects on behavior, but how they interact to produce those effects. For ethologists (students of the evolution of behavior) have shown that even the seemingly most rigid "fixed action patterns" (loosely, formerly called "instincts") require proper rearing in order to develop. Conversely, even the seemingly most learned of learned traits require the evolution of a brain capable of learning them. There can be no doubt that genes and environment interact to produce all behaviors.

But *how* genes and environment interact is a topic of intense controversy today. Is the interaction different for different behaviors? Does the interaction always produce behaviors which are "adaptive" (beneficial by some criterion), or can it produce maladaptively behaving individuals? If adaptive, by what criterion?—what function, if any, is maximized? What can go wrong in this process? Is there any way to distinguish a genuine case of "going wrong" from one in which things simply "went different"?

When this controversy focuses on homosexuality, there are two camps. One—call them the environmentalists—tends to stress the arbitrary nature of the connection between environment and homosexual behavior. This camp acknowledges that genes help create a human being with the capacity to fall in love in homosexual as well as heterosexual ways, that genes create

---

Author's Note: *Michael Ruse and Seymour Reichlin kindly served as referees for earlier drafts of the chapters in this section.*

genital structures and many nerve connections, and that genes permit a great deal of cortical control over sexual impulses. Many environmentalists also are willing to consider evidence of more precise, genetically based constraints on the process—for example, by considering predispositions for people to learn some kinds of love easily, with difficulty, or not at all. But other environmentalists are not so willing. Unfortunately, it is this unwilling subgroup that stereotypically comes to represent environmentalists as a whole—who thus are characterized as trying to explain everything in terms of learning and learning alone.

The other camp—call them the geneticists—tends to stress the nonarbitrary, genetically determined nature of the connection between environment and behavior. The geneticists have also come to be stereotyped—in this case, as the group trying to explain everything in terms of genes and genes alone. Although most geneticists stress predispositions in learning, they are also willing to consider genetically more deterministic models if the evidence seems to warrant them, and often look for behavior that is (subconsciously?) goal-directed when it seems otherwise on the surface. A subgroup of the geneticists, the sociobiologists, work with the hypothesis that genotype-environment interaction should produce behaviors adaptive according to the criterion of evolution by natural selection.

The stereotyping of the two camps is asymmetrical. Although nowadays there are many environmentalists who write as if environment and culture are all that need be considered in understanding homosexuality, there are no geneticists today willing to assert that genes are the only important factors. Nor, to the best of my knowledge, have there ever been any such claims in the history of serious, biologically based theories of homosexuality (Weinrich, Note 1).

This asymmetry is important because it explains the uneasiness about the social uses of biologically based models. Proponents of extreme genetic determinism have indeed existed, and have often had unfortunate (and worse) results—the most obvious example being the Holocaust, which was buttressed intellectually by racist and sexist theories linguistically based in biology. Social Darwinism is another prominent example. It is not surprising that people familiar with such gross misuses of biology, and also familiar with the opposite extreme position of some environmentalists, would project this trite nature versus nurture stance onto the geneticists, and view with alarm *any* statement implying that genes are more than trivial.

The three chapters in this section present what might be called the modern geneticists' viewpoint, although not all the authors are from that camp. Indeed, the first is a strongly critical review of the theories that come closest to complete genetic determinism—those that try to discover average hormonal differences between homosexual and heterosexual men and women. As Gartrell shows, these theories by and large have been proven false. I believe the evidence is now strong enough to conclude that there is no general hormonal correlation of hormones with adult homosexuality. Conceivably, there may be a subgroup of gay men or lesbians in which hormone levels are atypical in comparison with the heterosexual majority. But Gartrell's survey shows that if this subgroup exists at all, it cannot amount to a very large percentage. (For comments on the only exception to this trend, see Chapter 18.)

The second chapter exemplifies the renaissance in biologically based models of homosexuality. Kirsch (a zoologist) and Rodman (a botanist) are both trained evolutionists, and they insist that human behavior—especially a behavior that is so closely connected to the process of getting genes into the next generation—*must* at times be interpreted within the framework of evolution by natural selection, just as is the behavior of animals. (Of course, this framework fits looser around us humans, but it does exist and cannot be ignored with impunity.) Their chapter shows how homosexuality could conceivably—and paradoxically (in some people's minds)—be positively selected over the course of evolution. Some of their models imply that bisexuality is biologically most adaptive, with heterosexuality and homosexuality both inferior, but technically necessary, byproducts. Other models hypothesize, loosely speaking, that androgyny can help one's reproductive success, or at least the reproductive success of one's relatives. None of these models has been rigorously tested, much less proved, but their plausibility has important consequences.

The third chapter draws on the first two and is devoted specifically to applying these and other findings in society. I begin by reviewing homosexual behavior in animal species, and then discuss other arguments about whether homosexuality is biologically "natural." Then I consider how answers to these questions, and to the questions posed in the first two chapters, have an effect on social debates. My somewhat surprising conclusion is that they probably have little or no effect. Why? "The facts" have often been used merely to dictate the choice of argument used to justify a conclusion already decided on, not to determine the conclusion itself. Chapter 18 applies this insight to the nature-nurture discussion engaged in in this introduction.

REFERENCE NOTE

1. Weinrich, J. D. *Psychology and sociobiology: Adaptive models of homosexuality and their social consequences.* Paper presented at the meeting of the American Psychological Association, New York, September 4, 1979.

· 15 ·

Hormones and Homosexuality

Nanette K. Gartrell

The factors responsible for homosexual behavior have puzzled scientific researchers for more than a century. Until recently, many investigators believed that human sexual orientation was strictly a psychosocial phenomenon. However, the development of new and sophisticated techniques for measuring biologic substances in blood has stimulated a broad reevaluation of the contribution of hormones to sexual behavior.

Often implicit in the search for a hormonal explanation of homosexuality is the belief that homosexuality is maladaptive and requires treatment. Since this philosophy reflects many of our cultural prejudices against homosexuals, it is not surprising that hormone measurements which confirm differences between homosexuals and heterosexuals are widely publicized, whereas those which report no differences are generally overlooked. There is a great need for a scientific review of the studies on hormones in homosexuals which will permit unbiased responses to the following questions:

(1) Do homosexual males have lower levels of testosterone (a masculinizing hormone) than heterosexual males?

(2) Do lesbians have higher testosterone measurements than heterosexual women?

(3) Do excesses or deficiencies of hormones of the fetus in the uterus lead to adult homosexual behavior?

This chapter reviews the current literature on hormone measurements in male and female homosexuals.

Author's Note: This work was supported in part by NIMH—Psychiatry Education Branch, Grant #1 T01 MH-15455-01. References begin on page 181.

HORMONE MEASUREMENTS

Scientific interest in hormonal correlates of homosexuality can be traced to the early 1930s when homosexual males were unsuccessfully treated with large quantities of testosterone and other masculinizing hormones (Glass & Johnson, 1944; Meyer-Bahlburg, 1977). This treatment was based on the theory that homosexual males suffered from testosterone deficiencies—a theory presumably derived from observations of effeminate behavior in some male homosexuals. Testosterone treatments were abandoned when researchers found that testosterone increased the sex drive in male homosexuals but did not change their sexual orientation.

Studies of castrated and hypogonadal[1] males also failed to substantiate the testosterone deficiency theory of male homosexuality. Investigators found that castration (hormonal or surgical) did not increase the incidence of homosexuality in adult males (Meyer-Bahlburg, 1977; Bancroft et al., 1974; Bremer, 1958; Money, 1970; Murray et al., 1975; Tauber, 1940). Likewise, there have been very few reported cases of homosexuality in hypogonadal males (see also Heller & Maddock, 1947).

Until recently, the techniques for measuring hormones were crude and unsophisticated. Hormone levels in blood could be estimated only by measurements of hormone metabolites in the urine. Since most hormones do not have unique metabolites in the urine (for example, several sex hormones have the same metabolites in urine as does testosterone), the urinary measurements were not considered an accurate indication of the amount of testosterone in blood (Lipsett & Korenman, 1964; Lipsett et al., 1968; Southren et al., 1965). Improved methods for measuring hormone levels directly from blood have reopened the controversy about hormonal determinants of human sexual behavior. Most of the research has been devoted to hormone analysis in homosexual men; very little research on hormone measurements in lesbians has been published to date.

TESTOSTERONE

In 1971, Kolodny et al. (1971) reported that plasma (blood) testosterone measurements in predominantly to exclusively homosexual males (Kinsey Scale Numbers 5-6) were significantly lower than testosterone measurements in exclusively heterosexual male controls (Kinsey Scale Number 0). A particularly noteworthy finding was the almost linear negative correlation between testosterone level and sexual orientation: the testosterone measurements decreased as the degree of homosexuality increased (Meyer-Bahlburg, 1977). In other words, the more exclusively homosexual a subject was in his behavior, the lower his testosterone level was likely to be. The low testosterone measurements were also associated with decreased sperm counts and elevated gonadotropins, Luteinizing Hormone (LH) and Follicle Stimulating Hormone (FSH),[2] in some homosexual subjects (Kolodny et al., 1972). Although Kolodny et al. were among the first to report information on *plasma* testosterone measurements in homosexuals, the methodological problems in their study allowed only tentative conclusions. Many of their homosexual subjects were heavy marijuana users, and it has subsequently been shown by Kolodny et al. (1974) that marijuana lowers testosterone levels. Also, the four homosexual subjects with low testosterone measurements and elevated gonadotropins were azoospermic (i.e., no sperm were found in their semen), which suggests they were suffering from primary testicular disease. Azoospermia occurs in homosexuals and heterosexuals with similar frequency (Meyer-Bahlburg, 1977), and males with primary testicular disease would be expected to have low testosterone measurements regardless of sexual orientation.

Since Kolodny's data were first reported in 1971, thirteen studies in which plasma or serum (blood) levels of testosterone have been measured in male homosexuals and one study in which testosterone was measured in lesbians have appeared in literature. Data from the studies on male homosexuals are summarized in Table 15.1. In the lesbian study, Gartrell et al. (1977) reported that the mean plasma testosterone in 21 lesbians (Kinsey Scale Number 6) was significantly higher than the mean in 19 heterosexual women (Kinsey Scale Number 0). Gartrell et al. also found that the testosterone ranges for the two groups of women overlapped considerably, and that the testosterone measurements in all subjects fell within the expected range for healthy women.

Four general conclusions can be drawn from the data in Table 15.1 and the author's study:

(1) The great majority of homosexual males had testosterone measurements which are considered normal for healthy males; all lesbian subjects had testosterone measurements which are normal for healthy females.
(2) The negative correlation between degree of homosexuality (Kinsey Scale Number) and testosterone level which was found in the Kolodny study has not been substantiated by other investigators (Meyer-Bahlburg, 1977).
(3) The studies, as a whole, suggest that male homosexuals and heterosexuals have comparable total testosterone measurements.

Eight investigators report no differences in mean total testosterone between male homosexuals and heterosexuals (Doerr et al., 1973; Tourney & Hatfield, 1973; Barlow et al., 1974; Pillard et al., 1974; Parks et al., 1974; Dörner et al., 1975; Stahl et al., 1976; Livingstone et al., 1978). Two studies found that mean testosterone was significantly higher in male homosexuals than heterosexuals (Birk et al., 1973; Brodie et al.,

TABLE 15.1 Male Homosexuality: Testosterone Measurements (Blood)*

| | | SUBJECT CHARACTERISTICS | | RESULTS | |
AUTHOR	N	Sexual Orientation	Age Range	Mean Total Testosterone	Significance (H vs. C)
Kolodny et al. (1971)	4	Kinsey 2		775 ng/100ml	No difference
	6	K 3		681 "	" "
	5	K 4	H 18-24	569 "	" "
	7	K 5		372 "	H < C **
	8	K 6		264 "	H < C **
	50	Heterosexual	C 17-24	689 "	
Birk et al. (1973)	19	Homosexual (K 0-6)	H 22-40	1024 "	H > C **
		Kolodny (1971)	C	689 "	
Doerr et al. (1973)	32	K 3-6	H 20-63	537 " (Median)	No difference
	46	Not Assessed	C 20-33	536 " (Median)	
Tourney and Hatfield (1973)	13	K 5-6	H 18-32	920 "	No difference
	11	Heterosexual	C	650 "	
Barlow et al. (1974)	15	K 5-6	H 15-35	Range 330-1183 "	No difference
		Kolodny (1971)	C		
Brodie et al. (1974)	19	K 6	H Mean 26.0	800 "	H > C **
	20	Heterosexual	C Mean 23.4	604 "	
Pillard et al. (1974)	28	K 5-6	H 19-34	695 "	No difference
	36	Heterosexual	C	787 "	
Parks et al. (1974)	6	K 4-6	H 15-19	Range 383-979 "	No difference
	6	K 0-2	C 16-19	Range 483-936 "	

Study	N		Group	Age	Testosterone	Result
Dörner et al. (1975)	11	H	Homosexual	17-62	595 "	No difference
	20	C	Heterosexual		585 "	
Stárka et al. (1975)	18	H	Homosexual (a)	16-74	498 "	H < C **
	3		Homosexual (b)		449 "	H < C *
	79	C	Not assessed	16-60	739 "	
Stahl et al. (1976)	35	H	Homosexual	19-40	590 "	No difference
	38	C	Heterosexual	20-40	562 "	
Livingstone et al. (1977)	9	H	Homosexual	19-33	471.3 "	No difference
		C	Heterosexual		455 "	
					Mean Free Testosterone	
Doerr et al. (1976)	26	H	K 3-6	20-33	10.7% (Median)	H > C *
	26	C	Not assessed		9.7% (Median)	
Stahl et al. (1976)	35	H	Homosexual	19-40	10.7 ng/100ml	H < C **
	38	C	Heterosexual	20-40	13.3 "	
Friedman et al. (1977)	20	H	K 6	Mean 32	7.46 "	No difference
	18	C	K 0	Mean 28	6.50 "	

*Adapted from Meyer-Bahlburg (1977).

Abbreviations: N = Number
H = Homosexual Subjects
C = Control Subjects
K = Kinsey Scale Number

(a) = Effeminate
(b) = Masculine
*   p<0.05
**   p<0.01
*** p<0.001

1974), and two studies found significantly lower testosterone in male homosexuals (Kolodny et al., 1971; Stárka et al., 1975).

(4) The results of *free*[3] testosterone measurements in males are inconclusive.

Doerr et al. (1976) showed that homosexual males had elevated free testosterone, Stahl et al. (1976) showed that homosexual males had reduced free testosterone, and Friedman et al. (1977) showed that homosexual males had no differences in free testosterone when compared to heterosexual male controls.

Scientists often fall into the trap of assuming that correlation implies causality. The publication of the Kolodny data in 1971 led to a rapid search for testosterone variations which could be implicated in the genesis of homosexual behavior. Despite many methodological shortcomings in the Kolodny and subsequent studies,[4] available evidence fails to support the theory that adult excesses or deficiencies of testosterone produce homosexual behavior.

Gonadotropins and Other Hormones

Measurements of plasma gonadotropins (LH and FSH) in homosexuals also fail to show consistent results (see Table 15.2). As discussed previously, Kolodny et al. (1972) reported a significantly elevated mean LH in 15 homosexual male subjects. However, when the azoospermic males (who have predictably high LH levels) are excluded from their data, the remaining homosexual subjects had LH levels which fell within the normal to low range.[5] The azoospermic males in Kolodny's study were the only homosexual subjects who had elevated FSH measurements. Four subsequent investigations found no differences between homosexual and heterosexual males in LH measurements (Parks et al., 1974; Dörner et al., 1975; Friedman et al., 1977; Tourney et al., 1975), although two (Doerr et al., 1976; Rohde et al., 1977) found homosexual males to have elevated LH levels. Parks et al. (1974) and Tourney et al. (1975) reported normal FSH levels in homosexuals, whereas Rohde et al. (1977) reported elevated FSH in their homosexual subjects. Livingstone et al. (1978) found that the brain output of LH and FSH after stimulation by another hormone (LH releasing hormone) was similar in homosexuals and heterosexuals.

Very few studies on other hormones in homosexuals have been reported. Doerr et al. (1973, 1976) found elevated estrogens (feminizing hormones) in one group of homosexual males, whereas Friedman et al. (1977) found normal estrogens in another homosexual group. Both Kolodny et al. (1972) and Friedman and Frantz (1977) reported normal prolactin (hormone which stimulates milk production) levels in their homosexual male subjects. Isolated reports of elevation in other hormones—dihydro-testosterone (Doerr et al., 1976) androstenedione and cortisol (Friedman et al., 1977)—in homosexual males have yet to be replicated.

Although there is no consistent evidence for gross abnormalities of go-nadotropins or other sex hormones in homosexuals, elevated gonadotro-pins were found in some homosexual subjects. Further studies are needed before conclusions can be drawn about the relationship between pituitary hormones and homosexual behavior.

Discussion

An examination of the methodological problems in the current studies on hormones and homosexuality provides some explanation for the diversity of results. Few investigators carefully assessed the meaning of sexual orien-tation or matched demographic variables in the selection of subjects. For example, homosexual subjects included prison inmates, psychiatric pa-tients, students, and volunteers from homophile organizations; controls were laboratory technicians, military officers, students, and undefined groups of men. Their sexual orientation was assessed by means of the Kinsey Scale, which does not provide an accurate indication of the pattern of erotic feelings and behavior over time. The shortcomings of the Kinsey Scale are particularly apparent with prison groups, who may behave homo-sexually while incarcerated but are often heterosexual after release. Poorly matched groups, such as those found in many of the present studies, would be expected to differ not only in psychological makeup but also, perhaps, in hormone measurements as well (Meyer-Bahlburg, 1977). In such cases, it is impossible to determine whether sexual orientation or some other demo-graphic variable is responsible for the differences.

The studies reported differ greatly in the extent to which they controlled factors which are known to affect hormone measurements. Changes in hormone levels in the body have been associated with stress, mood, sleep patterns, dietary habits, physical activity, sexual activity, and drug use. For example, stress and marijuana use have been independently shown to lower testosterone levels (Kolodny et al., 1974; Kreuz et al., 1972). Inade-quate screening for many of these factors may have been responsible for the heterogeneity of results.

The unreliability of single hormone measurements in most studies was another major methodological problem. Sex hormone levels fluctuate in response to periodic secretion, to breakdown and elimination by the liver and kidneys, and to levels of other hormones in the body. The study by Parks et al. (1974) was the only one in which more than three blood samples were utilized for hormone measurements. This study found that testoster-one and gonadotropin levels varied by 6 to 22 percent over one month.

TABLE 15.2 Male Homosexuality: Gonadotropin Measures*

		SUBJECT CHARACTERISTICS			RESULTS		
AUTHOR	N	Sexual Orientation	Age Range	LH	Significance (H vs. C)	FSH	Significance (H vs. C)
Kolodny et al. (1971, 1972)	4	K2		8.5 mIU/Ml	No difference		
	6	K3		8.8 "	"		
	5	K4	H 18-24	6.8 "	"		
	7	K5		27.8 "	H > C **	12.3 mIU/ml	
	8	K6		46.5 "	H > C **	24.9 "	No difference
	50	Heterosexual	C 17-24	8.3 "		Range 4-25 "	
Parks et al. (1974)	6	K4-6	H 15-19	Range 10.2-13.5 "	No difference	Range 6.3-9.3 "	No difference
	6	K0-2	C 16-19	Range 10.0-12.0 "		Range 5.1-9.6 "	
Dörner et al. (1975)	21	Homosexual	H 20-59	13.5 "	No difference		
	20	Heterosexual	C 17-62	14.7 "			
Tourney et al. (1975)	14	K5-6	H 18-32	3.26 µg/100ml	No difference	17.5 µg/100ml	No difference
	11	Heterosexual	C	3.46 "		11.68 "	
Doerr et al. (1976)	26	K3-6	H 20-33	35.1 ng MRC (Median) 69/104/ml	H > C ***		
	26	Not assessed	C	24.9 " (Median)			
Friedman et al. (1977)	20	K6	H Mean 32	54 ng LER 907/ml	No difference		
	18	K0	C Mean 28	64.2 "			

Study	N		H/C	Age	LH		FSH	
Rohde et al. (1977)	50	K 5-6	H	20-49	28.2 mIU/ml		6.89 mIU/ml	
	40	Heterosexual	C	20-45	12.6 "	H > C**	4.17 "	H > C**
	24		C					
Livingstone et al. (1978)	9	Homosexual	H	19-33				
		Heterosexual	C					

Mean LH and FSH response to LH releasing hormone (LRH) not significantly different.

*See Table 15.1.
Abbreviations: See Table 15.1.
LH = Luteinizing Hormone
FSH = Follicle Stimulating Hormone

The laboratory techniques for hormone measurements were also quite diversified—radioimmunoassay, competitive protein binding assay, gas-liquid chromatography, and thin-layer chromatography—which make comparisons across studies difficult. Also, the use of statistical quality control, blind analyses, and duplicate determinations varied from study to study (Meyer-Bahlburg, 1977).

In the future, sex hormone measurements might be more reliable if the following requirements are met: (1) homosexuals and heterosexuals are carefully matched for demographic variables, socioeconomic status, sexual activity, physical health, mental health, physical activity, sleep patterns, and drug use; (2) precise definitions of sexual orientation, which include assessments of erotic feelings and behavior over time, are employed in the selection of subjects; and (3) a standardized laboratory procedure with multiple hormone measurements for each subject is utilized. In view of the inconsistencies and methodological problems in most of the current studies, it is premature to speculate on the causes of sex hormone variations in isolated homosexual subjects (Meyer-Bahlburg, 1977).

PRENATAL HORMONE THEORIES

An extension of the idea that hormone variations in adults produce homosexual behavior is the theory that *prenatal* excesses or deficiencies of certain sex hormones predispose individuals to later homosexual orientation. This theory suggests that testosterone deficiency at certain critical times in the uterine development of the male fetal brain leads to adult male homosexual behavior. Likewise, excess testosterone stimulation in the developing brain of a female fetus is hypothesized to be responsible for adult lesbianism. The studies which attempt to demonstrate the prenatal hormone theory of homosexuality follow two basic approaches: those which search for evidence of prenatal hormone abnormalities in the hormonal makeup of adult homosexuals, and those in which infants with suspected sex hormone abnormalities in the uterus are followed longitudinally in order to observe the possible long-term effects of these hormone abnormalities on adult sexual behavior. Data from these studies will be summarized in subsequent sections.

Prenatal Testosterone Deficiency in Males

Dörner's research group, in Germany, has been investigating the effect of estrogen injections on the pituitary production of LH in adult male homosexuals and heterosexuals. Dörner et al. (1975, 1977a, 1977b) report that homosexual males respond to estrogen injections with an LH increase which is more characteristic of females than their control heterosexual males. From this finding, Dörner et al. theorize that homosexual males have experienced a deficiency of testosterone at some time prior to birth which allowed their brains to develop along predominantly female lines. They submit their data as evidence of the prenatal testosterone deficiency theory of male homosexuality.

Dörner's data have yet to be replicated by other investigators. Since they provide no information about demographic, sexual, physical, or behavioral (e.g., drug use) characteristics of the homosexual and heterosexual subjects, it is not possible to evaluate their matching procedures for the two subject groups. Also, a careful examination of Dörner's data reveals that the LH response to estrogen in the homosexual subject is *not* identical to that found in women (1975). The response in the homosexual men who demonstrated the LH elevation (some homosexual subjects did not show the response; a number of heterosexual subjects did show the response) was not only much weaker, but it was also much slower than the LH response to estrogen in adult women. Without additional information on subject characteristics or verification by other investigators, Dörner et al.'s data can only be interpreted as suggestive of a variation in LH response to estrogen in some homosexual males.

Money and his co-workers have been investigating the effects of prenatal testosterone deficiency on adult male sexual orientation. One group of androgen-deficient males studied by Money are those who suffered from a chemical abnormality which makes their bodies partially resistant to the masculinizing effects of testosterone.[6] These males are born with genitalia which appear more characteristically female than male; many of them also develop breasts at puberty. Despite the strong developmental influence of prenatal and pubertal feminizing hormones in the absence of effective testosterone stimulation, these males were found to be exclusively heterosexual in erotic imagery and behavior as adults (Money & Ogunro, 1974). Although this finding seems incompatible with the prenatal testosterone deficiency theory of homosexuality, it must be noted that a hormone resistance or deficiency of the fetus in the uterus can only be *inferred* from postnatal observations. Furthermore, testosterone resistance in male external genitalia and breasts does not necessarily imply a testosterone resistance or deficiency in the developing brain.

Prenatal Testosterone Excess in Females

In the adrenogenital syndrome, females have an enzymatic problem in the adrenal gland which results in excess production of testosterone and other steroid hormones. The excess testosterone leads to a masculinization of the female genitalia at birth and, if untreated, a masculinized body appearance (lack of breast development, excessive hairiness, deepening of the voice) at puberty. In a group of 17 early-treated (i.e., treated since birth) adrenogenital females who were followed longitudinally to adulthood, Money and Schwartz found an 18 percent incidence of lesbian experiences (Money & Schwartz, 1977). Among 23 adrenogenital females who began treatment at a mean age of 26 years (most postpubertal females in this group had developed a masculinized body appearance), 17 percent reported lesbian experiences (Ehrhardt et al., 1968). Only one subject in the early-treatment group defined herself as exclusively lesbian, whereas no subject in the late-treatment group saw herself as exclusively lesbian.

The frequency of lesbian sexual behavior in adrenogenital females is slightly higher than Kinsey's estimation for the adult female population. Kinsey et al. (1953) found that 13 percent of women had lesbian experiences at some time during adult life. Although Money's data may suggest a hormonal predisposition to lesbianism in some adrenogenital females, there is no explanation for the fact that most adrenogenital females reported no lesbian experiences. Furthermore, it is difficult to draw conclusions about a prenatal hormonal disposition to lesbianism without (1) replication of Money's data by other investigators and (2) precise measurements of hormones in the uterus.

CONCLUSIONS

Overall, the evidence for a hormonal theory of homosexuality is weak. Researchers have failed to establish that male homosexuals or lesbians are characterized by abnormalities in plasma testosterone levels. Data on gonadotropins and other hormone measurements in homosexuals are also inconsistent and inconclusive. An increased incidence of homosexuality in adults who had suspected prenatal hormone abnormalities (testosterone-resistant males and testosterone-overstimulated females) has not been consistently demonstrated.

When one considers that approximately 4-10 percent of the adult population is homosexual, it is not surprising that hormone measurements on a small number of homosexuals fail to provide a simple biologic explanation for what most psychologists consider a complex social behavior. Masters and Johnson repeatedly remind investigators that our understanding of human sexuality is still in its infancy (personal communication, 1973). The current hormone data suggest that more sophisticated pre- and postnatal studies will be needed to sort out the biological, psychological, social, and cultural determinants of human sexual behavior.

NOTES

1. Hypogonadal males suffer from a deficiency of sex hormone production in the body.
2. LH and FSH, hormones which are produced by the pituitary gland in the brain, regulate sex hormone secretion by the testes and ovaries.
3. Approximately 95 percent of the "total" testosterone measured in blood is bound to plasma proteins and, therefore, chemically inactive; only the "free" or unbound testosterone is chemically active.
4. See the discussion section.
5. Kolodny et al. (1972, p. 20) report that nine homosexual subjects have "inappropriately low" LH measurements, but they do not provide numerical data. Since a low testosterone output from the testes usually triggers the release of increased amounts of LH and FSH from the brain, the observation that LH is not elevated in these subjects presumably led to the conclusion that the brain output of LH is "inappropriately low."
6. This is a "partial" testosterone deficiency, since the normal amount of testosterone is present in these males, but their bodies are physiologically unresponsive to its effects.

REFERENCES

Bancroft, J., Tennent, G., Loucas, D., & Cass, J. The control of deviant sexual behavior by drugs. 1. Behavioral changes following estrogens and anti-androgens. *British Journal of Psychiatry,* 1974, *135,* 310-315.

Barlow, L. H., Abel, G. G., Blanchard, E. B., & Mavissakalian, M. Plasma testosterone levels and male homosexuality: A failure to replicate. *Archives of Sexual Behavior,* 1974, *3*(6), 571-575.

Birk, L., Williams, G. H., Chasin, M., & Rose, L. I. Serum testosterone levels in homosexual men. *New England Journal of Medicine,* 1973, *289*(23), 1236-1238.

Bremer, J. *Asexualization: A follow-up study of 244 cases.* Oslo: Oslo University Press, 1958.

Brodie, H. K. H., Gartrell, N., Doering, C., & Rhue, T. Plasma testosterone levels in heterosexual and homosexual men. *American Journal of Psychiatry,* 1974, *131*(1), 82-83.

Doerr, P., Kockott, G., Bogt, H. H., Pirke, K. M., & Dittmar, F. Plasma testosterone, estradiol, and semen analysis in male homosexuals. *Archives of General Psychiatry,* 1973, *29*(6), 829-833.

Doerr, P., Pirke, K. M., Kockott, G., & Dittmar, F. Further studies on sex hormones in male homosexuals. *Archives of General Psychiatry,* 1976, *33,* 611-614.

Dörner, G. Hormones, brain differentiation and fundamental processes of life. *Journal of Steroid Biochemistry,* 1977, *8,* 531-36. (a)

Dörner, G. Hormone dependent differentiation, maturation, and function of the brain and sexual behavior. *Endokrinologie,* 1977, *69*(3), 306-320. (b)

Dörner, G., Rohde, W., Stahl, F., Krell, L., & Masius, W. G. A neuroendocrine predisposition for homosexuality in men. *Archives of Sexual Behavior,* 1975, *4*(1), 1-8.

Ehrhardt, A. A., Evers, K., & Money, J. Influence of androgen and some aspects of sexually dimorphic behavior in women with late-treated adrenogenital syndrome. *The John Hopkins Medical Journal,* 1968, *123*(3), 115-122.

Friedman, R. C., Drenfurth, I., Linkie, D., Tendler, R., & Fleiss, J. L. Hormones and sexual orientation in men. *American Journal of Psychiatry,* 1977, *134*(5), 571-572.

Friedman, R. C., & Frantz, A. G. Plasma prolactin levels in male homosexuals. *Hormones and Behavior,* 1977, *9,* 19-22.

Gartrell, N. K., Loriaux, D. L., & Chase, T. N. Plasma testosterone in homosexual and heterosexual women. *American Journal of Psychiatry,* 1977, *134*(10), 1117-1119.

Glass, S. J., & Johnson, R. W. Limitations and complications of organotherapy in male homosexuality. *Journal of Clinical Endocrinology,* 1944, *4,* 540-544.

Heller, C. G., & Maddock, W. O. The clinical uses of testosterone in the male. *Vitamin Hormones*, 1947, *5*, 393-342.

Kinsey, A. C., Pomeroy, W. B., Martin, C. E., & Gebhard, P. H. *Sexual behavior in the human female*. Philadelphia: W. B. Saunders, 1953.

Kolodny, R. C., Jacobs, L. S., Masters, W. H., Toro, G., & Daughaday, W. H. Plasma gonadotrophins and prolactin in male homosexuals. *Lancet*, 1972, *2*(776), 18-20.

Kolodny, R. C., Masters, W. H., Hendryx, J., & Toro, G. Plasma testosterone and semen analysis in male homosexuals. *New England Journal of Medicine*, 1971, *285*(21), 1170-1174.

Kolodny, R. C., Masters, W. H., Kolodner, R. M., & Toro, G. Depression of plasma testosterone after chronic intensive marijuana use. *New England Journal of Medicine*, 1974, *290*(16), 872-874.

Kreuz, L. E., Rose, R. M., & Jennings, R. Suppression of plasma testosterone levels and psychological stress. *Archives of General Psychiatry*, 1972, *26*, 479-482.

Lipsett, M. B., & Korenman, S. G. Androgen metabolism. *Journal of the American Medical Association*, 1964, *190*(8), 147-152.

Lipsett, M. B., Migeon, C. J., Kirschner, M. A., & Barden, C. W. Physiologic basis of disorders of androgen metabolism. *Annals of Internal Medicine*, 1968, *68*(6), 1327-1344.

Livingstone, I. R., Sagel, J., Distiller, L. A., Morley, E., & Katz, M. The effect of luteinizing releasing hormone (L.R.H.) on pituitary gonadotropins in male homosexuals. *Hormone Metabolism Research*, 1978, *10*(3), 248-249.

Meyer-Bahlburg, H. F. L. Sex hormones and male homosexuality in comparative perspective. *Archives of Sexual Behavior*, 1977, *6*(4), 297-325.

Money, J. Use of an androgen-depleting hormone in the treatment of male sex offenders. *Journal of Sex Research*, 1970, 165-172.

Money, J., & Ogunro, C. Behavioral sexology: Ten cases of genetic male intersexuality with impaired prenatal and pubertal androgenization. *Archives of Sexual Behavior*, 1974, *3*(3), 181-205.

Money, J., & Schwartz, M. Dating, romantic and nonromantic friendships, and sexuality in 17 early-treated adrenogenital females, aged 16-25. In P. A. Lee et al. (Eds.), *Congenital adrenal hyperplasia*. Baltimore: University Park Press, 1977.

Murray, M. A., Bancroft, J. H., Anderson, D. C., Tennent, T. G., & Carr, P. J. Endocrine changes in male sex deviants after treatment with anti-androgens, estrogens or tranquilizers. *Journal of Endocrinology*, 1975, *67*, 179-188.

Parks, G. A., Korth-Schütz, S., Penny, R., Hilding, R. F., Dumars, K. W., Farasier, S. D., & New, M. I. Variation in pituitary-gonadal function in adolescent male homosexuals and heterosexuals. *Journal of Clinical Endocrine Metabolism*, 1974, *39*(4), 796-801.

Pillard, R. C., Rose, R. M., & Sherwood, M. Plasma testosterone levels in homosexual men. *Archives of Sexual Behavior*, 1974, *3*(5), 453-458.

Rohde, W., Stahl, F., & Dörner, G. Plasma basal levels of F.S.H., L.H. and testosterone in homosexual men. *Endokrinologie*, 1977, *70*(3), 241-248.

Southren, A. L., Tochimoto, S., Carmondy, N. C., & Isurugh, K. Plasma production rates of testosterone in normal adult men and women and in patients with the syndrome of feminizing testes. *Journal of Clinical Endocrinology*, 1965, *25*, 1441-1450.

Stahl, F., Dörner, G., Ahrens, L., & Graudenz, W. Significantly decreased apparently free testosterone levels in plasma of male homosexuals. *Endocrinologie*, 1976, *68*(1), 115-117.

Stárka, I., Sípová, J., & Hynie, J. Plasma testosterone in male transsexuals and homosexuals. *Journal of Sex Research*, 1975, *11*, 134-138.

Tauber, E. S. Effects of castration upon the sexuality of the adult male. *Psychosomatic Medicine*, 1940, *2*, 74-87.

Tourney, G., & Hatfield, L. M. Androgen metabolism in schizophrenics, homosexuals, and normal controls. *Biological Psychiatry*, 1973, *6*(1), 23-26.

Tourney, G., Petrilli, A. J., & Hatfield, L. M. Hormonal relationships in homosexual men. *American Journal of Psychiatry*, 1975, *132*(3), 288-290.

· 16 ·

Selection and Sexuality
The Darwinian View of Homosexuality

John A. W. Kirsch
James Eric Rodman

One of the lessons of the history of science is that getting the Right Answer is, as often as not, a matter of asking the Right Question—or posing it in a scientifically testable way. Much of the controversy about the cause of homosexuality results, in our opinion, from asking wrong questions and from attempting to answer them in an essentially unbiological manner. In this chapter we will outline the reasons for our dissatisfaction with traditional psychoanalytic notions of homosexuality and indicate how evolutionary theory and methodology provide a more comprehensive framework for understanding "the love that dare not speak its name."[1] It should be clear that we are offering only a perspective on the issue and not a coherent, detailed theory of sexuality, which must ultimately provide the context for an understanding of human sexual experience.[2]

The essence of evolutionary biology is comparison—of individuals within a species, of different species, of communities of species. If a structure, function, or behavior occurs in a number of individuals or species, and if it persists through several generations, then that feature can be presumed to serve some evolutionarily advantageous function. That is, it must contribute to the persistence of the species by giving an advantage (or at least equivalent reproductive fitness) to the individuals possessing that feature. Thus, if the characteristic is to be explained in causal terms, one must form a

Authors' Note: *This essay is a modified version of one entitled "The Natural History of Homosexuality," which appeared in the* Yale Scientific Magazine, *1977, 51(3), 7. We are grateful to the editors of* Yale Scientific *for permission to use that material in the present chapter.*

hypothesis about its value to the organisms and test this notion against what is known of the natural history of the animals or plants which have it—and of those which do not. In favorable circumstances (for example, with small organisms having short generation times and high fecundity), experiments can be performed to manipulate environmental variables and thereby test reproductive success. Only in this manner can one separate the evolutionarily advantageous and genetically determined from the spurious, the transitory, and the monstrous.

The Right Questions, therefore, are: (1) Does homosexuality occur widely in our species and in other species? (2) If so, what useful function or functions can it serve in an evolutionary sense?

DIFFICULTIES OF THE PSYCHIATRIC VIEW

The chief difficulties with most psychoanalytic attempts to elucidate the causes of homosexuality are that they ignore the first question and subvert the second by starting from the premise that homosexuality is dysfunctional.[3] Since, the argument runs, the purpose of sex is procreation, behavior that does not (cannot!) produce offspring must be unnatural, therefore sick (see Chapter 11). Necessarily, the conclusions that result from this line of argument must be directed toward showing what has gone wrong in either the physical or hormonal machinery determining normal sexual behavior, or—more usually—in the personal history of the individual. Whether the final explanation rests on the grounds of "nature" (a genetic error, hormonal imbalance, anomalous development) or "nurture" (warped upbringing, traumatic seduction, or whatever), it is bound to reflect that initial prejudice, which is reinforced by Western ethnocentrism.

Given that one is naturally impressed by the rich and variable emotional life of human beings, it is understandable that the genetic factors in the causes of homosexuality are generally ignored. And it is safer for political reasons to avoid characterizing any group genetically. However, the resulting explanations based on nurtural analysis suffer because they rarely account for all instances of homosexuality or provide a unifying hypothesis of causality. Psychiatric scenarios stressing personal history often apply as well to heterosexuals as to homosexuals; yet, the "causes" of heterosexuality are rarely considered.[4] This inadequacy is compounded by a definitional error that does not make adequate distinction between "situational homosexuality" (for example, under conditions of deprivation, as in prison or the military) and true substitution of the same sex for the opposite sex in an affective relationship.

The problem of definition is critical. Behaviorists and ethologists recognize that much behavior can serve multiple ends; but clearly this complicates the attempt to dissect out, and then explain, what is fundamentally "homo-sexual" (that is, an affective, often erotic interest in the same sex) as against that behavior which seems primarily directed toward achieving nonsexual goals. Examples of the latter include aggressive behavior to achieve domi-nance or defend territories, "play" behavior in children and adolescents that is part of the process of gender identification and may continue through adulthood, ritualized behavior in religious ceremonies or initiation rites, and opportunistic behavior for economic gain.

The social sciences have gone a long way toward describing these various behaviors and the environmental context in which each occurs, and identi-fying the goals these behaviors purportedly serve. But they have fallen far short of constructing heuristic overviews of human behavior, largely be-cause of a narrow focus on special aspects of particular human societies (usually urban, Western, and recent).

In any event, the data do not stand up to the expectations of prejudice. Homosexuality is not correlated with any particular racial or socioeconomic group, or with any one cluster of factors in an individual's history. Moreover, nurtural explanations often ignore the considerable body of information on the cross-cultural occurrence of homosexuality.[5] For those human societies showing homosexuality (which is to say, nearly all), the implication of the premise of dysfunction is that they are all, to some degree, sick. That seems an incredible conclusion, especially in view of the long-term persistence of some of them. We have no doubt that human behavior is very malleable, and that in some individuals a purely circumstantial explanation of homo-sexuality may be adequate. But the comparative anthropological phenom-ena alone suggest a strong genetic component.

THE GENETIC CONTRIBUTION . . .

Explanations based on the belief that homosexuality results from a devel-opmental error in expounding the genetic program for normal sexuality, or from a mistake in the program itself, are not much more satisfactory than those derived from the loose cultural—and class—biased correlations of personal life histories. There are no convincing data supporting the view that a physiological, hormonal, chromosomal, or anatomical anomaly underlies homosexuality (see the preceding chapter). The problem with this style of argument lies partly in its oversimplification of the nature-nurture dichot-omy, a naive view which most psychologists and ethologists are now careful to avoid. Traditionally, being a geneticist means first searching for differ-ences among individuals. Finding them, one attempts to discount environ-mental causes for variation by controlling environmental variables and test-ing for the persistence of differences through subsequent generations (as, for example, growing the seeds of apparently different plants in a single garden). If differences do persist in similar environments, then there is a strong presumption that the traits are genetically controlled. Moreover, when contemporary advocates of hereditary causes state that homosexuality is genetically determined, what they mean is not that an individual is necessarily programmed to act homosexually under all circumstances, but that under some conditions that individual but not others will so behave.[6]

This way of presenting the possibility of a genetic basis for homosexuality would help to explain why apparently identical life histories may characterize both homosexuals and heterosexuals. It would also explain the classic twin studies showing that, when one of a pair of identical twins is homosexual, the other is homosexual more often than would be expected statistically.[7] Most significantly, a genetic component in sexual preference can exist independently of physical differences between homosexuals and heterosexuals; thus there need be no direct correlation between anatomical gender and choice of sexual partner.

. . . AND THE EVOLUTIONARY PARADOX

The evidence for a genetic component of homosexuality—from ethological studies of animal species, anthropological accounts of diverse human societies, and the statistical correlation in twin studies—is strong, we believe. If this conclusion is true, then it is mandatory to seek an evolutionary explanation for the appearance and maintenance of homosexuality in humans and other animals, because genetically determined characteristics are the subject of natural selection.

This presents a paradox: The criterion of evolutionary success is number of offspring (reproductive fitness) and consequently the continued (and sometimes increasing) representation of genetically determined traits in succeeding generations. How can homosexual behavior persist if, as is certainly true, exclusive homosexuals do not reproduce as frequently as heterosexuals? By definition, natural selection ought to eliminate any gene predisposing toward such behavior.

Three mechanisms, to our knowledge, have been advanced whereby the paradox is resolved: (1) density-dependent population control, (2) balanced polymorphism, and (3) kin selection for a type of altruistic behavior associated with homosexuality.

Density-Dependent Maintenance of Homosexuality

It has been suggested that homosexual behavior is useful (and therefore selected for in humans) precisely *because* homosexuals leave fewer offspring—that homosexuality is a natural, density-dependent, population control measure that comes into operation when numbers become too great. This would explain why, for example, rats begin to display homosexual behavior in situations of overcrowding.[8]

Superficially, this is an attractive hypothesis, but its chief difficulty is that under conditions of high density the frequency of any gene disposing toward homosexuality would be drastically reduced, since individuals bearing it would not breed. Consequently, the representation of such a gene would decline in subsequent generations; eventually homosexuality would disappear.

Moreover, the problems of overpopulation seem to be relatively new for humans, and it is thought that homosexuality was as common in uncrowded societies as it is in ours. One would expect a positive correlation between the incidence of homosexuality and overcrowding, but this is apparently not the case in human societies. Furthermore, this explanation ignores comparative information from the natural history of other species, which in most cases do not face the problem of keeping populations down, yet often display homosexuality.

Balanced Polymorphism

A more plausible hypothesis has been advanced by G. E. Hutchinson, who, recognizing the significance of the data on twins, was the first biologist to attempt to place homosexuality in an evolutionary context.[9] Hutchinson suggested that the persistence of a gene for homosexuality might be explained by positing some special advantage for heterozygotes. The presumption is that there is a gene determining sexual preference and that there are two alleles (or alternative forms; see "A Primer of Genetics," next page) of that gene which determine, in one case, a disposition toward heterosexuality and, in the other, toward homosexuality. Exclusive homosexuals or heterosexuals would carry a double dose of the corresponding allele; such uniform individuals are termed "homozygotes." If the heterozygotes (individuals with both kinds of allele) had increased fitness (that is, left more offspring than did homozygotes), it would explain why the allele for homosexuality is maintained even though homozygous homosexuals are unfit.[10]

This selection for heterozygosity is the essence of balanced polymorphism, where an allele which would be deleterious in the homozygous state is maintained in a population due to the advantage it confers when in combination with the alternate allele. In humans, for example, the allele causing sickle-cell anemia is lethal in homozygotes, but in heterozygous combination with the "normal" allele confers resistance to malaria, thus explaining the high incidence of sickle-cell anemia in populations exposed to malaria. Such heterozygous advantage is the *least* we must demand from a "homosexual gene" if it is to be maintained in a population, for it is surely

A PRIMER OF GENETICS

Every genetically determined characteristic has its ultimate physical basis in a fragment of the long, twisty molecule known as DNA, located somewhere on the chromosomes which are found in the nuclei of living cells. Each individual has two rather similar sets of chromosomes in each cell, except in the eggs or sperm, where special cell division halves the number of chromosomes to one representative of each pair. Thus, at fertilization the normal double number is re-established: One set is contributed by the father's sperm and one by the mother's egg. Since every person has two of each kind of chromosome, he or she also has two "doses" of each *gene,* which may be exactly alike or somewhat different. Alternative forms of the same gene are known as *alleles,* and are the reasons for variation in some traits, such as eye color, which is genetically determined to be blue or brown. If the alleles received from mother and father are the same, an individual is said to be *homozygous;* for an eye color gene there are two kinds of homozy- • gotes: double-blue or double-brown. But if the contributions of the parents are unlike, the offspring is said to be *heterozygous.* For many familiar traits like eye color, one allele—in this case that determining brown pigment—is expressed at the expense of the other. Thus, a heterozygous person has brown eyes: there are three distinct genetic combinations, but only two visible results. However, for other features, especially biochemical ones like blood types, both alleles may be expressed in a heterozygous combination, such as that underlying type AB. The example of blood groups is complicated by the fact that there are other types than A, B, and AB—in human populations there are often more than two alleles for a particular gene. During reproduction any two of the several alleles may be drawn from the common pool in forming a new individual. But, once again, no particular person may inherit more than two kinds of alleles. Establishing the possible genetic basis for behavioral characteristics such as sexual preference is enormously more complex than doing so for eye color or blood type, and if there is such a basis, almost certainly many different genes play a role in determining the trait. Nevertheless, the simple genetic model involving a few basic kinds of response and their genetic causes provides at least a starting point for study and discussion.

too much to expect that repeated mutation maintains the conspicuous incidence of homosexuality.

Unfortunately, there has been no test of Hutchinson's hypothesis (the paper in which it was advanced itself seems little known), and it would be difficult to construct a crucial experiment. For one thing, it hardly seems likely that only a single gene is involved in determining sexual preference. Nevertheless, we conceive of one test deriving from a related kind of explanation which focuses on the uses of homosexual behavior in a nonsexual context. This explanation assumes that such an expanded behavioral repertoire might contribute to social—and hence ultimately reproductive—success. For example, a large percentage of observations of homosexuality in other animals does involve the transfer of superficially sexual behavior to situations involving territory maintenance or dominance displays. Ritual mountings of subordinates by dominant males are common in primates and several other orders of mammals, and Trivers reported male-male mountings in lizards which seem to be a consequence of territoriality.[11]

It might not be apparent that the advantages of being a heterozygote may lie in rewards that are not explicitly sexual, but heterozygous advantage could account for some homosexual behavior in human societies. For example, it is clear that a good deal of homosexual behavior in prisons, fraternities, and the military is really about territory and dominance, and not primarily for sexual gratification. If there is any heterozygous advantage, it might well be connected with the ability of those individuals (heterozygotes) who are capable of homosexual behavior, as well as inclined to reproduction, to secure a dominant position in the social hierarchy, maintain a territory, and secure mates. It ought to be possible to construct an experiment to test for this correlation, and we suspect that information is already available for animal and even human societies.

Altruism and Kin Selection

After all examples of the nonsexual use of homosexuality are considered, there remain, particularly among humans, many instances of homosexual relationships that must be considered simply loving and erotic. If there are fewer examples of these in animals, it is probably because ethologists have traditionally avoided imputing emotions to other organisms.[12] Purely loving homosexual relationships between individuals are harder to explain genetically, yet we think this can be done if the question of selective advantage is not posed so simply. The context of evolutionary argument (including the foregoing) has, until recently, been one in which only sexual behaviors leading directly to reproductive fitness of the *individual* were considered subject to natural selection. In fact, natural selection often operates more subtly than this.

As with many issues in evolutionary biology, we may profitably return to Darwin's work for insight. He recognized a class of hereditary behaviors which, benefiting other individuals, apparently reduce the behaving organism's own reproductive output. Phenomena such as the species of ants which allow themselves to be enslaved by other kinds of ants provoked Darwin's comment that it would be fatal to the theory of natural selection should any species be shown to do something solely for the benefit of another.[13]

If competition between species is vigorous, it is even more intense between members of the same species, which are directly competing for space and energy. Behavior that seems evolutionarily inexplicable is presented when individuals appear to be acting altruistically—that is, are performing actions which are of benefit to other members of the same species but seem to detract from the altruist's own reproductive fitness. Examples are numerous and in social species include situations in which one individual may utter an alarm call that alerts its fellows to the approach of a predator (while endangering the signaler), cooperative breeding or care of young as in many primates, food sharing in some species of insects and mammals, and suicidal defensive behavior by certain insect castes (for example, bees).[14] Once again, it would seem likely that genes predisposing toward such behavior ought to be speedily eliminated by natural selection.

Yet altruism is characteristic of many species; it must be the case that altruistic behavior is genetically determined and is therefore favored by natural selection. Of necessity, altruism is correlated with sociality, and understanding how altruism can evolve and be maintained depends on appreciating this fact, its connection with sexuality, and the importance of mating between genetically different individuals.

Every member of a sexually reproducing species carries two alleles representative of each gene, derived from each of its two parents, and there is a sense in which the members of a population may be said to share these genes in their various forms. During each bout of reproduction the members of the interbreeding group "pool" their alleles (in the form of gametes— eggs and sperm—each containing one allele for each gene), from which the next generation's individuals, with their allelic combinations, are constructed.

The hypothesis of kin selection introduced by Hamilton[15] accounts for altruism by showing that if the recipients of altruistic acts are close relatives of the altruist, the altruist is in effect favoring its own success because its kin will very likely share many of the altruist's alleles, drawn from the common and limited gene pool. Thus, if an altruistic act increases the recipient's likelihood of leaving or raising offspring, then the chances of multiplying the representation of "altruism genes" is also increased—because, in the terminology of kin selection, the "inclusive fitness" of the group has been raised. In acting altruistically, the individual is really serving its own interests (or those of its genes, which amounts to the same thing evolutionarily).

As Wilson points out, such analysis "has taken most of the good will out of altruism."[16] Altruism then becomes a misleading, if convenient, term for all such indirectly selfish acts. And so, within species as well as between them, nobody seems to be doing anything for nothing.

The mechanism of kin selection, developed in the context of comparative ethological studies of numerous species of social animals, is directly applicable to humans, who are and probably always were intensely social. Wilson has suggested[17] that homosexuality might be one expression of the genetic component of altruism in humans: In primitive societies, he argues, homosexuals may have formed a kind of "sterile caste" which, freed from the need to direct energy toward raising their own offspring, gave a special advantage to their kin by providing various forms of help which would not have been available in kin groups lacking homosexuals (since all members would be competing to raise their own offspring). Increase in the fitness of the homosexuals' near relatives would have favored the continued representation of helpful individuals whose helpfulness was correlated with possession of "homosexual genes." Of course, there is a tradeoff of advantages and disadvantages here, since too many individuals with such genes means no reproduction at all, but a balance between heterosexuals and homosexuals would have been struck by natural selection.

There is a string of "ifs" in Wilson's argument, but it is worth noting that in primitive societies homosexuality is often valued in the sense that shamanism is frequently associated with homosexual behavior.[18] Moreover, Wilson's idea is scientifically sound in that it predicts certain consequences of the hypothesis under changed environmental conditions. One is that with the trend away from close kin groups consequent on modern transportation, human beings will become even more mixed genetically as they tend to live more distantly from near relatives. Selection for altruistic acts then can no longer operate according to a model requiring close relatedness of altruist and recipient. Thus, the number of homosexuals should decrease as the conditions favoring selection for homosexuality become rarer. Any observation of a diminution in genetically based homosexuality will be difficult to disentangle from the presumably opposite effects of sexual liberation, since such cultural changes are so much more rapid than those alterations which occur on an evolutionary timescale.[19]

CONCLUSIONS: BEYOND BIOLOGY

Despite the difficulties of testing evolutionary explanations such as Hutchinson's or Wilson's, they appeal to us because they go a long way toward explaining the cross-cultural occurrence of homosexuality, the failure of classic psychoanalytic explanations, and the lack of clear-cut physical determinants of sexual preferences. In suggesting how homosexual behavior may have contributed to the real evolutionary success and unique adaptations of human beings, they make homosexuality a very *natural* thing.

If homosexuality is therefore part of the range of behavior that has molded *Homo sapiens,* then it is clear that homosexuality is not a disease, and certainly the general object should not be to "cure" it. At the same time, should Wilson's hypothesis be shown to have factual support, we would hope that its acceptance would not lead to a narrow expectation of how homosexuals should behave: that homosexuals are "justified" by public expression of "altruistic genes" would set prescribed behavior as the price for indulging sexual preferences formerly prohibited. There is always a real danger of this kind in the narrow genetic characterization of a minority group—a danger that the group will be tolerated only because of the social advantages that are incidentally associated with its inherent characteristics. Such a line of argument reveals a decision to use scientific conclusions to justify ethical choices, although biology and ethics may quite legitimately be decoupled. If, however, the biologically natural *is* used to support ethical decisions, it is important that the facts be correct. Thus, our aim in this essay has not been to justify homosexual behavior on biological grounds, but rather to show that the frequent condemnation of gay people because homosexual behavior is unnatural must be rejected because the premise of unnaturalness is false.

We do believe that an understanding of biology should inform the conduct of one's life, but we recognize that one has *every* right to construct a code of ethics independent of biological considerations. Biology need not be destiny—there should be room for the genuinely selfish homosexual as well as the apparently altruistic one. The fundamental and profound paradox of human biology is that it frees us to act sometimes unbiologically. With due respect for the environment and for each other, that ought to be possible: Part of the joy of being human often lies in transcending the biological constraints which have, nevertheless, shaped us.

NOTES

1. It is perhaps not well known that this famous phrase is from the last line of a poem by Lord Alfred Douglas, entitled "Two Loves," which appeared in the single published issue of the Oxford undergraduate magazine *The Chameleon,* December 1894. The poem is available in Reade (1970).

2. At least it must be admitted that a "unified-field theory of sexuality" should give equal consideration to the distinct problems posed by female and male homosexuality (see Michael Ruse's review of E. O. Wilson's *On Human Nature* in *The Advocate,* 1979, No. 266, p. 18, for a

consideration of lesbianism in the context of the kin-selectionist theory outlined later). We are aware that our article is slanted toward explaining the etiology of gayness in men, but the literature is overwhelmingly concerned with males: It is regrettably true that even consideration of what is often called "unmasculine" behavior in men is tainted with a sexist bias.

3. We are necessarily oversimplifying the psychoanalytic position because of space, and do not mean to imply that the profession is monolithic in its attitude toward homosexuality.

4. But see Bonnell (1976) for an amusing satire. Actually, Bonnell's article raises a serious point—the failure of most early studies of homosexuality to fulfill a basic scientific principle: namely, the need for a control in drawing conclusions from any experiment (presumably a comparison group of heterosexuals or at least nonpatient homosexuals). Until recently, this fundamental need was met in only a few studies (e.g., Weinberg & Williams, 1974).

5. Churchill (1967).

6. That the nature versus nurture controversy arises at all stems from the assumption that genes must always direct development, or at least set limits on its outcome. One of us [Kirsch, in H. Feldman and A. P. Eggleston (Eds.), *Current Issues in Human Sexuality,* publisher and date to be announced] has argued that the contradictory evidence for environmental and genetic determination may be resolved by imagining instead that some genes operate on the *products* of individual ontogeny. Since gender (the sense of one's sex) is clearly learned, and in humans at least need not be correlated with the definitive chromosomal differences between males and females, it seems possible that the alleles of the putative gene for sexual orientation dispose one to be attracted to the gender opposite to (or the same as) that one *imagines* oneself to be. "Sexual" preference is thus really gender preference. Whether this is a reasonable idea or not, that the same environment can produce different results with regard to human sexual preference makes it almost mandatory that there be a genetic influence. Although we are aware that some biologists believe that there is no convincing evidence of a genetic basis to homosexuality (e.g., Futuyma, 1980), their contention reveals a tendency to apply more stringent standards of evidence to genetic than to environmental explanations. Operationally, this means that any observed difference may be accounted for by an environmental variable, no matter how subtle or arcane, while the possible genetic factors are dismissed out of hand. The quickness to prefer nurtural explanations in the face of reasonable alternatives seems contrary to the traditional procedures of genetic investigation sketched in the text. We have tried to remain unbiased, but applying equally rigorous standards to the types of causal explanation inclines us to favor a genetic component. For a recent survey of the prenatal hormonal influences on the etiology of gender-related behavior, an essential part of any complete biological treatment, see Ehrhardt and Meyer-Bahlburg (1981). Their paper is part of an important special issue dealing with sexual dimorphism.

7. The classic references are F. J. Kallmann (1952a, 1952b). Most of the twins in Kallmann's studies were raised together, and this has been a primary criticism of his work, for the obvious reason that the same environmental influences obtained for both individuals. However, this was also true for fraternal twins included by Kallmann, yet the co-occurrence of homosexuality in these was about the same as in the population as a whole, a result overlooked by proponents of environmental explanations. One cannot have it both ways: If environment is the primary determinant of sexual orientation, there should be no such dramatic disparity between mono- and dizygotic twins. Moreover, other investigations since then gave similar results for siblings reared apart (e.g., Heston & Shields, 1968). In neither study is it the case for all identical pairs that both twins were homo- or heterosexual; one reason may be that identical or monozygotic twins are not always certainly distinguished from fraternal ones. Beyond that technical difficulty, practicing biologists are alive to the necessity of viewing experimental results in a statistical framework. Studies of the kind we are considering here usually do not involve large enough numbers to permit statistical tests, although major investigations (such as the Minnesota Twin Study) are under way and should provide more decisive results when published. We also wish to note our awareness of the criticism that even when twins are reared apart the separate environments themselves may be correlated—that is, may be sufficiently similar to evoke the same psychosexual profile in both siblings. Of course, this argument is another instance of structuring a "no-win" situation for the genetic hypothesis by environmentalists. Weinrich's comments (this volume) about the futility of so simply posing the nature/nurture dichotomy

should be read carefully (see also note 6). Money (1980) provides further trenchant comments on studies of the sexuality of twins.

8. The idea that homosexuality can provide a mechanism to limit population size may be traced back at least to Aristotle. In his comments on the Cretan constitution in *Politics* (1272^a 23-26), Aristotle states that "companionship" or "intercourse with males" was encouraged among Cretan men in order to reduce population pressure on the food supply. Dover (1978, p. 186) argues that the passage refers certainly to sexual intercourse, which is further supported by Aristotle's concluding remark that he intends to discuss later the morality of the Cretan custom (but does so nowhere in *Politics*).

9. Hutchinson (1959). This important paper, in which Hutchinson adopted the useful term *paraphilia* ("a tendency to substitute in . . . sexual behavior, goals which cannot lead to reproduction"), has been strangely neglected, especially in view of the fact that it occurs in the same volume as one of Hutchinson's most famous papers—indeed, we came across it while paying homage to Santa Rosalia.

10. The extreme phenomenon of exclusive homosexuality clearly raises a question of reproductive fitness. Less-than-exclusive homosexuality, however, may not obviously reduce fitness. Historical study (Boswell, 1980) demonstrates that homosexuality in association with heterosexuality may have been common and even valued in certain societies; consequently, homosexuality in these contexts may not have reduced individual fitness. In the oft-cited example of ancient Greece, men were ordinarily expected to marry and breed as well as take male lovers. As for the United States, the well-known studies of Kinsey and his associates (1948) showed that only four percent of American males were exclusive homosexuals for a period of three years prior to being interviewed. In 1948, this low percentage might well have been an effect of the strong societal pressures against homosexuality; in a climate of opinion that then, more than now, valued the nuclear family and rejected unreproductive behavior of any kind, it is hardly surprising that most homosexuals were at least sometimes functionally heterosexual. Today, given the excellent chances for survival of any offspring, and the related tendency to have small families, homosexuals would only need, on average, to replace themselves in order to avoid negative selection. Thus the combination of historical pressures to be at least operationally bisexual, and current standards of infant care, may undermine the basis of the apparently obvious conclusion that homosexuals must be selected against. Nevertheless, Hutchinson concluded that sufficient reduction of fertility probably occurred to raise the question of why the frequency of homosexuals has not decreased.

11. Trivers (1976) suggests that a subordinate male may benefit from submitting to such mountings because, like females, it is not chased away, and "an occasional buggery might be a small price to pay for the advantages of remaining within the large male's territory" (p. 266).

12. But the usefulness of ascribing emotions and consciousness to animals is argued positively by Griffin (1976). The young males of many mammalian species often live together in "bachelor herds" and frequently engage in homosexual behavior; sometimes the bonding between pairs of males is quite strong (see Churchill 1967, chapter 3 for a compilation of examples of homosexuality in animals). Dagg and Foster (1976) discuss the function of "necking" between male giraffes, and further examples of animal homosexuality will be found in Chapter 17 by Weinrich. One of the first catalogues of examples of homosexuality among nonhuman animals, covering an extraordinary range of phyla, was André Gide's platonic dialogue, *Corydon*, published in 1926. We would like to have quoted from this work, but all English-language copies we know of in the Yale libraries have disappeared—testimony, perhaps, to its enduring status as an underground *succès de scandale*.

13. See Darwin (1975).

14. The first resort of all persons interested in animal behavior and its ecological significance must be Wilson's *Sociobiology* (1975a); a thorough treatment of altruism with numerous examples will be found in Chapter 5 of that book.

15. As Wilson points out, Darwin introduced a concept of kin selection in *Origin of Species* to explain the evolution of sterile castes in insects; Hamilton developed the algebra in a series of papers between 1964 and 1972, of which the last is an excellent review. A superb popular account is that by Dawkins (1976).

16. Wilson (1975a, p. 120). Humanists will argue that there is a residuum of altruism not covered by the kin-selectionist's austere definition, including acts performed without any conscious thought or apparent possibility of reproductive gain. We remain uncommitted on this point, since Trivers (see note 19) is extremely clever in attempting to account for even these. In any event, we stress that our use of altruism is in the accepted, if unfortunate, biological style involving concepts of group selection.

17. See Wilson (1975a, chapter 27; 1975b, 1978). Trivers (1974) also accounts for homosexuality in the context of kin selection, but by suggesting that it is an outcome of the clash of interests between parents and their offspring. He shows that there are situations in which it will be to parents' advantage not to allow their young to reproduce; evolution may have selected for the ability of young to become homosexual in such circumstances. Although Trivers's explanation bears a formal resemblance to psychoanalytic ones accounting for homosexuality as a result of early experiences, the environmental situation which a psychiatrist would interpret as pathological is, in Trivers's interpretation, a necessary outcome of the maximization of inclusive fitness, under the strict control of natural selection.

18. See Churchill (1967). In his Ph.D. thesis, Weinrich (1976) presents for the first time a detailed analysis of kin selection for nonreproductive behavior, including homosexuality. His thesis also includes an extensive summary of the anthropological literature demonstrating an association between shamanism and homosexuality.

19. But Wilson fails to consider that there might be aspects of the new human ecology favoring homosexuality for other reasons. One such is suggested by the occurrence of "reciprocal altruism" in humans (Trivers, 1971). Trivers argues that unrelated humans (and members of other species), with their long memories and persistent relationships, perform altruistic acts with the expectation that sometime in the future those acts will be reciprocated, and in the knowledge that the possible consequences of *not* acting altruistically may be disagreeable. While reciprocal altruism must have evolved in a situation where the participants were closely related, such behavior need not be limited to kin groups, and has now become characteristic for our species (which is fast producing the most dispersed gene pool imaginable). At least during the evolutionary process of *becoming* reciprocally altruistic, and certainly in contrast to groups of the same species which do not so behave, everyone gains fitness if they cooperate. This being the case, we might predict not that homosexual behavior would disappear among humans, but rather (following the argument for heterozygous advantage presented above) that we might see the eventual emergence of a universal bisexuality. At least, more of us might consider the advantages of being, from time to time, a little gay.

· 17 ·

Is Homosexuality Biologically Natural?

James D. Weinrich

1. *For this cause God gave them up unto vile affections: for even their women did change their natural use into that which is against nature: And likewise also the men, leaving the natural use of the woman, burned in their lust one toward another; men with men working that which is unseemly* [Romans 1:26-27].

As the quotation above suggests, people have often discussed whether homosexuality is "natural" or "unnatural." What basis, if any, have these discussions had in the facts we know about the world derived from the study of biology? And what consequences does this knowledge have, if any, for the social debate on the acceptability of homosexuality?

Answering these questions in light of the most up-to-date biological information is the task of this chapter. Since many people (see quotations 2, 3, and 4, below) believe that what animals do is important in answering this question, I will begin by summarizing some of the most recent information gathered by modern biologists on homosexual behavior in animals. Many people (see quotations 5 through 10) have also paid much attention to biological evidence that does not depend on the behavior of animals, so I will next consider these definitions of "natural." I will not discuss theories of

Author's Note: *I thank Sarah Hrdy for permission to report her unpublished observations, and for much discussion and reference trading. I thank James J. Moore for permission to report his work also. For comments on earlier drafts I thank Clinton Anderson, John Boswell, Suzanne Chevalier-Skolnikoff, Ralph Hexter, John Kirsch, William Koelsch, Toby Marotta, Paul Robinson, Roger Swain, and Richard Wrangham. I thank Robert Trivers for pointing out the two recent gull references to me. The Society of Fellows, Harvard University, supported me for much of the time I was developing these ideas.*

naturalness in which biology does not play an explicit role. Boswell (1980, especially chap. 11) has written the definitive discussion on this topic, and concluded that in the religious discussions of homosexuality's naturalness, Aquinas and other medieval theologians responded "more to the pressures of popular antipathy than to the weight of the Christian tradition" (1980, p. 329).

But knowing what the facts are does not necessarily tell society what should be done. This point is so often missed that I will pay special attention to it. People often talk as if the connection between a scientific finding and its social consequence is obvious. In fact, the correct consequence can be deduced only by moving up to a higher level of discussion: what philosophers of science call the metascientific level of talking about biology itself, rather than the scientific level of talking about animals and their behavior. How this relates to homosexuality's naturalness is the final topic I will consider.

HOMOSEXUAL BEHAVIOR IN ANIMALS

2. *PLAYBOY: How do you explain homosexuality to a nine-year-old?*

BRYANT: . . . I explained in simple terms to the little ones that some men try to do with other men what men and women do to produce babies; and that homosexuality is a perversion of a very natural thing that God said was good, and that it is a sin and very unnatural. I explained to the children that even barnyard animals don't do what homosexuals do.

PLAYBOY: That's simply untrue. There is a lot of evidence proving not only that barnyard animals do engage in homosexuality but that . . . many primitive cultures [do too]. . . .

BRYANT: Well, I've never heard of it. The point is that God says it's an abomination of nature and it's wrong.

PLAYBOY: That's a different point—we're saying that among various species, human and animal, it is a common occurrence.

BRYANT: That still doesn't make it right [Kelley, 1978, p. 82].

In quotation 2, Anita Bryant asserts that barnyard animals don't perform homosexual acts. But consult the footnotes in Chapter 11 of Kinsey et al. (1953) and you will discover that homosexual behavior in the barnyard has been observed in bulls, cows, stallions, donkeys, cats, rams, goats, and pigs, and has been observed outside the barnyard in antelope, elephants, hyenas, monkeys, apes, rabbits, lions, porcupines, hamsters, mice, and porpoises.

The problem with most observations made by 1953 is that they came from watching animals living in captivity—zoos or cages. Even though a behavior seen in captivity is almost always also seen in the wild, it is often seen at an atypical frequency or in an atypical context. So it is very difficult to use these observations to reach conclusions about a behavior's evolution or function. This distinction can be crucial in certain definitions of "natural" (see my discussion below under "Other Dismissals").

To answer these objections, I recently reviewed instances of homosexual behavior in the animal kingdom, considering only observations that could clearly be related to free-ranging populations living with little human interference (Weinrich, 1980). In this chapter, I will summarize only those cases most relevant to human homosexuality.

HOMOSEXUAL BEHAVIOR IN ANIMALS: A SUMMARY

By the term "homosexual behavior," I mean any behavior involving the mechanisms of sexual arousal (e.g., erection in males, or vaginal lubrication in females) between two members of the same sex. With this definition, animals can exhibit their own species' version of homosexuality, just as they exhibit a version of heterosexuality—though either may be quite unlike *human* sexuality. (For more details on the propriety of this definition, see Weinrich, 1980.)

Homosexuality as a Component of Bisexuality—*Anolis* Lizards

In a species of lizard *(Anolis garmani;* see Trivers, 1976), females maintain small territories in trees, several females per tree. Mature males maintain large territories (one to two trees), enclosing those of several females. Each male mates with females within his own territory. But sometimes there lives within a male's territory another male—one who is sexually mature but not yet grown large enough to be clearly distinguishable from females. (Males grow larger than females in this species.) Until such a male grows too large to look female-sized, he can copulate with females nearby. However, such a small male also has to act like a female in copulation when the larger male comes around. Indeed, two such homosexual copulations between males in a wild population were observed by Trivers (1976, p. 266).

Although this pattern is not precisely copied in human homosexuality, Paul Larson (personal communication) has pointed out to me that there is a similarity with some cases in humans of homosexual behavior between an adolescent male and a higher-status adult man who, in exchange for sex and affection, provides the youth with a head start in life (see, e.g., Boswell, 1980, chaps. 1 and 2, for the extent to which this pattern was idealized by the ancient Greeks and Romans).

Homosexuality as an Expression of Dominance—Mountain Sheep

In mountain sheep (*Ovis dalli stonei;* see Geist, 1971), we find homosexual behavior performed as an expression of the dominance (superior strength, access to food or mates, etc.) of one animal over another. Male-male battles end with the losing ram being treated sexually as a female by the winning ram, who mounts the loser with an erection. Intromission is suspected (Geist, personal communication), but is hard to document because of the coyness of other authors and because these observations were made at a distance. Another author (Denniston, 1980, p. 34) stated that feral male goats have been observed ejaculating in homosexual encounters.

This pattern, too, is not a precise copy of human homosexuality, but again it is similar to one aspect of it. In men's prisons, stronger or more dominant men often treat weaker or less dominant men as women, by taking the "insertor" role in anal intercourse with them. Both kinds of men usually perform in the typical heterosexual male role with women once they are released.

Homosexual Pair Bonds in Birds

The vast majority of mammal species are not at all monogamous. However, a few mammals—and over 90 percent of bird species—are at least as monogamous as are humans.

Since heterosexual pair bonds are most common in birds, it is in that group of animals that we might expect to find most easily examples of homosexual pair bonds, even though birds are phylogenetically more distantly related to us than are mammals. Indeed, homosexual pair bonds are frequently reported for certain shore birds in captivity (Meyer-Holzapfel, 1968, p. 494). Reports from the wild are just beginning to be published, in spite of quotation 3.

> 3. *Homosexual behavior has never been the main choice, or even a customary minor part of the sexual pattern, of any mammal living in the free state* [Hunt, 1974, p. 299].

In western gulls (*Larus occidentalis;* see Hunt & Hunt, 1977), most pairs are heterosexual: one male and one female. But in the population studied, 8 to 14 percent of the mated pairs cooperating in incubating the eggs laid in a given nest were female-female. These pairs engaged in most of the courtship and territorial behaviors shown by male-female pairs, and a few performed mounting and attempted copulation. There are now reports from two other species that show similar patterns in wild populations (ring-billed gulls and California gulls; see Ryder & Somppi, 1979; Conover, Miller, & Hunt, 1979).

These examples, too, are not precisely like human homosexuality. However, they are closer than any others of which I am aware to human preferential homosexuality, in which a member of one's own sex is preferred to members of the opposite sex. In the best-studied case (Hunt & Hunt, 1977), seven of eight female-female pairs stayed together over more than one breeding season.

Homosexuality as Affection or Practice—Primates

Field biologists studying the behavior of wild primates have occasionally reported observing homosexual interactions in the wild, but virtually none of them has pursued or published these findings. Often, the homosexual behavior observed has been dismissed as mere dominance assertion:

> 4. *The occasional mounting of male animals by other males—apes in particular—is not true homosexuality but is in part playful and learning behavior in the immature, and in part a way of avoiding violent fighting between two males. The weaker one signifies submissiveness by "presenting" his rear, the stronger signifies dominance by mounting and making a few routine penile thrusts without intromission or ejaculation* [Hunt, 1974, p. 299].

Sometimes such a dismissal is legitimate, for primates (like many mammals) often do exhibit routine dominance mounts. But other kinds of homosexual mounts also take place. Dr. Sarah Hrdy has observed both male and female homosexual behavior in wild langurs *(Presbytis entellus)*, a kind of monkey. She observed a few male-male mounts when an all-male group (composed of males too low in dominance rank to attract females) encountered a "harem group" of females (who normally live with a single, dominant male) whose male was looking for food elsewhere. Hrdy (personal communication) said that this male-male mounting often involved high levels of excitement, frequent embraces, and other reciprocal acts unrelated to mere perfunctory dominance interactions. She tentatively interpreted it as a means for members of an all-male group to enlist cooperation for an attempt to "steal" copulations from the harem male. It is as if the males were trying to show off to the females what good copulators they were. James J. Moore (personal communcation) has confirmed these observations, seeing well over 40 male-male interactions in three months.

Again, notice that this behavior is not precisely like human homosexuality but bears a strong resemblance to certain forms of human homosexual behavior. These langurs seem to be practicing for later heterosexuality, although they are themselves sexually mature. One similar phenomenon in humans is adolescent homosexual experimentation.

Homosexual behavior between primate females has also been observed, and (in the reports I have been able to gather) assumes a remarkably consistent form. Typically, one female mounts another in a way that stimulates her own and/or her partner's genitals. Sexual excitation ensues, and sometimes orgasm is reached. (See Goldfoot, Westerborg-van Loon, Groeneveld, & Slob, 1980. This report perforce came from a captive colony in which behavioral correlates of orgasm were established which have also been observed in wild females.) Usually, a female's estrous state correlates with her role in the activity. And less clearly sexual interactions (like "hide-and-seek" games) often invite or follow sex. (These generalizations were made from the following sources: langurs, Hrdy, 1975, p. 237 and personal communication; rhesus monkeys, Akers & Conaway, 1979; stumptail macaques, Chevalier-Skolnikoff, 1974, 1976; and Goldfoot et al., 1980.)

Again, note that these homosexual patterns do not duplicate human homosexuality but do resemble certain aspects of human homosexual behavior. Most or all of the females engaging in homosexual relationships also engage in heterosexual ones—although it would be hard to demonstrate which they prefer. Individual females certainly do have preferences, and pursue them, among both males and females. A situational bisexuality is one human parallel, as are certain affection-based forms of homosexuality.

WHAT DOES THIS EVIDENCE MEAN?

From the above discussion, it should be clear that animal homosexuality covers an enormous range of behaviors, just as does human homosexuality. There is scarcely any aspect of human homosexuality that does not have at least a moderately close parallel in some animal species (for more detail, see Weinrich, 1980). But what consequences does this evidence have for humans, as we address the question of what society should do about homosexual behavior?

First, certain statements about homosexuality in animals have to be changed. For example, views expressed in quotations 2, 3, and 4 are no longer tenable.

But suprisingly, this does not necessarily mean that society will be forced to change its conclusions. This is clear from examining Figure 17.1 together with the logic, or lack thereof, in quotation 2. Bryant begins by asserting that homosexuality is unnatural because it does not occur in animals (upper left box), and concludes that homosexuality should be discouraged in humans (upper right box). The logic used (arrow #1) seems unassailable: For if homosexuality is unnatural, wouldn't it make sense to discourage it in humans?

Not necessarily. After being challenged, Bryant essentially changes her argument over to arrow #3, concluding that even if homosexuality does occur in animals, "that still doesn't make it right."

This same game can be played on the other side, too, of course: Since

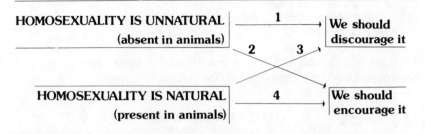

FIGURE 17.1 The Four Possible Relationships Between Facts of Nature and Attitudes Toward Homosexuality American society adopts argument #1: that homosexuality is unnatural, and that it should thus be discouraged. A quotation attributed to Lucian adopts argument #2: that homosexuality's very unnaturalness means it is a higher human trait and should be encouraged. Had the facts been considered different (lower left box), one would still be able to arrive at whichever conclusion one wished (arguments #3 and #4); see text. Most discussions implicitly assume that naturalness is directly related to presence in nonhuman animals (parentheses); for the consequences of assuming this is not the case, see text. Diagram © 1977 by James D. Weinrich.

every variation of human homosexuality takes place in some animal species, then homosexuality must be natural in humans—and should be allowed or encouraged. Once again, the logic presented (arrow #4) sounds fine until the alternative possible fact and argument (arrow #2) is considered. Just this was done in a fictional debate from ancient Greece as to whether gay love or straight love is better (see pseudo-Lucian, in Macleod, 1967, pp. 205-206). In this debate, the advocate for the homosexual side argued that homosexuality does not exist in animals and heterosexuality does—and hence that nonprocreative homosexuality is superior to base, procreative, heterosexual lust. Clearly, even arrow #2 has had its adherents.

In fact, the whole enterprise—as symbolized in Figure 17.1—is bogus. When one rises above the *scientific* level of the truth or falsity of any one "fact," or the appropriateness of any one arrow, one attains the *metascientific* level and asks: Are any of these arguments valid? I take a jaded view and answer in the negative. When animals do something that we like, we call it natural. When they do something that we don't like, we call it animalistic. What we like or don't like has been decided by a process outside the boundaries of Figure 17.1.

Kinsey and his co-workers reached a similar conclusion over 30 years ago:

Whether such biologic inheritance is an adequate basis for considering any activity right or wrong, socially desirable, or undesirable, is an issue which we do not raise, and one which we have never raised. We do contend, however, that sexual acts which are demonstrably part of the phylogenetic heritage of any species cannot be classified as acts contrary to nature, biologically unnatural, abnormal, or perverse [Kinsey et al., 1949, p. 24].

It is a pity—and, I suspect, not an accident—that such sound advice has been overlooked by so many people for so long.

OTHER DISMISSALS

I have now established the basis for my jaded view of arguments reasoning from animals to human acceptance or disapproval. Thus, I feel justified in extending this jadedness to the other anti-homosexual arguments listed below—and to their pro-homosexual, but equally unthinking, counterparts.

5. *Biologically, moreover, homosexuality is abnormal in the sense that no children can be born of it* [Hunt, 1974, p. 299].

Consider quotation 5. A diagram similar to figure 17.1 is easy to construct here, too. Equating normality or naturalness with reproductiveness is, to put it charitably, weak (see Chapter 16 by Kirsch & Rodman)—that is a "fact" from the left side of the diagram. Even assuming that naturalness is equivalent to reproductiveness, this does not mean that heterosexuality is much better—for there are many arrows leading to the right side of the diagram. For what of celibate priests and nuns? Or contraception? Wouldn't all these be condemned by this criterion? Few systems of belief of which I am aware oppose both of these nonreproductive choices.

6. *It is true, of course, that even contraception is abnormal in this sense, but the heterosexual couple using contraception has it within their power to be fertile or not, as they choose;* . . . [Hunt, 1974, p. 299].

The author of quotation 5 answered the point about contraception in his immediately following sentence, quotation 6. This cites *choice* as the essential component of naturalness. But consider heterosexual cases where choice is absent: coitus after sterilization, coitus by postmenopausal women, and attempts at coitus by diabetically permanently impotent men. Or a case where choice is present but homosexuality is not involved: masturbation by heterosexuals after marriage. To be consistent, quotation 6 would have to judge all these phenomena unnatural, too.

Moreover, the modern technology of artificial insemination makes another argument possible—one that makes homosexual acts interpretable in a framework of choosing to forego reproduction. Male homosexuals' ejaculating *could* be viewed as their making the choice not to father babies by artificial insemination. Lesbians' making love without the presence of a live penis *could* be viewed as making the choice not to have donor sperm involved this time. If this argument strikes readers as being forced, it is only because it has rarely appeared; think back to the argument in the previous section by pseudo-Lucian.

> 7. . . . *and even when they choose not to, they are still employing the neural, hormonal and muscular responses of sexuality in the fashion which evolution, with the goal of reproduction, cunningly designed to provide maximum reward* [Hunt, 1974, p. 299].

My less forced rebuttal, above, was also anticipated by the author of quotation 6, in quotation 7. Here, *teleology* enters the fray. Teleology is the doctrine that things are directed toward an end or shaped by a purpose. In this quotation, "evolution" by natural selection is stated to have "the goal of reproduction," and has "designed" sexual processes to feel the best when used for reproductive ends. Teleology also lies behind quotation 8 (written by an evolutionary biologist, alas), its presence signaled by the words "absurd" and "ridiculous," which require some system to make sense of or give a goal to heterosexual acts.

> 8. *Homosexuality is biologically absurd and anatomically ridiculous* [Swanson, 1974, p. 108].

The ultimately sensible system referred to implicitly or explicitly in these two quotations is evolutionary biology. Many evolutionary biologists believe it is illegitimate to inject teleological arguments into biology; for these biologists, quotations 7 and 8 are inadmissible on their face. Other evolutionary biologists—including myself—admit teleological arguments, and these biologists have to face up to their use in these quotations.

We do so by noting that if heterosexuality is natural because it has an evolutionary purpose or function, then homosexuality must also be natural if it has an evolutionary purpose or function. As shown by Kirsch and Rodman in Chapter 16 (and by Weinrich, 1977, Pt. 2, and Wilson, 1978, chap. 6), biologists do consider such purposes to be tenable. The anatomically *un*ridiculous fit of penis in vagina suggests that coitus is one natural use of the sex organs. But this does not preclude other uses, any more than using one's tongue for eating makes its use in speech or sex unnatural.

> 9. *There is also recent evidence that homosexuality may be related to certain biological pathologies: Research on animals and human beings . . . has shown that virilizing hormonal imbalances in the mother during gestation lay down important male patterns of reactivity in the developing neural*

structure of a female fetus, who later on, in childhood and beyond, exhibits classically male patterns of play and aggressiveness. Comparable congenital "errors," it is thought, may underlie some or much of the classically female behavior of some male homosexuals [Hunt, 1974, pp. 299-300].

The evidence referred to in quotation 9 is reviewed in this section in the chapter by Gartrell. Most of it (especially the blood-hormone-level studies excised from my version of the quotation) has been disproven. As Gartrell shows, the rest (relating to neural patterns laid down in the fetus) is controversial. Even if it turns out to be true, one still must fit the facts into scheme like that shown in Figure 17.1. On what grounds are the prenatal hormones judged to be "imbalances" and "errors"? It's not much help to define the precursors to be imbalanced and in error just because the results produce (in theory) homosexuality; that would be circular. Once again, a teleological rationale (such as that lying behind quotations 7 or 8) must be provided, from outside a similar scheme.

10. *Heterosexual object choice is determined from birth due to cultural and environmental indoctrination. It is supported by universal human concepts of mating and the family unit with the complementariness and contrast between the two sexes* [Socarides, 1970, p. 1201].

There are several variations of the argument in quotation 10, all of them assuming in common that homosexuality *must* be unnatural because there is no conceivable socialization mechanism by which it could occur—only a pathological version could have produced it. This argument falls on the border between biology and psychology, because it invokes psychological theories as to the development of sexual orientation, but conceals a biological assumption about how the human central nervous system works.

This assumption can be made explicit by considering the history of a concept called masturbatory insanity. (This argument, I believe, was first made by Kinsey et al., 1949, pp. 31-32.) For a long time in the West, it was widely believed that masturbation could drive people insane. Doctors wrote learned treatises preaching the evils of "self-abuse" and "self-pollution." Parents were sold spiked devices designed to be worn by their sons which physically prevented any erections, even at night. Some doctors advocated clitoridectomies for their female patients. (Hare, 1962, and Bullough, 1975, summarize this era well.) Yet although the frequency of masturbation might have changed, people continued to have sexual feelings that they sometimes relieved by masturbating. Masturbation was, to some extent, resistant to socialization pressures against its expression.

This is not far from the current status of homosexuality. Both homosexuality and masturbation were (are) strongly condemned, not mentioned in polite company, considered grounds for severe medical treatment, and occasionally reinforced in adolescent peer groups—but otherwise reinforced only by the pleasure they can bring. In order to conclude that these behaviors are "unnatural" on their face, we have to make some assumptions about how the central system learns. That is, we must prove that a person acted upon by these socializing agents in these ways turns out *not* to exhibit these behaviors (homosexuality or masturbation). Only then can the existence of the behavior be considered, in and of itself, evidence of pathology.

But such a theory of human learning is far from proven. Psychological theories of learning that assert that socialization is all there is to learning do exist, but they are at least premature, and will probably turn out to be quite wrong. Recent psychological theories conclude that learning patterns differ from species to species, and cannot be understood without references to evolution and biological predispositions in learning (Seligman, 1970, and Lockard, 1971, provide reviews).

What is the consequence of this trend for psychological theories similar to that embodied in quotation 10? Unless one rejects completely any influence of biology on the learning of sexual behaviors, one cannot sustain the notion that homosexuality today (and masturbation a hundred years ago) is (was) on its face a symptom of psychological pathology. Indeed, should any one of the several biologically based theories of homosexuality prove true for even a small percentage of homosexuals, then the point of view espoused in this quotation would collapse.

CONSEQUENCES

There is a long and sordid history of statements of human uniqueness. Over the years, I have read that humans are the only creatures that laugh, that kill other members of their own species, that kill without need for food, that have continuous female sexual receptivity, that lie, that exhibit female orgasm, or that kill their own young. Every one of these never-never-land statements is now known to be false. To this list must now be added the statement that humans are the only species that exhibit "true" homosexuality. Does anyone ever state that we alone exhibit true heterosexuality?

Yet I take a skeptical view of efforts to make some kind of simple connection between facts about nature and conclusions about social policy. My rebuttals of the quotations in this chapter should be taken merely as rebuttals, and not as advocacy of the opposite position: that homosexuality is "natural" and should be permitted.

Human homosexuality is *as biologically natural as is human heterosexuality.* That is a very carefully worded statement. Its only social consequence is that arguments based on nature cannot be used to distinguish between homosexuality and heterosexuality. Like left- and right-handedness, the two are expressions of a single human nature that can be expressed differently in different individuals.

The alert reader will have noticed that of the 10 quotations listed in this chapter, I have discussed only 9 in detail. Quotation 1, from the King James translation of the Bible, has until now escaped my scrutiny. Note that this quotation doesn't really present an argument, but merely the opinion that homosexual acts are "against nature," "vile," and "unseemly." Frankly, I believe that the only tenable arguments against homosexuality are overtly opinionated, like this one. They are, of course, only tenable for those who hold them. And even this passage has been rebutted by Boswell (1980, p. 109), who interpreted it as an invocation against heterosexuals "turning against" *their* "natural use" by performing homosexual acts. Many writers have suggested that deep and uncomprehended opinion is the ultimate source of anti-homosexual arguments—and, in particular, that arguments relying on biological unnaturalness stem proximately from religious precepts. Although such ideas seem plausible to me, evaluating them is far beyond the scope of this chapter. I leave their proof or disproof to the future.

CONCLUSIONS

1. Essentially every type of human homosexual behavior also occurs in some species of animal, to a close approximation.

2. Essentially every biologically based argument that homosexuality is unnatural fails, either when confronted by the evidence of conclusion 1, when compared with "control" statements about heterosexuality, or when account is taken of new theories in evolutionary biology.

3. Human homosexuality is thus as biologically natural as is human heterosexuality.

4. Even if biology were to present conclusive evidence that homosexuality is natural or unnatural, the question of what society should do as a result is independent of this information (see Figure 17.1).

5. Opinion rooted in causes outside biology probably accounts for attempts to use biology in arguments against homosexuality.

· 18 ·

Summary and Conclusions

James D. Weinrich

In these three chapters, four authors have given us the evidence from biology. How can we summarize their disparate viewpoints and reach some conclusions about what society should do about homosexuality as a social issue?

Some conclusions are clear. Gartrell showed that homosexual men and women apparently do not suffer from hormone abnormalities any more than do heterosexuals. If there were any simple connection between the adult level of hormones and the adult sexual orientation, we really should have found it by now. However, as she notes, there is one suggestive finding that might connect *prenatal* hormone levels with adult sexual orientation in at least some individuals. This finding, so far the product of only one research group (albeit a highly respected one), deserves further study.

In a similar vein, Kirsch and Rodman argue that the evolution of homosexual behavior by natural selection deserves further study. Their prognosis is brighter than Gartrell's is for the prenatal hormone theory, however. They argue that there has been, despite scant evidence on both sides, a higher propensity to accept explanations stressing environment than those stressing genes in explaining any given behavior. They conclude that the plausibility of adaptively based genetic models of homosexuality casts doubt on the widely held view that homosexuality is unnatural.

In these respects, their views nearly coincide with the ones I express in my chapter. I conclude that homosexuality is in every sense as biologically natural as is heterosexuality; yet I caution (as they do) that moving from this statement to a social conclusion is not a simple matter.

Practitioners of the so-called hard sciences like biology have been slower than social scientists in dealing with the social consequences of their findings. Like all good scientists, they value truth above all else, and are highly suspicious and hurt when accused of bias, especially by advocacy groups with axes to grind. There are groups, of every conceivable persuasion, which accept uncritically any scientific finding that can be plugged into their social influence apparatus; but they subject all other findings to the most meticulous, withering scrutiny.

But axes sometimes really do need sharpening, especially when we are confronted with scientists who don't realize how much their research is influenced by nonscientific outside forces. Money must be raised, tenure committees must be satisfied, and (often) legislators must be kept voting the right way. Pure truth is so much easier to pursue when the pursuers avoid applying their findings to the real world.

Here is a proposal for settling the legitimate worries each side has about the other. Each side should pay closer attention to the lack-of-intellectual-controls phenomenon summarized in Figure 17.1. Just as each scientific experimental group should have a control group to make sure the findings are not spurious, so should each scientific or social argument have a control to make sure it is not fallacious.

So when scientists think of the hypothesis that male homosexuality might be linked to low testosterone levels, they should also think about why they did not ask if it could be linked to high testosterone levels. If they are really interested in doing pure science, then they must find some way to look at both possible sides, rather than just the socially less controversial one.

Similarly, when academics argue that there is something unnatural about homosexuality, they should also think about whether there is something unnatural about heterosexuality, and whether there are aspects of homosexuality that are *more* natural than heterosexuality. If this second control example sounds absurd, recall the following quotation:

> What will strike some readers as a partisan point of view is chiefly the absence of the negative attitudes on this subject ubiquitous in the modern West; after a long, loud noise, a sudden silence may seem deafening [Boswell, 1980, p. xvi].

Thus jolted, recall (for example) that homosexual individuals have no need for the modern armamentarium of contraceptive technology, and can perform sex acts in ways that contracepting heterosexuals would otherwise find interfering with what evolution cunningly designed to provide maximum reward.

Conversely, on the advocates' side, one must apply the same standards to the studies with results one likes as to the studies with results which one does not like. If one criticizes a study for failing to have a double-blind controlled trial, one must also be willing to evaluate other studies' methodologies without first noting their results. One must also avoid the trap of Figure 17.1 and think self-critically of what arguments one would have used had the facts been different than one currently presumes them to be. Advocate groups should also add scientists or philosophers to their staffs to help sketch out long-range strategies, immune from the momentary status of the battle between nature and nurture (say), or biology and psychology. Research money waxes and wanes, scientists change their minds, academic fashions come and go. But Figure 17.1s endure, and advocates should place their arguments into such a framework to understand for themselves where they are weak.

In short, advocates must realize that they are doing not science but metascience—they are thinking about science, not proving or disproving facts. Scientists must realize that science is shaped by metascientific forces but should be judged as science independent of those forces. Lack of bias is approximated, not attained. But in order to approximate it, one must look at the broader metascientific picture.

I close this section by beginning to apply this strategy to the nature-nurture debate. In the introduction, I argued that this debate is dead. I took a metascientific overview and said (as Kirsch and Rodman put it) that nature-or-nurture is not the "right question" to ask. I also suggested that the distaste with which many people view modern biological models of homosexuality arises from the justified distaste with earlier misuses, such as social Darwinism or Nazism.

I must now ask the people who react with such distaste to think out the appropriate control arguments. Social Darwinism and Nazism are genuine examples of misuses of biology; what about good results from biology, and bad results from other fields that oppose themselves to biology?

Answers come quickly to mind. Biological models of homosexuality in general, and sociobiological ones in particular, leave a decidedly pro-homosexual taste in one's mouth (Ruse, 1979). Only environmentalistic arguments, not biological ones, are currently used by groups opposing gay rights. And right now, people in psychotherapists' offices and in prisons are having their wits shocked out of them or their dinners vomited out of them by behavior-modification therapies based entirely on simplistic, environmentalistic, stimulus/response theories.

There is no longer any excuse for overlooking biologically inspired models in future research about homosexuality. This is not to imply that these models must prove true—just that they may very well be necessary to arrive at a complete picture. It is time to move from metascience back down to science, and go get some more facts.

· IV ·

Life Adaptations

Edited by
Mary E. Hotvedt

· 19 ·

Introduction

Mary E. Hotvedt

There are commonly held assumptions about the lifestyles of gay men and lesbians, broadly drawn caricatures that are deep within the social and sexual mythology of our culture. We learned them from adults and other children as we grew into our own sexual identities. The images have been reinforced by jokes, books, films, and plays which depict homosexuals to be gender-confused, lonely, pathetic, or silly individuals incapable of having meaningful relationships.

The myths serve as propaganda for anti-gay movements in which heterosexuals actively seek to eliminate all homosexual expression in our society. Most often these myths are accepted by heterosexuals who have had little conscious interaction with homosexuals. When even well-intentioned heterosexuals hold these attitudes, they inadvertantly make life more restrictive for homosexuals by failing to respond to needs for personal support, useful social services, and political and legal change. They can also pass on the same mythology to their own children. This perpetuates confusion not only for future heterosexuals but for homosexuals as well, for these ideas sometimes are held by homosexuals who are aware of their sexual and emotional needs but are not yet involved in some identifiable part of a gay community. The stereotypes then can cause personal conflict for an individual who cannot imagine him/herself conforming comfortably to such patterns and accepting the general social approbation for them.

Let's delineate four commonly held ideas about homosexuals' lifestyles. I invite you, the reader, to search your memory for when you last heard some variation, even subtle, on the following themes:

(1) "You can always tell a fag." The assumption implies there are always styles of dress, speech, and mannerisms that distinguish all homosexuals

from all heterosexuals. Choices of certain occupations, for example, are thought to be indicators of homosexuality while others are considered to be realms of exclusive heterosexuality.

(2) "Homosexuals have unhappy personal lives because they cannot develop permanent relationships." The image is one of all the homosexuals in the United States going to gay bars each night in lonely quests for a passing fling or some impersonal sexual contact. A correlate of this is that aging is especially traumatic to homosexuals because the prevailing mode of casual sex emphasizes youth and attractiveness. Lesbians are generally thought to fare somewhat better than gay men in finding permanent relationships and masking them in some socially accepted way—i.e., "roommates"—but even these situations will be seen for what they really are because of Myth #3.

(3) "In homosexual relationships, somebody is always 'male' and the other is 'female.'" Several popular movies and plays have supported the notion that homosexual pairing is associated with sex-role patterns even more rigid than those in heterosexual relationships. Associated with this idea is another that views "feminine" men and "masculine" women as automatically homosexual and therefore in search of a same-sex partner who will play the other role.

(4) "Homosexuals very seldom want or have families—which is just as well because they'd probably be poor parental models." Their children will have confused sex roles, will feel ostracized by their peers, and may themselves become homosexuals. Their parents may sexually abuse them or simply neglect them in their pursuit of sexual satisfaction.

Be honest. Whether you accepted these ideas or not, have you ever heard them and wondered if, at least in part, they were true? This section is an opportunity for you to test these issues in some detail. The authors of the chapters that follow report empirical data from several studies on the structure and content of gay lifestyles and relationships. We invite your curiosity so that you can alertly assess what is presented.

The authors will be giving, whenever possible, measured comparisons between homosexuals' and heterosexuals' varied lifestyles and relationship values. Many recent studies on sexual orientation have used matched groups to assess differences and similarities between samples. Patterns will emerge, but also a great diversity.

Recent information will be given about the formation, functioning, and dissolution of relationships between gay men and between lesbians. Ways people meet, what each is looking for in another person, strengths and problems of relationships, sexual compatibility and conflicts will be discussed. Aging and age groups will also be considered.

Much data will be given on the degrees of sex-stereotyped role-playing versus egalitarianism in homosexual relationships. The influences of feminism and the gay rights movement on sex roles will be presented.

We will consider the homosexual parent. Two chapters will cover issues of parenting, mothers' support networks, children's and mothers' sex roles, and children's development.

It is hoped that readers will be given a strong sense of the way social institutions affect gay men and women's personal lives as they function as lovers, family members, parents, and workers. Authors will suggest social and legal changes that would decrease discrimination against homosexuals.

As in earlier sections, the problem of sampling technique should be pointed out to the reader. Random samples of committed gay male couples and lesbian mothers are impossible to find. Several of the recent studies on which the authors report attempt to address these problems by the use of matched samples, more ingenious techniques for soliciting subjects (than simply going to a gay bar with a questionnaire), and better research instruments to investigate sex roles, relationship values, love, sex, and parenting. The result is a diversified and sophisticated view of gay relationships, having both strengths and problems. All the authors will point out areas where additional research would be helpful, but the work they have done should help move us from mythology to reality.

• 20 •

Gay Male Relationships

Paul C. Larson

The purpose of this chapter is to review the literature on gay male relationships and present an integrated summary of the current research. To facilitate this task a temporal perspective will be used, tracing the natural course of relationships from their inception through the various possible end points. Then a number of issues underlying gay male relationships, regardless of their stage of development, will be discussed. Finally, the implications for social policy will be explored.

TIME AND RELATIONSHIPS

Contact Points

The necessary conditions for any gay male relationship are the meeting of two men and their mutual identification of each other as homosexual. Given the stigmatized nature of homosexuality, this is frequently a difficult task. Since most states still have laws against adult homosexual behavior, there is an initial legal barrier to gay male relationships that may have a chilling effect on their continuance and growth. The degree to which legal or police involvement may be a hindrance is related to whether the setting is public, semiprivate, or private, whether there are few or many people involved, and the time of day when the most activity occurs.

Bars (Weinberg & Williams, 1974), bath houses (Weinberg & Williams, 1975), public restrooms (or "tearooms" as they are known in gay argot—Humphreys, 1970), gay organizations (Hooker, 1957, 1967; Saghir &

219

Robins, 1973), private parties, and friendship networks (Warren, 1974), as well as public recreational locations such as parks, beaches, and movie theaters (Rechy, 1962, 1967, 1977), are some of the more common locales where meetings between gay men can occur (and where researchers recruit subjects). Another source of partners is advertisement in gay-oriented magazines and newspapers (Lee, 1973, 1976; Laner & Kamel, 1977; Laner, 1978). This list, of course, is not exhaustive—though it may be taken as representative of the range of sites used.

The term "cruising" is used by gay men to describe the purposive search for potential sexual partners and friends. It also refers to the particular rituals used for identification of people as prospective partners. Recently the use of variously colored bandana handkerchiefs to identify a person as gay and to specify the type of sexual activity preferred has become common. Key rings on one or the other hip, various hair styles, fads in dress, and other physical symbols have been used to identify other men as possibly gay and therefor approachable. These are not new practices. Bullough (1976) reported that red neckties were a sign of recognition used by homosexual males in nineteenth-century Chicago. What appears new is the variety of physical cues used to represent the subcultural diversity among gay men.

Saghir and Robins (1973) noted a relationship between age and the frequency of cruising at a given locale. Among younger males, school and private parties were the dominant settings. As age increased, a variety of public locales (parks, bars, and restrooms) supplemented the other forms of contact. Weinberg and Williams (1974) confirmed Saghir and Robins's conclusions that male homosexuals cruise more frequently than lesbians. They found that bars, baths, and private parties were the most frequent locales and that parks, beaches, movie theaters, and tearooms were less often used. Since that study focused on a large city with a gay ghetto (Levine, 1977), it was not surprising that cruising on the streets was a high frequency event—though it would be expected to be less so in smaller communities. Bell and Weinberg (1978) found that age was related to frequency of cruising in white males; younger males cruised more often than older males. Among blacks, occupational status was related to the frequency of cruising; those in higher-status jobs cruised more often than those in lower-status jobs.

The nature of the contact point is related to the type of relationship that follows. Tearooms and gay baths are the chief source of casual impersonal sex (Humphreys, 1970; Weinberg & Williams, 1975). Those wishing more permanent relationships often seek similarly inclined men in contexts where more social rather than sexual interaction can occur, such as bars, private parties, and gay organizations. Though much of the life of the gay bar involves brief "one-night stands," Humphreys (1971) noted that there is at least the aim of finding "deeper and more enduring personal relationships."

Second Encounters and Sexual Identity

Participation in variant sexual practices which are highly stigmatized forces some adaptations in self-concept (Warren, 1974). Most of the research in this area has been conducted by sociologists who are interested in deviance. A major interest has been how an individual moves from performing deviant behaviors to having a deviant identity. This concept was first introduced by Lemert (1951) and applied to the situations of homosexuals by Farrell and Nelson (1976). The acquisition of a homosexual or gay identity is a process by which self-attributions, perceived rejection by "straight" society, growing self-definition as homosexual, and associations with gay people begin to coalesce into a coherent sense of self.

This process of self-acknowledgement is termed "coming out" in gay slang. The social relationships that facilitate this process are quite important. Dank (1971) noted that 50 percent of his subjects "came out" in the presence of other homosexuals. Private behavior frequently became accessible for labeling in the company of other gay men and was reinforced. Much has been made of the importance of secrecy in the gay world and its effect on gay social interactions (Leznoff & Westley, 1967). The homosexual group is one of the few places, if not the only one, where protective public roles and masks can be let down. Other gay men are available as role models for appropriate behavior, gay knowledge (Warren, 1974), adopting a normalized attitude about homosexuality, and becoming more committed to homosexuality (Weinberg & Williams, 1974).

The transitional period most often occurs in the late teens and early twenties for males (Dank, 1971). The experimentation with alternate lifestyles may continue over the course of many years with no specific commitment given to the labels "homosexual," "bisexual," or "heterosexual." Most achieve some degree of self-definition which may or may not be congruent with actual behavior.

An example of an individual who performs homosexual acts yet does not identify himself as gay is the "hustler" or male prostitute (Reiss, 1967). These men or youths often maintain a strong macho heterosexual identity even though much of their sexual activity may be with other men. One of the ways by which separation of behavior from identity is maintained is the exchange of money. Saghir and Robins (1973) noted that older men generally were customers of the younger men, when money is exchanged at all.

Another example of behavior at variance with identity is the man involved in a heterosexual marriage who identifies himself as heterosexual yet frequents public restrooms for anonymous sex with other men (Humphreys, 1970). Either risk of exposure and loss of their current social position, or having only a peripheral interest in homosexual contacts (having a rating of 1 or 2 on the Kinsey scale of heterosexual-homosexual behavior) serve to make such contacts more desirable than the public involvement that might come from going to a gay bar or organization.

Harry and DeVall (1978) found that having a more heterosexual identity was related to lower desires for intimacy with other homosexuals, though it did not affect the incidence of sexual behavior. One of the most important means of establishing a positive gay identity is social involvement with other homosexuals. Weinberg and Williams (1974) found that those men who had closer ties with the gay community had fewer psychological problems than those who had little or no social contact with other homosexuals. For men who come to identify themselves as gay, *social* contact with gay men and participation in the broader gay community are important in the development of their sexual identity. These nonsexual relationships among gay men appear to be important for psychological health.

Bonding: Friendships

Hooker (1967) noted that early problems in researching homosexuality centered on the difficulty in gaining access to a community that is largely unseen and not readily recognizable. Her research into the nonclinical aspects of the homosexual community led her to find subjects through a variety of friendship networks. Leznoff and Westley (1967) were among the first researchers to seek out this group of homosexuals. They found a number of differences between social groups that were relatively more open or secret about their homosexuality. In particular, those in higher-status occupations were less open and tended to have a less noticeable and less flamboyant lifestyle than those with lower-status occupations.

Bell and Weinberg (1978) found that gay men socialize more frequently with other men—regardless of sexual orientation—than with women. Furthermore, almost half of their sample said all of their male friends were homosexual. They described five modal types in their study: close-coupled, open-coupled, functionals, dysfunctionals, and asexuals. The degree and type of socialization varied among these groups. For example, individuals in closed couples tended to go out less often than those in open couples or the singles described as functional. Overall, the majority of their subjects spent four or five nights a week at home. Frequent activities were contact with friends and attendance at movies, theater, or other cultural activities. Participation in or attendance at sporting events was uncommon. Both black and white males went to a gay bar with some frequency, though blacks were more likely than whites to have done so within the past week. Baths and homophile organizations were also low in the hierarchy of social outlets.

Several authors have observed that sexual contacts within an individual's social network were not common (Leznoff & Westley, 1967; Hooker, 1967;

Warren, 1974), and in some cases appeared similar to an incest taboo (but see below, under "Promiscuity Versus Love"). This was interpreted by Leznoff and Westley as support for viewing the friendship network as the primary source of social support and justification of "deviancy." For whatever reason, the social group may function similar to the family as the primary basis of support and identity formation.

Bonding: Primary Relationships

Despite the prevailing image that homosexual men spend most of their free time looking for sexual contacts (cruising) and have multiple casual sexual encounters, virtually all of the homosexuals studied by Bell and Weinberg (1978) had had extended affairs with other men, including intense emotional involvement. About half were currently involved in an affair.

Saghir and Robins (1973) likewise found that gay men had a wide variety of relationships. They classified them as "one-night stands," liaisons (lasting 4-12 months), and affairs (lasting over one year). Most but not all of the affairs ended within three years. Compared with lesbians, gay men had more sexual partners and participated in casual sex more often. They also had briefer relationships. Only one-quarter of those reporting relationships had sex only in the primary relationship, while three-quarters had never been monogamous or had been so only during the early stages of the relationship. Thus, gay male relationships vary considerably in length, degree of emotional involvement, and number of partners.

Of the five modal types that Bell and Weinberg (1978) found in their study, two describe couples. The close-coupled relationships involved a higher degree of sexual and social satisfaction derived from within the relationship. They were the best adjusted, did less cruising, had fewer sexual problems, and were unlikely to regret their homosexuality compared with the other groups. Open-coupled homosexuals sought greater social and sexual contacts outside the primary relationship; consequently, they went out more. Their adjustment was intermediate between the close-coupled and the dysfunctional homosexuals.

Harry and DeVall (1978) classified their subjects in terms of an analogy with heterosexual marital status. They termed those not in a relationship as "single," those who had a lover but were not living together as "engaged," those who were living with their lover as "married," and those who did not have a lover now but had one in the past as "divorced" or "formerly engaged" depending on whether they lived with their former lover. The number of singles declined with age, and the number married never exceeded 50 percent, ranging from 39 to 46 percent across the various age groups. Like others, they found that sexual exclusivity was not common. However, they also found support for Warren's (1974) hypothesis that a mature gay relationship included some acceptance of sexual diversity and made accommodation to outside contacts, frequently agreeing to casual impersonal sex where there would be no disruptive romantic or social consequences for the primary relationships. In this regard their conclusions are inconsistent with Bell and Weinberg's findings, previously cited, concerning the superior adjustment of close-coupled gay relationships. However, Harry and DeVall did not make a direct assessment of adjustment by marital status, so the apparent inconsistency is uncertain.

Recently, Silverstein (1981) conducted extensive interviews with 55 gay male couples and an additional 62 men who had been but were not currently coupled. He asserts that there are two general types of gay men: "excitement seekers," who have a high need for independence and sexual diversity, and "home builders," who seek more permanent relationships based on emotional intimacy. Most gay men are a combination of these types, though some men are totally one or the other polar type.

It is clear that the stereotype of the gay man as a lonely, neurotic individual incapable of intimacy or stable relationships does not conform to reality. All the studies cited support the conclusion that gay men show a diversity of relationship styles. How that diversity is described is another matter. Harry and DeVall (1978) chose terms taken from heterosexuality, Bell and Weinberg (1978) focused on whether the relationship was open or closed to outside sexual contact, and Silverstein (1981) emphasized the preference either for sexual diversity or for continuity in relationships. Describing gay male relationships in ways that facilitate comparisons to heterosexual relationship patterns is understandable but may not offer any advantage. It may also distort the truth by imposing categories that ignore differences between homosexual and heterosexual lifestyles.

Dissolutions

Several authors have addressed the issue of why gay male relationships appear to be less durable than heterosexual ones. Factors such as the lack of social and legal recognition for gay couples and the plentiful opportunity for casual sexual activity have been advanced (Harry & DeVall, 1978). Another author (Tripp, 1975) suggests that partner similarity in general plays a role in dissolutions.

Another interesting finding by Harry and DeVall (1978) concerned the hypothesis that dominance conflicts are responsible for the instability in many gay male relationships. They did not find evidence to support this assumption. The modal type of relationship was egalitarian (60 percent of the total sample) rather than structured into complementary roles. Where dominance was present, income disparity between partners was often a major contributing factor. They concluded that the cultural model around which most gay men structure their relationships could better be termed "friendship" than "marriage," and pointed out that gay men typically refer to their lovers as "friends" rather than adopting heterosexual terminology. Since one can have many friends, sexual relationships structured as friendships rather than as marriages could more readily accommodate sex outside the primary relationships.

The reasons why relationships end might be indirectly understood by examining the factors in successful relationships. Tuller (1978) found that the factors that led to satisfaction in homosexual couples were those also cited by heterosexual couples (e.g., love, understanding, mutual interests). Jones and Bates (1978) studied 14 gay male couples and concluded that "it is reasonable to describe the successfulness of gay relationships in ways that are similar to those used to describe straight relationships" (p. 223). Sexual fidelity was not one of their variables, so their conclusions apply only to the interpersonal or larger social dynamics of relationships.

Bell and Weinberg (1978) found that most gay men reported feeling sadness and distress over the breakup of a relationship, and most felt they grew or benefited in some way from their former relationship. Silverstein (1981), however, reported on one man, whom he classified as an "excitement seeker," who expressed relief at the end of a relationship that lasted "too long." Bell and Weinberg observed that two-thirds of those living with a male roommate were having sex with each other, and half of those who were not currently having sex with their roommate had done so in the past. Thus, one end point of gay male love affairs is the friend/roommate relationship—where emotional and social needs are met within the primary relationship, while sexual needs are met elsewhere.

Another end point, particularly for long-term relationships, is the death of one partner (Silverstein, 1981, chap. 11). The lack of legal recognition of gay relationships often complicated this process, especially when parents or other relatives strongly disapproved of the relationship. Sometimes hospital or family have limited visits to blood relatives only, or barred the surviving partner from making funeral arrangements.

ISSUES AND THEMES

Promiscuity Versus Love

The fact that gay men as a group have more sexual partners and briefer relationships has given some support to the stereotype of gay men as promiscuous. The evidence also suggests that long-term relationships with deep love and commitment are possible. One reason gay men may appear to be more promiscuous is that couples are less visible in public gay institutions such as bars and baths which cater to singles (Tripp, 1975). The term "promiscuous" reflects a bias against multiple sexual relationships and conveys a pejorative appraisal of such a lifestyle. Silverstein (1981) argues that viewing "excitement seekers" as less mature is wrong; it is less a matter of whether they are capable of long-term relationships than whether they choose that lifestyle. Both diversity and continuity of partners can be satisfying.

Lee (1973, 1976) has written on the diverse patterns by which love can be expressed in the context of gay relationships. These patterns are clusters of needs, behavioral styles, and values that characterize five modal types: *Eros,* which is primarily based on physical attributes and admiration for an ideal body type; *Ludus* is a type where more playful and noncommital attitudes prevail and physical characteristics may be less restrictively enforced; *Mania* characterizes the desperate search for fulfillment of deficient self-esteem, resulting in relationships troubled by jealousy and insecurity; *Storge* describes a pattern of gradual growth of intimacy rather than a sudden falling in love; *Pragma* is a search for a high degree of compatibility, a shopping list approach to love. His data came from classified advertisements in the *Advocate,* a national gay biweekly newspaper.

Lee (1976) also speculated that the advent of gay liberation may be changing gay male relationships. He observed that the "incest taboo" noted earlier by Leznoff and Westley (1967) as a norm in friendship circles is not necessarily present. Those authors also emphasized the differences between "overt" and "secret" groups, the latter being careful to prevent exposure of their members' homosexuality. It is possible that the increased acceptance for those who come out has made secrecy less important in many gay friendship networks. Distinctions between the roles of friend, sexual partner, and lover may be less noticeable now than when Leznoff and Westley gathered their data.

Age and Identity

At each period of life there are certain characteristic problems, situations, central issues, and desired outcomes by which behavior is organized (Erikson, 1950, 1968). Consistent with this perspective, it could be expected that sexual identity, behavior, and patterns of relationship would show changes with age.

In fact, all major empirical studies of gay relationships showed age differences. Younger men had more sexual partners, greater frequency of sex, spent more time cruising, and had shorter relationships than older men (Saghir & Robins, 1973; Weinberg & Williams, 1974; Bell & Weinberg, 1978; Harry & DeVall, 1978). Homosexual responsiveness peaks in the early teens (Kinsey et al., 1948) and declines slowly as age increases. A form of bisexuality often seen in gay men is most prevalent in early adulthood and may represent a transitional phase (to homosexuality) where preferences are tested through experimentation with different lifestyles and relationships.

These age-related differences relate to the task of identity formation. Overall sexual identity is a complex unity of gender identity, sexual orientation, and social sex-role preference (Shively & De Cecco, 1977; Larson, 1981). The process by which a person acquires a gay identity has only recently begun to be explored.

Cass (1979) proposed a six-stage model of homosexual identity formation. She based her work on interpersonal congruency theory, which holds that the process of identity formation and maintenance serves to maximize congruence between the person's perceptions of self, perceptions of others, and his or her own behavior. Homosexual identity begins with a period of confusion where the individual has few clear perceptions and may be inexperienced in sexual relationships. The next stage involves trying out different alternative identities, and, as a result, some are ruled out or in. At some point identity foreclosure can occur as the person chooses a particular label with which to identify. As a gay identity develops there are stages of tolerance, then acceptance, of the self as homosexual. As the person begins to identify more with other homosexuals, a stage of pride in being gay comes about, where differences between "gay" and "straight" lifestyles are emphasized in a "them-us" philosophy. The final stage (identity synthesis) results in greater acceptance of individual differences; there is still pride in homosexual identity, but it is coupled with tolerance for the world's diversity.

As mentioned earlier, the movement through these stages is termed "coming out" in the gay world. In Dank's (1971) study, the average age of coming out was 19.3 years: 15 percent of his subjects between 10-14, 44 percent between 15-19, and 29 percent between 20-24. There was an average of six years between age of first homosexual awareness and age of deciding that one was gay. There has been relatively little attention given to examining the differences between those who come out in teens or early adulthood and the "late bloomers" who come out later in life, though Silverstein (1981) has recently provided some coverage of this latter group. Their process of acquiring a gay identity is often complicated by heterosexual marriage, divorce, and resolution of custody and visitation rights with children.

The homosexual subculture is generally thought to be youth-oriented (Hoffman, 1968). Consequently, older gay men are viewed as becoming increasingly alienated, socially isolated, lonely, and suffering from accelerated aging. But Minnegerode (1976) failed to find any differences between homosexuals and heterosexuals in age status labeling.

Weinberg and Williams (1974) also failed to confirm the negative stereotypes about older homosexuals. They found older men were less concerned about exposure of their homosexuality, had more stable self-concepts, and were less effeminate. More masculine homosexuals appear to be better adjusted and have a better self-concept (Brown, 1958; Siegelman, 1972b; Stringer & Grygier, 1976; Larson, 1981). The same concerns of older persons in general are also experienced by aging homosexuals (Kelly, 1977): fear of loss of partner and fear of institutionalization. Kelly also found that 63 percent went to gay bars to some extent, and most continued social contact with other homosexuals. This does not necessarily contradict Weinberg and Williams (1974), who found that older males went to bars less frequently and live alone more than younger males. Though participation in the public aspects of gay culture may become less frequent, there is continued involvement through gay friendship networks and with one's partner. Kelly found that coupling tended to peak between the ages of 45 and 55, decreasing afterward, frequently due to death of the partner or change in the desire for a single lifelong partner.

Harry and DeVall (1978) found that there was not necessarily a strong youth orientation among gay males. There was a pronounced interest of younger men (18-24) in partners older than themselves, and of older men (35 or older) in partners younger than themselves. Age as a factor in relationships was found to be more important for those of lower educational or occupational status and among those who attended bars frequently. They also noted that the bars often have a "singles" atmosphere where youth may take on more importance than in other contexts.

Role Differentiation Versus Diffusion

One consequence of viewing homosexual relationships in categories derived from heterosexual relationships is the assumption that gay male couples structure their relationships into complementary masculine and feminine roles. Over the years numerous typologies of male homosexuals have been constructed around such dichotomies as active/passive, dominant/submissive, "butch"/"femme," or inserter/insertee in genital activity. Current views stress more of a "both/and" attitude rather than an "either/or" one; that is, role differentiation is seen as more diffuse in recent studies.

Saghir and Robins (1973) found that for all age groups, the majority of homosexuals tended to interchange roles as inserter and insertee in sexual activity. Only a minority of the couples tended to conduct their affair in a "husband and wife" pattern. Harry and DeVall (1978) found a larger degree of egalitarian relationship styles than would be expected from the stereotype. They concluded that the dominance/submission dimension was not characteristic of gay male relationships because of individual differences in commitment to various aspects of male sex roles.

Also, the concept of masculinity/femininity as a single bipolar dimension has been challenged recently (Block, 1973; Bem, 1974, 1975; Heilbrun, 1976; Spence & Helmreich, 1978). In its place, it is suggested that masculinity and femininity are separate dimensions, and an individual can show high or low amounts of either or both sex roles. Persons high on both masculinity and femininity are termed "androgynous" (Bem, 1974) after the Greek roots for male (andros) and female (gyne). Bem and others have found androgyny related to greater flexibility and adaptiveness. No study has yet assessed gay male relationships in terms of this new view, and studies of homosexuals as a group (McDonald & Moore, 1978) or compared with heterosexuals (Larson, 1981) have resulted in different conclusions.

Isolation Versus Organization

One difference between the gay situation today and that of twenty years ago is the increased number and visibility of homophile organizations, businesses catering to homosexual clientele, and community organizations. Many American cities have some form of gay organization other than bars, baths, and other cruising areas. The potential for other types of interaction besides looking for a prospective sexual partner is enhanced in these larger urban areas. Harry and DeVall (1978) have noted the importance of urbanization for the creation of social and cultural alternatives to the sexual marketplace. They observed that many gay men who were born in rural areas migrated to larger cities in search of a better-developed gay community.

Weinberg and Williams (1974) found that those gay men who socialized more with other homosexuals had fewer psychological problems than those who were relatively uninvolved with the gay world. Greenberg (1976), however, found that participation in a homophile organization did not increase self-esteem. It did decrease alienation in the short run, though the effect was minimal for those members who had been involved for over a year. The author's conclusions were guarded, as his sample was small. Perhaps there is an initial effect as the new member experiences the solidarity of numbers but then becomes less active as he or she builds up a network of friends through the organization. As anyone who has been a member of a voluntary group knows, interest and attendance fluctuate; for a variety of causes, activists experience "burn out" after long periods of involvement. So the impact of gay groups on its members, like all similar groups, would tend to vary.

As gay communities have developed in several large urban areas, the process of differentiation and proliferation of gay organizations has led to what Harry and DeVall (1978) termed increased "institutional completeness." This refers to the degree to which the needs of its individual members are met through other group members (i.e., having gay doctors, laundries, financial institutions, music and art centers, and other retail or service organizations). This diversity allows a truly gay culture to emerge. Levine (1977) has described predominantly gay neighborhoods in large metropolitan centers, where the social life of gay men finds the greatest variety and institutional support. The role of residential concentration is crucial—it is easier to patronize a gay business if it is conveniently located where an individual lives or works. Furthermore, such proliferation allows the gay community to provide more employment for its own members.

The impact of these developing gay communities on the behavior and consciousness of individual gay men or women has not yet been explored. It is also not known what effect the diversification of gay culture has on couples. There is clearly a wider range of relationships available other than lover or friend. Each new organization or business adds a different context within which gay male relationships can occur.

TRENDS

Humphreys (1971) was the first of many authors to note the virilization of the gay male subculture. Swish and camp have been eclipsed by beards, Levi's, and an emphasis on more masculine appearance. This represents a self-conscious rejection of earlier heterosexual expectations that gay men would act and appear feminine; now a conscious hypermasculinity asserts the feeling that gay men are really men.

This celebration of masculinity comes at a time when the gay liberation movement is seeking allies to continue its campaign for social equality for homosexuals. Its closest ideological ally is the feminist movement, since both challenge traditional sex roles and values. Many in the women's movement view highly masculine gay men as embodying the ideals that demean and oppress women. There are critics in the gay community who view this development as moving from the Scylla of limp-wristed femininity to the Charybdis of macho masculinity; gay men are still trapped by stereotypes, and therefore there is no advancement toward liberation.

Perhaps, though, a dialectical process is at work. After being oppressed with the feminine image, gay men are exploring the image they were denied. Soon another alternative, a synthesis, might emerge. The attempt to level differences with a unisex culture appears to be waning. But androgyny does not necessarily entail the leveling of differences; a comfortable integration and appreciation of different sex roles might require a period of exaggerating different roles to test their limits.

Another trend in gay male relationships is the increased comfort with aging. As more men come out and live openly gay lifestyles, there will be more visibility of middle-aged and older homosexual men. Already gay newspapers and magazines are including more models in their thirties or forties. Baldness or grey hair is less of a barrier in the eyes of advertisers; indeed, it increases the market appeal to a group that is growing in numbers as the population ages. Indeed, the trend toward acceptance of aging is a product of the increased self-acceptance of gay men.

The relationships between love, sex, and affection may also be undergoing change. As Lee (1976) noted, the incest taboo that seemed prominent in earlier studies of gay male friendship circles may be diminishing. He also mentioned exploration of alternatives to two-person coupling—communes and group marriage. These possibilities will continue to be a minority expression within the gay community. However, the growing acceptance by heterosexuals of nonpermanent sexual relationships opens up wider avenues for intimacy between men as well.

A more serious look needs to be taken at short-term relationships, not as failures of coupling but as alternatives to coupling. Clearly, many gay men experience satisfaction from such relationships. However, in a culture that extols permanent unions as the only model of intimacy, the value of short-term relationships may be inadequately understood. To the extent that friendship and sexual involvement are less separate in the gay world, the function of each may change.

POLICY IMPLICATIONS AND CONCLUSIONS

The research reviewed in this chapter suggests a number of areas in which social policy should be changed.

The laws against consenting adult sexual activity need reform. Though often unenforced, they make it difficult for gay men to meet each other, and affect the society in ways detrimental to gay men (see Chapter 27). Also, the status of gay couples needs attention, both from the law and from the church. Only the Metropolitan Community Church (which has a large gay following) regularly offers a service of "union" for those couples who wish some liturgical recognition of their commitment. No state has a mechanism available to most gay couples whereby each member can be treated even as the other's next of kin—not to mention the problems with joint ownership of property, discrimination in accommodations, and so on. In short, there are a myriad of ways society recognizes and gives advantage to heterosexual couples that are not available to gay couples. That so many gay couples endure without such support is a testimony to the strength of gay love.

Some would argue that such unequal treatment is justified—for example, by society's need to promote the family. This question is addressed in other chapters in this volume. Here I will note only that the cost in human suffering and productivity should be entered into the equation; equal treatment would only result in more social cohesion as sources of alienation are removed. The fuller participation of gay citizens in the political, economic, and social life of the nation is a benefit not to be ignored. Such participation should, of course, include attempts to portray more accurate images of gay relationships in the media.

These considerations are suggestive rather than exhaustive. They may seem unrealistically optimistic in a period of social retrenchment. But any movement for social justice must be persistent despite changes in political or social currents. Gay male relationships are in a period of flux due to the changes in the sexual attitudes of many Americans. Despite the lack of full opportunity, there has never been as favorable a climate in America for the growth of a strong, positive, and healthy gay identity. The continuance of this climate is essential if society wants the maximum possible from its gay citizens.

• 21 •

Understanding Lesbian Relationships

Letitia Anne Peplau
Hortensia Amaro

Although love may not "make the world go 'round", the lives of most adults are powerfully affected by their experiences in intimate relationships. It is commonly believed that the psychologically healthy adult must have the capacity for work and love. The importance of intimate relationships is no less great for lesbians than for heterosexuals. Yet, whereas heterosexual women can readily find information about the joys and problems of relationships with men in advice columns, scholarly books, and college courses on marriage and family, lesbians have few comparable sources of accurate information. For anyone interested in understanding lesbian lifestyles, factual information is essential.

In this chapter we review scientific knowledge about lesbian love relationships. Although fiction, biographies, the impressions of therapists, and other sources (e.g., Berzon & Leighton, 1979; Vida, 1978) can provide useful insights into lesbian relationships, we have restricted our review to empirical research. We are acutely aware of the methodological problems of conducting research in the gay community—or among members of any partially hidden group (Morin, 1977; see Gonsiorek's introduction, Chapter 5). The most serious problem in this area has been the impossibility of obtaining representative samples of lesbians. As a result, it is imperative that research results be interpreted cautiously.

Authors' Note: *Our sincere appreciation goes to Emilia Bellon, Betty Berzon, Susan D. Cochran, Maria Diaz, Steven L. Gordon, Christine Padesky, and Karen Rook for their helpful comments on an earlier version of this chapter.*

In attemping to portray lesbian relationships, it is important to curb the impulse to oversimplify the complexities of women's experiences. There is no such thing as the "typical lesbian couple." Most empirical research has concentrated on a limited segment of the lesbian population: Typical respondents have been younger, educated, middle-class white women. Unfortunately, very little is known about lesbians from other backgrounds. Existing research contributes little to our understanding of the role of such factors as age, education, social class, religion, ethnicity and culture in lesbian relationships.

With these cautions in mind, we reviewed the available empirical research. We began with the question of how many lesbians are currently involved in steady relationships. Seven studies[1] provide information on this issue. Among these studies, the proportion of women who were currently in a steady relationship ranged from 45 to 80 percent. In most studies, the proportion of women in ongoing relationships was close to 75 percent. Furthermore, the same studies indicate that many lesbians are living with their partners; estimates range from 42 to 63 percent of all lesbians surveyed living with their partners.

Although these figures should not be taken as representative of all lesbians, they do suggest that at any particular point in time many lesbians are involved in an intimate relationship. What these statistics do not tell us, of course, is what these relationships are like—whether or not lesbian couples are happy, loving, or committed. Later in the chapter we probe more deeply into the quality of lesbian relationships. It is important to recognize that those lesbians who are *not* currently in a steady relationship are a diverse group. They include women who have recently ended a relationship through breakup or through the death of a partner, women who are eager to begin a new relationship, and others who do not want a steady relationship.

A related question concerns the average length of lesbian relationships. Do most lesbians have fairly short-lived affairs or longer-term relationships? This is a difficult question to answer. For an adolescent—whether lesbian or heterosexual—a relationship of three months may seem "long"; for a 50-year old person, a relationship of 15 years may be long. In other words, a person's age determines to some extent the length of time that a relationship can have endured and subjective perceptions of whether or not a relationship has lasted a "long" time.

A recent study by Bell and Weinberg (1978) of 283 lesbians living in San Francisco inquired about the length of women's *first* lesbian relationship. On the average, women in this sample were 22 years old when they had their first "relatively steady relationship." Nearly 90 percent said they had been "in love" with this first partner, and the typical first relationship lasted for a median of one to three years. For less than 8 percent of the women did this first relationship end in three months or less. This pattern of establishing relatively enduring relationships characterizes not only lesbians' first intimate relationships but also their subsequent relationships.

Several studies[2] have asked lesbians to describe the length of their current love relationship. In these studies, most participants have been young lesbians in their 20s. The typical length of their relationships was two to three years. Studies of older lesbians would be especially useful in understanding the length of relationships, but such research is strikingly absent from the existing literature. Studies that have included small numbers of older lesbians[3] document that relationships of 20 years or more are not unusual.

The relative stability of most lesbians' relationships is further reflected in data on the total number of different partners lesbians have had. In the Bell and Weinberg (1978) study, in which nearly half the white lesbians sampled were over age 35, the majority of women had had fewer than 10 different lesbian sexual partners during their lifetimes. One-time or brief sexual liaisons occurred but were uncommon.

Thus, the picture that tentatively emerges from these statistics is that the majority of lesbians experience relatively stable, long-term relationships. Important exceptions to this pattern should be noted, however. A minority of lesbians have shorter relationships and a greater number of different partners. For example, in two studies (Bell & Weinberg, 1978; Jay & Young, 1977), 15 percent of respondents reported that they had had sexual relations with 25 or more lesbian partners. It seems likely that for some lesbians this reflects a pattern of choice—a rejection of committed relationships as a personal goal. For other lesbians, casual sexual affairs may occur concurrently with a committed relationship. For still others, a pattern of many partners may reflect difficulties in establishing intimate bonds; such problems might be based on the internalization and acting out of the culture's rejection of lesbian relationships and of stereotypes that lesbians are unable to develop long-term relationships (compare Ettorre, 1980).

Having seen that most lesbians spend much of their adult lives in intimate love relationships, we next turn to findings about the nature of lesbian relationships. We begin with an examination of lesbians' attitudes and values about relationships, and look at issues of commitment and permanence in lesbian couples. In a later section we investigate role-playing in lesbian relationships and present findings debunking the myth that lesbian couples adopt characteristically "masculine" and "feminine" roles. This is followed by a discussion of research on power in lesbian relationships and an examination of the sexual lives of lesbian couples.

ATTITUDES ABOUT RELATIONSHIPS

For most lesbians, love relationships are important. Bell and Weinberg (1978) asked lesbians how important it was to them to have a "permanent living arrangement with a homosexual partner." One-quarter of lesbians said that this was "the most important thing in life" and another 35 percent said it was "very important." Less than one woman in four said that a permanent living arrangement was not important to her. So, again, we see a range of views, with a couple orientation being most common.[4]

It has frequently been speculated that lesbian relationships are more "romantic" than those of heterosexuals. For example, Hyde and Rosenberg (1976) suggest that "homosexual women live almost an idyllic love relationship with their partner, with more intense emotion and imagination than the typical heterosexual relationship" (p. 176). Only one study has examined this issue empirically. Peplau et al. (1978) administered a six-item romanticism scale to a sample of 127 lesbians in Los Angeles. Items assessed adherence to the belief that "love conquers all." Included were statements about true love lasting forever and love overcoming barriers of race, religion, and economics. As a whole, lesbians in this sample were not strongly romantic in their beliefs. Further, when lesbians' romanticism scores were compared to those of matched samples of heterosexual women, gay men, and heterosexual men, no significant differences were found among any of the groups (Cochran & Peplau, 1979). So, while some lesbians may indeed have a highly romanticized or idealized view of love relationships, this orientation does not appear to be any more common among lesbians than among other adults.

Given that most lesbians want a steady relationship, what are the characteristics they seek in such partnerships? The single most consistent theme to emerge from empirical research is the strong importance most lesbians place on emotional intimacy and expressiveness. In this regard, lesbians are quite similar to heterosexual women. For example, Ramsey, Latham and Lindquist (1978) asked members of lesbian and heterosexual couples to rank the importance of 11 possible relationship goals. Lesbians ranked the sharing of affection as most important, with personal development and companionship next. The same three goals topped the list of heterosexual women. Further, women in both groups gave least importance to economic security, community standing, and religious sharing. In another study (Peplau et al., 1978; Cochran & Peplau, 1979), 127 lesbians rated the importance they personally gave to 16 features of love relationships. Again, lesbians gave greatest importance to "being able to talk about my most intimate feelings" and "laughing easily with each other." These same features were also given greatest importance by a matched group of heterosexual women.

A second theme that recurs is the value lesbians place on equality in relationships. In one study (Peplau et al., 1978), lesbians strongly endorsed the importance of "having an egalitarian (equal-power) relationship" and strongly rejected the idea of "having more influence than my partner in our joint decision-making." Similar findings have been reported in ethnographic studies of lesbian communities in California (Wolf, 1979) and Oregon (Barnhart, 1975). For many lesbians, an emphasis on egalitarianism is linked to a more general endorsement of feminist values. Feminist lesbians may be more conscious of the power dimension in close relationships and more concerned about equality as a goal than are nonfeminist lesbians.

There is more diversity of opinion among lesbians about the desirability of other features of love relationships. Two important dimensions along which the relationship values of lesbians differ have been identified by Peplau et al. (1978). A dimension of "dyadic attachment" concerns the importance women give to having a close-knit, exclusive, relatively permanent relationship. Some women are strong proponents of attachment who want to spend most of their free time with their partner, share many activities, preserve sexual exclusivity, and know that the relationship will endure. Other women reject many of these goals, preferring instead to have a lesser degree of togetherness in their relationship. A second dimension, "personal autonomy," concerns boundaries between the individual and her relationship. While some individuals prefer to immerse themselves in a relationship to the exclusion of outside interests and activities, other women prefer to maintain greater personal independence.

Lesbians' attitudes about relationships are affected not only by their personal histories but also by the social context in which they live. Ethnographic studies of particular lesbian communities illustrate how group norms can affect relationship values. For example, in the early 1970s Barnhart (1975) studied intensively a counterculture community of lesbian women in Oregon. Among women in this group, an ideology had developed emphasizing that the individual's first loyalty should be to the community; couple relationships should be secondary. The community further encouraged women to reject the idea of sexual exclusivity because, in their analysis, it conflicted with norms of equality and sisterhood. As Barnhart points out, many women experienced some difficulty in reconciling their preexisting beliefs about monogamous relationships with the newer attitudes endorsed by their social group. Further research on variations among different lesbian groups and communities in relationship values would be useful.

Satisfaction, Love, and Commitment

Given that many lesbians would like to establish a satisfying, close relationship, how successful are they in achieving this goal? Unfortunately, information about satisfaction, love, and commitment in lesbian relationships comes from a few studies based on fairly small samples and using self-report measures. So the following results are presented cautiously. They suggest that most lesbians find their relationships to be highly satisfying.

One study (Cardell, Finn, & Marecek, in press) compared a small Pennsylvania sample of lesbians, gay men, and heterosexuals on a measure of couple adjustment. They found that lesbians did not differ from the other two groups in adjustment; most couples were very satisfied with their relationship. Another recent study (Ramsey et al., 1978) compared 26 lesbian couples to 27 gay male couples and 25 heterosexual couples. All couples had lived together for at least six months; the average length of cohabitation for lesbian couples was over six years. Relationship satisfaction was measured by the widely used Locke-Wallace marital adjustment scale. The lesbian couples scored in the "well-adjusted" range and did not differ significantly from couples in the other two groups.

Only recently have social psychologists attempted to measure love systematically, spurred by Zick Rubin's development of scales to measure "love" and "liking" for a romantic partner. Cochran and Peplau (1979) compared matched samples of younger lesbians, gay men, and heterosexuals, all of whom were in steady relationships. On Rubin's measures, lesbians reported high love for their partner, indicating strong feelings of attachment, caring, and intimacy. They also scored high on the liking scale, reflecting feelings of respect and affection toward the partner. On other measures, lesbians rated their current relationship as highly satisfying and very close. When comparisons were made among lesbians, gay men, and heterosexuals on these measures, no significant differences were found. Also included in this research were open-ended questions asking participants to describe in their own words the "best things" and "worst things" about their current relationship. Systematic analyses (Cochran, 1978) found no significant differences in the responses of lesbians, gay men, and heterosexuals, all of whom reported similar types of joys and problems. To examine the possibility that more subtle differences existed among groups that were not captured by the coding scheme, the statements were typed on cards in a standard format with information about gender and sexual orientation removed. Panels of judges were asked to sort the cards, separating men and women and heterosexuals and homosexuals. Judges were not able to distinguish correctly the responses of lesbians from those of heterosexual women, heterosexual men, or gay men.

Taken together, these findings suggest that many lesbian relationships are highly satisfying. Lesbian couples appear, on standardized measures, to be as well-adjusted as heterosexual couples. This does not, of course, mean that lesbians have no difficulties in their relationships. They undoubtedly have some of the same problems as heterosexuals—for example, in coordinating joint goals and resolving interpersonal conflicts. Lesbian couples may also have special problems arising from the hostile and rejecting attitudes of many people toward lesbians. Overall, however, existing research suggests that lesbian relationships are as likely to be personally satisfying as are heterosexual ones.

Correlates of Satisfaction

Researchers are only beginning to examine factors that promote personal feelings of love and satisfaction in lesbian relationships. A study by Peplau, Padesky, and Hamilton (1982) is a first step in this direction. They found that among a group of relatively young lesbians from Los Angeles, satisfaction was strongly related to equality of involvement in the relationship. Those relationships in which partners were equally committed and equally "in love" tended to be the happiest. In contrast, lopsided relationships in which one partner was much more involved than the other were less satisfying. This pattern is quite similar to results of studies of heterosexual relationships (e.g., Hill, Rubin, & Peplau, 1976).

A second factor contributing to satisfaction in the lesbian relationships in this study was equality of power. We saw earlier that most lesbians are strong proponents of egalitarianism in relationships. Perhaps not surprisingly, those women who perceived their current relationship as egalitarian were significantly more satisfied than were women who thought their relationship was not. Third, evidence was also found indicating that similarity of attitudes and backgrounds facilitated successful relationships. This is consistent with the widely replicated finding among heterosexuals that similarity increases attraction.

It is also interesting to note factors that were *not* related to satisfaction in lesbian relationships. In the Peplau, Padesky, and Hamilton (1982) study, satisfaction was not related to the extent of involvement in lesbian or feminist groups and activities; nor was it related to the degree to which women were open versus closeted about being lesbian. Finally, the three studies that have examined satisfaction have looked for age-related differences. Results indicated, however, that older and younger lesbians are equally likely to have satisfying relationships.

The Ending of Relationships

Why do lesbian relationships break up? Probably for many of the same reasons that heterosexual relationships end (see Levinger & Moles, 1979). Permanence and commitment are affected by two major factors. First, relationship bonds are strengthened by the positive, rewarding features of relationships. The complex set of ingredients that makes a particular partner and relationship appealing—whether it be sexual attraction, feelings of compatibility, or shared goals and activities—contributes to the stability of the relationship. It is possible in any relationship that attractions wither and that passions and interests subside; lesbians have no special immunity to falling out of love.

A second set of factors affecting the permanence of relationships consists of barriers that make the termination of the relationship costly, either psychologically or materially. For heterosexuals, marriage usually creates many barriers to the dissolution of a relationship—including the cost of divorce, the wife's financial dependence on her husband, joint investments in property, children, and so on. Such factors may encourage married couples to work on improving a declining relationship, rather than to end it. In some cases, they may also keep partners trapped in an empty relationship. Lesbians probably encounter fewer barriers to the termination of their relationships. Lesbian relationships are not, for example, typically formalized by legal contracts, and lesbians are less likely to be financially dependent on a partner. Whereas family and friends often encourage heterosexual spouses to work out their relationship problems, lesbians may have less social support for their relationships. Because of these lower barriers to breaking up, lesbians are less likely to become trapped in hopelessly unhappy relationships. But they may also be less motivated to rescue deteriorating relationships. All of these speculations about commitment in lesbian relationships are in need of empirical verification.

ROLE-PLAYING

A false stereotype of lesbian relationships is that they mimic traditional sex-typed heterosexual patterns, with one partner adopting a "masculine" role and the other a "feminine" role. Such role-playing is supposedly manifested in the division of household tasks, style of dress, patterns of dominance-submission, and preferences about sexual behavior. In popular thinking, such role-playing is seen as reflecting a desire by some lesbians to be men. Research clearly discredits all of these common beliefs.

Research indicates that sex-typed role-playing is rare in contemporary lesbian life. Most lesbians say they dislike such categories as "butch" and "femme," and reject the idea of role-playing (Barnhart, 1975; Jay & Young, 1977; Tanner, 1978). For example, one lesbian wrote:

> I strive to eliminate all vestiges of role-playing in my relationship with women, as the opportunity to do so is one of the major reasons I am a lesbian. My lover and I have constantly shifting roles . . . depending on the needs of the mo-

ment. If ever I felt we were getting locked into any roles, especially those of butch/femme, I would run . . . to escape from this relationship [Jay & Young, 1977, p. 320].

The theme reflected in this quotation and in other anecdotal accounts is that lesbian relationships permit women to avoid limitations imposed by traditional male-female role-playing that occurs in many heterosexual relationships.

Several studies[5] have examined role-playing patterns in the division of household tasks, style of dress, and sexual conduct of lesbians. The consistent finding is that most lesbians do *not* conform to rigid masculine-feminine roles. Instead, role shifting and role flexibility are the predominant pattern. A reasonable estimate would be that only about 10 percent of lesbians today engage in clear-cut role-playing. One lesbian explained her participation in role-playing:

When I am with a younger girl, I like to . . . protect her, and I like it very much if she lets me buy drinks, etc. . . . What I like best about the "male" or "butch" role is the protective angle, even though I realize intellectually that this is a lot of sexist shit [Jay & Young, 1977, p. 322].

It appears that role-playing was more prevalent in the "old gay life" (Wolf, 1979), a period before the 1950s evolution of homophile organizations and the more recent effects of feminism in the lesbian community. Cultural stereotypes about lesbian role-playing may have developed during this earlier period, when the straight community's knowledge of lesbian life was largely derived from behavioral patterns observed in gay bars. We do not know how prevalent role-playing used to be, since most research is of recent vintage. Two studies based on data collected before 1969 (Bass-Hass, 1968; Jensen, 1974) reported that a majority of respondents engaged in role-playing. Ethnographic accounts (e.g., Wolf, 1979) contain descriptions by lesbians of the old bar scene in major cities. It appears that there has been a historical decline in role-playing among American lesbians.

Nevertheless, let us examine factors that may foster the adoption of these sex-typed patterns. Four possibilities are suggested by existing studies. First, role-playing may be more common among older women who were or continue to be part of the old gay life. Second, role-playing may be more common among lesbians from lower socioeconomic levels (Gagnon & Simon, 1973; Wolf, 1979). Although virtually no data exist on blue-collar and working-class lesbians, research has suggested that lower-income heterosexuals have more sex-typed behavior patterns than do higher-income heterosexuals (e.g., Komarovsky, 1967). It may be that stronger adherence to masculine-feminine roles is found among women who have traditional values, perhaps based on religious and cultural socialization. Third, role-playing may be related to the coming-out experiences of some lesbians (Gagnon & Simon, 1973; Saghir & Robins, 1973). For example, a young woman who is new to the lesbian community may initially dress in a stereotypically butch manner in order to be more easily identified as lesbian and to conform to her perception of group expectations about behavior. Fourth, in some cases, role-playing may result from temporary situational factors. Saghir and Robins (1973) found that 12 percent of their lesbian respondents had engaged in role-playing; the majority had developed such roles because one partner was temporarily unemployed or attending school.

In summary, masculine-feminine role-playing is another area in which variations among lesbians have been found. While the great majority of lesbians rejects role-playing, a minority continues to behave in sex-typed ways. What should be remembered, of course, is that the greatest amount of role-playing has always been and continues to be found among heterosexual couples.

POWER

In the earlier discussion of lesbians' attitudes about relationships, we saw that most gay women consider equality an important relationship goal. How successful are women in achieving this egalitarian ideal? There has been only one empirical investigation of power in lesbian relationships (Caldwell & Peplau, in press), based on questionnaire responses from a sample of 77 younger Los Angeles lesbians who were in a steady relationship. When asked directly who they thought should have more power in their relationship, 97 percent of these women said that both partners should have "exactly equal" say in their relationship. Not all women believed that their relationship attained this ideal, however. When asked to describe the overall balance of power in their current relationship, 64 percent reported equal power, but a sizable 36 percent minority reported that one partner had greater influence than the other.

Caldwell and Peplau investigated factors that tip the balance of power away from equality in lesbian relationships. Some years ago sociologist Willard Waller (1938) proposed the "principle of least interest"—suggesting that when one partner in a relationship is relatively less interested or committed, she/he will have greater power. Clear evidence was found for such a link between imbalances of involvement and imbalances of power in lesbian relationships. Social psychological theory also suggests that power is likely to accrue to the partner who has greater personal resources, in terms of greater education or income or other desirable characteristics. In this study, women who had relatively greater income and education than their partner tended to have relatively greater power. Thus, both relative dependency and personal resources affected the balance of power. Further research is needed to confirm these findings about power in lesbian relationships.

SEXUAL BEHAVIOR

A cultural stereotype depicts lesbians as highly sexual people. Perhaps because of this myth, much of the research on lesbians has investigated their sexuality. Yet research suggests many commonalities—and a few differences—between the sexual attitudes and experiences of lesbians and of heterosexual women.

Studies of physiological aspects of sexuality (Kinsey et al., 1953; Masters & Johnson, 1979) have found no differences in the pattern of sexual response of lesbians and heterosexual women. It is hardly surprising that the physiological mechanics of sexual arousal and orgasm are similar for all women, regardless of sexual orientation.

It may also be useful in this context to recognize that the majority of lesbians have had sexual relations with men as well as with women. In one study of 151 lesbians (Schaefer, 1976), 55 percent of respondents had had heterosexual coitus prior to their first lesbian experience. Studies[6] suggest that close to 80 percent of lesbians have had sex with men at some point in their lives. For many lesbians, these heterosexual experiences occurred in the context of dating or marital relationships. One study found that a majority of lesbians had dated men (Peplau et al., 1978). A significant minority of lesbians (perhaps 25 percent) has been heterosexually married.[7]

Lesbians' evaluations of their sexual relationships with men vary considerably. Jay and Young (1977) found that 23 percent of lesbians rated their past heterosexual experiences as positive, 21 percent as neutral, and 55 percent as negative. One factor contributing to this may be that for some lesbians, sexual activities with men did not lead to orgasm (e.g., for 33 percent of lesbians in Bell and Weinberg's study). Equally important, however, may be differences in the emotional tone of sexual experiences with female and male partners. Schaefer (1976) asked the 57 lesbians in her sample who had had sexual relations during the past year with both women and men to compare these experiences. Major differences were reported. Most women said that compared to sex with men, sex with women was more tender (94 percent), intimate (91 percent), considerate (88 percent), partner-related (73 percent), exciting (66 percent), diversified (52 percent), and less aggressive (71 percent).

Studies of lesbians' sexual experiences with women have identified two patterns. First, for many lesbians, sex and love are closely linked. In a survey of 962 lesbians (Jay & Young, 1977), 97 percent of women said that emotional involvement was important to sex, and 92 percent said that in their own personal experiences, emotional involvement always or very frequently accompanied sex. Consistent with this emphasis on affection, Bell and Weinberg (1978) found that 62 percent of lesbians had never had sex with a stranger, and 81 percent said that they had felt affection toward most of their sexual partners. Gundlach and Reiss (1968) found that equal proportions of lesbians and heterosexual women—64 percent—said they could have sex only if they were in love with the partner. So, whereas a minority of lesbians enjoys casual or "recreational" sex, the majority prefers to limit sexual activities to partners toward whom they feel at least affection. Given this pattern, it is not surprising that many lesbians draw their sexual partners from people they already know as friends (Peplau et al., 1978; Schaefer, 1977; Tanner, 1978), and that the incidence of cruising—meeting casual partners in bars and other settings—is quite low (Jay & Young, 1977).

Research also shows that most lesbians find their sexual interactions with women highly satisfying. Lesbian love-making typically leads to orgasm.[8] For example, lesbians in one study said that they seldom had difficulty achieving orgasm during sex (Jay & Young, 1977). Only 4 percent said they never had an orgasm and 5 percent said they had orgasms infrequently. Comparative studies suggest that lesbians achieve orgasm more often during love-making than do heterosexual women. Kinsey et al. (1953) compared heterosexual women who had been married for five years with lesbians who had been sexually active for an equal number of years. Among these women, 17 percent of the heterosexuals compared to only 7 percent of the lesbians never had an orgasm. And only 40 percent of heterosexuals had orgasm easily (i.e., 90-100 percent of the time they had sex), compared to 68 percent of lesbians. These differences may, as Kinsey suggested, reflect differences in the knowledge and sexual techniques of women's partners. But differences in the emotional quality of sexual experiences may be equally important.

Studies examining sexual behavior in steady lesbian relationships find that for most women, sex is an enjoyable part of such relationships. In one study (Peplau et al., 1978), three-quarters of lesbians said that sex with their steady partner was "extremely satisfying," and only 4 percent said that it was not at all satisfying.

Available data[9] suggest that lesbian couples have sex about as often as do heterosexual couples. Among the younger lesbians typically studied by researchers, the average frequency of sex is about two to three times per week. This figure varies widely from couple to couple, however. Among the lesbians studied by Jay and Young, only 5 percent reported having sex daily. Most women (57 percent) had sex two to five times per week, 25 percent had sex once a week, and 8 percent had sex less often with their partner.

Little is known about the factors that influence the actual or desired frequency of sex in lesbian relationships.

Sexual exclusivity is a controversial issue for many American couples, both lesbian and heterosexual, as discussed above. The predominant pattern reported in available studies[10] of lesbians is serial monogamy—women participate in a series of sexually exclusive relationships. But other patterns are also common. Commenting on sexual openness, a lesbian explained, "I have sex outside the relationship, and we talk about it openly. So far it has had a positive effect. We both agree to be nonmonogamous" (Jay & Young, 1977, p. 326). One study (Peplau et al., 1978) found that sexual openness was not related to dissatisfaction within women's primary relationship. Women in sexually open relationships were just as satisfied with their steady partner as were women in monogamous relationships. More needs to be known about how different lesbian couples handle this contemporary issue.

Finally, it is important to note that although many lesbians are happy with sex in their relationships, some lesbians do have sexual difficulties. The myth that all lesbians have perfect sex can be quite harmful to women who experience problems. No systematic research exists on sexual difficulties faced by lesbians, but observations by clinicians offer a few speculative clues. Toder (1978) suggested that lesbians share some of the same sexual problems as heterosexual women, including orgasmic dysfunction and differences in the desired sexual frequency of partners. But lesbians may also have some special problems, such as discomfort in taking the initiative in making love to a partner or sexual inhibitions about such activities as oral sex. More research on lesbian sexuality is needed to understand this aspect of lesbian relationships, and to provide information for counselors who seek to help lesbian clients.

CONCLUSIONS

Our review of research on lesbian relationships has found wide variations in the experiences of individual lesbians. For every general pattern that can be identified, there are many exceptions.

When possible, we have compared the attitudes and experiences of lesbians and heterosexual women. It is important to understand why such comparisons are useful. We do *not* assume that heterosexuality or heterosexual marriage is an ideal pattern to be used as the standard in analyses of lesbian relationships. Rather, such comparisons highlight similarities in the values and experiences of all women. For example, childhood socialization experiences of girls in this culture often emphasize emotional expressiveness and love as central to close relationships, and these themes can be seen in the adult relationships of both lesbians and heterosexuals (Cochran & Peplau, 1979; Gagnon & Simon, 1973; Schaefer, 1976; for similar issues in male homosexuality, see Peplau & Gordon, in press). Second, comparisons of lesbian and heterosexual relationships point to basic issues that confront all intimate couples, regardless of sexual orientation. For instance, imbalances of dependency can tip the balance of power away from equality in lesbian and heterosexual relationships alike. Finally, such comparisons help to identify those unique qualities of lesbian relationships that make them a positive and desirable lifestyle for women.

There is a long list of needed research about lesbian relationships. Because virtually all of the research we have reviewed is based on white women (exceptions are Bell & Weinberg, 1978 and Hidalgo & Hidalgo-Christensen, 1976), findings cannot be generalized to ethnic lesbians. Existing research says little about the impact of cultural, ethnic, economic, and religious factors on values and behavior in lesbian relationships. Yet it is obvious that relationships reflect both the personal experiences of the partners and the social context in which the relationship exists. The nature of satisfaction, commitment, sexuality, or power may differ for a Hispanic couple living in the barrio, a Black professional couple, a first-generation Asian couple, and the white respondents typically studied in previous research. Ethnic lesbians find themselves part of two minorities, each of which may reject the other. In ethnic communities, traditional values often result in hostility toward lesbian relationships (Hidalgo & Hidalgo-Christensen, 1976; Mays, 1980). Similarly, within the lesbian community, cultural insensitivity—or worse, racism—may lead to the exclusion of ethnic couples. Clearly, investigations of the relationships of minority lesbians are needed (Mays, 1980).

Many questions about lesbian relationships remain unanswered. For example, what impact do children have on lesbian relationships? How do the social support networks of lesbians affect the development of love relationships, and how do these networks respond when relationships end? What role do family ties play in lesbian relationships, especially for women from cultures where familial bonds are strong? What issues arise in lesbian couples where partners differ in race, religion, class, or age? What impact does social oppression have on lesbian relationships? What factors foster happiness and commitment in lesbian couples?

Most studies of lesbians have not focused specifically on relationships, and so we have had to gather relevant pieces of information as best we could. Research directly investigating lesbian relationships would be useful to lesbians themselves, and to relatives, friends, counselors, and others who want to understand lesbians' lives. We hope this review will soon become outdated as better research provides a more complete picture of the diversity of lesbian relationships.

NOTES

1. The percentage of lesbians currently in a steady relationship varies across studies: Bell and Weinberg (1978), 72 percent; Cotton (1975), 83 percent; Jay and Young (1977), 80 percent; Oberstone and Sukoneck (1977), 80 percent; Peplau et al. (1978), 61 percent; Raphael and Robinson (1980), 45 percent; and Schaefer (1976), 72 percent. These variations reflect differences in the wording of questions, the sampling procedures, the date of the research, and the lesbian populations themselves.

2. The average or median length of lesbians' current relationship varies across studies: Bell and Weinberg (1978), 1-3 years; Oberstone and Sukoneck (1977), 22 months; Peplau et al. (1978), 2.5 years; and Gundlach and Reiss (1968), 1-9 years.

3. Several studies have included a small proportion of older lesbians (Bell & Weinberg, 1978; Jay & Young, 1977; Saghir & Robins, 1973). Only one study (Raphael & Robinson, 1980) has explicitly focused on older lesbians.

4. An emphasis on emotional bonds in relationships is described by Bell and Weinberg (1978), Cotton (1975), Hidalgo and Hidalgo-Christensen (1976), Peplau et al. (1978), and Ramsey et al. (1978).

5. Studies investigating role-playing include Bass-Hass (1968), Bell and Weinberg (1978), Caldwell and Peplau (in press), Cardell et al. (in press), Cotton (1975), Gagnon and Simon (1973), Jay and Young (1977), Jensen (1974), Ponse (1980), Saghir and Robins (1973), Tanner (1978), and Wolf (1979).

6. Studies of sexual behavior include Bell and Weinberg (1978), Jay and Young (1977), Gundlach and Reiss (1968), Peplau et al. (1978), and Schaefer (1976).

7. The proportion of lesbians who have been heterosexually married varies across studies: Bell and Weinberg (1978), 35 percent; Gundlach and Reiss (1968), 29 percent; Saghir and Robins (1973), 25 percent; Schaefer (1976), 14 percent.

8. Data on orgasms are found in Bell and Weinberg (1978), Gundlach and Reiss (1968), Jay and Young (1977), Kinsey et al. (1953), and Masters and Johnson (1979).

9. Data on sexual frequency in lesbian relationships are found in Jay and Young (1977), Peplau et al. (1978), and Schaefer (1976).

10. Serial monogamy has been described by Cotton (1975), Peplau et al. (1978), Saghir and Robins (1973), Tanner (1978), and Wolf (1979). Exceptions to this pattern are discussed by Barnhart (1975), Bell and Weinberg (1978), Ettorre (1980), Jay and Young (1977), and Peplau et al. (1978).

· *22* ·

Everything in Its Place
The Coexistence of
Lesbianism and Motherhood

Ellen Lewin
Terrie A. Lyons

Being a mother, to me, being a mother is more consuming than any other way
that I could possibly imagine identifying myself. . . . I am a lesbian mother, I am
a working mother—mother hardly ever modifies any other thing. Mother is
always the primary—it's always some kind of mother, but it's never a mother-
anything. Mother is—mother, for mothers, is always the thing that is more
consuming. Because being a mother is so big, I have much more in common
with all mothers than I have in common with all lesbians. It's just so big. It starts
out as a 24-hour-a-day job, and it just goes on and on and on.

Secrecy has been a well-established part of the homosexual world for as
long as stigma has been attached to the expression of homoerotic preference (see Goffman, 1963; Ponse, 1977). Lesbians and gay men have traditionally avoided revealing their sexual orientation to outsiders, justly fearing
the hostility such disclosure might provoke, expressed in ostracism, loss of
employment, and sometimes physical violence. While the growth of the
homophile movements, and the more recent and more militant gay rights
and women's liberation movements, have made efforts to validate gay lifestyles and to convince the heterosexual majority that it has nothing to fear
from peaceful coexistence, only limited progress has been made toward
erasing the stereotypes and altering the prejudices which gay people regu-

Authors' Note: *The research reported in this chapter was carried out under NIMH Grant No.
MH30890.*

249

larly confront. The growth of these organizations, however, as well as that of other institutional supports (e.g., gay religious congregations, gay newspapers, gay mental health clinics) which offer homosexual men and women social support and a sense of community, have encouraged many to "come out of the closet"; and it is, of course, in the wake of this energetic wave of self-disclosure that volumes such as the present one find their audience.

Despite these efforts to gain wider recognition for and acceptance of the multitude of gay lifestyles, the lesbian mother continues to be a particularly invisible person. In part, this reflects the more general imbalance in knowledge about male as compared with female homosexuality; overall, homosexuality among women has less often been the subject of research than has male homosexuality (Hooker, 1972; Morin, 1976, 1977). The lesbian is defined not only by the public but by those who purport to study her primarily in terms of her sexuality and her emotional problems (Caprio, 1967; Cory, 1965; Kinsey et al., 1953; Saghir & Robins, 1973; Bell & Weinberg, 1978). This preoccupation has deterred attempts to study the whole person, her social situation, and the role of her sexuality in her larger social adaptation by concentrating research efforts on sexual practices, etiology, and "cures."[1]

Beyond these difficulties, a primarily sexual view of the lesbian and one which views such sexual definitions as fixed and immutable puts the lesbian mother in a theoretically impossible category. How, the average person wants to know, can a lesbian possibly be a mother? If heterosexual intercourse is the usual prerequisite for maternity, how is it possible for women who by definition do not engage in heterosexual behavior to be mothers? If motherhood is a state which requires the expression of nurturance and altruism, and the sacrifice of sexual fulfillment, how can a lesbian, a being thought to be oversexed, narcissistic, and pleasure-oriented, perform the maternal role? How can women who are "masculine," aggressive, and assumed to be confused about their gender be able to behave appropriately within its boundaries, or to assume the quintessentially womenly task of motherhood? If lesbians are women whose lives are organized in terms of the relentless pursuit of clandestine pleasures, if lesbians are women who behave as quasi-men and who have been poorly socialized into their gender roles, then how can they expect to provide adequate models of feminine behavior to their children, to prepare them for their own sexual and parental careers?

Before the recent publicity accorded to some lesbian mother custody cases (see Gibson, 1977) and the activities undertaken by lesbian and feminist organizations to publicize the existence of the lesbian mother and to gather support for her in her struggles with custody, lesbian motherhood did not seem to have presented itself to the minds of even the most sensitive investigators. Even when scholars have suggested that a more holistic view of the lesbian's (and gay man's) life might be in order, requiring an examination of family relationships, work, friendships, and other daily activities, lesbian motherhood has typically been overlooked. Gagnon and Simon (1973), for example, criticize previous descriptions of lesbians as being too preoccupied with sexual conduct, and remind their readers that lesbians' socialization to both sexuality and adulthood follows typical feminine lines and that lesbians, accordingly, organize their lives according to typically "female" patterns. They do not, however, mention lesbian motherhood at all.

Similarly, Bell and Weinberg (1978) collect some evidence of motherhood in the course of compiling demographic data on homosexuals in the San Francisco area, but they fail to investigate it further even in their section on "social adjustment," which takes up such issues as work, religion, politics, friendship, and social activities. In the same vein, their chapter on "social difficulties" focuses on the low incidence among women of problems known to be more pervasive among gay men, such as arrest, blackmail, and extortion; no discussion of loss of child custody and other family law problems appears. Although these findings indicate that lesbians organize their lives differently from men, so much is missing that similarities lesbians' lives bear to those of women in general are lost.

Bearing these problems in mind, it is appropriate at this point to consider how many lesbian mothers actually exist. The total population of lesbian mothers is unknown, and estimates range from 200,000 to 3,000,000 (Hoeffer, 1978; Martin & Lyon, 1972). All of these figures are, of necessity, highly speculative, and not just for the usual reasons—few people suspect mothers of being lesbian. Elsewhere in this volume (e.g., Chapter 3 by Paul and Weinrich) is considered the question of who is and is not a lesbian; answering this question definitively is beyond the scope of this book (see also Ponse, 1978).

SINGLE MOTHERS

If we assume that the majority of lesbian mothers are not currently living in a heterosexual marriage, then it is appropriate to consider the structural factors which govern their situation in the light of those which derive more generally from single motherhood.

Over the last two decades, the proportion of American families headed by women has increased dramatically and has been the subject of commentary from social and behavioral scientists, demographers, and those responsible for the planning of human services (Keniston, 1977; Ross & Sawhill,

1975). Despite widespread concern that female-headed households do not present the optimal conditions for child development (Wynn, 1964; Herzog & Sudia, 1970; Glueck & Glueck, 1962; Hoffman & Nye, 1974), the female-headed family with children has increased ten times faster than two-parent families during the past ten years (Waldman & Whitmore, 1974). In 1973, 6.6 million families with children under 18 were headed by women; the 9.2 million children living in female-headed households in that year represented a 76 percent increase over 1960 (U.S. Bureau of the Census, 1974).[2] According to Ross and Sawhill's figures for 1974, about two-thirds of all female-headed families include minor children (Ross & Sawhill, 1975, p. 13). Census figures for 1979 reveal that 17 percent of all families with children are now female-headed as compared to 9 percent in 1960 (U.S. Bureau of the Census, 1980). Since women move in and out of head-of-household status over time as a result of marital disruption, remarriage, departure of children from the home, and other life cycle changes, statistics on single-parent or female-headed households for any particular period may fail to reflect the broader impact of such families on the population as a whole. Current estimates are that four out of every ten children born in the 1970s will spend some portion of their childhood in a one-parent family, most likely one with a female head of household (Bane, 1976).

Single mothers, regardless of their sexual orientation, can be expected to face many of the same kinds of problems. Perhaps the most pervasive of these are economic, reflecting not only the fact that the poor are more likely to divorce (Ross & Sawhill, 1975) but also the economic consequences divorce has for women. Even women from middle-class backgrounds whose ex-husbands are relatively affluent may find themselves in diminished financial circumstances following divorce (Winston & Forsher, 1971; LeMasters, 1970). Ross and Sawhill cite a Wisconsin study which showed that within one year of divorce, 42 percent of fathers had made no court-ordered child support payments, and that after 10 years the percentage had risen to 79 percent (1975, p. 47). Other studies corroborate these findings (Citizens' Advisory Council, 1972) and also reveal that alimony payments, which figure prominently in the popular image of divorce, are in fact rarely awarded and even more rarely paid. A 1975 study commissioned by the International Women's Year Commission indicated that only 14 percent of divorced wives in America are awarded alimony and that fewer than half of these collect it regularly (Gates, 1977, p. 225). Mothers who have never been married, of course, are not eligible for even these precarious benefits.

While women's participation in the labor force has increased dramatically over the past three decades, and has grown most rapidly for mothers and married women (U.S. Department of Labor, 1975; U.S. Bureau of the Census, 1976), working mothers are unlikely to earn at a level approaching the standard of living provided by their former husbands (Kreps, 1971). Despite highly publicized efforts by feminists to improve opportunities for women in male-dominated occupations, women workers still tend to be clustered in traditionally "feminine" (and low-paid) clerical and service occupations (Lipman-Blumen, 1976, p. 69). Lipman-Blumen reports that the 1972 median annual income for female-headed families with children under 18 was $4,000, as compared with $11,600 for all families (1976, p. 88). In 1974, moreover, unemployment rates for female family heads were more than twice as high as those for husbands in husband-wife families (U.S. Department of Labor, 1975, p. 21). Besides reflecting pervasive occupational segregation, these discrepancies often result from the problems women experience in reentering the labor force, especially if they had been full-time homemakers (Gates, 1977). Further, the difficulty of obtaining adequate, affordable child care and help with homemaking duties often undermines women's ability to earn by limiting them to part-time and seasonal employment (Kreps, 1971). These problems can be particularly troublesome during summers and school vacations when the built-in child care provided by schools is no longer available and competition is intense for places in low-cost recreational programs.

Although female-headed families are now found at all income levels, the majority of poor families with minor children are headed by women (Ross & Sawhill, 1975, p. 15). In 1971, 45 percent of female-headed families had incomes below the poverty line. Despite the lengthy investigation process required to obtain welfare and the sparse income it provides, more and more families are taking advantage of AFDC benefits (Durban, 1975). In 1971, for example, 94 percent of eligible families participated in the Aid to Families with Dependent Children (AFDC) program (Ross & Sawhill, 1975, p. 103). While many of these cases reflect long-term reliance on public assistance, many welfare families are headed by single mothers who experience rapid downward mobility at the termination of their marriages. Women from middle-class backgrounds may receive support from their families, but this kind of dependence may foster interpersonal difficulties (Goode, 1956). Similarly, for those who do receive adequate child support or alimony payments, insecurity and anxiety may be the price of economic solvency. Spousal support (alimony) is now often awarded for a limited time to permit the mother to prepare herself for the job market; its temporary nature and the fact that it may be withdrawn capriciously by the ex-husband makes complete reliance on such support less than desirable.

These economic pressures not only limit single mothers' opportunities for financial security, but exacerbate already serious problems they may have in obtaining adequate housing. About two-thirds of poor, female-headed families live in central cities, where many occupy overcrowded, substandard housing (U.S. Department of Housing and Urban Development, 1976, p. 87). After divorce many mothers find that they must leave their homes, either because the house has been sold as part of the property division or because they find themselves unable to afford the costs once the husband is no longer the principal wage earner. For these families, purchase of a new home with conventional financing is likely to be out of the question, particularly as few divorcing women have established their own credit ratings. Renting, however, is also likely to be a problem, as many landlords are unwilling to rent to female-headed families or to people "on welfare" (U.S. Department of Housing and Urban Development, 1976, p. 88).

In general, then, the economic picture for formerly married mothers is one of downward mobility (Kriesberg, 1970), resulting not only from the reluctance or inability of the father to meet his obligations but also from a pervasive societal pattern of economic discrimination against women (Ferris, 1971). In fact, the opportunity structure for single mothers is so barren that acquiring a male household head is most frequently the most effective way for female-headed families to avoid poverty (Ross & Sawhill, 1975, p. 113). Not only do divorced mothers need to scale down their consumption to live within reduced incomes, but they often find that they must move into less costly housing in poorer neighborhoods, spend less time with their children, and in general subject their family situation to greater environmental pressures than they are used to managing (Brandwein, Brown, & Fox, 1974).

Exacerbating the material difficulties associated with economic distress is the problem of isolation. Many single mothers report that family headship means that they have little or no relief from constant responsibility for every aspect of family functioning (Weiss, 1975, 1979). These problems take several forms. Some mothers experience something that might be characterized as "role conflict" in which their responsibilities to their other areas of activity (e.g., employment) and personal commitments (e.g., sexual or romantic relationships) conflict with their maternal obligations. Others describe feelings of isolation deriving from having to make all family decisions and having no other responsible adult with whom to share the problems and joys of child rearing. Still others may encounter difficulties establishing and maintaining reliable systems of social support. Because married people tend to have married friends, separation may lead to the collapse of an individual's friendship network. Both men and women who end their marriages may find that their friendships "depended on their marital status as well as their particular interests or qualities" (Weiss, 1975, p. 153). Many separated women who go to work find that their new schedules preclude keeping up with old friends. In other cases, married people who experience divorce as threatening or anxiety-provoking may reject or avoid their divorced and separated friends (Bohannan, 1970; Hunt, 1966; A. Miller, 1970).

LESBIAN MOTHERS

When single mothers are also lesbians, they may face special problems forming social support systems. Despite a greater societal tolerance in recent years for sexual diversity, homosexuality is still severely stigmatized. Families that are aware of a member's homosexuality may experience shame and embarrassment; "coming out" to one's family, especially to one's parents, may result in a lengthy or even permanent break in relations (Martin & Lyon, 1972). The difficulty gay people experience disclosing their sexual orientation to their families is reflected both in its centrality as a conversational theme in gay social circles and in the development of psychotherapeutic approaches to helping families of homosexuals to resolve their conflicts (see Silverstein, 1977; Wirth, 1978). A common feature of these coming-out situations seems to be that the family feels discredited by the deviance of the child; parents may wish, accordingly, to keep knowledge of their child's homosexuality strictly secret so that they themselves do not suffer discrimination. Disclosure of sexual orientation, then, is likely to be particularly risky for the lesbian mother. Not only must she consider the personal difficulties she is likely to face with family, friends, and employers, but the possible harassment of her children also enters into decisions she makes about disclosure.

Most important, child custody may be problematic for lesbian mothers. Child custody settlements are never considered final (they may be challenged whenever a "material change in circumstances" is claimed), and because the purposefully vague standard of the "best interests of the child" forms the basis for custody determinations, judges are permitted a great deal more latitude and discretion than they are in other areas of the law. Nearly any kind of evidence may be considered by a judge in deciding with which parent (or party) to place a child and with what frequency and under what circumstance to permit or demand visitation (Hunter & Polikoff, 1976; Goldstein et al., 1973; Boggan et al., 1975; see also the chapters on legal issues in this volume).

When lesbianism is raised in a custody dispute, then, it tends to be considered sufficient evidence that the mother is an unfit parent, jeopardizing her claim to custody. Even when the grounds for denying custody to a lesbian mother do not rest on the presumption of immorality, she may expect revelation of her lifestyle to prompt fears that her children will grow up to be homosexual, unsure of their gender identity, or developmentally damaged. She may also encounter concern on the part of the court with the stigma which her children might experience because of her homosexuality, as the courts often justify removing children from the custody of lesbian mothers because of fears that the children would suffer from teasing and other forms of ridicule at the hands of their peers. These issues are especially likely to be raised when the mother's sexual orientation is relatively publicly known; in particular, publicity mothers may use to gain support for their cause is often seen as inappropriate and likely to expose the child to damaging notoriety (Hunter & Polikoff, 1976, pp. 700-701).

Beyond these concerns, however, decisions against lesbian mothers in custody disputes often seem to rest on the assumption that homosexuality cannot be combined successfully with the ongoing process of child rearing. The lesbian sexual relationship is implicitly viewed as competitive with or polluting of motherhood and likely to undermine the provision of proper maternal care. This view has led to a number of cases in which the lesbian mother was awarded custody, but only with the stipulation that she limit or terminate her relationship with her lover. The same assumptions, then, which contribute to the relative invisibility of the lesbian mother in the wider culture and in the scholarly literature also are involved in judicial decisions to deny custody to lesbian mothers or to award custody only under particular conditions.

It might be expected, then, that the special stigma with which homosexuals in our society are burdened and its economic and legal ramifications may create some adaptive differences between heterosexual and lesbian mothers whose situations do not differ greatly in other respects. Both heterosexuality and homosexuality potentially engage the individual in particular patterns of social relationships, and these, in turn, both modify the options open to mothers for meeting their various obligations, and affect the values and world view with which they organize their lives. Subjective feelings about stigma may have as profound an effect on the decisions made by both heterosexual and lesbian mothers as the "actual" experiences of discrimination they face. Further, both homosexual and heterosexual lifestyles may affect single mothers' adaptations by expanding or contracting access to relationships and networks which may help mothers meet their obligations as heads of families. Mothers of either orientation form sexual and affectional relationships, make choices about where they will live and with whom, maintaining or dissolving ties with kin, in-laws, friends, and neighbors, and participating in community, religious, political, or therapeutic activities.

In the research which we will describe in the following pages, we sought to explore the impact of both heterosexuality and homosexuality on the adaptations women make to single motherhood. Because the majority of single mothers are heads of families as a result of divorce or separation (Ross & Sawhill, 1975), and because custody disputes are more likely to arise in the course of marital dissolution and to be instituted by the father/former husband, we have concentrated on describing the situations of formerly married mothers. However, it should be noted that motherhood among women who have not married is on the rise in the United States (Ross &

Sawhill, 1975), both because of higher rates of teenage pregnancy and because of the growth of intentional single motherhood, and might be expected to give rise to somewhat different patterns than those which we will present.

METHODS

The research to be reported in this chapter was conducted in the greater San Francisco Bay area between August 1977 and July 1979 and is part of a four-year study of adaptive strategies employed by lesbian and heterosexual single mothers. Participants were located through personal and professional referrals, as well as through publicity carried out in the local media, feminist and women's publications, and newsletters published by child care and single-parent organizations. Notices were also posted in some child care centers, women's centers, bookstore, coffee houses, and bars.

Because one portion of the study population is a highly stigmatized group, obtaining a statistically representative sample of the lesbian mothers is not a realistic goal. Rather, we have made use of purposive sampling (D. Miller, 1964; Goode & Hatt, 1952), selecting informants so that the study population would be stratified by four major variables: sexual orientation, age of children, achieved socioeconomic status, and presence or absence of a coresident sexual partner.

This chapter reviews data gathered in interviews with 80 formerly married[3] mothers, 43 lesbians and 37 heterosexuals,[4] who have children ranging in age from 1 to 20 years. Approximately half of the lesbians and one-third of the heterosexuals have a coresident sexual partner. The mothers themselves range in age from 26 to 47, with a mean of 35.2 for the lesbians and 34.3 for the heterosexual women. The average family size is similar for both groups: 1.7 children for the lesbians and 1.8 for the heterosexuals, although the lesbians are more likely than the heterosexuals to have no more than one child in the family (51 percent of the lesbians and 41 percent of the heterosexuals have one child).

Although all of the mothers have been married, not all were legally divorced at the time of the interview. Among the lesbians, 32 (74 percent) are divorced, with 10 of the remaining women being informally separated from their husbands but still legally married. One lesbian mother's marriage had been annulled. The proportion of women who are legally divorced is greater among the heterosexuals: 31 women (or 83.8 percent) are divorced and only 6 separated from their husbands. None of the mothers in either group had obtained a legal separation prior to divorce.

Most mothers in both groups have legal custody of their children and live with them full-time. Among both groups, however, a small percentage (11.2

percent) have joint custody (five heterosexual and four lesbian mothers) and an even smaller percentage (3.7 percent) have paternal custody (one heterosexual and two lesbian mothers). These legal arrangements, however, are not necessarily directly mirrored by the living arrangements of the families involved: In a small number of cases the father took primary responsibility for some of the children and the mother for the others; in some other families, joint custody had been established despite the lack of a formal determination at the time of the divorce. In about 15 percent of the cases, mothers retain de facto custody of their children either in the absence of any legal arrangements (as when there has been no formal divorce action) or in contrast to the legal custody determination. Since our research concerned the situations of parents whose children lived with them, we limited our informants to those who have at least half-time physical custody of one or more minor children.

As socioeconomic status was one of the independent variables by which the sample was stratified,[5] mothers in the study represent three populations: those whose primary support comes from professional employment (N = 29), those employed nonprofessionally (N = 31), and those whose incomes derive principally from sources not involving employment (N =20). The actual occupations claimed by informants (although not all earned their livings at these) represent a wide range, from traditional women's work in clerical positions (nurses, teachers, librarians, waitresses) to relatively non-traditional work both in the professions (physicians, lawyers, college professors) and in blue-collar trades (gardeners, mechanics, bus drivers, construction workers). Included in the sample as well are a substantial number of self-employed (interior designers, advertising consultants, shopkeepers, self-employed typists, and carpenters). A number of the mothers describe themselves as students, and several of them attend school (either graduate or undergraduate) on a full-time basis. Nearly all of the participants in the study are white; there are two black and two Hispanic women among the lesbian informants. Most mothers who participated in the study are well educated: only 13.8 percent have educational levels lower than "some college." Looking at the sample as a whole, 28 percent had attended some college, 33 percent were college graduates, while some 26 had completed post-baccalaureate work, including five with doctoral and higher professional degrees. Lesbians and heterosexuals in the sample do not differ in their educational attainments.

In-depth, semi-structured interviews lasting between three and six hours were conducted with each mother, focusing primarily on the adaptive strategies pursued by the mothers and the influence of sexual orientation on the resources available to mothers and to the choices they make in using these resources. Although the interviews were conversational and were broadly structured by informants' life histories, each covered a similar range, concentrating on economic issues, interpersonal support systems, institutional support systems, and beliefs and values held by informants about their situations as single mothers. Particular attention was directed toward discussion of informants' relations with kin, lovers, friends, and ex-husbands; on their management of financial difficulties and role conflicts; and changes they perceive in their situations as mothers since the dissolution of their marriages. For the lesbians, the interview included some discussion of the degree to which they disclose their sexual orientation to others (relatives, co-workers, children, ex-husbands), and the ways in which they handle problems which they view as connected to the stigmatization of homosexuality.

VARIATIONS AMONG LESBIAN MOTHERS

The most important findings of this research are those which show overall similarities between lesbian and heterosexual mothers' adaptations to single parenthood and family headship. Both lesbian mothers and other single mothers identify themselves according to a variety of affiliations, including those provided by ethnicity, religion, occupation, social class, political ideology, and their status as mothers. While their lesbianism has been the characteristic that most captures the curiosity of outsiders, many lesbian mothers report that other aspects of their identity are more troublesome than their sexual orientation. For example, a Jewish informant, who had spent her formative years as a refugee, is more attuned to the difficulties which she had experienced as a Jew than those which might be caused by her homosexuality. Another lesbian mother, whose regular activities include active participation in two different religious groups and in a therapeutic self-help group, is more involved in the round of activities associated with these memberships than with anything that might be called the "gay life." Her friends reflect the eclectic nature of her interests, and comprise other members of the religious congregations and the self-help group, both of her ex-husbands, a heterosexual roommate (also a single mother), and several relatives (all heterosexual). A third mother, who works at a nontraditional blue-collar job with only male co-workers, finds herself more involved in trying to prove her skills as a woman in this all-male and somewhat hostile domain than with her status as a lesbian. Her work keeps her away from home for long and largely irregular hours and is the single most consistent organizing principle in her daily life. In the work environment, femaleness is her most salient identity and the one which her co-workers force her to consider at all times.

The variability lesbians exhibit with respect to the place of homosexuality in the organization of daily life is also reflected in the wide variety of personal "coming out" histories related during the interviews. While some of the lesbian mothers had their first homosexual experience prior to their marriage or while they were still married, about half said that their first relationship with a woman had taken place after the dissolution of the marriage. This suggests that other sources of identity, and particularly that of mother, are likely to have been well-established prior to entry into a homosexual lifestyle. Further, not all of the women participate in the activities of the "gay community"; many said that they rarely visit lesbian bars, do not belong to gay or lesbian organizations, and do not regularly attend lesbian cultural events, such as concerts, dances, and poetry readings. For some, these patterns are dictated by problems associated with obtaining child care or by financial difficulties. In many cases, however, the mothers indicate that these activities hold no intrinsic attraction for them.

SALIENCE OF MOTHERHOOD

The area of perhaps greatest commonality between lesbian and heterosexual mothers is found in their accounts of the salience of motherhood in their lives. Mothers in both groups report that motherhood influences the conduct of their lives in ways which generally overshadow the influences of other factors. One lesbian mother, who explained to the interviewer that most of her friends are single mothers, persons who understand the pressures and limitations of parenthood, was asked if these were limited to other lesbian mothers.

> No, I have friends that are straight mothers. The mothering thing, the thing about being a mother seems to be more important to me than my sexual orientation. . . . I just prefer being with people who have some sense of what it's like to be me, and I understand where they are, too.

While perusal of some of the more visionary feminist and lesbian literature might give rise to the expectation that lesbian and feminist single mothers have banded together throughout the country to support each other as parents and as women, many of the informants painted a rather different picture of the kind of community response they experienced. Some feel that women's centers, bookstores, coffeehouses, and feminist cultural events are generally insensitive, or even hostile, to mothers and their children and demonstrate this by failure to provide adequate child care facilities and other amenities, as well as by a lack of what might be called a welcoming attitude. One lesbian mother says that she rarely goes to feminist or women's events because of feeling that she is treated as an invisible person; the problem, as she experiences it, is less one of active hostility than "an absence of recognition."

Another lesbian mother described unsuccessful efforts to involve lesbians who are not mothers in activities with children, including developing a "big sister" role for such women. Her conclusions about the "lesbian community" ring with bitterness.

I think the lesbian community is organized around the single lifestyle only. I've heard more than a hundred times from a . . . lesbian—"I chose not to have kids, so don't push yours off on me." I have a lot of anger about it . . . real anger that they can't make a commitment to their kids—I mean, I consider them everybody's kids. . . . It really turns me against the lesbian community. I do nothing in the lesbian community now whatsoever.

Still another lesbian mother had had similar experiences at the meeting of a lesbian organization.

The mothers in the group were trying to get all the women to donate for child care expenses. And a lot of the women, one in particular that I remember, got up and said, "I don't ask you to pay for babysitting my dog, I'm not going to pay for babysitting your kid." . . . There's nothing you can say to a person like that.

These experiences are not limited to lesbians. One heterosexual mother, who works in a feminist publishing firm, spoke about her experiences with her all-women co-workers. Because of her responsibilities to her son, she has been unable to put in as many hours as her co-workers, none of whom had children, and found that they were not particularly sympathetic to her situation.

For a couple of years, people were working seven days a week and I simply couldn't do it. I felt that there was some lack of understanding as to that reality as there is often in many movements; there is a kind of divergence between what people espouse and what they're able to practice. And it was a struggle. I had been the only mother. And that was hard for me. . . . I guess that I have this kind of ironic sense that in many ways, men are more sympathetic of the plight of women who have children because they themselves often have children. I'm not sure that I ever believed the cliché that women are easier to work with than men as a class but I certainly know now that I don't think that's right.

SUPPORT FROM KIN

To the extent that they encounter barriers of this type between other women and themselves, both lesbian and heterosexual mothers tend to limit their dependence on community support and to rely more generally on the resources provided by immediate personal networks. Despite the expected tendency for the exposure of homosexuality to put considerable strain on family relations, both lesbian and heterosexual mothers depend heavily on close relatives, especially parents and siblings, as primary sources of social, emotional, and economic support. These ties are particularly central for mothers whose relatives provide daily child care or regular babysitting. For others, the connection with kin offers a sense of stability, an opportunity to continue family tradition, and emotional comfort.

One lesbian mother described the reestablishment of her relationship with her mother, which had been disrupted for a time after her mother learned of her homosexuality. Now, however, the relationship is close and characterized by mutual support. This informant sees her mother on the average of once a day. Her child goes to his grandmother's house each day after school and is cared for in the evenings by his grandmother. This relationship is maintained despite the fact that the grandmother refuses to visit the informant's house or to interact with her lover.

Another lesbian mother sees her parents as her most important source of support. Although they live on the east coast, she can send her child to them for extended visits and thus be able to take time off herself.

> I would always feel like, at this point anyway, that I could turn to them if something was going on for me, and they'd certainly do whatever they could to try and help me. . . . There's just some sense that they care about me, that to me is most helpful. I can really feel miserable and everything, and I always feel like well, I could go to my parents' and my mother will take care of me and cook for me and be glad I'm there.

Similar feelings are also expressed by a heterosexual mother who looks to her parents as a financial support and for help in times of crisis.

> They're very supportive. I could certainly ask them for money and they've given me money. . . . In fact, I have to tell them not to give me the money sometimes. . . . When John, my ex, was causing a lot of problems and threatening me and the kids, I left him and I went down there. So I have gone to them in crisis situations. . . . I can't think of anything I wouldn't ask them.

While considerable turmoil may be generated by the revelation of a mother's homosexuality to her family, most families described in the interviews seem to adjust to the situation after a period of time. One mother describes a period of several weeks during which her parents either refused to speak to her or harangued her on the phone, begging her to change her ways. After several weeks they relented, and asked her, in essence, to return to the fold.

> Once in a while it will come up, and we'll talk about it. It's real painful for them. They don't want to hear it. So most of the time I don't talk about it. . . . It's a

very tight family and my mother says that we can't disown you. We can be really sad and unhappy about what you're doing, and you are making a big mistake, but we love you and that's that.

The compromises mothers make with their parents are frequently linked to their relationships with the children. Although relatives are not the most common source of child care, they are used at least as often as older children and co-ops or babysitting exchanges, and are named at least as often by lesbian mothers as by heterosexuals as their first preference for child care. In the case just mentioned, for instance, the lesbian mother's parents and adult siblings took responsibility for almost all her child care and babysitting needs.

ROLE OF FRIENDSHIP TIES

Both lesbian and heterosexual mothers also place great emphasis on friendship ties as the foundation for important and reliable systems of social support. In most cases, the relationships are formed with other women, and frequently a requirement is that the friend also be a single mother. As one lesbian mother explained:

There is a difference between people who have children and people who don't have children. People who don't have children, to my way of thinking, are very selfish. . . . They needn't consider anyone other than themselves. They can do exactly what they want to do at any given time. And though I admire that, it's not possible for me to do that and I guess for that reason most of my friends are single mothers, because it's hard for me to coordinate my needs and my time with someone who's completely in a different head set.

Some mothers define these relationships primarily as emotional resources, with more instrumental tasks being handled through the kinship network or through the use of institutional facilities. Others describe friendships with one or two women with whom all manner of mutual exchange is carried out, with few limits or boundaries on the kinds of demands that might be made. Some of these are friendships that antedate the mothers' marriages and which continue to be viable despite the many changes in both friends' lives.

One heterosexual mother, for example, describes her friendship with other single mothers who live nearby.

There are a group of single women friends here in the neighborhood. . . . We do a lot for each other, in just needing somebody to get drunk on wine with, or jam with, date with, caring for the kids. Somebody to jog with in the morning. They're just there. There's no ceremony involved. You can call them up any time of the day or night, doesn't matter if they're entertaining or not. We basically have open house for each other constantly.

For other mothers, friendship involves assistance with child-rearing problems.

> I think we all feel like we participate in our kids' lives, because we all know that one parent isn't really enough. And we feel very comfortable disciplining each other's children, taking them on.

Friendships with other single mothers can also aid mothers in meeting a variety of instrumental needs; friends go to each other for assistance with the everyday emergencies that punctuate life—a broken-down car, an unexpected need for babysitting, small loans of money. Some women describe their friendships as providing a buffer against poverty, a kind of protection against the isolation that would otherwise characterize their situations. "None of us has everything we need, but as a group, we do. . . . So collectively our needs are met, but individually they wouldn't be."

While friendship with other women appears, as a consistent theme in the accounts both lesbian and heterosexual mothers give of their lives and the emotional resources that are important to them, such friendships are not necessarily to be relied on for ongoing, day-to-day assistance with the business of child rearing and family headship. Friendships with women appear to provide an emotional context within which the more individual duties of motherhood are carried out. For mothers who lack a partner, in particular, the opportunity to talk, to share ideas and feelings with another adult, and to gain perspective in the process is a vital need which friends—especially women friends—can fulfill. While these friends may be called on in emergencies, they are not used by mothers as the cornerstones of their support systems; typically, friends are either too busy with their own parental obligations to be the source of constant support or too insensitive to the needs of mothers because they don't have children of their own. Excessive reliance on friendship for constant assistance would not only yield an unreliable support system but would very likely place intolerable strains on the friendship itself.

INTIMATE RELATIONSHIPS

The presence of a coresident sexual partner has an important effect on the extent to which reliance on either kin or friends is central to a mother's adaptation. Among both lesbian and heterosexual mothers, lovers are generally expected to provide on-the-spot child care, to step in under emergency conditions as a substitute parent, and to share financial difficulties that might otherwise have been presented to family or friends for assistance. While some partners take on the role and responsibility of a coparent, some mothers among both lesbians and heterosexuals report conflicts between children and lovers, and sometimes between their perceptions of their roles as mothers and lovers.[6]

One lesbian, for example, described a series of extreme difficulties between her daughter and her lover of four years. The lover, she felt, was consistently hypercritical of the child and resentful of the time and energy the mother needed to devote to her. Another lesbian sees motherhood as virtually precluding the formation of intense affectional relationships.

> A lot of times I feel like I can't really have a relationship 'til she's 18 and out of the house. . . . You can't just take the mother; you've got to take the mother and the kid, too, in a relationship. That's two people to get along with, and it's hard enough to get along with one. I can't imagine anybody else coming into it.

Similarly, a number of heterosexual mothers feared that intimate relationships with men might hurt their children. Some are concerned that the child might experience a loss if the new relationship didn't work out and that this could be especially damaging in the wake of marital disruption. One heterosexual mother, for example, has avoided having men spend the night while her daughter is present and sees no way to reduce the conflict which the two levels of relationship present.

> Unless it's a relationship of substance and seriousness, there's no point in involving her in it. She can only stand to be hurt if she develops an attachment to the person.

For some mothers, the difficulties they encounter integrating a lover into the household with their children heighten feelings of isolation and discourage them from trying to establish romantic relationships. For others, no expectation of integration seems to exist; rather, they organize their lives so as to separate their sexual-emotional involvements from the daily conduct of their domestic lives. This solution appears to be workable for some of the heterosexual mothers who believe that the introduction of a man into the home would be particularly obtrusive and likely to engender anxiety in the children.

> For a long time, I wouldn't have a man sleep over when I was seeing someone, based largely on my sense that it was an unwarranted intrusion on Johnny, and didn't deserve to be done unless it was someone that I cared about that I felt comfortable doing it with. I think it's traumatic for a kid to have someone suddenly or to have a man suddenly in his mommy's bed. And it was.

Another put it this way:

> I don't feel that any of these men are going to be part of my life. I feel like they're diversions I need and . . . I treat them as friends, but for me to talk to my son about them would have to mean that I have a commitment to some man, and I've never felt that with these three or four people.

One mother described the difficulties she encountered when her boyfriend moved in.

> It was a lot of hard times, but I realized it was a period of adjustment, to live with somebody. And it was harder on him, to adjust to living with three kids and somebody else. . . . He was feeling a lot of pressure. He wasn't accustomed to having to devote so much time to a family. . . . Finally he just decided it was too much, he didn't want to handle it, he didn't want to live here.

Lesbian mothers also felt that their relationships with their children placed a strain on intimacy and sometimes undermined the relationship with the lover.

> From the very beginning it was not too good. My lover . . . just was not into it. She was not into having a child around, and she really resented the energy I had to put into my daughter. That was sad . . . I would have liked for her to put some energy into raising her, you know. Some positive energy. But she didn't put any positive energy into it, for four years.

This relationship finally broke up, leaving the mother with this resolution.

> I will never live with anybody again that doesn't have their own relationship with her aside from me. . . . Those were terrible, awful, painful years. It was very painful for me to put myself out as a mother, to really try and get across how oppressed I feel to be a mother, and how hard it is to be a mother, and how hard it is to do it alone, and still get shit from a person that I want to get support from.

While the presence of a live-in lover reduces the extent to which both lesbian and heterosexual mothers see their families as their primary line of defense against financial disaster, lovers are not necessarily expected to assume parental responsibilities if the mother becomes ill or cannot carry out her maternal duties for some other reason. Although many mothers say that they would leave their lover in charge of the children in the event that they were not able to meet their responsibilities, a substantial number prefer to assign this duty to the relatives or to the children's father. This hesitancy to cast the lover fully in the role of coparent suggests that this level of obligation might place an intolerable burden on the romantic connection, threatening not only the continuation of this relationship but the fulfillment of the mother's expectations for the care of her children.

It should be noted here that heterosexual relationships which appear to be successful and in which a satisfactory coparenting role has been assumed by the lover are likely, at least in our sample, to move in the direction of legal marriage after a relatively short period of coresidence. Since this particular way of legitimizing a relationship is not, of course, available to lesbians, it's difficult to determine whether expressions of long-term commitment put forth by homosexual informants constitute equivalent behavior. In one lesbian family interviewed, in which two lesbian mothers have been living together for ten years, both mothers maintain that they refer to all the children as "ours" and make no distinctions between the children in terms of decision-making and discipline. They distinguish themselves from a stereotypical married couple in that no specific, sex-typed roles are reserved for either of them, although a relatively consistent division of labor does characterize their organization of household tasks. Other lesbian informants describe their situations in ways which emphasize the value placed on permanence, fidelity, and planning for the family's economic future (e.g., joint investment, buying a house, owning insurance). Only a few of these adopt the language of conventional relationships in attaching the label of "marriage" to committed relationships.

RELATIONSHIPS WITH EX-HUSBANDS

Although the formerly married are unlikely to count their former husbands among their closest associates, both lesbian and heterosexual mothers in our study seek to strengthen the children's relationships with their fathers. Often, these efforts are made despite ongoing displays of disinterest on the part of the fathers. Some of the mothers report that their ex-husbands are unwilling to schedule regular visitation, forget children's birthdays, call the children in the middle of the night, and behave in other ways which suggest to the mothers that their feelings for the children are, at best, ambivalent.

Interviewer: So he could visit if he wanted to?

Informant: Yeah. But he chooses not to. It's kind of weird, 'cause he always felt that his father only gave money and never really was there for him. . . . And it wound up that in his case, it's the most blatant of that that you could possibly be. All he does is give money, in his case.

Maintaining connections with the children's father may be especially troublesome when he has remarried and has a second family.

> George has evidently adopted his new wife's kid. He's just taken on this whole new family, and I feel his kids—my kids—have gotten real short shrift. . . . It's turned out that these two weekends a month originally agreed upon have become about one weekend a month. . . . If somebody doesn't want to see his kids, you can't really make him.

Despite these difficulties, most of the mothers in both groups continue to be firm believers in the importance of male role models in child development, and most expect their ex-husbands to be a central source of such modeling for the children. While heterosexual mothers may also consider boyfriends and other men of their acquaintance capable of providing the image of adult maleness they think their children need, lesbian mothers may not have access to very many men. They are most likely, then, to rely on the ex-husband to perform this function, even when relations with him are particularly strained. Their belief that children need some amount of contact with an adult male, and especially with their father, if they are to develop successfully militates against their individual need to reduce contact that may be personally stressful.

> Were it not for the money and the child support thing, I probably would have really told him off a long time ago—just told him to go jump, and it would be fine if I didn't see him again, ever, or hear from him again, ever. But with the kids, I don't feel like I can do that. I know that I maintain a certain kind of pleasantness, probably with an edge to it, because he's totally capable of never paying another cent. That, in some ways, is the only tie the kids have. They're able to say, well, sure he cares about us—look. You know? And I don't want to be responsible for severing that line.

Even for heterosexual mothers, however, the presence of another adult male who can provide a masculine image does not diminish the mother's emphasis on the maintenance of a relationship between the children and their father. One mother describes her boyfriend's relationship with her son:

> He's a surrogate father. In fact, he's really spent more time with Mike than his real father has, in terms of we have him for nine months and his dad gets him for three months. But I think—it just seems to me like to blood ties—it's really amazing, the blood tie business. No matter how much time is spent, the real father is the father. All that's saying that no matter what, I think Paul will always be second. He will not be the real father.

The emphasis placed on fortifying the relationship between the children and their fathers persists among most of the mothers, both lesbian and heterosexual, despite the difficulties they experience obtaining child support payments from their former husbands. Besides those who report erratic and late payments of court-ordered support, several women receive no financial assistance of any kind.[7] Although child support is not generally their sole or primary source of income, it may make the difference between bare subsistence and the ability to meet some of the special needs children have, especially as they grow into adolescence. Mothers in the study frequently report, for example, that the amount of child support originally awarded remains the same despite inflation and the changing demands older children make on family finances. Many are quite sympathetic to the difficulties their ex-husbands face in meeting their obligations and accept the assignment of primary financial responsibility to themselves. They view the husband's new obligations as legitimately diminishing the extent to which he should remain responsible for the financial welfare of his children. Others, however, fail to share this sympathy and speak bitterly of their inability to combat what they view as paternal capriciousness. Nevertheless, they are often unwilling to demand more money because of the legal expenses and complications involved or because they believe it is virtually impossible to collect because of the way the husband has manipulated his finances.

Despite the financial hardships they face, however, they generally continue to encourage the children's contact with their father. This contact may be achieved in many instances, but not without difficulties for the mother.

> If he has a headache, the kids come home. If one of the children has the sniffles, the kids come home. He puts up with the fun, but he doesn't quite know how to handle the inconvenience.

THREATS TO CHILD CUSTODY

The legal difficulties they might encounter are not the only reasons mothers fail to seek legal remedies for child support problems. Many fear that such action might prompt a child custody challenge or some other form of retaliation on the part of the ex-husband. This fear is particularly acute for lesbian mothers, as reviewed earlier in this chapter. We found this fear to be common among the lesbian mothers in our sample. One mother, for example, whose ex-husband had shown no interest in his son since the divorce settlement, said she still worries about his challenging custody: "I'm always concerned, it's always in the back of my mind, that he's going to want to go back to court for custody." Another lesbian mother agreed to a property settlement which involved dividing the equity in the family home equally, despite the fact that nearly the entire purchase amount had come from her own funds. Looking back on the financial aspects of her divorce she said: "I think I would have done much better if I hadn't been afraid of the lesbian issue. . . . I traded my equity in the house for that issue not being raised at the time."

For some mothers, the need to balance their fear of exposure against their commitment to provide paternal interaction for their children leads to contradictory situations. One lesbian mother, for example, has accepted her ex-husband's offer of daily babysitting in her home while he is unemployed and she is working. While the arrangement provides the child with an opportunity for extensive contact with his father, it also severely compromises the mother's need for privacy. This mother is extremely secretive about her lesbianism, keeping the information not only from the ex-husband but also from her child, and confining her social interactions with other lesbians to contacts outside her home. She is resigned to having to forego serious intimate involvements with women until after her child is grown and the threat of custody litigation is less intimidating.

These anxieties are not limited to lesbians. Heterosexual mothers who have experienced custody litigation are likely to be extremely cautious in the way they interact with their ex-husbands, and they, too, may compromise their economic interests to assure them freedom from legal difficulties. One heterosexual mother who had already been through a custody battle with her former husband said she cannot discuss problems she has with the children with their father.

> When I do present problems to him, he points out what I'm doing wrong. And it makes me feel that he's gathering evidence for another custody suit. He will reveal nothing of what he perceives as problems to me. So we don't communicate at all. . . . My happiness I want to share as much as the problems, and it makes me sad that I can't share that with him. But there's too much of a wall of bitterness to talk about us sharing the good things about our kids.

While lesbian mothers may believe themselves more vulnerable to custody challenges, and may, in fact, stand a poorer chance of winning custody if their sexual orientation is brought out in court, heterosexual mothers who face such litigation are likely to adopt similar strategies for protecting themselves from scrutiny. Further, in view of the tendency of recent custody decisions to show less preference for the mother as custodial parent than was the case in the past (Derdeyn, 1976; Watson, 1969), mothers of either sexual orientation are realistic when they assess their chances of retaining custody after a challenge as poor. Mothers' desires, moreover, to promote a durable relationship between their former husband and their children undermine their ability to challenge arrangements which deprive them of resources to which they are legally entitled.

CONCLUSIONS

Our research suggests that single motherhood among both lesbians and heterosexuals gives rise to a single adaptive system, one which is unified by the salience of motherhood as a central organizing force. Despite mothers' tendencies to identify their difficulties as aspects of their particular situations, the interview data reveal a more general and pervasive pattern of conflict between maternal and other aspects of the women's lives. These are resolved, in most instances, in a manner which enhances maternal performance but which may lead to the sacrifice of personal goals. In some cases, for example, the desire to encourage the formation of a relationship between her ex-husband and her children may lead a mother to compromise her financial needs and to moderate her criticisms of paternal capriciousness in the payment of child support and other benefits. Helping children to maintain an ongoing connection with their father may also require a mother to forego the need to terminate her own relationship with him, and thus undermine, in essence, the finality of their divorce.[8]

In other cases, the mother may postpone or altogether sacrifice the formation of intimate relationships unless a partner can be found who can be harmoniously integrated into her family. Some lesbian and heterosexual mothers in our study have overcome this problem, establishing supportive intimate relationships and building these into the ongoing family system; others, however, have not found lovers to be sources of reliable support. Although it cannot be said that lesbian and heterosexual liaisons should be considered similar in every respect, it appears that their readiness to be integrated into single-mother families and their ability to provide regular social, economic, and emotional support may be subject to parallel stresses.

These difficulties have similar consequences for both homosexual and heterosexual mothers. Within both groups there are women who perceive single motherhood to be fundamentally lonely, isolated, and unlikely to provide them with recognition for their successes in raising children outside of the supports traditionally supplied by the nuclear family. While most also feel that they are competent at their maternal tasks and that they can rightfully be proud of their ability to overcome obstacles, many describe feeling overwhelmed by their obligations and regret that they must acquit their responsibilities in solitude. Friendship and lover relationships sometimes provide support for mothers, but there is nothing about the structure of either homosexual or heterosexual networks that assures either success or failure in these attempts. It seems, in addition, that in the absence of a solitary, coresidential lover relationship, a network of friends who share similar parental obligations will come to play a central role in mothers' support systems.

For both lesbian and heterosexual mothers, however, the difficulty of establishing such reliable sources of support increases the importance of kinship-based relationships and even leads to an emphasis on continuing ties with the former husband. It is those who have a direct kinship to a mother's children that are likely to be judged reliable and most worthy of trust.

Our research indicates that while homosexuality may be a significant aspect of a lesbian mother's identity, her obligations to her children are likely to overshadow its expression and to mitigate the degree to which she sees her homosexuality as distinguishing her fate from that of other single mothers. Although a substantial proportion of the lesbian population are mothers, lesbian communities and lifestyles do not generally present features that encourage lesbians to adapt distinctively to single parenthood. Rather, it is motherhood that alters women's experience of homosexuality, providing a matrix within which other dimensions of identity are structured.

These findings not only inform us about the complex motivations and pressures which enter into the ongoing adaptations of lesbian mothers, but they suggest that new strategies for the study of homosexuality must be developed. Just as homosexuality does not provide the central, or single, driving force behind the organization of lesbian mothers' lives, neither can information about sexual orientation or sexuality provide definitive understanding of the wide variety of behavior that appears among homosexual individuals. Researchers need to consider the wide range of social, economic, cultural, intrapsychic, and situational factors which intersect with sexuality and sexual orientation to produce particular behavioral and experiential patterns. By building a more holistic and dynamic framework for the study of homosexuality, we may begin as well to understand the larger issue of the relationship between the sexual and nonsexual dimensions of human life and thus place homosexuality in its most meaningful human context.

NOTES

1. A further problem derived from a primarily sexual view of the lesbian has emerged in the area of research design: Most studies do not even attempt to control for socioeconomic status, employment, or marital/relationship status in matching homosexual subjects with heterosexual controls (see Adelman, 1977, for a noteworthy exception).

2. Ross and Sawhill (1975, pp. 14ff) analyze demographic data on the female-headed family and demonstrate that, despite the recent rise in illegitimate births, marital disruption due to divorce or separation is the primary source of female family headship. Rising divorce rates have paralleled falling death rates, so that a decreasing proportion of female family heads are widows.

3. The women in the study had all been legally married to the father of their first child when they conceived or gave birth. Inclusion in the sample required that they be divorced or separated and no longer living with the ex-husband for a minimum of one year prior to the interview. Some women had subsequent offspring through other unions, whether legal or consensual.

4. Individuals chosen for interviews identified themselves as either lesbian/homosexual or heterosexual, and either had had sexual relationships of the corresponding type during the past year or expressed a preference for same-sex or opposite-sex partners in the event they began a relationship. Persons who labeled themselves bisexual or who rejected all labels were excluded from the sample, as were those whose stated sexual behavior directly contradicted the sexual orientation label they had selected.

5. Because conventional measures of socioeconomic status are more applicable to men than to women, the investigator devised a measure of SES that would be more appropriate for women and would further the research goals of the project. Each potential participant was asked both her occupation and her primary source of income. Informants were then categorized according to (a) whether or not their income was derived primarily from earnings or from funds paid by other persons/agencies (e.g., AFDC, child support, spousal support, investment income) or (b) if income was derived mainly from earnings, whether the work involved was professional (including the so-called semiprofessions, high-level managerial work, and the arts) or nonprofessional (including service, clerical, sales, and blue-collar employment). These measures were used to provide a sample that would include women dependent on a potentially capricious source of income, women whose work involved relatively high levels of commitment, and women whose incomes came from work requiring less training and less personal commitment. Although this measure did permit segregation of informants into relatively discrete subgroups, some women were difficult to categorize, either because they did several different kinds of work or because particular kinds of work could be interpreted as either professional or nonprofessional.

6. These difficulties are similar to those which have been reported for stepparents (Bernard, 1971).

7. Recall from the literature review at the beginning of this chapter that fathers tend to be extremely unreliable in meeting their child support obligations.

8. Joint custody arrangements very likely intensify these conflicts by structuring a high degree of continuing interaction into the relationship between former spouses; on the other hand, by decreasing the emphasis in these divorces on mutually exclusive assignment of custody and child support, the potential for serious conflict may be reduced (see Roman & Haddad, 1978).

• 23 •

Children of Lesbian Mothers

Mary E. Hotvedt
Jane Barclay Mandel

During this decade the American public's awareness of the diversity of family units in our society increased greatly. The family unit consisting of a lesbian mother, her children, and her female partner has come to the public's attention primarily as a result of publicity given to child custody cases. The issues raised by the courts in such custody trials have implications which reach far beyond the particular features of an individual case. They encompass questions about the sources of adult sexual orientation, the criteria by which adequate parenting should be evaluated, and the constitutional issue of a parent's rights to raise children according to her/his own values.

The family court which handles custody discussions has typically raised several issues in the case of lesbian mothers and their children; these cases are more numerous than those involving gay fathers. The standard view of the court has been that merely being a lesbian renders a mother unfit, and that it is therefore "in the best interest of the child" to remove the child or children from a lesbian mother's home. In states where homosexual behavior is still against the law, an avowed homosexual has admitted to a felony, which means that fitness as a parent is severely compromised.

Anti-homosexual spokespersons have even contended that homosexuals are child molesters, even though reputable studies show that only a minuscule fraction of sexual assaults on children are committed by women or by homosexual males. If homosexuality is not illegal (as is the case in 20 states having adopted "consenting adults" legislation), homosexuality may still be viewed as immoral according to Judeo-Christian teachings. The

275

family court judge may believe this "immorality" generalizes to all aspects of living and therefore renders the homosexual parent unfit.

In cases where a parent's homosexuality is discussed in the courtroom, or in cases where pains have been taken to ascertain the psychological and emotional status of the children as well as of the parents in making the custody decision, the issues are more specifically drawn: Will a parent's sexual interests overshadow his/her concern for the child so that actual physical, emotional, and intellectual neglect will occur? Will the child be stigmatized by his/her peers for having a homosexual parent? Will the child, due to exposure to an atypical parent and friends, have an inappropriate sex role orientation (i.e., a boy being "feminine," and girl "masculine")? Will the child also adopt a homosexual orientation?

The purposes of this chapter are to review literature pertinent to the issues of child custody concerns and to report in greater depth on research projects involving lesbian mothers and their prepubescent children. The custody rights of gay fathers are also pertinent, but to date the professional literature contains only a few articles of anecdotal nature (Babuscio, 1976; Clark, 1977; Mager, 1975) and only two research studies (Miller, 1979; Bozett, 1980) about them. Both studies used in-depth interviews with fathers to investigate the issue of "coming out" to children. Miller (1979) also interviewed 14 children (ages 14-33) who knew their fathers' sexual orientation. Miller's data indicate that the gay fathers did not practice child molestation, subject their children to social harassment, or raise them to be homosexual. There is still a need for research parallel to the lesbian mother studies, looking at the whole process of the child's development in a gay father's household and comparing that with heterosexual single-father families. Putting together a sample could be difficult, because the courts still do not commonly award child custody to fathers, and the prejudice against gay fathers can prevent them from keeping visitation rights—much less obtaining custody. While the number of households headed by gay fathers is probably much smaller than those headed by lesbian mothers, the assumptions about unfitness to parent are the same and therefore need to be examined scientifically.

In order to assess the impact on children of being raised by a mother whose sexual orientation is homosexual, we must examine several areas of research. A majority of children of lesbian mothers are also children who have experienced a parental divorce, so we must turn to the literature on the effects of divorce and father absence on children and examine this carefully, so that we do not confuse the effect of divorce, for example, with the effects of the mother's sexual orientation. We will also review studies of children being raised in households with a parent of atypical sexual orientation—research on families headed by lesbian mothers.

DIVORCE, FATHER ABSENCE,
AND CHILDREN'S ADJUSTMENT

Father Absence

Prior to the mid-1970's, research on children of divorced parents centered on the effects of father absence, rather than on the impact of the divorce itself. Furthermore, the social climate of the 1950s and 1960s (when many of the data were collected) was such that strong sex role differentiation in marriage was still the predominant pattern, with fathers as breadwinners and mothers as housewives. Much of the research has been directed toward discovering the father's role in the development of the child's sex role orientation, intellectual development, and social maturation.

What do these studies tell us? By far the majority of studies on the effect of father absence have focused on the effects on male children. In a review of 60 studies which met minimal research criteria, Herzog and Sudia (1970) summarized the effects of father absence on masculine identity as the failure of the male children to develop an adequate sense of their own masculinity, resulting in feminization, sex role "confusion," or overcompensation leading to extreme aggressiveness and delinquent behavior.

Green (1976) noted that 40 percent of his sample of boys exhibiting extreme feminine behavior were separated from their biological fathers before their fifth birthday. For boys, father absence has also been related to poor peer group relationships (Mitchell & Wilson, 1967; Lynn & Sawrey, 1959) or to overdependence on peers in adolescence (Hetherington, 1966).

Studies exploring the effects of father absence on girls are few. By far the most thorough research in this area is that of Hetherington (1972). Girls from families whose fathers were absent as a result of death or divorce were unable to relate in a trusting and comfortable manner to men and male peers. Age at onset of heterosexual activities was also affected. No differences were found between father-absent and father-present girls in sex role preference or femininity.

Summarizing the literature on the effects of father absence, boys show changes in masculinity, aggression, competitiveness, and physical activity. The boys' peer relations may also be affected. The female child may be unable to engage in trusting relationships with males, and may be more dependent on her mother; however, her femininity does not seem to be affected. The earlier in the life of the child and the more prolonged the absence of the father, the more likely that the child (especially the male) will experience adjustment problems.

Divorce

Some researchers have studied the process of divorce (most particularly the first two years after separation) on family functioning. The effects of divorce on specific age groups of children have also been researched. However, there are still relatively few studies of these areas, given the magnitude of the phenomenon. It has been estimated that 25-30 percent of all American children born in this century have experienced a separation or divorce, and that the projected figure for the next few decades is 40 percent (Bane, 1976).

In a clinical study of children from divorced homes, McDermott (1970) found that the children commonly went through a period of depression after their parents separated. Custody battles worsened behavioral and emotional problems for some children. Hetherington, Cox, and Cox (1976) have reported that few of the parents in their study were prepared for the family traumas experienced after divorce. They had assumed that the most stressful period would be over with the actual separation. Within the first year after divorce, commonly reported problems were children's increased disobedience, less affection between parents and children, and parents' sense of loss of control. After two years, problems (as perceived by both children and adults) had decreased. However, mothers of boys "at the end of two years are feeling less competent, more anxious and angry . . . than married mothers or divorced mothers of girls." Hetherington et al. found that after two years, many divorced families still had disturbed parent-child relations when compared to intact families; however, many parents reported better parent-child relationships than prior to the divorce. Initially after divorce, father-child contact may increase, but it declined steadily over the two-year period during which their families were followed.

Wallerstein and Kelly (1974, 1976) investigated the effects of divorce on different age groups of children, interviewing their subjects at the time of divorce and a year later. In preadolescent school-age groups, half the children reported that their personal problems about the divorce had decreased. The other children had begun to show signs of phobias and delinquency and continued to be depressed. All the preadolescents had a hard time juggling good relationships with both parents. Even among the better-adjusted children, bitterness over the divorce and nostalgia for the old family form were common (Wallerstein & Kelly, 1976). Adolescents, on the other hand, went through this most difficult period at the time their parents divorced. For the most part, their feelings improved within the year, adjusting in proportion to their personal independence from their parents. However, teenagers who had gone through their preadolescence in a stressful household had more difficulty adjusting to a later divorce (Wallerstein & Kelly, 1974).

Studies of children in divorced households, then, indicate that the effects of parents' separations are manifested somewhat differently in boys and girls and in different age groups. Also, the emotional and behavioral effects are longer lasting for some, although the first year is traumatic for parents and children alike.

As we begin to review the studies concerning lesbian mother households and comparative groups of heterosexual single-mother-headed families, we will note similarities and differences in the divorce experience for the two groups. We will also indicate whether or not the children in those studies exhibit the effects of father absence as seen in earlier research.

STUDIES OF LESBIAN MOTHERS AND THEIR CHILDREN

Until recently, very few studies of homosexual parents existed in the scientific literature. The earliest reports of homosexual women raising children are anecdotal, ranging from Martin and Lyon's (1972) description of lesbian mothers to case reports in the psychiatric literature. These accounts are general or individual histories of lesbian mothers, emphasizing the mother's concern about when and how much she should disclose about her lifestyle to her children, her concerns about losing custody of her children, and questions about the impact of father absence.

Pagelow (1976) compared lesbian mothers with heterosexual mothers in urban areas. The study focused on the problems encountered in custody, child rearing, housing, and employment. All subjects, both heterosexual and homosexual, indicated problems on all four issues, but lesbian mothers reported special difficulties resulting from societal attitudes toward homosexuality. They also showed counterbalancing behaviors, such as relatively higher levels of self-reliance than the heterosexual controls, particularly in financial matters.

Lewis (1977) reported on a study of 21 children of homosexual mothers ranging in age from 9 to 26 years. She concluded from the interview data that emotional difficulties and communication problems occurring in the family unit were the major source of stress for family members and that concerns about the mother's sexual orientation were secondary. Lewis found that older adolescent boys reacted most negatively to their mother's homosexuality.

One report in the psychiatric literature (Weeks, Derdeyn, & Langman, 1975) reported on two disturbed adolescents, each of whom had homosexual parents. The authors' conclusion was that the children's conflicts resulted more from the difficulties of divorce than from reactions to their parents' sexual preference.

Green (1978) reported on the examination of 35 children of sexually atypical parents, 21 of whom were being raised by lesbian women. His conclusion, based on interview data with parents and children and children's responses on tests that have shown gender identity and sex role preference, indicated that 20 of 21 children had no gender identity problems. All of the children showed clear, typical sex role preferences and, in the case of adolescent and older children, reported romantic interest in opposite-sex peers. No control group was used.

In one of the few studies using a carefully matched control group, Kirkpatrick, Smith, and Roy (1981) tested matched samples of 20 children of lesbian single mothers and 20 children of single heterosexual mothers. There were 10 boys and 10 girls aged 5-12 in each group. This study found that none of their measures was able to differentiate the two groups of children, although children in each group did exhibit emotional conflicts typical of children of divorce. Interviews and testing of the children were conducted by a child psychiatrist and child psychologist, who were unaware of the type of family to which the children belonged. Neither the playroom interview nor psychological tests given to assess the degree of pathology in the children could distinguish between groups.

Another important study has already been reported in this volume. In the previous chapter, Lewin and Lyons described their study of 80 previously married mothers (homosexual and heterosexual) from the San Francisco area. The main focus of their research has been the ways in which women adapt to single motherhood and how, if at all, sexual orientation differentiates adaptive strategies.

In a preliminary report on a study of single mothers with preadolescent children (Mandel & Hotvedt, 1980), data from a sample of 50 lesbian mothers and their 58 children (aged 3-11) were compared with responses from a matched group of 20 heterosexual single mothers and their 25 children. Major emphasis of the study was on the psychosocial adjustment of the children, including assessment of their gender identity/sex role orientation. Data were also gathered on the mothers' experiences of single parenting and on their own role orientation.

METHODS

Participants in the study were from ten states in the Northeast, Midwest and South; families from both rural and urban areas in those states were visited at home by the researchers. For inclusion in the lesbian sample, women had to be self-designated as homosexual, have custody or joint custody of at least one child between ages 3 and 11, and have been living with no adult male in the home for at least two years. This last criterion allowed some control for assessing the effects of father (or father substitute) absence.

The heterosexual matches were collected from approximately 500 responses to requests for single-mother subjects. A heterosexual mother and her family were matched to a lesbian mother and her family on age (±5 years) and race of mother, age and sex of children, length of time separated from father, marital status of mother (never married, divorced, separated, widowed), income level of family, educational level of mother, and (when possible) mother's religion of upbringing.

All adult subjects were white women aged 25-46 at the time of interview who had been living as single parents for at least two years, with a mean of 4-5 years. While the majority (88 percent homosexuals and 88 percent controls) were separated or divorced, three unmatched homosexuals were widowed, and 10 percent in both samples were never married.

Income and occupation ranged from unemployed women on welfare to professional women earning \$1200-\$2000 per month. The majority worked full-time for substantially less (median = \$500-\$850/month). Education ranged from grade school to graduate degrees; most subjects completed at least one year of college.

Each accepted adult filled out questionnaires and attitude scales pertaining to her parenting experiences, upbringing, marital and relationship patterns, and attitudes toward divorce, sex roles, sex education for children, and discipline. Personality scales such as the Bem Sex Role Inventory and Jackson PRF were also included. An audio-taped interview with each mother was made. The interview reviewed the material from the questionnaires, adding depth to several areas, and included a sexual history of the mother.

Children were interviewed and tested in the home. The battery included the WPPSI or WISC-R; several tests for sex-role behavior and gender identity, including instruments developed by Green (1974); the Bene-Anthony Family Relations Test; and interviews on play preferences, friendships, television habits, and thoughts about their own adulthood. A child was not asked to discuss his/her mother's sexual identity or his/her own reaction to mother's marital status.

RESULTS

The study was designed to test several of the specific issues brought up in lesbian mother custody cases, as well as to look at the effects of father absence and divorce on children. In order to interpret the social relevance of the data, we present the preliminary findings of the study and of others' research in response to those issues.

Will a mother's sexual orientation, the pursuit of her lifestyle, result in neglect of her child? The data from the study support the findings of Lewin and Lyons that there are more similarities than differences between homosexual and heterosexual single mothers' experiences, and that motherhood is the central theme in their lives.

Field notes were used to make some observations on attention given to children in their homes. No evidence of neglect or child abuse was seen. To the contrary, despite serious income restrictions in many families which affect the size and furnishing of homes, the children always had pleasant rooms. In several homes this meant the mother slept in the living room, giving up some of her own privacy for her child's sake. Children were anxious to show their room and favorite toys. Research dates were planned around numerous extracurricular activities such as dance and music lessons, sports events, and tutoring.

The majority of children spent 25 percent or less of their time with their fathers. Field observations showed that generally positive feelings were expressed toward fathers during the child interviews. Negative feelings toward fathers were centered on perceptions of a few fathers' disinterest because of inconsistency of visitation or broken promises about time together.

Will the child have poor peer group relationships because of mother's sexual orientation? Children in the study were asked who their best and second best friends were. There were no significant differences in sex of child chosen, the majority of children choosing same-sex best friends. They were also asked their impression of their popularity both at school and in the neighborhood with children of their sex and of the opposite sex. Some of these items differentiated the female children. In the preliminary report, daughters of lesbian mothers rated themselves more popular with other girls both in the neighborhood and at school, as well as with boys in the neighborhood, than did the daughters of heterosexual mothers. No differences were found between the two groups of sons' self-ratings of popularity with other boys and girls.

Will the child have a confused gender identity or sex role orientation because of mother's sexual orientation? Traditionally, femininity in childhood is expressed by interest in doll play, identification with female figures in fantasy games, women's dress, and avoidance of rough-and-tumble play (for example, see Brown, 1957). Masculinity contains sex role traits that are instrumental, dominant, goal oriented, and cognitive (Kelly & Worrell, 1976). Masculinity in children is associated with rough-and-tumble play; preference for toys such as trucks, cars, and guns; identification with male figures in fantasy games; and men's dress. The individual with sexual identity conflict perceives himself/herself to be the opposite gender, and supports that self-labeling by fulfilling the opposite traditional sex role. In some adult cases, the person seeks surgery and hormonal treatments to effect a transsexual change (Green & Money, 1969). Using Green's (1974) criteria, there were no signs of gender identity confusion in sons or daughters in either group in our study. Several measures of gender identity and role preference were used.

For boys, particularly, there was great similarity between the two groups on all tests and measurements; that is, boys consistently chose traditional masculine preferences in play activities, toys, dress, role models, and careers.

The two groups of daughters differed somewhat. First, girls in each group showed a wider range of scores than did boys, indicating possibly more flexible sex roles than boys are encouraged to have. Second, daughters of lesbian mothers scored as less traditionally feminine, but still not masculine, on a number of items. For example, daughters of lesbian mothers tended to pick possible careers that are not traditionally feminine, and to engage in a somewhat wider variety of play. Daughters of heterosexual mothers had a stronger preference for traditional feminine play than did the lesbian mothers' daughters. Findings on sex role orientation were consistent with those reported earlier by Green (1978) and Kirkpatrick et al. (1981).

Will the child become a homosexual if the parent is a lesbian? The children in the study had not yet reached an age where they were openly expressing sexual interest. A follow-up study on the families will obtain answers to this question. The current study reports only about gender identity and sex role orientation for each child. Green's earlier sample (1978) included adolescent children of lesbian mothers, all of whom reported heterosexual fantasies and interests.

Next, what of the effects of divorce and father absence? Earlier we said that father absence studies had shown that boys in single-mother homes were significantly more likely to have an uncertain sex role orientation, increased aggressiveness, or poor peer relationships. This one sample of boys from single-mother households does not replicate these findings. There are several possible explanations for this. One is that the vast majority of children in the study had a father or other male living at home throughout infancy, followed by a steady decline in father presence due mainly to divorce and separation. Also, both lesbian and heterosexual mothers encouraged father-child contact; when fathers were not involved, other males were sought by the mothers as role models for their children.

Kirkpatrick et al. (1981) indicated emotional disturbances in their child subjects that they considered typical of children of divorce, using a projective measure (Koppitz' scoring of the Draw-A-Person Test) to test for emotional problems. They found a number of indicators of emotional problems consistently in both sons' and daughters' tests, but there were no significant differences based on mothers' sexual orientation.

DISCUSSION

To date, research by several teams has not supported the assumptions often made in family court that being a lesbian makes one an unfit parent. Comparative studies of lesbian and heterosexual single-mother households have not demonstrated that a mother's homosexual orientation results in the child's neglect, unpopularity, confused gender identity, or homosexuality.

It is also important that we take a broader look at what a typical family in our society today is like. Keniston (1977) notes that in March 1976, 54 percent of mothers of school-aged children worked outside the home, and 37 percent of mothers of preschool children worked as well. So we no longer live in a society where the majority of children have a mother who is at home with them during the day or at home between the hours of 9 a.m. and 5 p.m. Keniston also notes that currently one in three marriages ends in divorce, and comments: "Four out of every ten children born in the 1970's will spend part of their childhood in a one-parent family, usually with the mother as head of the household." Forty percent, then, of the children in our culture will be living in a single-parent family for at least part of their childhood. These experiences must be borne in mind when assessing what is typical and atypical in terms of family style during custody decisions.

Dr. Allison Clarke-Stewart (1977, p. 98), in her study of children for the Carnegie Corporation, stated: "The lack of a father (or mother) is not as bad as *having* a father or mother is good." She writes: "If the single parent can share the burden of child care with another adult—who is not necessarily a spouse or even of the opposite sex—it will benefit both parent and child." Indeed, two parents are better than one; that is really not under debate here. But her suggestion that a child's care need not be performed by a heterosexual mother and father in marriage provides new insight into the kinds of models that can be effective for parenting.

CONCLUSIONS:
FAMILY COURT POLICY AND LESBIAN MOTHERS

We recognize that family court policy is usually formulated on the merits of each case as perceived by the judge or, occasionally, the jury. So it is important to familiarize divorce lawyers, judges, and child welfare professionals with current research on single-parent households and lesbian mother families. Equally important is helping the child welfare professional, often responsible for making a psychological assessment for the court, to be able to differentiate the stressful effects of a divorce and custody battle from an issue related to sexual orientation. In the absence of that assurance, we would recommend that a lesbian mother or gay father seek expert witnesses who can interview the child as well as the parents to ascertain strengths and problems.

In those states where active homosexuality is still a felony, the homosexual parent's case is jeopardized. To ensure that "the best interests of the child" and "fitness to parent" can be truly ascertained, these laws must be repealed. Our research and that of others does not support the usual concerns raised in family courts, which typically regard the homosexual as an unfit parent. No evidence of gender identity conflict, poor peer relationships, or neglect was seen in two matched nonclinical samples of children of lesbian mothers and heterosexual single mothers.

24

Summary and Conclusions

Mary E. Hotvedt

In Dr. Larson's discussion, literature that indicates many of the ways in which gay men meet, pair, stay together, and break up has been reviewed. He examined several kinds of relationships, running the gamut from a one-night stand to an established relationship that may last 20 or more years. In reviewing the values and compromises that go into establishing such varieties of relationships, the research has shown similarities with heterosexual males and their relationship values. Research further indicates that equality, rather than traditional sex role playing, is extremely important in the majority of relationships. Larson emphasized the importance of both the women's movement and the gay rights movement on this egalitarianism, and discussed the modern trend toward masculinity as opposed to the traditional image of "femme" attitudes and behaviors for gay males. The idea that the aging homosexual male is at a distinct disadvantage for a satisfying life has also been called into question.

Peplau and Amaro examined the literature on women in relationships, finding strong similarities between homosexual and heterosexual women. Differences and similarities with Larson's findings emerge. As an example of differences, we see that lesbian women often choose partners out of circles of friends and stay together for a longer period of time than reported in research on gay men, although relationships again run the gamut from one-night stands to long, committed relationships. For similarities, once again we see that sex role stereotyping is considered passé by large segments of lesbian communities; instead, egalitarianism in relationships is considered the desired and common form of partnership. Again, the influence of feminism and the gay rights movement on personal sex role expression is clear.

287

Some myths on the reasons why women become lesbians are challenged by the information that a majority of lesbians in several studies have had sexual relationships with males with varying degrees of satisfaction, ranging from completely nonorgasmic to orgasmic. We find, however, that lesbians report a high degree of orgasmic response with same-sex partners.

With the chapter by Lewin and Lyons, we move into the realm of lesbians in other social relationships, most particularly their experience as mothers. The research suggests that single motherhood among both lesbians and heterosexuals gives rise to a single adaptive system, one in which motherhood is the cental organizing issue. That is, lesbian and heterosexual single mothers solve problems similarly and make use of the same range of resources. For both lesbian and heterosexual single mothers, the emphasis is on the maintenance of family ties, and they strongly encourage their children's relationships with relatives and with their fathers.

The conclusions of all three chapters strongly support the importance of considering sexual orientation in the context of other dimensions of individuals' lives and of considering the many ways in which people of different sexual orientations manufacture basic lifestyle features and fail to demonstrate important behavioral differences. To summarize, we have seen that heterosexual and homosexual men react similarly in a number of situations, and homosexual and heterosexual women likewise show more similarities than differences.

In the chapter by Hotvedt and Mandel, we turn attention away from the adult and parent to the child living in an alternate lifestyle: the lesbian mother or gay father home. We have looked in some detail at the concerns that are raised in custody cases regarding homosexual parents, taking care to separate out the children's and parents' reactions to divorce. Once again, the similarity between heterosexual and homosexual single-parent experiences indicates that the homosexuality of the parent has not been demonstrated to be deleterious or not "in the best interests of the child."

In the introduction to this section, four common and interrelated myths about homosexual lifestyles were discussed. Let's review them in the light of the authors' findings.

The first myth was that homosexuals are always alike and identifiable and therefore very different from heterosexuals. The research presented in these chapters does not support the assumption; instead, it has shown the overall similarities in goals, values, and experiences of homosexuals and heterosexuals as adults, both in seeking relationships with other adults and in experiencing parenthood. To simplify, men are like men and women are like women despite differences in sexual orientation. Furthermore, lifestyles show great variation; there is not a single "gay lifestyle" any more than there is a single "straight lifestyle." As to identifying characteristics of homosexuals, several pieces of research indicate that "femme" males and "butch" females are not synonymous with homosexual orientation, nor are they necessarily images with sexual appeal to all prospective partners. Rather, there is the same emphasis on sensitivity plus masculinity, and on self-assuredness plus womanliness, that is prized by many heterosexuals these days.

The next myth was that homosexuals have unhappy personal lives because they cannot develop positive relationships. The research presented in the chapters (particularly those by Larson and by Peplau and Amaro) indicates that the value of long-term commitment and the compromises between monogamy and open relationships are issues handled successfully by many homosexual men and women. The issue of commitment is a burning one, not only for homosexuals but for heterosexuals in our culture as well. While there is some indication that lesbians do have a greater proportion of long-term relationships than do homosexual males, both groups experience the same gamut of relationships. In considering the needs for social support for gay relationships (for example, counseling and meeting places), we see that homosexuals experience very similar relationship problems, including sexual ones, that heterosexual couples experience.

The image of the sad, aging homosexual has also been discussed in the first two chapters. Aging appears to be of no greater concern to homosexuals than it does to heterosexuals; it is the context of the relationships one experiences that determines whether or not aging is a painful or satisfying experience. Furthermore, all the authors stress that one's sexuality is embedded in the rest of one's life as a friend, parent, worker, and partner.

The third myth, related to the first, was that in homosexual relationships someone is always "male" and one is always "female." This popularly held assumption may have been based on a parody of the rigid sex roles held by heterosexual couples in the late 1940s and 1950s. However, research has clearly indicated that the preferred mode of interaction in homosexual relationships is that of equality and shared responsibility in the relationship rather than a rigid dichotomization into masculine and feminine behaviors. Likewise, in the lesbian mother research, these values of equality and androgyny are those values parents desire for their children as well. As in heterosexual relationships, the importance of the women's movement on the content of sex roles and relationships has been shown. The gay rights movement reinforces this message, particularly for gay males.

Finally, we consider the myth that homosexuals could not be good parents. Two chapters have dealt specifically with the issues of parenting. We have learned from them that there are more similarities than differences between the parenting experiences of single heterosexual mothers and fathers and gay parents. It would be fitting to note again that some gay parents do not raise their children as single parents, but rather raise them in the context of a committed relationship in which the child has at least two parental figures in addition to the parent who does not live in the household. We have seen that lesbian mothers are deeply concerned that their children have more than sufficient contact with their fathers and with relatives, and that their peer relationships be satisfying for the child. The support networks made up of friends and families are similar for both lesbian and heterosexual single mothers. All the mothers experience problems of income change and the need to juggle work, family, and personal obligations. Parenthood and its responsibilities take precedence over other concerns.

The research reviewed in these chapters leads us to some of the central issues surrounding the social institutions that bring pressure to bear on the effective functioning of gay women and men in their personal lives and as members of society. If one can accept the findings of the research and can see one's way to removing the barriers to full involvement of homosexuals and all social institutions, what changes would need to be made? The authors suggest several possibilities.

The legal and extralegal restrictions which currently handicap gay people in meeting each other must be removed. Even in states where homosexual acts between adults are legal, a few highly visible but temporarily "safe" bars are not enough. Larson suggests that churches and social organizations could take a leadership role in establishing alternatives to the bar scene—as they have for heterosexuals—so that abuse of alcohol, fear of harassment, and the promiscuous image of singles' bars could be avoided.

A second area which all the authors point out is the need for counseling services that are nonjudgmental and sympathetic for singles, gay couples, parents, and children. Several communities have such counseling centers specifically set up to meet the needs of gay clients. Furthermore, therapy networks often have a system for referrals to therapists who are particularly empathetic and experienced in dealing with homosexuals' concerns. However, this is not enough. It is important to remove the heterosexual bias from the services given by public agencies so that a gay person is not barraged with questions which assume a heterosexual identity whenever he/she approaches an institution dealing with the common needs for education, child welfare, and employment.

In the area of domestic law, education of judges, lawyers, and mental health professionals needs to take place so that "the best interests of the child" criterion is not assumed to exclude a gay man or lesbian from parenting. Rather, sound custody decisions need to be made on the issues of parenting skills rather than on sexual orientation.

Other legal steps which would be of benefit to gay relationships are similar to those which would clarify a number of heterosexuals' living arrangements as well. For example, documents could indicate, at the formation of a relationship, what is joint property and what is individual property, and what is to be done in the case of a breakup. Custody and visitation rights for two gay parents could be ensured by similar agreements.

Finally, there is a general social change that needs to be made that could relieve the greatest stresses on homosexuals. Heterosexuals need to rethink the stereotypes we have discussed in these chapters, to become aware of the great variations in gay lifestyles and also of the many similarities between homosexuals and heterosexuals. But they need to do more than think. If they have come to terms with their own fears and believe in human rights for all people, regardless of sexual orientation, the next step is to act. Action can take many forms: honest conversation with friends and children to disman-tle the mythology; application of these research findings to decisions made in one's professional work; support at church meetings for gay social events; recognition in one's language and social interactions that heterosexuality does not define the whole world; political activity on behalf of platforms, candidates, and organizations committed to civil rights for gay men and lesbians.

A stronger alliance, formal and informal, of people of all sexual orienta-tions has obvious benefits to gay men and lesbians. With greater attitudinal and institutional changes, one could live without the fear of loss of employ-ment, harassment of personal relationships, blackmail, loss of one's chil-dren, and social exclusion and censure. But what of benefits to heterosex-uals? There is, first, the satisfaction of acting on one's beliefs. Moreover, the development and preservation of the human rights of any one group strengthen the concept of human rights for everyone; the twentieth century has seen several examples where tolerated harassment of one minority has led to persecution of other variations. That may sound like a doomsday prediction, likely or not. It can be stated more palatably: In rejecting the simplified assumptions about straights and gays, about the roles of men and women, we see similarities that foster a sense of belonging—and variations, which imply a sense of options in creating social relationships. The amalgam of these two senses allows us, as a society and as individuals, to work toward a future true to our beliefs.

· V ·

Social and Cultural Issues

Edited by
William Paul

· 25 ·

Introduction

William Paul

This section is a collection of articles which not only provide evidence directly pertinent to some current social issues but also deal with some of the consequences inflicted on human lives by social reactions toward homosexuality and Gay people. As apparent in the preceding section on life adaptations, homosexuality as a social issue is very much about everyday people—a fact we should not forget when considering evidence, however remote the subject.

The chapters in this section—and, indeed, the entire book—are by no means a complete array of evidence on the issues. However, they were selected for their usefulness as direct evidentiary resources, and also as sources of perspective; all tend to deal primarily with current events and related controversies. This introduction also provides some brief reviews of findings on issues not examined elsewhere in this volume but adequately dealt with in a number of current works.

The chapters which follow deal primarily with homosexuality as a social issue in modern America. These accounts are about social conflict: historical backgrounds of oppression and fear colliding with emerging social identities and values.

The first two examine homosexual orientation and the law, questions which involve not only the laws but how the courts treat Gay citizens. The first, "Homosexuals and the Constitution," was prepared by David Stivison when he was at the Civil Liberties Research Center of Harvard Law School, and deals specifically with constitutional rights—especially questions of equal protection, due process, and separation of church and state. The second, "Homosexuality and the Law," was written by Rhonda Rivera,

Associate Professor of Law at Ohio State University. This deals with a number of issues pertaining to homosexuality: judicial bias and discrimination, employment rights, child custody, and similar problems.

A passing familiarity with news reports over the past several years provides evidence of discrimination against Lesbians and Gay men. Stivison and Rivera present considerable evidence of how the legal system has denied equal protection to Gay people. There is a range of available evidence related to legal issues. Hearings conducted by the U.S. Civil Rights Commission (1980) gathered a variety of documentation and testimony demonstrating discrimination especially in terms of employment, due process, and equal protection. Research on the structure of such discrimination in private and public institutions is nearing completion at the Center for Research and Education in Sexuality (CERES, at San Francisco State University). The questions addressed by our two legal scholars involve not only whether discrimination on the basis of personal sexual orientation exists but whether it should exist.

Readers interested in more comprehensive analyses of legal issues may refer to an excellent recent anthology (Knutson, 1980).

Chapter 28 gives a historical and sociopolitical account of the San Francisco White Night riots of 1979. The author is David Thomas, Professor of Political Science at the University of California at Santa Cruz, who was an eyewitness to the events described. His account and analysis confer a sense of realism on issues that too often seem remote and academic. The dramatic images of several thousand Gay men and Lesbians in the streets demanding equality informed many Americans for the first time that there are social costs to oppression. The events also made clear the historical fact that Gay people are not simply a collection of isolated individuals, but a large and potentially powerful social group.

The concluding article on issues of minority status for Lesbians and Gay men examines precisely this issue of social identity and majority oppression. This final analysis of conflict, organized hatred, and social change should not be read in isolation from the other highly relevant studies in this volume.

SOCIAL CONTEXT AS A NECESSARY BACKGROUND

As seen in several earlier chapters, the application of scientific evidence to social issues is a process deeply influenced by the historical and social conditions which envelop such debates. An examination of this social context is a necessary background for understanding how accurate information from disciplines like psychology can illuminate the issues. Debates about sexual orientation transpire in a context of social conflict over Gay civil rights that is highly volatile. For this reason alone, some discussion of contemporary political and social conflict is a necessary perspective. Academic debates are embedded in this context.

As the title of this section suggests, American society is no longer dealing simply with issues of individual sexual orientation and behavior, but with the historical emergence of Gay people as an increasingly visible and important social group. Members of the growing Gay communities are enormously diverse, representing nearly every major element of socioeconomic, cultural, racial, and ethnic life in contemporary American society (Voeller, 1980). A corollary of this diversity is that Gay men and Lesbians are also present within those other elements. There is a sociological reality behind the motto expressed by Gay civil rights activists: *"We are everywhere!"*

This heterogeneity of group composition and social distribution has profound social and cultural ramifications. Among these is a real potential for economic and political power, already manifest in certain cosmopolitan areas of the country and visibly applied in statewide politics.

More fundamental in historical significance is the enormous process of cultural change well under way now for over a decade, of which liberated Gay people are at once an initiating force and a human outcome. Hence, the Gay civil rights movement is a social and political force, whereas Gay Liberation is a *process*—of self-definition, of expanding roles and identities, and of very deep psychological and cultural transformation.

Political pendulums swing left then right, or so says the conventional wisdom. What is not so apparent, however, is that the pendulum itself is attached to a cultural base which is drifting in directions that may be neither right nor left, but perhaps toward pluralist diversity and validation of human variation.

A number of independent observers concur that whatever the immediate political climate, American society is moving toward greater social diversity in values, identity, and personal lifestyles, quite consistent with the nation's long-term historical development. Toffler, in *Future Shock* (1970), described this diversification as a process of acceleration. He cites research by Gruen (1968) indicating that what he terms "the American core culture" is already evolving toward pluralism of basic ideas about living: "Diversity in beliefs was more striking than the statistically supported uniformities." Klapp (1969) has given a persuasive account of a pluralism in contemporary American society in which individuals and groups can select new social identities and reformulate old ones to the extent that multiple social allegiances and roles have emerged.

Traditionalists, especially among the coalition of religious and political groups termed the "New Right," correctly ascertain the magnitude of change this portends but tend to perceive alternative values and social identities as hostile threats. In reaction to these perceived attacks on their value system, they have declared an ideological war in which social and cultural issues are the cause, in defense of traditionalist Christian values as a dominant ideology, and in which political weapons are forged from generalized fear and apprehension among large segments of the population in response to economic problems and perceptions of social instability.

A number of journalistic accounts have documented the escalation of organized anti-Gay campaigns by this movement (e.g., Bush & Goldstein, 1981; Ross, 1978). These accounts suggest that Gay civil rights issues have been associated with other issues (such as abortion) and with generalized public apprehensions about such social problems as crime, violence, drug use, and instabilities in conventional nuclear families. The Family Protection Act, introduced in Congress in July 1981, would codify the dominance of traditionalist Christianity as a quasi-official value system while virtually annihilating all equal government services and protections for homosexuals.

This law would explicitly prohibit all federal funding for any program conducted by an individual or organization which accepts Gay people or their orientation on the basis of equality. Statements by some of those who formulated the bill leave little doubt that social pluralism itself is seen as a danger, and that beyond an ultimate goal of codified religious morality enforced by the state, the bill is designed to restrict civil rights for Gay citizens.

Gary Potter, representing Catholics for Christian Political Action, helped formulate the Family Protection Act, and describes its ultimate objectives explicitly:

> There will be no Satanic churches, no more free distribution of pornography, no more abortion on demand, no more talk of rights for homosexuals. When the Christian majority takes control, pluralism will be seen as immoral and evil, and the state will not permit anyone the right to practice evil [quoted in Bush & Goldstein, 1981, p. 10].

As will be shown in related chapters on issues and the section's conclusion on Gay minorities, the rhetoric and the tangible reactions can range to violent extremes. It is therefore prudent to examine briefly some of the older persisting popular beliefs about homosexuality to the degree that they form some part of the issues as posed in forums of law, public policy, and mass media.

SOME PERSISTING POPULAR ISSUES

As indicated in Chapter 4 on issues and themes, many of the issues amount to popular beliefs, folklore, or allegations that are embedded to varying degrees in public opinion. A number of questions raised in debates about some of these issues have, in fact, been previously answered with solid evidence and therefore need not be continuously treated with serious consideration in comprehensive new studies. On certain older issues, persistent in the mass media and propaganda, the preponderance of factual evidence is simply so overwhelming that conclusions serve superficially to summarize the existing knowledge while providing some useful references.

THE SOCIAL MEANINGS OF HOMOSEXUALITY

Sociologist Peter Berger has insightfully described social life as a series of reality definitions (Berger & Luckman, 1967). Reality is socially constructed according to Berger and a number of social psychologists, who have produced experimental evidence that perceptions of events—of others, and of oneself—can be molded by social context and group influence. It is also a maxim of social science that what people believe about social behavior tends to influence that behavior.

In this view, homosexual behavior or identity is not necessarily good or bad—it simply exists and is shaped or defined by externally imposed sociocultural meanings. How a given society views homoerotic experience and sexuality in general can make a vast difference in what kinds of human consequences emerge. If, say, in the Midwest of the 1950s, there is an almost universally perceived image of Gay people as pathetic, sexually obsessed, and frustrated individuals loitering around public places in search of anonymous sex, then it can be reasonably understood how at least some homosexuals might assimilate such a role and live out the script provided by society. Indeed, findings by a number of researchers and clinicians indicate that many homosexual males do assimilate popular misconceptions about homosexuality and Gay people (Hoffman, 1968; Tripp, 1975; May, 1974). This general view and related problems of identity in the context of a hostile social environment are ably articulated in a recent analysis by Humphreys and Miller (1980). See also Chapter 10 in this volume.

From the perspective of homosexualities in the plural, variously defined and organized in response to the overwhelming social and cultural pressures, there are forms of homosexual behavior that could be described in highly negative terms. Indeed, much of the previous scholarship purporting to give an objective account has been highly negative and biased. Morin's review of heterosexual biases in psychological literature (1977) is but one documentation of this slant.

The following brief and rather superficial survey of certain old issues not adequately covered elsewhere in this volume may appear to lean toward a positive view of homosexual behavior. This is due to a definite tilt in the evidence on certain issues that should be righted.

NOTIONS OF HOMOSEXUALITY AS SOCIAL PATHOLOGY

There is simply no substantial evidence that homosexual behavior is either a cause or a symptom of social decline or decadence. No valid study exists that can demonstrate or describe a society that has been destroyed or undermined by widespread acceptance of homosexual behavior. Nor has any valid evidence been produced indicating that homosexuality in any way attacks the family. In 1956, the British Wolfenden Commission refuted such notions on the basis of findings from a number of scholars, and successfully recommended the decriminalization of homosexual behavior in England. Beliefs that homosexuality has destructive effects on society persist, however. In 1970, Levitt and Klassen (1974) found that 84 percent of those surveyed agreed that "homosexuality is a social corruption that can cause the downfall of civilization." These assertions are currently promoted on a mass scale in publications and the media under general claims that homosexuality is part of an "attack on the family" (e.g., Robison, 1980). As Hotvedt's section in this volume indicates, Lesbians and Gay men often belong and give support to families. It requires no sociological sophistication to discern that biological reproduction itself is not necessary for one to contribute love and material support to a family. Especially in the more traditional extended families, it was common to find unmarried childless family members who were deeply valued by the group. The inclusive nature of extended families is such that it is also common to find "spinster aunts" and "bachelor uncles" who may not even be genetic relatives, yet belong in the strongest sense. The major ingredient in happy families seems to be love.

Ford and Beach (1951), in their classic cross-cultural study, found that in the majority of societies and cultures they surveyed, some form of homosexual behavior was approved. These widely diverse societies, with relatively higher tolerance of homosexuality, flourished in conditions of relative stability, producing healthy, productive members comparable to other enduring social systems (Bullough, 1979). Carrier's findings (1980) are similar. He finds that wide variations in permissible homoerotic and gender role behavior appear all over the planet.

It has been widely supposed in certain popular beliefs about homosexuality that tolerance of homoerotic love was a cause and/or symptom of the fall of the Roman Empire. Actually, no recognized historians or classical scholars devoted to the study of Rome have ever seriously proposed such a theory (e.g., Gibbon). In his recent comprehensive history of homosexuality in relation to Christianity, Yale historian John Boswell (1980) provides several sources of factual evidence thoroughly disproving such notions.

This evidence on homosexuality as it has appeared in other times and places gives us a factual vantage point with a larger and longer view of current issues which generate such anger and alarm over Gay people and their lovemaking. A balanced and thorough study of the historical and cross-cultural data yields several compelling conclusions: (1) Human societies are quite capable of considerable flexibility in what is defined as valid sexual activity. (2) The only common sexual rules seem to be taboos against incest and requirements that sufficient numbers reproduce offspring. (3) Homosexual love and eroticism can coexist in people who also fulfill their duties of social reproduction; hence the widespread bisexuality found studies by Ford and Beach (1951), Dover (1979), Carrier (1980), and other investigators.

When discussing homosexuality, it is necessary to remember that we are dealing with people and their lives. Therefore, a fair question to ask of history, literature, and anthropology is not only whether approval of homosexual behavior somehow decays or damages society, but what kind of people are thereby produced. Rowse (1977), a senior scholar at Oxford, finds that tolerance and validation of homoerotic love have flourished during some of the highest points of civilization. This was the view of Westermarck (1908). Renaissance Italy and classical Greece were hardly periods of decadence or decline. Rowse (1977), Katz (1976), Bullough (1979), and other contemporary historians have placed the question of social pathology in a humane focus by examining some of the people who have emerged during eras of relative sexual freedom.

As a final point of historical and cross-cultural comparison, Japan is a most instructive example of a highly esteemed and productive society that validated and often idealized homoerotic love during periods of high civilization such as the Ukiyo or "Floating World" period (as reported by Kaempher). Ihara Saikaku, Japan's greatest novelist of that time, idealized romantic homoerotic love in *Comrade Loves of the Samurai*.

HOMOSEXUAL DANGER TO CHILDREN: MYTH AS PROPAGANDA

Arguments opposing social equality for Gay and Lesbian citizens become volatile when civil rights legislation is portrayed as a threat to little children. In congressional hearings on the inclusion of homosexuals under protections afforded by the 1964 Civil Rights Act, evidence of such mass appeals was presented by the National Organization for Women. Mass mailings by *Christian Voice* were cited:

Thousands of innocent American children may soon be molested by sex deviates—if Congress votes for a proposed "civil rights" law now being considered—including precious Christian children in your Sunday school.

NOW representatives described these tactics as attempts "to incite hatred and fear" (San Francisco Chronicle, Jan. 28, 1982, p. 13).

As seen in the analysis of arguments, "danger to the young" is a prominent anti-homosexual propaganda theme. This translates into the widespread belief that Gay people are likely to sexually molest young children.

It is only as a persistently promoted accusation that this myth remains an issue. Recognized researchers in the field of child abuse, including law enforcement research, almost unanimously concur that homosexual people are actually *less* likely to sexually approach children (Burgess et al., 1978). Groth and Birnbaum conclude, for example: "It appears then, that the heterosexual adult constitutes more of a threat to the underage child than does the homosexual adult" (1978, p. 180). Dr. Groth, Director of the Sex Offender Program for the Connecticut Department of Corrections, finds child molesters typically hostile toward Gay people and homosexuality in general (Groth & Birnbaum, 1978).

Laboratory experiments by Freund et al. (1973) physiologically measured actual sexual arousal in response to various erotic displays. Heterosexual male subjects were found somewhat more likely to be sexually aroused by photos of little girls than were homosexuals viewing photos of boys—the latter was found to be as unlikely a source of arousal as landscapes.

There is such an immense body of evidence refuting the myth of Gay people as a sexual danger to children that it is simply inappropriate as an issue. Were it not for lurid media distortion and the lack of public access to reliable information on sexual orientation, and sexuality at large, this kind of anti-homosexual vilification would not merit a serious response.

DISCUSSION

Vilification of an entire category of people, with frightening but easily disproven labels like "potential child molester," is made possible in part because of the immense mystery surrounding homosexual life. Mystery, in turn, flourishes in the absence of factual information that is readily available to the public. As evident in the thematic view of anti-Gay positions (Chapter 4), avoidance is a common reaction to taboo. Avoidance of the entire topic is perhaps the most widespread social response to anything deemed "homosexual"—an enforcment of taboo against knowing about people and their communities aside from their sexualities.

If there is a common goal shared by the contributors in this section, it is to provide the reader with a variety of reasons why we must begin to know these mysterious people, who are not so different really, and why we must begin to understand them.

• 26 •

Homosexuals and the Constitution

David Stivison

A dozen years have now passed since courts first recognized constitutional limits to discrimination against homosexuals in the federal civil service[1] and in the teaching profession.[2] This last decade has been characterized by the increasing willingness of homosexuals—and their opponents—to turn to the courts and legislatures to achieve their goals.

Areas affected by this new awareness span the whole range of human interactions—from immigration to employment, from marriage to the military, from student groups to new churches, and from city council chambers to the national legislature.

In the middle of this struggle, with gains and losses for both sides, it is important not to lose sight of the fact that "a homosexual is after all a human being, and a citizen of the United States despite the fact that he finds his sexual gratification in what most consider to be an unconvential manner. He is as much entitled to the protection and benefits of the laws and due process fair treatment as are others."[3] Homosexual men and women are as fully protected in the exercise of their recognized constitutional rights as any other citizens. Our courts now face the problem of defining those rights and applying established methods of constitutional analysis to situations new to most judges, and the difficulty many judges have in separating personal biases from legal standards.

To date, constitutional principles have been applied primarily to claims of homosexuals in the areas of due process, freedom of association and speech, and equal protection, and the following discussion is organized along these lines.

WHAT PROCESS IS DUE?

The earliest cases to directly address discriminatory practices against homosexuals involved the right of homosexual public employees to keep their jobs unless and until their homosexual activity was shown to render them unfit to work.

The starting point for this analysis was Morrison v. State Board of Education,[4] decided by the California Supreme Court in 1969. Mr. Morrison, an exemplary teacher with many years' experience, had a friend, Fred Schneringer, also a public school teacher, who often turned to him for advice. As Mr. Schneringer's finances and marriage both deteriorated, the two men became closer, and "for a one-week period in April (1963), during which [Mr. Morrison] and Mr. Schneringer experienced severe emotional stress, the two men engaged in a limited, noncriminal physical relationship which [Mr. Morrison] described as being of a homosexual nature." That was all. After Mr. Schneringer's separation from his wife, Morrison suggested several women his friend might want to date, and generally helped him get his life back in order. After a year Mr. Schneringer reported this incident to Mr. Morrison's superintendent, and Morrison resigned on May 4, 1964.

And there the case normally would have ended. Few teachers or other public employees are willing to focus public attention on their sexuality by going to court; they move on to another job and hope their history does not follow them.

On August 5, 1965, an accusation was filed with the State Board of Education to revoke Mr. Morrison's teaching certificate, and on March 11, 1966, his teaching certificate was revoked "because of immoral and unprofessional conduct and acts involving moral turpitude." This action would have made it impossible for him to teach in any California public school for the rest of his life. Morrison went to court.

The California Supreme Court ordered his teaching credentials reinstated, and held that a teacher could be discharged only after a finding that the "immoral, unprofessional" conduct in question rendered the teacher unfit to teach. The court said,

> in determining whether the teacher's conduct thus indicates unfitness to teach the board may consider such matters as the likelihood that the conduct may have adversely affected students or fellow teachers, the degree of such adversity anticipated, the proximity or remoteness in time of the conduct, the type of teaching certificate held by the party involved, the extenuating or praiseworthiness or blameworthiness of the motives resulting in the conduct, the likelihood of the recurrence of the questioned conduct, and the extent to which disciplinary action may inflict an adverse impact or chilling effect upon the constitutional rights of the teacher involved or other teachers.

The Morrison decision underlies other cases involving homosexual teachers and requires that some "nexus," or logical connection, exist between the teacher's acts and the teacher's ability to teach. Mere status as a homosexual is not enough.

Though the teacher is entitled to notice and a hearing to decide whether this nexus exists, such a hearing falls short of a full court trial. For instance, evidence of a previous arrest and trial for sexual conduct can be introduced against a teacher, even if the teacher was acquitted in the earlier trial.[5] And evidence which could not be admitted into a criminal trial may be allowed in a teacher dismissal hearing.[6]

Even after Morrison, however, some lower courts in California continue to show a strong homophobia. Consider the case of Jack Millette[7]: On October 19, 1972, he was arrested for an alleged homosexual solicitation in a public restroom. No charges were ever filed against him. He steadfastly denied the charge, and no one was present except the arresting officer. A psychiatrist testified that he was not a homosexual. Yet the school board by which he was employed went to court seeking to dismiss him as a teacher. The trial court decided that the solicitation charges were in fact true, but that it had been an isolated incident unlikely to recur and therefore did not show unfitness to teach. The school was ordered to reinstate Millette.

The school appealed. The appeals judge stated:

> The criminal nature of the defendant's conduct constitutes, as a matter of law, sufficient grounds for dismissal. . . . Evidence of homosexual behavior in a public place constitutes sufficient proof of unfitness for service in the public school system. . . . It is immaterial that the defendant is or is not convicted of the criminal offense. It is the act, not the conviction thereof, that formed the basis of his dismissal and evidences his unfitness. . . . *His act remains criminal by definition and entirely disgusting and abhorrent by any reasonable standard of decency* [emphasis added].[8]

This decision was sharply rebuffed by the state supreme court: Justice Tobriner, the author of the Morrison opinion, also wrote the high court's opinion in this case. The court found that the trial judge had reasonable grounds for his decision, ordered Millette reinstated, discussed the errors of laws the appeals judge had committed, and then vacated his opinion.[9]

Unfortunately, this protection of substantive due process rights is not as well settled in some other states.

On October 18, 1971, Peggy Burton was dismissed from her teaching position because the mother of one of her students informed the school that Peggy was a lesbian, a fact which she did not deny when questioned by school officials. Ms. Burton filed a civil rights complaint against the school and asked for summary judgment. Judge Solomon granted her request, in one of the shortest opinions on record. Omitting the statement of facts, citations, and quotations, the entire decision reads:

> I find [the Oregon teacher dismissal] statute unconstitutionally vague. . . . This statute vests in the school board the power to dismiss teachers for immorality. However, the statute does not define immorality. Immorality means different things to different people, and its definition depends on the idiosyncracies of the individual school board members. It may be applied so broadly that every teacher in the state could be subject to discipline. The potential for arbitrary and discriminatory enforcement is inherent in such a statute. . . . A statute so broad makes those charged with its enforcement the arbiters of morality for the entire community. In doing so, it subjects the livelihood of every teacher in the state to the irrationality and irregularity of such judgments. The statute is vague because it fails to give fair warning of what conduct is prohibited and because it permits erratic and prejudiced exercises of authority. . . . No amount of statutory construction can overcome the deficiencies of this statute.[10]

Judge Solomon's wisdom was recognized by the appellate court, which upheld his decision to award damages to Ms. Burton of the balance of her salary for the year she was discharged and half that amount for the following teaching year, plus lawyers' fees.[11] The majority on the appellate panel believed Ms. Burton should not be reinstated because she was a nontenured teacher on an annual contract and the monetary award made her whole for the school's breach of contract. Judge Lumbard strongly dissented, arguing that reinstatement was appropriate whenever the teacher's constitutional rights had been violated,[12] quoting with approval another case's assertion that "enforcement of constitutional rights frequently has disturbing consequences. Relief is not restricted to that which will be pleasing and free of irritation."[13] Judge Lumbard also noted:

> It is questionable whether a monetary award is sufficient to deter the school board from taking similar unconstitutional action in the future. After all, what the board wanted was to be rid of Ms. Burton and the district court judgment allows it to accomplish that. If a similar situation arises in the future it might well conclude that it would be willing to pay a few thousand dollars in order to be rid of an unwanted teacher.[14]

A similar argument based on the vagueness of "immorality" as grounds for teacher dismissal was given short shrift by the Supreme Court of the state of Washington in Gaylord v. Tacoma School District No. 10.[15] The trial court "concluded in substance Gaylord was properly discharged for immorality because he was a homosexual, and as a known homosexual, his ability and fitness to teach was impaired with resulting injury to the school." James Gaylord had been a teacher in the same school district for over twelve years and had always received excellent evaluations. A former student disclosed to school authorities his suspicion that Gaylord was a homosexual, and, when asked, Gaylord admitted that he was. There was no public knowledge of this fact until the school made it public; Gaylord had never been arrested for illegal sexual activity, nor was there any charge that he had attempted to take liberties with any of his students. Yet the trial court found that an admission of homosexuality connotes illegal as well as immoral acts, because "sexual gratification with a member of one's own sex is implicit in the term 'homosexual,'" and such acts would be prohibited by Washington's lewdness and sodomy statutes.[16] This kind of argument from status (homosexual) to criminal act (sodomy and lewdness) with no evidence of the commission of any criminal act was forbidden by the United States Supreme Court in 1962,[17] yet the Washington Supreme Court upheld Gaylord's dismissal. The Court reasoned: "If Gaylord had not been discharged after he became known as a homosexual, the result would be fear, confusion, suspicion, parental concern and pressure on the administration by students, parents and other teachers."

The Washington Supreme Court supported its ideas that all persons admitting to being homosexual are criminals by quoting from the *New Catholic Encyclopedia,* among other sources. The Court then declared that Gaylord was to be considered guilty of any act he did not specifically deny.

> If Gaylord meant something other than homosexual in the usual sense, he failed to explain what he meant by his admission of homosexuality or being a homosexual so as to avoid any adverse inference; although he had adequate opportunity at trial to do so. He clearly had a right to explain that he was not an overt homosexual and did not engage in the conduct the court ascribed to him which the court found immoral and illegal.

The question of the immorality of homosexuality was settled by the Court's conclusion that "Homosexuality is widely condemned as immoral and was so condemned as immoral during biblical times."

That settled, the Court then decided that, while homosexuality is not inborn, "nevertheless it is a disorder for those who wish to change their homosexuality which is acquired after birth. In the instant case plaintiff desired no change and has sought no psychiatric help because he feels comfortable with his homosexuality. He has made a voluntary choice for which he must be held morally responsible." Thus, Gaylord's acceptance of his own homosexuality was turned into a weapon against him.

The Court rejected an argument that the decriminalization of private homosexual acts among adults in Washington state had voided this entire line of argument: "Generally the fact that sodomy is not a crime no more relieves the conduct of its immoral status than would consent to the crime of incest." The Court also expressed a fear that "students could treat the retention of the high school teacher by the school board as indicating adult approval of his homosexuality." The Court felt it was an "unacceptable risk" to require school officials to "wait for prior specific overt expression of homosexual conduct before they act to prevent harm."

A strong dissenting opinion was filed by Justice Dolliver,[18] who pointed out that there "is not a shred of evidence in the record" that Gaylord had committed any crime.

> The trial court essentially found that, as an admitted homosexual, unless Mr. Gaylord denied doing a particular immoral or illegal act, he can be assumed to have done the act. . . . Presumably under this reasoning, an unmarried male who declares himself to be heterosexual will be held to have engaged in "illegal or immoral acts." The opportunities for industrious school districts seem unlimited.

Justice Dolliver concluded: "To base a dismissal on the proof of a status with no showing of conduct and no showing of an actual detrimental effect on teaching efficiency violates the constitution due process rights to which Mr. Gaylord is entitled."

Mr. Gaylord's own reaction is easily understood:

> I quite frankly find it rather galling to have sat through the school board hearing and once again through this trial and hear administrators say that I'm a good teacher, I've been a very good teacher, and yet be without a job, particularly when I see other people who still hold their jobs who haven't read a book or turned out a new lesson plan or come up with anything creative in years.[19]

Like Mr. Gaylord, the individual in all these cases suffered simply for *being* a homosexual, or even for being a heterosexual person who had engaged in limited homosexual activity. The Courts essentially analyzed the rights of these persons using these criteria: Was the statute or rule invoked clear enough to give fair warning of its prohibitions? Was there any logical relationship between the statement, "This teacher is homosexual" and the statement "This teacher is unfit to teach"?

SPEAKING OUT

Many homosexuals in the 1970s, however, went far beyond the model of the discreet, closeted life of the "hidden homosexual" and began to organize and speak openly about the repression and fear they felt, and to seek public acceptance of a diversity of lifestyles and a public forum for self-affirmation. Though the proportion of homosexuals who are "out of the closet" and actively working for greater acceptance of alternative lifestyles is still small, their impact on public consciousness has been dramatic, and the courts have been increasingly involved in defining the scope of constitutional protection for that expression.

One of the first such confrontations arose from the attempt by James McConnell and Jack Baker to secure a marriage license in Minneapolis in 1970. They were denied the license but received newspaper publicity about their attempt. Mr. McConnell subsequently saw his promised employment by the University of Minnesota as a librarian evaporate before the anger of the university's Board of Regents. The Regents' position was that even though McConnell might be a very capable librarian,

> his professed homosexuality connotes to the public generally that he practices acts of sodomy, a crime under Minnesota law; that the Regents have a right to presume that by his applying for a license to marry another man, [McConnell] intended, were the license to be granted, to engage in such sodomous criminal activities; that the Regents cannot condone the commission of criminal activities; that the Regents cannot condone the commission of criminal acts by its employees and thus plaintiff has rendered himself unfit to be employed.[20]

McConnell sued the Regents, and District Court Judge Neville found that his rejection by the Regents violated his due process rights. The Court stated:

> What [McConnell] does in his private life, as with other employees, should not be his employer's concern unless it can be shown to affect in some degree his efficiency in the performance of his duties. . . . A homosexual is after all a human being, and a citizen of the United States despite the fact that he finds his sex gratification in what most consider to be an unconventional manner. He is as much entitled to the protection and benefits of the laws and due process fair treatment as are others, at least as to public employment in the absence of proof and not mere surmise that he has committed or will commit criminal acts or that his employment efficiency is impaired by his homosexuality. . . . Plaintiff does not have an inalienable right to be employed by the University but he has a right not to be discriminated against under the Fourteenth Amendment due process clause.[21]

The U.S. Court of Appeals for the Third Circuit sharply reversed the District Court and dismissed McConnell's case against the Regents.[22] Referring to McConnell's attempt to obtain a marriage license as "this antic," the Court quoted the headlines greeting this attempt: "Prospective Newlyweds Really in a Gay Mood"; "'Gay' Marriage Refusal Fought"; "Homosexual Marriage License Denial Urged"; "Two Homosexuals Plan to Wed."

The heart of the Court's opinion then read:

> We need only to observe that the Board was given the unenviable task and duty of passing upon and judging McConnell's application against the background of his actual conduct. So postured, it is at once apparent that this is not

a case involving mere homosexual propensities on the part of a prospective employee. Neither is it a case in which an applicant is excluded from employment because of a desire clandestinely to pursue homosexual conduct. It is, instead, a case in which something more than remunerative employment is sought; a case in which the applicant seeks employment on his own terms; a case in which the prospective employee demands, as shown both by the allegations of the complaint and by the marriage license incident as well, the right to pursue an activist role in *implementing* his unconventional ideas concerning the societal status to be accorded homosexuals and, thereby, to foist tacit approval of this socially repugnant concept on his employer, who is, in this instance, an institution of higher learning. We know of no constitutional fiat or binding principle of decisional law which requires an employer to accede to such extravagant demands. We are therefore unable fairly to categorize the Board's action here as arbitrary, unreasonable or capricious [emphasis added].[23]

A parallel case with a parallel conclusion arose in the state of Washington not long thereafter: John F. Singer, a typist employed by the Equal Employment Opportunity Commission (EEOC) office at Seattle, and known to be gay at the time of his employment, applied for a marriage license with another man on September 20, 1971.[24] The denial of the license was unsuccessfully appealed through the Washington state courts.[25] Because of this and other actions publicly acknowledging his homosexuality, Singer was fired. He appealed through the administrative structure of the Civil Service Commission, where the opinions at each level were nearly identical:

There is evidence in the file which indicated that appellant's actions establish that he has engaged in immoral and notoriously disgraceful conduct, openly and publicly flaunting his homosexual way of life and indicating further continuance of such activities. Activities of the type he has engaged in are such that general public knowledge thereof reflects discredit upon the Federal Government as his employer, impeding the efficiency of the service by lessening general public confidence in the fitness of the Government to conduct the public business with which it is entrusted.[26]

Though there was no evidence that anyone had complained about Singer's behavior and no indication that any disruption or tension existed with his co-workers, the District Court dismissed his suit against the Civil Rights Commission, and the Court of Appeals for the Ninth Circuit affirmed.[27]

The U.S. Supreme Court, however, vacated this ruling[28] for reconsideration in the light of changed civil service regulations. In 1969, the Court of Appeals for the District of Columbia had found discharge from the Civil Service on the sole ground of the employee's homosexuality constituted a denial of due process.[29] The Northern District Court of California had reinstated an employee so discharged, with the additional order to the Civil Service Commission to

forthwith cease excluding or discharging from government service any homosexual person whom the Commission would deem unfit for government
employment solely because the employment of such a person in the government service might bring that service into the type of public contempt which
might reduce the government's ability to perform the public business with the
essential respect and confidence of the citizens which it serves.[30]

The Civil Service then revised its regulations and removed the discriminatory language.

As cases arose more directly involving political activity, the courts have
begun to analyze them using traditional "free speech" categories and have,
reluctantly at first, begun to vindicate the right of "gay activists" to speak out
and still hold their jobs in public employment, and have increasingly required equal access to public forums for gay political action groups.

Early activists fared poorly. Consider, for example, the career of Joseph
Acanfora III. He was treasurer of the Homophiles of Penn State as a student
and was co-plaintiff in the law suit that won official status for the group at that
university. Six weeks into his student teaching he was suspended by the
dean of the College of Education because of his membership in that group.
Another lawsuit followed; he was reinstated and completed his student
teaching with a satisfactory evaluation. After graduation, and without revealing his homosexuality, he was hired as an eighth-grade earth science
teacher at Parkland Junior High School in Montgomery, Maryland. Acanfora had applied for teacher certification in Pennsylvania, but because his
homosexuality was an issue in that proceeding, the final decision to certify
him was made directly by the Pennsylvania Secretary of Education. Instead
of quietly sending a letter to Acanfora about his certification, the secretary
called a press conference and announced it publicly. The story ran in the
New York Times and the *Washington Post.*

Acanfora was transferred to a nonteaching position "pending investigation," and sued to be reinstated to the classroom. Students and faculty
separately petitioned for his reinstatement, and his transfer became a media
event. He conducted telephone interviews with newspaper reporters, appeared on both commercial and educational TV, gave a long radio interview, and appeared on CBS's "Sixty Minutes."[31]

During the interview on "Sixty Minutes," Acanfora stated:

Many of my friends have asked me why I am doing this, why I just don't go
someplace and be a teacher and not let the gayness enter into it at all. But the
fact is that I'm gay, just like the fact is that other teachers are straight or
heterosexual. But I'm sure a heterosexual teacher isn't going to live his life a
complete lie and hide what he is and I have no intentions of doing that either. I
have every right to be what I am. I have every right to be a teacher. And I plan
on doing both.[32]

Unfortunately, the courts did not agree with him. The District Court stated: "The time has come today for private, consenting, adult homosexuality to enter the sphere of constitutionally protectable interests. Intolerance of the unconventional halts the growth of liberty. . . . [I]t follows from the First Amendment that public speech, organization and assembly in support of that goal by ordinary citizens is also protectable."[33] But the Court then stated that "to some extent every teacher has to go out of his way to hide his private life, and that a homosexual teacher is not at liberty to ignore or hold in contempt the sensitivity of the subject to the school community." Though "the homosexual teacher need not become a recluse, nor need he lie about himself," "a sense of discretion and self-restraint must guide him to avoid speech or activity likely to spark the added public controversy which detracts from the educational process." The District Court judge then decided that Mr. Acanfora's public appearances were beyond any protection offered by the Constitution, and therefore he had no right to be reinstated.[34]

The Court of Appeals ruled that Acanfora's public statements were protected by the First Amendment guarantee of free speech, but threw his case out because he had not mentioned his affiliation with the Homophiles of Penn State in his job application.[35] Though he had correctly guessed that the board would not hire him if he admitted his homosexuality in his application, Acanfora "cannot now invoke the process of the court to obtain a ruling on an issue that he practiced deception to avoid."

Even if a teacher is not fired for his political activity, a school board may find other methods of harassment nearly as serious to the teacher.

An English teacher in Paramus, New Jersey, John Gish, assumed the presidency of the New Jersey Gay Activists Alliance in June 1972. Though he had been with the school system seven years without incident, on July 10, 1972, the school board directed Mr. Gish to undergo a psychiatric examination because of his "overt and public behavior." He was later informed that "the Board of Education has determined that your conduct during said period evidences a harmful, significant deviation from normal mental health affecting your ability to teach, discipline and associate with students of the Paramus Public Schools." The Court noted that the sole basis for the board's demand was Gish's political activities and "the reasons do not include a single instance of any undue conduct or actions in the classroom or out of the classroom with respect to a particular student."

Nevertheless, the Court upheld the board, stating: "A requirement that apellant subject himself to a psychiatric examination can hardly be classified as a penalty or a sanction. . . . The submission by Gish to a psychiatric examination takes nothing from him except his time." Thus, in New Jersey at least, participating in open political activity alone is such strong evidence of "harmful, significant deviation from normal mental health" that it justifies a court-sanctioned psychiatric examination.

This decision and those involving Acanfora and McConnell may well represent a line of cases destined to die out. Two years before Gish was decided, the Court of Appeals for the First Circuit upheld the right of the students of the University of New Hampshire to organize into a Gay Students Organization and to have university recognition and equal, even-handed treatment with all other student organizations.[37] Media coverage of a dance and play sponsored by that group had produced an outcry by many citizens and the threat from Governor Meldrim Thomson that if the University trustees did not "take firm, fair and positive action to rid your campuses of socially abhorrent activities" he would "stand solidly against the expenditure of one more cent of taxpayers' money for your institutions." The university banned social events sponsored by this group, and the Court lifted the ban because it violated the freedom of association guaranteed by the First Amendment to the U.S. Constitution.

This same resolution has occurred in other cases in which university refusal to fully recognize homosexual student groups has been challenged in the courts. The Gay Alliance for Students, for example, received full privileges as a student group at Virginia Commonwealth University only after appealing to the Fourth Circuit Court of Appeals.[38] A concurring opinion in that case declared:

It is of no moment, in First Amendment jurisprudence, that some ideas advocated by an association may to some or most of us be abhorrent, even sickening. The stifling of advocacy is even more abhorrent, even more sickening. It rings the death knell of a free society. Once used to stifle "the thought that we hate", in Holmes' phrase, it can stifle ideas we love. It signals a lack of faith in people, in its supposition that they are unable to choose in the marketplace of ideas.[39]

Likewise, Gay Lib received vindication of its rights on the University of Missouri campus only after appearing before the Eighth Circuit Court of Appeals, and almost facing a day before the U.S. Supreme Court. The university president had rejected recognition, saying, "The organization of Gay Lib by applying for recognition is attempting to obtain the tacit approval of homosexuality by the University of Missouri. Homosexuality is generally treated in the State of Missouri as being a socially repugnant concept as is evidenced by the criminal statutes of the State of Missouri."[40] The Board of Curators, through its Academic Affairs Committee, appointed a hearing officer who heard "both lay and expert testimony on such subjects as the history of the Gay Lib movement, whether orgies were standard homosexual practice, the alleged homosexual propensities of a mass murderer in Houston then much in the news, and the detrimental effects on children of 'mothers who are overly protective or hostile and rejecting or clinging.'"

The conclusions of the Board of Curators were that "formal recognition by the University of Gay Lib will "tend to cause latent or potential homosexuals who become members to become overt homosexuals; . . . tend to expand homosexual behavior which will cause increased violations of (Missouri's sodomy statute); . . . [and] constitute an implied approval by the University of the abnormal homosexual life-style as a normal way of life."

The Board also found that "a homosexual is one who seeks to satisfy his or her sexual desires by practicing some or all of the following: fellatio, cunnilingus, masturbation, anal eroticism and perhaps in other ways . . . [and that] homosexuality is an illness and should and can be treated as such and is clearly abnormal behavior."

The District Court quoted as part of its decision testimony by Dr. Harold M. Voth and Dr. Charles Socarides's statement that "sodomy . . . is one of the most prevalent forms of sexual expression in homosexuality. . . . Any gathering would certainly promote such sexual contact."[41]

Although the District Court upheld the University, the Eighth Circuit Court of Appeals reversed this decision, ordering the University to grant full recognition to Gay Lib and awarding them attorney's fees,[42] with a concurring opinion noting:

> There is absolutely no evidence that appellants intend to violate any state law or regulation of the university or even that they will advocate such violations. . . . I have no doubt that the ancient halls of higher learning at Columbia will survive even the most offensive verbal assaults upon traditional moral values; solutions to tough problems are not found in repression of ideas.[43]

The U.S. Supreme Court refused to review the case, but just barely. Chief Justice Burger and Justices Rehnquist and Blackmun voted to consider it, but four votes were needed to place it on the docket. By phrasing the question as "whether a university can deny recognition to an organization the activities of which expert psychologists testify will in and of themselves lead directly to violations of a concededly valid state criminal law," Justice Rehnquist left little doubt as to his position.

This opinion, however, and others in this chapter point up the effect of the existence of a state sodomy statute on First Amendment constitutional analysis. Thus, even if such a law is not enforced—if not removed from the statute books—it could well provide the basis for curtailment of the free speech and free association rights of homosexual citizens.

The right of a faculty member to serve as advisor to a student group of homosexuals, without fearing for his job, was established in 1977 by an unusually complete and detailed decision of the U.S. District Court of Delaware.[45] Richard Aumiller, a nontenured lecturer in theater arts at the University of Delaware, accepted an offer to serve as faculty advisor to a student group known as the Gay Community. He was so identified in newspaper articles and interviews, with photographs showing him in the university's theater building.

When Aumiller's contract came up for renewal, President Trabant refused to reemploy him, and Aumiller sued. The Court concluded that "Aumiller did not intentionally or recklessly attempt to create the false impression that he was acting as a University spokesman," nor was he advocating any kind of sexual activity or experimentation, or exceeding his role as a faculty advisor to a campus student group.[46]

Because of the university's impermissible infringement upon Aumiller's First Amendment rights, the Court awarded him his year's lost salary, $10,000 for mental distress, humiliation, and embarrassment, and expungement of all reference to this incident from any university records or future university replies to employment inquiries about Aumiller. Further, $5,000 punitive damages were assessed personally against the university president for his "wanton disregard for Aumiller's constitutional rights" and his "pernicious insensitivity." Though this result would not be surprising in a context of racial or sexual discrimination, it appears to be the first case involving a homosexual in which punitive damages were awarded. The judge's awareness of the novel nature of his decision may be seen in the care with which he constructed his opinion: It fills 46 printed pages and is a model of a decision written to withstand review and reversal. As part of a posttrial settlement the university agreed not to appeal the decision.[47]

The right of campus gay groups to organize, to be treated the same as other campus groups, to have active faculty advisors, and to use university facilities seems to be well established now.

Further, the free speech rights of gay students in high school settings were upheld by the decision of the Rhode Island Federal District Court to allow a gay student to take his male date to the school prom.[48] After careful analysis, the judge concluded that this action constituted political speech, and was protected by the First Amendment. Responding to claims that discipline could not be maintained if the youth brought his chosen data, the judge said "the first amendment does not tolerate mob rule by unruly school children," and suggested the school provide adequate chaperones.

Recent years have seen the growth of homosexual rights groups off-campus as well as on, and the following cases have arisen defining their rights in differing contexts.

A Mississippi court has upheld a decision of student editors of a campus newspaper to reject an advertisement submitted by an off-campus group sponsoring a social and discussion center for homosexuals.[49] The judge's analysis was that

"since there is not the slightest whisper that the University authorities had anything to do with the rejection of this material offered by this off-campus cell of homosexuals, since such officials could not lawfully have done so, and since the record really suggests nothing but discretion exercised by an editor chosen by the student body, we think the First Amendment interdicts judicial interference with the editorial decision."

Community groups seeking recognition of their First Amendment rights have included the "Toward a Gayer Bicentennial Committee," which won the right to use the Old State House in Rhode Island for a "Congress of People with Gay Concerns" in a last-minute, cliff-hanger decision.[50] Plans for the Congress and a Gay Pride parade to be held during national Gay Pride Week in 1976 were submitted to the Rhode Island Bicentennial Foundation on July 11, 1975. The request to recognize these events was denied on August 21, and after unsuccessful efforts were made to resolve the dispute, suit was instituted.

On June 9, 1976, the District Court of Rhode Island gave the Bicentennial Commission one week to approve the use of the Old State House or "promulgate in writing, in clear and precise terms capable of even-handed application, the standards to be used in evaluating the plaintiff's request for endorsement." The judge stated:

I cannot help but note the irony of the Bicentennial Commission expressing reluctance to provide a forum for the plaintiff's exercise of their First Amendment rights because they might advocate conduct which is illegal. Does the Bicentennial Commission need reminding that, from the perspective of British loyalists, the Bicentennial celebrates one of history's greatest illegal events?[51]

The commission chose to issue new standards on June 16, 1976. On June 18, the Toward a Gayer Bicentennial Committee submitted a new proposal under these standards. On June 22, the commission again rejected the proposal and, on June 23, wrote a letter to the Court informing it of the disapproval, stating: "The general sentiment of the Commission and the principal reason for denial of this proposal appeared to be that endorsement would involve approval." The Court replied: "This is a totally unacceptable reason for the Commission's action. The United States Supreme Court has held on numerous occasions . . . that government officials may not restrict access to a public forum simply because they disagree with, or disapprove of, the views to be expressed there."[52] Thus on June 25, 1976, the Court ordered the Bicentennial Commission to approve the "Congress of People with Gay Concerns" to be held the very next morning.

A similar exclusion of a gay group from use of a public forum arose in Alaska. The Mayor of the City of Anchorage cut out a description of the Alaska Gay Coalition from the 1976-77 *Anchorage Blue Book,* a municipally financed directory of service organizations in the Anchorage area.[53]

The trial court upheld the city, but the state Supreme Court reversed, stating:

> The *Blue Book* was clearly an appropriate place for the communication of the type of information submitted by the Gay Coalition. . . . The *Blue Book* was designed for and dedicated to expressive and associational use and therefore, once it was opened for such use, the government could not deny [the Gay Coalition] access to it based solely on the content of its beliefs.

Finding that the municipality's actions violated the Gay Coalition's constitutional rights to freedom of speech and association and equal protection, the Court ordered that the city be enjoined from further distribution of the book without inclusion of the coalition's description.

Finally, police harassment of a gay conference was stopped when members of several gay organizations in Fort Worth, Texas, sued the police for an injunction to end police harassment, which included surveillance of a statewide conference, recording license numbers of cars present, questioning persons coming in and going out of the building, and driver's license checks. The plaintiffs alleged that the numbers and names were then given by the police to Fort Worth newspaper reporters. The Court certified several specific groups to proceed in this class action, and the action was settled out of court by a consent decree which prohibited the police from further harassment of this kind.[54]

EQUALLY PROTECTED?

The cases discussed above in which university student groups and other groups asserted violation of their First Amendment rights to free speech and free association were also, in fact, equal protection cases. To allow one group access to a public forum and deny such access to another group because of the content of its ideas and goals both restricts speech and discriminates between the two groups. The courts have usually been able to avoid facing this question of equal protection by their resolution of the First Amendment claims.

The first direct affirmation of equal protection rights of homosexual citizens occurred quite recently in a California Supreme Court decision which held, among other things, that the equal protection provision of the California State Constitution operates to bar Pacific Telephone and Telegraph from arbitrarily discriminating against homosexuals in its employment decisions.[55] After reviewing the status of public utilities in general and the size and importance of PT&T in particular, the Court concluded that "from the standpoint of the individual employee, the potential for employment discrimination by a public utility is high, and the effect of such discrimination, when it occurs, is devastating." Further, "the general public cannot avoid giving indirect support to such discriminatory practices" because of the utility's monopoly position, which "derives directly from its exclusive franchise provided by the state." Therefore the Court concluded "that in this state a public utility bears a constitutional obligation to avoid arbitrary employment discrimination."

Besides running afoul of the California statutes regarding the policies of regulated utilities, the Court also found that discrimination against homosexuals and members of homosexual groups violated the state's labor code, as interfering with political activity. The Court found that

> the struggle of the homosexual community for equal rights, particularly in the field of employment, must be recognized as a political activity. Indeed the subject of the rights of homosexuals incites heated political debate today, and the "gay liberation movement" encourages its homosexual members to attempt to convince other members of society that homosexuals should be accorded the same fundamental rights as heterosexuals. The aims of the struggle for homosexual rights, and the tactics employed, bear a close analogy to the continuing struggle for civil rights waged by blacks, women, and other minorities [citations omitted].

> A principal barrier to homosexual equality is the common feeling that homosexuality is an affliction which the homosexual worker must conceal from his employer and his fellow workers. Consequently one important aspect of the struggle for equal rights is to induce homosexual individuals to "come out of the closet," acknowledge their sexual preferences, and to associate with others in working for equal rights.

This decision was based on California's state constitution (partly to preclude review by a hostile U.S. Supreme Court) and thus is limited to full application only in California. However, other courts are showing similar understanding.

CONCLUSIONS

It is fitting to close this chapter with the ringing affirmation of the "right to be different" as stated by a federal magistrate in an Ohio case arising when a high school guidance counselor openly acknowledged her bisexuality:[56]

> In this case, Defendants conceded that a person who is homosexual or bisexual may be capable of performing properly as a high school guidance counselor. They argued that Mrs. Rowland was not fit to be a guidance counselor because of her statements, her actions and her mode of dress. They claimed that she was a "free spirit" who had embarked on an "uncharted course" and was operating in an unconventional manner. . . .

Apparently the jury felt, as does the Court, that in our public educational system, which should have as one of its highest values the free expression of thoughts and ideas, there is room for the "free spirit," the unconventional person who marches to the beat of "a different drummer."

Although no court has yet ruled on the specific issues set forth in this opinion, we believe that such a person has the constitutional right to be different; to express her innermost personal thoughts, her doubts, her fears, her insecurities, her likes, and her loves to fellow workers and friends so long as she does not impede the performance of the public school function. . . .

Speech is often provocative and challenging. It may strike at prejudices and preconceptions and have profound unsettling effects as it presses for acceptance of an idea. That is why freedom of speech, though not absolute [citation omitted], is nevertheless protected against censorship or punishment, unless shown likely to produce a clear and present danger of a serious substantive evil that rises far above public inconvenience, annoyance, or unrest [citations omitted]. There is no room under our Constitution for a more restrictive view.

NOTES

1. Norton v. Macy, 417 F.2d 1161 (D.C.Cir. 1969).
2. Morrison v. State Board of Education, 1 Cal. 3d 214, 461 P.2d 375, 82 Cal. Rptr. 175 (1969).
3. Judge Neville in dissent, McConnell v. Anderson, 316 F.Supp. 809, 814 (D.Minn. 1970).
4. Morrison v. State Board of Education, supra, note 2. The principles of Morrison have been applied also to the California State Highway Patrol, Warren v. State Personnel Bd., 94 Cal.App.3rd 95, 156 Cal.Rptr. 351 (1979). The court held that homosexuality alone would not justify firing a patrolman. However, being picked up at a raid on a party featuring sex for hire, a history of associating with the transvestite prostitutes sponsoring the party, and lying to his superiors about it *did* justify firing the patrolman. See also Childers v. Dallas Police Department, 513 F.Supp. 134 (1981).
5. Board of Education of El Monte School District of Los Angeles County v. Calderon, 110 Cal. Rptr. 916, 35 Cal.App.3d 490 (1974), appeal dism'd. 419 U.S. 807.
6. Governing Board of Mountain View School District of Los Angeles County v. Metcalf, 111 Cal.Rptr. 724, 36 Cal.App.3d 546 (1974).
7. Board of Education of Long Beach Unified School District of Los Angeles County v. Millette, Cal.App., 133 Cal.Rptr. 275 (1976).
8. Long Beach v. Millette, supra, 133 Cal.Rptr. at 277-280.
9. Board of Education of Long Beach Unified School District of Los Angeles County v. Jack M., 139 Cal.Rptr. 700, 19 Cal.3d 691, 566 P.2d 602 (1977).
10. Burton v. Cascade School District Union High School No. 5, 353 F. Supp. 254 (1973).
11. Burton v. Cascade School District Union High School No. 5, 512 F.2d 850 (9th Cir. 1975), cert. den., 423 U.S. 839 (1975).
12. Id. at 512 F.2d 854ff.
13. Id. at 512 F.2d 855, citing Sterzing v. Fort Bend Independent School District, 496 F.2d 92, 93 (5th Cir. 1974) (per curiam).
14. Id. at 512 F.2d 856.
15. Gaylord v. Tacoma School District No. 10, 88 Wash.2d 286, 559 P.2d 1340 (1977).
16. Gaylord v. Tacoma School District No. 10, 88 Wash.2d 286, 559 P.2d 1340 at 1342 (1977).
17. Robinson v. California, 370 U.S. 660 (1962). See also Powell v. Texas, 392 U.S. 514 (1968).
18. Id. at 1348.

19. Id. at 1351. The Gaylord decision has been uniformly criticized by commentators—see, for example, "Civil Rights—Homosexual Teacher Dismissal: A Deviant Decision," 53 Wash. L. Rev. 499, May 1978.

20. McConnell v. Anderson, 316 F.Supp. 809, 811 (D.Minn. 1970).

21. Id. at 814.

22. McConnell v. Anderson, 451 F.2d 193 (8th Cir. 1971).

23. Id. at 196. The U.S. Supreme Court refused to review the case. 405 U.S. 1046 (1972).

24. Singer v. United States Civil Service Commission, 530 F.2d 247, 249 (9th Cir. 1976).

25. Singer v. Hara, 11 Wash.App. 247, 522 P.2d 1187 (1974).

26. Singer v. U.S. Civil Service Commission, 530 F.2d 247, 250-251 (9th Cir. 1976).

27. Singer v. U.S. Civil Service Commission, 530 F.2d 247, (9th Cir. 1976).

28. Vacated 429 U.S. 1034 (1977).

29. Norton v. Macy, 135 U.S. App. D.C. 214, 417 F.2d 1161 (1969).

30. Society for Individual Rights v. Hampton, 63 F.R.D. 399, 402 (D.C.N.D.Cal. 1973), aff'd. in part 528 F.2d 905 (1975); see 40 Fed.Reg. 2047-48, (July 3, 1975).

31. Statement of facts found in Acanfora v. Board of Education of Montgomery County, 359 F.Supp. 843 (D.Md. 1973), aff'd. on other grounds 491 F.2d 498 (4th Cir. 1974), cert. den. 419 U.S. 836 (1974).

32. Acanfora, supra, 359 F.Supp. at 846, quoting from transcript of "60 Minutes," p. 8.

33. 359 F.Supp. 843 at 851, 854.

34. 359 F.Supp. 843 at 857.

35. Acanfora v. Board of Education of Montgomery County, 491 F.2d 498 (4th Cir. 1974).

36. Gish v. Board of Education of Borough of Paramus, Bergen County, 145 N.J. Super. 96, 366 A.2d 1337, 1340-1341 (1976), U.S. cert. den. 434 U.S. 879.

37. Gay Students Organization of the University of New Hampshire v. Bonner, 509 F.2d 652 (1st Cir. 1974). In accord, see Wood v. Davidson, 351 F.Supp. 543 (D.C.Ga. 1972) (University of Georgia); Student Coalition for Gay Rights v. Austin Peay State University, 477 F.Supp. 1267 (D.C.Tenn. 1979); and Gay Activists Alliance v. Board of Regents of the University of Oklahoma, (Oklahoma 1981) 638 P.2d 1116. See also Associated Students of Sacramento State College v. Butz, Civil No. 200795 (Super. Ct. Sacramento, Calif., Feb. 15, 1971 Order) (cited at 351 F.Supp. 546); Gay Student Services v. Texas A&M University, 612 F.2d 160 (5th Cir. 1980), cert. den. 449 U.S. 1034 (1980). An unreported decision in the Tenth Circuit Court of Appeals is said to have allowed the "denial of recognition as a campus organization to a 'gay front' group." Lawrence Gay Liberation Front v. University of Kansas, Civil No. T-5069 (D.Kan. Feb. 10, 1972) aff'd. Civil No. 72-1159 (10th Cir. March 12, 1973), quoted in Maryland Public Interest Research Group v. Elkins, 430 F.Supp. 387, 393 (D.Md. 1976). For annotation see 50 ALR Fed. 516-524.

38. Gay Alliance of Students v. Matthews, 544 F.2d 162 (4th Cir. 1976).

39. Concurrence by J. Markey, 544 F.2d at 168.

40. Gay Lib v. University of Missouri, 416 F.Supp. 1350, 1358 f.n. 6 (W.D.Mo. 1976).

41. Id. at 1369.

42. Gay Lib v. University of Missouri, 558 F.2d 848 (8th Cir. 1977), cert den. 434 U.S. 1080 (1978), reh. den. 435 U.S. 981 (1978).

43. Concurrence of Circ. J. Webster, 558 F.2d at 857.

44. 434 US 1080, 55 L.Ed.2d 789, 790 (1978), reh. den. 435 US 981 (1978).

45. Aumiller v. University of Delaware, 434 F.Supp. 1273 (D.Del. 1977).

46. Id. at 1297, 1301.

47. Aumiller v. University of Delaware, 455 F.Supp. 676 (D.Del. 1978).

48. Fricke v. Lynch, 491 F.Supp. 381 (D.R.I. 1980).

49. Mississippi Gay Alliance v. Goudelock, 536 F.2d 1073 (5th Cir. 1976) reh. den. 541 F2d 281 (1976), cert. den. 430 U.S. 982 (1977).

50. Toward a Gayer Bicentennial Committee v. Rhode Island Bicentennial Foundation, 417 F.Supp. 632 (1976) and 417 F.Supp. 642 (1976).

51. Id. at 642 (citations omitted).

52. Id. at 645 (citations omitted).

53. Alaska Gay Coalition v. Sullivan (Alaska 1978) 578 P.2d 951.

54. Cyr v. Walls, 439 F.Supp. 697 (1977) and phone conversation March 24, 1980, with James C. Barber, Esq., Dallas, Texas, counsel for plaintiffs.

55. Gay Law Students Association v. Pacific Telephone and Telegraph Company, 24 Cal.3d 458, 156 Cal.Rptr. 14, 595 P.2d 592 (1979). This employment protection is *not* provided by federal civil rights statutes, see, e.g. Blum v. Gulf Oil Corp., 597 F.2d 936 (5th Cir. 1979), DeSantis v. Pacific Telephone and Telegraph Co., 608 F.2d 327 (9th Cir. 1979) and cases discussed there. But see Valdes v. Lumbermen's Mutual Casualty Co. 507 F.Supp. 10 (S.D. Fla. 1980) (Title VII Claim stated in allegation that firing of employee as lesbian was mere pretext for sexual discrimination).

56. Rowland v. Mad River Local School District, Case No. C-3-75-125, D.C.S.D. Ohio, Western Div., Slip Opinion, October 22, 1981.

· 27 ·

Homosexuality and the Law

Rhonda Rivera

What legitimate interest the government, employers, and others in official and semiofficial societal positions have in the private, sexual behavior of individual adults perplexes many persons. However, whether the interest is legitimate or not, it is pervasive.[1] Today in the United States, private consensual sexual activities between adults of the same sex—that is, homosexual behavior—cause them to be subjected to various criminal penalties and to experience discrimination in their employment and housing situations as well as in innumerable other situations in their daily lives.[2]

The word "deviant" used in its technical, statistical context refers merely to behavior which lies so many standard deviations from the norm.[3] However, the word as used today is pejorative. The "deviant" person in America has been labeled as either sick, criminal, or immoral. Thus, society "legitimately" could seek to cure, jail, or shun the person involved. The homosexual person has had the singular honor of having all three labels applied. For years homosexuality was considered a mental illness[4] and mental health workers could use shock treatments, aversion therapy, or milieu therapy to cure this illness. Not only were homosexual individuals sick, they were also sinful and immoral. This characterization provided a justification for not renting them apartments, firing them, and taking custody of their children. Last, but hardly least, they were criminals and could be jailed, often as felons, for their sexual behavior.

How has the law fit into this pattern and practice of discrimination? Legal matters are either civil or criminal. Criminal acts are those punishable by the state—for example, murder, robbery, and so on. Behaviors are labeled criminal when they endanger not only individuals but our collective society.

323

Civil matters are private matters, usually disputes between individuals, which the legal system attempts to resolve by providing a settlement mechanism.

In the criminal area, the societal attitude toward homosexuality has resulted in the use of affirmative sanctions by courts, legislatures, and administrations. In the civil area, the societal attitude toward homosexuality has resulted in affirmative nonaction by various governmental agencies. The government has refused to intervene in private disputes to ensure that homosexual persons are treated fairly and equitably.

Let us turn first to the current state of the law in the criminal area. Until 1962, sexual behavior between persons of the same sex was criminal in all 50 states.[5] Sexual acts between married heterosexuals in other than "missionary" position were also outlawed.[6] However, laws against heterosexual behavior were generally ignored. Laws against homosexual behavior were enforced, albeit selectively.[7] Selective enforcement kept the average homosexual person fearful and closeted. Since 1962, with the adoption of the Model Penal Code in Illinois,[8] private, consensual, adult sexual behavior has been decriminalized in 21[9] states. Thus, homosexual persons in those states are no longer criminals. It should be noted that at least one state, after decriminalizing adult, consensual, private sex, specifically recriminalized homosexual sodomy.[10] Today in 29 states the sexual behavior of homosexual persons is criminal.[11] There are a variety of laws ranging from the prohibition of sodomy[12] to the prohibition of "gross indecencies between two men" and "gross indecencies between two women."[13] These "crimes" are often felonies, carrying penalties of up to 20 years in prison.[14] Selective enforcement is still the rule. Moreover, behavior by police, bordering on entrapment, underlies most arrests for homosexual behavior.[15] Most "complainants" in courts are police decoys who testify to solicitation by the homosexual individual.

The criminalization of homosexual sexual behavior not only affects those apprehended but legitimizes discrimination by other sectors of society. A criminal record can be a justification for refusal to hire persons, rent them an apartment, deny them a professional license, or admit them to the military.[16] For years, the federal government justified its employment discrimination against gay persons on the grounds that since they were criminals who had to hide their activity or be arrested, they were particularly susceptible to blackmail and hence were poor security risks.[17]

The laws making homosexual behavior criminal have been attacked in many state forums as unconstitutional.[18] A number of these cases have succeeded.[19] However, this line of attack suffered a serious setback in 1976 when the U.S. Supreme Court summarily upheld the decision of Doe v.

Commonwealth's Attorney for Richmond.[20] In Doe, two gay men challenged the constitutionality of the sodomy statute of Virginia. A three-judge federal panel upheld the statute by a vote of two to one. The decision relied heavily on three arguments. The first argument was based on the longevity of the statute—the "it's always been like that" argument.[21] The second argument was religious in nature. The court quoted Leviticus and Deuteronomy.[22] The third argument was circular. The court said that since the state had a right to punish criminal behavior, it had a right to make homosexual behavior criminal.[23] The Doe decision has been heavily criticized by some commentators because the court ignored a whole line of constitutional privacy decisions.[24] However, the decision was upheld without comment by the U.S. Supreme Court. The effect has been to legitimize the current criminal sanctions against homosexual behavior.

EMPLOYMENT

What kind of legal protection does a gay person have today in his or her employment? Remember that gay people represent one of the largest minority groups in America.[25] It is popular to say, even among supposed liberals, that gay persons are not discriminated against[26] in employment (see Chapter 29). The real discrimination occurs when a gay person is open or discovered; it is then that he or she is refused employment or is fired.

Under current legal theory a private employer in the United States has an absolute right to hire and fire as he or she pleases for whatever reason he or she wishes.[27] The only limit on private employment actions is federal law. Title VII of the Civil Rights Act of 1964 forbids private employers from discriminating on the basis of sex and race.[28] Therefore, women and racial minorities, including Blacks, are protected by federal law. Sexual preference or orientation is not a category protected by Title VII. At least three major court cases have sought to include homosexual persons among those protected by Title VII and all have failed.[29] As of this writing, there is no federal or state legislation protecting the employment rights of homosexual persons who work for private employers. Such employees can be fired on whim, caprice, and for no reason other than bigotry.

There are two bright spots in this otherwise dismal picture. The National Gay Task Force has obtained a "no-discrimination" policy statement from many large corporations.[30] While such a policy gives the gay employee no legal recourse, it does reflect a societal change of attitude. Second, a few municipalities and counties have ordinances prohibiting discrimination against gays. Most of these ordinances do not speak to employment discrimination, but rather prohibit discrimination in public accommodations and housing.[31] A smaller number protect a gay person who is employed by the city or county,[32] and a few actually forbid discrimination by private employers.[33]

Public employment presents a slightly different picture. The federal government and state governments are bound by the protections afforded by the Fifth and Fourteenth Amendments to the U.S. Constitution. This means that a person cannot have a job taken away without the "due process of law." Stivison's article (Chapter 26) reviews this topic in its nonmilitary aspects.

It should be noted, however, that the military is not covered by Federal Civil Service regulations. The armed forces since the late 1940s have had a clear and harsh policy of immediate separation of discovered gays coupled with dishonorable discharges.[34] This policy, according to a study done by Williams and Weinberg, has resulted in the separation of approximately 2000 men and women from the military per year.[35] How many persons are refused enlistment is not accurately known. The same study indicated that the great majority of gay persons in the military are never discovered and serve honorably and productively.[36] Those gay persons who have been dishonorably discharged carry a stigma for the rest of their lives. A dishonorable discharge on the basis of homosexuality makes it extremely difficult for the person involved to become employed except in the most menial positions.[37]

Until recently, most gay military personnel did not fight the armed services on their policy of dishonorably discharging gay people. But since the early 1970s gay military personnel have begun to fight this policy in the courts. At present the main effect of this litigation has been a policy change whereby gays being separated from the service are more often given honorable discharges.[38] However, for many gay soldiers and sailors, this is simply not enough, because they wish to reenlist and have military careers. The now famous Sergeant Leonard Matlovich has fought this issue in the courts with some success.[39] Sergeant Matlovich was a much-decorated and exemplary member of the Air Force who announced his sexual preference to his commanding officer. He was immediately discharged, originally with a general discharge, which, after he sued, was upgraded to an honorable discharge. Sergeant Matlovich lost his first law suit—although Judge Gesell, who found for the Air Force, spent a large part of his opinion castigating the Air Force for its irrational but legal policy.[40] However, during this first lawsuit, the Air Force stated that its policy was not the immediate separation of all gays; on rare occasions "exceptional" gay soldiers could be retained.[41] On appeal, the Appellate Court remanded the case to the lower court. It directed the Air Force to justify the different treatment between "ordinary" gay soldiers and "exceptional" ones and to specify the criteria the Air Force was using to make these decisions.[42] This case was resolved after this chapter was written. Matlovich settled out of court for a sum of money; as a condition of the settlement, he did not seek reinstatement. Very recently, the Department of Defense has issued new and more stringent regulations against homosexual persons in the military. These regulations dim any hope raised by the appellate court in the Matlovich decision.

Meanwhile, a number of other cases have been decided at lower federal court levels which find the whole policy against gays by the military unconstitutional as a denial of equal protection, a violation of due process or an intrusion into one's right of privacy.[43] How these cases will fare on appeal is problematic. At the present time, known homosexual persons are still being denied entrance into the military and are still being discharged upon discovery.

One other employment area must be considered—public school teaching.[44] In no other area is homophobia so widespread. Gay persons, upon discovery, are routinely fired from teaching positions. The reasons generally given are the following: (1) homosexual persons molest children, (2) homosexual teachers will turn "normal" children into gays, (3) homosexual teachers are immoral per se and thus do not present a proper teaching model to students. The first is simply untrue. Statistics show that most child molestation is done by heterosexual males,[45] with homosexual males accounting for most of the rest. (Women, gay or straight, are seldom involved in such activity.) Child molestation is a mental illness (pedophilia) having no connection with sexual preference. With regard to turning children into homosexual adults, again reputable studies show that sexual preference is determined usually by five or six years of age—before school age.[46] Moreover, since heterosexual teachers do not seem to be able to change gay students' sexual preference, how the reverse is to be accomplished is yet to be explained. The third rationale is a reflection of how religious standards impinge on our legal decisions. Teacher certification in almost all states can be removed for "immorality" or "moral turpitude."[47] Many commentators would limit such phrases to apply to conviction for criminal activity and to exclude private, consensual, adult sexual behavior. However, this is not a pervasive view. At present, gay teachers are entitled to due process rights— that is, they are entitled to a hearing before they are fired. However, they generally lose at those hearings, and courts generally uphold their dismissal.[48]

Indeed, most gay teachers live in fear of losing their jobs. Father O'Neill, author of *The Church and the Homosexual,*[49] believes that this fact is extremely counterproductive to our society, because many gay persons are actively drawn to teaching as a vocation—and, according to Father O'Neill, have strong special abilities in this field.

CHILD CUSTODY

Another civil matter often before the court which involves discrimination against homosexual individuals is child custody. Many homosexual persons marry and have children. When the lesbian mother or gay father divorces his or her spouse, a child custody issue may arise. Until very recently, gay parents usually did not fight the demands of the nongay parent for custody because of threats of blackmail. The nongay parent often informed the gay parent that if he or she contested the custody issue, parents, friends, and employers would all be told, and the issue of the gay parent's sexual preference would be raised in open court. Many gay parents, wishing to protect their ability to earn a living as well as to protect their children from the trauma of an ugly court battle, gave in. Starting in the early 1970s, however, gay parents began fighting to keep their children. It has been a uphill battle.[50]

Custody decisions are made in domestic relations courts, the lowest level of our court system. The judges, for the most part, are white, male, middle class and over 50.[51] Except in Texas (where juries are used), the decisions are made by judges. Theoretically, the standard to be applied is "the best interest of the child."[52] However, this standard is so vague that most judges can, and often do, apply their own standards.[53] The decision is based mostly on facts. In our court system, facts are decided for all time at the original court level; appeals are only on matters of law. In custody decisions, which are highly factual and are limited only by a very vague legal standard, appealable issues are rare. An appeals court will overturn a trial court judge on the facts only if a gross abuse of discretion is shown. Therefore, a case won on appeal is extremely rare. The result is that almost all custody decisions are made at the trial court level by domestic relations judges. The homophobia of many of these judges is well documented.[54] In many cases the mere homosexuality of the parent is deemed sufficient to show that the best interests of the child lie in custody with the nongay parent.[55] Other than homosexuality per se being not in the "best interests" of the child, the courts cite child molestation, fear of the child becoming homosexual himself or herself, embarrassment from teasing by peers, and (once again) immorality as the usual reasons for finding against the gay parent.[56] In rare cases where the court permits custody to remain with the gay parent, that parent is often forbidden to live with another gay person in a loving relationship.[57] In one case, visitation was allowed only in the gay father's home when the father's lover was gone and no other gay person was in the house.[58]

Many gay parents have lost their children. Exactly how many is unknown because most child custody cases are not appealed and hence are unpublished and not available to legal scholars.[59] Some gay parents have won custody. However, the price is high. The strategy has been to educate the court about homosexuality and homosexual parents. Such a strategy entails expert witnesses, and such witnesses are extremely expensive. The second main cost is emotional: Parents who choose to fight long court battles suffer enormously. Because they admit their sexual preference, they often lose their jobs, lose the support of parents and supposed friends, and suffer physical abuse and harassment. There have been some victories for gay parents.[60] The Supreme Courts of Michigan[61] and California[62] in recent cases have declared that homosexuality per se is not a reason to remove a child from a parent or to refuse custody to a parent. But such victories are few and far between.

It should be noted that in the United States, no child custody decision is ever final, and custody remains an issue until the child is 18. A noncustodial parent can always challenge a custody decision by arguing that "a change of circumstances" has occurred and the "best interests" of the child would be served if the original order were changed. Thus even those gay parents who have won are never free from the fear of subsequent suits by homophobic ex-spouses, in-laws, and even their own parents.

The child custody issue does not end with disputes between divorcing parents. Gay persons have sought to adopt children and have been denied that right, solely on the basis of their sexual preference. Other gays have offered to be foster parents, usually for gay kids who need the special understanding another gay person can give. While in New York,[63] New Jersey,[64] and, reportedly, California, some social service agencies have recognized that gay persons are the logical choice as foster parents for gay kids, a number of courts in other states have refused to countenance such actions.[65] The theory seems to be that the gay child, if placed in a heterosexual home, will "straighten" out. The courts have ignored the recommendations of social workers, psychologists, psychiatrists, and others who recommend placement with gay parents.

A third issue in child rearing is the use of artificial insemination. Many lesbian women wish to be mothers and seek to be artificially inseminated.[66] There are no particular laws or regulations which govern artificial insemination. Hence all such decisions are made by doctors individually. Many doctors refuse to artifically inseminate lesbians, although they will perform the task for single heterosexual women.

MARRIAGE

Marriage is an issue for gay persons in two ways. First, many gays marry in the traditional sense and later wish to divorce their spouses. Interestingly enough, homosexuality on the part of one's spouse is not grounds for divorce.[67] Generally courts have granted divorces to the nongay spouse, holding that the other spouse's sexual preference represents "extreme cruelty."[68] A New York court refused to grant a woman a divorce from her husband even though she could prove his conviction for sodomy.[69] In that day adultery was the sole basis for divorce in New York, and the court found that sodomy was not adultery. Today, with the growing prevalence of no-fault divorce and dissolution, the question of homosexuality as grounds for divorce is becoming obsolete.

However, marriage as a legal status is an issue for gay persons in another way. Our society sets up innumerable formal and informal legal and economic benefits for married persons. For example, they may own property with special survivorship rights, enjoy in some circumstances a lower income tax rate, inherit automatically by statute, and receive a widow's or widower's allowance. Insurance companies which write medical and/or property insurance tailor programs for married persons and do not permit nonmarried cohabitors to enjoy these benefits. Pensions are treated in a similar manner. Moreover, "being married" is an important social status in our society. The commitment implies stability and responsibility. Marriage is also a public statement of family and love relationships. In no state are gay persons permitted to marry one another.[70] This is so even in those states (the majority) where the language of marriage statutes is gender neutral. Court decisions in a number of states have denied gay persons the right to marry.[71] The bases of these decisions have been tradition and religion.[72] As in other cases, biblical quotations abound to support the decision.[73]

What of the gay persons who do not seek traditional marriage but contract between themselves as to the legal and economic incidents of their relationship? These contracts stand a strong possibility of being unenforceable in courts of law.[74] Courts have held such contracts void as against public policy. The contracts theoretically offend public policy by promoting immorality and are "tainted" by the sexual relationship between the contacting parties. Given the recent Marvin v. Marvin[75] decision in California recognizing certain economic rights of heterosexual, nonmarried cohabitors, it is possible that in some states carefully drawn contracts between gay persons may be upheld. It is indeed ironic that on one hand gay persons may not marry and on the other that when they attempt to deal with the issues by contract, they are again denied the support of the courts.

IMMIGRATION

Gay persons have been systematically excluded from immigrating to the United States. Under current immigration law they can be excluded as sexual psychopaths.[76] Moreover, once admitted to the United States, an alien can have his or her visa revoked because of homosexuality.[77] Finally, a permanent resident may be denied citizenship based on his or her sexual preference.[78] In this area there have been some recent changes in Immigration and Naturalization Service (INS) policy that are favorable to gays. However, these are slight and subject to change with each administration. The most impressive change has been a few court decisions that have held that citizenship may not be denied to permanent residents who are gay.[79] The courts have held that same-sex sexual preference does not mean that the applicant cannot be of good moral character—which is a criterion for citizenship. Another change in INS procedure was caused by a change in policy by the U.S. Public Health Service (USPHS) when the American Psychiatric Association (APA) removed homosexuality from its diagnostic manual as a mental illness. The USPHS began refusing to certify to the INS that gay aliens were mentally ill; as a consequence, since mid-1979 the INS has been unable to exclude gay persons at the borders.[80] The INS is fighting this policy change.

INCORPORATION

Gay persons, like all others, wish to associate with one another and form organizations for charitable, educational, and research purposes. When such groups are formed by nongay persons, they are usually legally incorporated and then granted tax-exempt status as nonprofit corporations by the Internal Revenue Service. Gay groups have faced two legal hurdles in this area. A number of states have refused to allow the gay groups to incorporate on the basis that formal recognition of such groups was against public policy. The Ohio Supreme Court[81] actually upheld such a refusal, but subsequently the Ohio Attorney General reversed this opinion.[82] In most states today, gay organizations can be incorporated as nonprofit groups. However, only since 1978 has the Internal Revenue Service begun to routinely grant tax-exempt status to gay nonprofit organizations. After hard work and lobbying by the National Gay Task Force, the IRS issued a Revenue Ruling[83] which allowed gay organizations to be evaluated on the same basis as similar nongay organizations. Originally, gay organizations were refused tax-exempt status on the grounds that the organizations treated homosexuality as an acceptable, alternative lifestyle "rather than a sickness, disturbance or diseased pathology."[84]

GAY STUDENTS

Is there no bright spot on the legal horizon for gay persons before the courts in the United States? In one area of legal controversy gays have consistently won their legal battles at the appellate level. Gay students have sought to organize on campuses across the nation. Universities and colleges have almost uniformly sought to stop such organization by refusing the organizations access to university facilities, refusing them recognition as official student groups, and refusing them funding granted to other similar student organizations. Federal appellate courts across the country, when confronted with cases arising from these situations, have uniformly decided in favor of the student groups.[85]

CONCLUSIONS

What I have sought to illustrate in this chapter is that the law and its officers and institutions treat a significant portion of the American population differently, unequally, and unfairly. First and foremost, behavior that is private, consensual, and among adults is made criminal. Second, the state actively chooses not to protect its homosexual population from the bigoted, malicious, and ignorant actions of other citizens. The state chooses affirmatively to deny homosexual individuals a fair chance at a job, service in the country's armed forces, a chance to be an effective parent, and the status of formally recognized committed relationships. The policy of the state reinforces and promotes homophobia and homophobic actions by other Americans.

The curious dilemma that faces gay persons living in a discriminatory society is that until they are found out they can lead lives free from harassment. Unless gays "come out" in large numbers, they will be ineffective to change attitudes and effect political change to prevent discrimination. As Jill Johnston said, "what if every gay person in America turned purple for one day?"[86] But to come out forces gay individuals to do what no individual really wants to do—make one's private intimate life a public issue. As long as persons are presumed heterosexual unless they indicate otherwise, the laws will operate to support that presumption. It is a tough position for gay Americans.

NOTES

1. For a comprehensive documentation of discrimination against homosexual persons, see Rivera, "Out Straight-Laced Judges: The Legal Position of Homosexual Persons in the United States," 30 Hastings L. J. 799 (1979).
2. See Comment, "The Homosexual's Legal Dilemma" 27 Ark. L. Rev. 687 (1973); Note, "Homosexuality and the Law—An Overview," 17 NY L. Rev. 273 (1971).
3. *The American College Dictionary,* Random House (1955).
4. See Bowman & Engle, "A Psychiatric Evaluation of Laws of Homosexuality," 29 Temp. L. Q. 273 (1956).

5. This situation is described in M. Ploscowe, *Sex and the Law* (rev. ed. 1962) and Notes "The Constitutionality of Laws Forbidding Private Homosexual Conduct," 72 Mich. L. R. 1613 (1974). See also W. Barnett, *Sexual Freedom and the Constitution* (1973).

6. See Hefner, "The Legal Enforcement of Morality," 40 U. Colo. L. Rev. 199 (1968), at 200. All the sexual acts penalized when committed between persons of the same sex also can be performed by persons of the opposite sex. Laws forbidding certain sexual acts often do not differentiate as to heterosexuals or homosexuals, married or unmarried persons. Kinsey estimated that if all the laws then currently on the books forbidding various sex acts were enforced, 95 percent of all white American males would be subject to prosecution. A. Kinsey, W. Pomeroy, & C. Martin, *Sexual Behavior of the Human Male*, 390-93 (1948).

7. See "Decoy Enforcement of Homosexual Laws" 112 U. Pa. L. Rev. 259 (1963); "The Consenting Adult Homosexual and the Law" 13 UCLA L. Rev. 643 (1966).

8. 1961 Ill. Laws, p. 1983, § 11-2 (effective Jan. 1, 1962).

9. Rivera, supra, at 949-951.

10. Ark. Stat. Ann. § 41-1813 (1977).

11. Rivera, supra, at 949-951.

12. e.g. Md. Ann. Code §§ 27-553, 27-554 (Mich. Supp. 1977).

13. Mich. Comp. Laws §§ 750.338, 750.338a (1968).

14. Id.

15. "Clandestine Police Surveillance of Public Toilet Booth Held to be Unreasonable Search," 63 Col. L. Rev. 955 (1963); Jacobs, "Decoy Enforcement of Homosexual Laws," 112 U. Penn. L. Rev. 259 (1963); "Private Consensual Homosexual Behavior: The Crime & its Enforcement," 70 Yale L. J. 623 (1961); "The Consenting Adult Homosexual and the Law: An Empirical Study of Enforcement and Administration in Los Angeles County," 13 UCLA L. Rev. 647 (1966).

16. D. J. West, *Homosexuality* 91 (1967).

17. Note, "Security Clearances for Homosexuals," 25 Stan. L. Rev. 403, 410 (1973).

18. Rivera, supra, at 952-953.

19. State v. Pilcher, 242 N.W.2d 348 (Iowa 1976).

20. 403 F Supp. 119 (E.D. Va. 1975), aff'd mem, 425 U.S. 901, rehearing and denied, 425 U.S. 985 (1976).

21. Id. at 1202.

22. Id.

23. Id.

24. For commentary on this case, see Comment, "Constitutional Protection of Private Sexual Conduct Among Consenting Adults: Another Look at Sodomy Statutes," 62 Iowa L. Rev. 568 (1976); Comment, "Doe v. Commonwealth's Attorney: A Set-Back for the Right of Privacy," 65 Ky. L. J. 748 (1977); 15 Duq. L. Rev. 123 (1976). Many important civil cases explicitly refer to the court's decision in Doe. See Cyr v. Walls, 439 F. Supp. 697, 700-01 (N.D. Tex. 1977); Saal v. Middendorf, 427 F. Supp. 192, 198 (N.D. Cal. 1977); Matlovich v. Secretary of the Air Force, Civ. No. 75-1750 (D.D.C. July 16, 1976) reported in 2 Sex L. Rep. 53, rev'd, 47 U.S.L.W. 2361 (D.C. Cir Dec. 6, 1978).

25. See Chapter 3.

26. See Leo, Homosexuality: Tolerance vs. Approval," Time, Jan. 8, 1979, at 48, 51; Robinson, "Invisible Men: The Issue is Visibility, Not Discrimination," The New Republic, June 3, 1968, at 9.

27. United Elec. Radio & Mach. Workers v. General Elec. Co., 127 F. Supp. 934, 937 (D.D.C. 1954), cert. denied, 352 U.S. 872 (1956).

28. 42 U.S.C. §§ 2000e-2000e-17 (1970 & Supp. V 1975).

29. Voyles v. Ralph K. Danies Medical Center 403 F. Supp. 456 (N.D. Cal. 1975); Smith v. Liberty Mutual Insurance Co. 395 F. Supp. 1098 (N. DGA 1975); Parfitt v. D. L. Auld Co. et al. C.A. No. 74-437 (S.D. Ohio) 7-20-75.

30. National Gay Task Force Action Report 4 (April 1978).

31. Col. OH. Code § 2325.02 (1974).

32. The following cities have ordinances or executive orders banning discrimination against homosexual persons in municipal employment only: Amherst, MA; Atlanta, GA; Boston, MA;

Chapel Hill, NC; Cupertino, CA; Ithaca, NY; Los Angeles, CA; Mountain View, CA; New York, NY; Ottawa, Canada; Pullman, WA; Santa Barbara, CA; Sunnyvale, CA. *It's Time,* March, 1977, at 3.

33. The following ordinances prohibit private employment discrimination against homosexuals: Anchorage, Alas., Ordinance A077-75 (Jan. 20, 1976); Ann Arbor, Mich., Code ch. 112, §§ 9:151-9:155 (1972); Detroit, Mich., Code ch. 10, §§ 7-1004-7-1005 (1976); East Lansing, Mich., Code ch. 4 § 1.127 (1973); Madison, Wis., Code § 323(7) (a) (1976); Minneapolis, Minn., Code ch. 945 (1975); Palo Alto, Cal., Admin. Code § 2.22.050 (1969); Seattle, Wash., Ordinance 102, 562 (Sept. 18, 1973); Washington, D.C., Human Rights Law (Nov. 16, 1973).

The following cities and countries were reported by *It's Time,* the newsletter of the National Gay Task Force, in March 1977, to have laws prohibiting private employment discrimination against homosexuals: Alfred, NY; Austin, TX; Berkeley, CA; Cleveland Heights, OH; Marshall, MN; Portland, OR; San Jose, CA: Toronto, Ontario; Tucson, AZ; Yellow Springs; OH; Hennepin County, MN; Howard County, MD; Santa Cruz County, CA.

Since March 1977, other cities have passed ordinances prohibiting private employment discrimination: San Francisco, *see* National Gay Task Force Action Report 3 (May 1978); Aspen, CO, *see The Advocate,* Jan. 25, 1977, at 8; Champaign, IL, *see The Advocate,* Sept. 9, 1977, at 8; Iowa City, Iowa, *see The Advocate,* Feb. 8, 1978, at 11; Windsor, Ontario, *see The Advocate,* Feb. 8, 1978, at 11. However, a number of such ordinances recently have been repealed by referendum in Dade County, Florida; Wichita, Kansas; St. Paul, Minnesota; and Eugene, Oregon.

The following counties are reported to have laws forbidding discrimination against homosexual persons in private employment: Santa Cruz, California; Latah, Idaho; Howard, Maryland; Hennepin, Minnesota. *It's Time,* March 1977.

34. Note, "Homosexuals in the Military," 37 Fordham L. Rev. 465, 468 (1969). For a concise history of U.S. military attitudes prior to the 1940s *see* 465-46.

35. C. Williams & M. Weinberg, *Homosexuals and the Military* 53 (1971).

36. Id. at 60.

37. The armed forces are evidently well aware of the stigma attached to any discharge other than honorable. "Both officers and enlisted men who resign or accept an undesirable discharge must sign a waiver recognizing . . . that they expect to find difficulty in civilian life due to the character of their separation. *E.g.* SEC NAV Instruction 1900.0(6)(c)(2)(b)(1)(2), 20 April 1964." Note, "Homosexuals in the Military," 37 Fordham L. Rev. 465, 469 n. 36 (1969).

38. Rivera, supra, at 837-855.

39. Matlovich v. Secretary of the Air Force NO. 75-1750 (D.D.C. July 16, 1976), reported in 2 Sex L. Rep. 53 (1976) and 45 USLW 2074-75 (Aug. 17, 1976), rev'd 47 USLW 2361 (D.C. Cir. Dec. 6, 1978).

40. 2 Sex L. Rep. 53, 56 (1976).

41. "Exceptions to permit retention may be authorized only where the most unusual circumstances exist and provided the airman's ability to perform military service has not been compromised." Memorandum in Support of Defendants' Motion to Dismiss or, in the Alternative for Summary Judgment, and in Opposition to Plaintiff's Motion to Compel Discovery at 1, Matlovich v. Secretary of Air Force, No. 75-1750 (D.D.C. July 16, 1976).

42. 47 U.S.L.W. 2361 (Dec. 12, 1978).

43. Saal v. Middendorf 427 F. Supp. 192 (N.D. Cal. 1977); Martinez v. Brown 449 F. Supp. 207 (N.D. Cal. 1978).

44. While 56 percent of a population sampled agreed that homosexuals should have equal rights in terms of job opportunities, 65 percent of the population sampled felt homosexuals should *not* be hired as elementary school teachers. *"Homosexuals Move Toward Open Life as Tolerance Rises,"* New York Times, July 17, 1977, at 34, col. 1. See also LaMorte, "Legal Rights and Responsibilities of Homosexuals in Public Education," 4 J. Law-Educ. 449 (1975).

45. Child molestation is *not* a homosexual phenomenon. Pedophilia, a sexual preference for children, is distinct from homosexuality. See D. J. West, Homosexuality Re-Examined 212-17 (1977); D. J. West, Homsexuality 118-19 (1967); Comment, "Private Consensual

Homsexual Behavior: The Crime and Its Enforcement," 70 Yale L. J. 623, 629 (1961). Homo-sexual men primarily prefer men of their own age rather than children. Institute for Sex Research, Sex Offenders 639 (1965); M. Schofield, Sociological Aspects of Homosexuality, 147-55 (1965), cited in W. Barnet, Sexual Freedom and the Constitution 129-30 n. 51 (1973). In fact, child molesters tend to be heterosexual in orientation. Schofield, supra; Institute for Sex Research, supra at 277-79, 303-34, 332-34. Moreover, child molesters are almost never female, either heterosexual or homosexual. West, Homosexuality, supra at 115; Institute for Sex Research, supra at 9.

46. J. Money and A. Ehrhardt, Man and Woman: Boy and Girl, Johns Hopkins University Press (1972).

47. While it is well established that states have the power to set the standards for teaching certificates, Vogulkin v. State Bd. of Educ., 194 Cal. App. 2d 424, 15 Cal. Rptr. 335 (1961); People v. Flanigan, 347 I11. 328, 179 N.E. 823 (1932); Marrs v. Matthews, 270 S.W. 586 (Tex. Civ. App. 1925), there is no case law and little data on any initial exclusion of homosexual persons from the teaching profession. See Horenstein, "Homosexuals in the Teaching Profession," 20 Clev. St. L. Rev. 125 (1961) for interviews with school officials as to school policy with respect to the applications of homosexual teachers.

48. Rivera, supra, at 860-874.

49. J. McNeill, *The Church and the Homosexual* (1976).

50. Rivera, supra, at 883-904.

51. See generally Buxton & Dubin, "Family Court Judges are Only People: But More is Required," 1 Whitt. L. Rev. 177 (1979).

52. Finlay v. Finlay, 240 N.Y. 429, 433-44, 148 N.E. 624, 626, 211 N.Y.S. 429, 434 (1925).

53. See generally N. Lauerman; "Non-Marital Sexual Conduct and Child Custody," 46 U. Cin. L. Rev. 647 (1977).

54. Rivera, supra, at 883-904.

55. Chaffin v. Frye, 45 Cal. App.3d 39, 119 Cal. Rptr. 22 (1975).

56. Hall v. Hall, No. 55900 (C.P. Licking County, Ohio June, 1974).

57. Schuster v. Schuster & Isaacson v. Isaacson Nos. D-36867, D-36868 (Wash. Super. Ct., King County Dec. 22, 1974), aff'd in part, 585 P.2d 130 (Wash. 1978). On appeal, the Washington Supreme Court affirmed that part of the opinion that allowed the mothers to retain custody but ruled that the lower court had erred in modifying the custody order to allow the mothers to live together.

58. In re J.S. & C. 129 N.J. Super. 486, 324 A.2d 90 (1974). The court analogized the father to a bank robber who is allowed visitation rights only on the assumption that he will not expose his child to his "unacceptable line of endeavor." Id. at 497-98, 324 A.2d at 97. A homosexual parent who advocates breaking New Jersey's sodomy laws can, the court reasoned, be similarly restricted. Accordingly, the court imposed the following restrictions on the father's visitation rights: (1) during visitation the father may not cohabit or sleep with any individual other than a lawful spouse; (2) during visitation the father may not involve the children in any homosexual related activities or publicity; (3) during visitation the father *may "not be in the presence of his lover."* Id. at 498, 324 A.2d at 97 (emphasis added).

59. The nonpublication issue is so real and so controversial that noted scholar Herma Hill Kay, in her extremely well-regarded text, K. Davison, R. Ginsburg & H. Kay, *Sex-Based Discrimination* at 275 (1975), discusses unreported lesbian mother cases. Professor Kay applies the California standards with respect to certification for nonpublication to determine whether many of the child custody cases were properly denied publication.

60. M.P. v. S.P., 5 FLR 2855, (N.S. Sup. Ct. App. 1979). Bezaire v. Bezaire, 2 Fam. L.R. 51 (Sup. Ct. Ontario 1979).

61. People v. Brown 49 Mich. App. 358, 212 N.W.2d 55 (1973), Miller v. Miller.

62. Nadler v. Superior Court 255 Cal. App.2d 523, 63 Cal. Rptr. 352 (1967).

63. Franks, "Homosexual Foster Parents: An Advance or a Peril," *New York Times*, May 7, 1974, at 47.

64. See *New York Times*, Dec. 2, 1979.

65. In re Davis 1 Fam. L. Rep. (BNA) 2845 (Wash. Super. Ct. 1975).

66. The Advocate, Feb. 22, 1978, at 6. See generally, Note, "The Legal Status of Artificial Insemination: A Need For Policy Formulation," 19 Drake L. Rev. 409 (1970); Note, "Artificial Insemination: A Legislative Remedy," 3 West ST. U. L. Rev. 48 (1975).

67. Rivera, supra, at 879-80.

68. Crutcher v. Crutcher 86 Miss. 231, 38 So. 337 (1905) Currie v. Currie 120 Fla 28, 162 So. 152 (1935) Townend v. Townend No. 639 (Ohio Ct. App., Portage County Sept. 30, 1976).

69. Cohen v. Cohen 200 Misc. 19, 103 N.Y.S.2d 426 (Sup. Ct. 1951).

70. See generally, Note, "The Legality of Homosexual Marriage," 82 Yale L. J. 573 (1973).

71. Baker v. Nelson 291 Minn. 310, 191 N.W.2d 185 (1971); Jones v. Hallahan 501 S.W.2d 588 (Ky. Ct. App. 1973); Singer v. Hara 11 Wash. App. 247, 522 P.2d 1187 (1974).

72. Jones v. Hallahan 501 S.W.2d at 589.

73. Baker, 191 N.W.2d at 186.

74. Rivera, supra, at 799, 905.

75. 18 Cal.3d 660, 557 P.2d 106, 134 Cal.Rptr. 815 (1976).

76. 8 USC § 1182(a)(4)(1976).

77. 8 USC § 1251(a)(1)(1976).

78. For a detailed description of immigration and naturalization problems and procedures see C. Gordon & H. Rosenfield, *Immigration Law and Procedure* (1978).

79. In re Labady 326 F. Supp. 924 (S.D.N.Y. 1971); In re Brodie 394 F. Supp. 1208 (D. Or. 1975).

80. INS directive of Aug. 13, 1979.

81. Grant v. Brown 39 Ohio St. 2d 112, 313 N.E.2d 847 (1974).

82. Conversation with Powell Grant, President and Trustee of Greater Cincinnati Gay Society (Aug. 8, 1978).

83. Rev. Rul. 78-305, 1978-33 I.R.B. 10.

84. *It's Time,* Oct. 1977. at 1.

85. Wood v. Davison 351 F. Supp. 543 (N.D. Ga. 1972); Gay Students Organization of the University of New Hampshire v. Bonner 367 F. Supp. 1088 (D.N.H.), modified 509 F.2d 652 (1st Cir. 1974); Gay Alliance of Students v. Matthews 544 F.2d 162 (4th Cir. 1976); Gay Lib v. University of Missouri 558 F.2d 848 (8th Cir. 1977), cert. denied, 434 U.S. 1080 (1978). For further discussion of this case, see 46 U. Mo. Kan. City L. Rev. 489 (1978); 43 Mo. L. Rev. 109 (1978).

86. J. Johnston, *Lesbian Nation,* Simon & Schuster (1970).

San Francisco's 1979 White Night Riot
Injustice, Vengeance, and Beyond

David J. Thomas

In November 1978, Harvey Milk was the most prominent, publicly gay elected official in the United States. As such he was more than supervisor for San Francisco's geographically central District Five, which included colorful, bustling, and gay Castro Street. For gays he symbolized their new openness, assertiveness, and political clout, the end of closetry, servility, and political invisibility. For others—indeed for some gays—he was a deplorable model of brashness, impudence, and public immorality.[1] George Moscone, the liberal mayor of San Francisco, leader of a fragile coalition of the disadvantaged, openly backed gay causes and was staunchly supported by gays.

The rise of gay political activism and its first wave of success were remarkably recent and rapid. Harvey Milk had moved to San Francisco in 1969 and first run for supervisor in 1973. The Castro emerged as the dominant gay area in the seventies—a residential neighborhood, shops for necessities to frivolities, and a major cruising street. Moscone was elected in 1975 and narrowly survived a conservative recall attempt in 1977. The state of California decriminalized sexual activity between consenting adults in 1975, a measure strongly promoted by Moscone, who was then a senator. In 1976, while Milk lost a State Assembly race, San Francisco passed Proposition T, which replaced at-large supervisorial elections with separate districts. Fateful, progressive, and significantly gay District 5 was born.[2] In 1977 Harvey Milk was elected its first supervisor.

Mayor Moscone signed into law Milk's comprehensive gay rights bill in 1978, barring discrimination in housing and employment. On the Board of

Author's Note: I am indebted to Randy Alfred, without whose sound knowledge, sage advice, and splendid files I could not have written this chapter. Errors and interpretation are mine.

Supervisors only Supervisor Dan White opposed the measure. This was also the year in California of the Briggs Initiative (Proposition 6) which, if enacted, would have barred gay teachers, or those who advocated homosexuality as a normal way of life, from the public schools. Nationally, in the wake of Anita Bryant's crusade, gay rights ordinances were falling in popular votes: Miami, St. Paul, Wichita, Eugene. In the summer of 1978, many believed California would be next. Gays fought back, with extensive nongay support, Harvey Milk in the forefront debating state Senator John Briggs up and down the state—as always urging gays to come out, stand up, and fight. The measure was defeated statewide and handily in San Francisco. All districts opposed Proposition 6, but while District 5 swamped it with 87.3 percent voting no, District 8—Dan White's district—was the least opposed in the city with 60.7 percent no votes.[3]

With the defeat of the Briggs Initiative on November 7, with Harvey Milk's visible ascendancy and Dan White's unexpected resignation, and with Mayor Moscone looking good for a second term, the future of progressive gay politics in San Francisco had never shone brighter. Three weeks later Milk and Moscone were dead, shot in City Hall offices on Black Monday, November 27, by ex-Supervisor Dan White. With nine bullets San Francisco was ripped apart, its politics confounded, its progressives stripped of their two most prominent leaders, its gay community thrown into shock, hurt, fear, and disarray.[4] The massive, quiet, candlelit march and tribute to Harvey Milk and George Moscone that evening, as perhaps 40,000 people gathered from the Castro and elsewhere, flowed down Market Street and assembled at City Hall, showed how deeply the two leaders were grieved, Milk in particular. Marches down Market Street, from the Castro to City Hall, had become customary at times of major public events affecting gays.

Milk's killing, after only eleven months in office, was followed by a series of events which seemed to many gays to show that their only recently won gains were endangered and even slipping away. The new mayor, Dianne Feinstein, a rival of Moscone and a self-proclaimed centrist, had supported gay rights ordinances, but she was viewed as prissy and uncomprehending of gays' real concerns. Initially, for instance, she declined to repeat Moscone's crucial pledge to appoint a gay to the important Police Commission. The prescient Milk, anticipating a violent death, had tape-recorded a political testament to be played should he be assassinated. Cannily, he had named acceptable and unacceptable successors. This effectively tied the new mayor's hands, but her delay in the appointment and manner of its negotiation created ill will. Eventually Harry Britt, a gay leader acceptably close to Milk, was appointed the new District 5 supervisor.

Relations between gays and police, always edgy, worsened. Already in December, during a Feinstein-supported cleanup of the Tenderloin district, there was a brutal incident at the predominantly gay Crystal Hotel. An outraged public official protested: "Cops busting in doors, hauling people who were not involved out of their rooms, and inflicting corporal punishment is as raw as what we saw in Hitlerite Germany. It's a disgrace to the American people."[5] Uniformed police roughed up two lesbians outside Amelia's, a popular bar. Off-duty police crashed another well-known lesbian bar, Peg's Place, caused a row, and injured several people. It was widely believed that police now felt less constrained to mete out even-handed justice to gays and nongays alike, though Chief of Police Charles Gain, who endorsed gay recruitment to the force, had wide gay support. The district attorney was also seen as harassing gay businesses under a previously little-used red-light abatement statute.

On the afternoon of May 12, a "mini-riot" suddenly welled up on Castro Street. Hundreds quickly gathered at the intersection of Castro and 18th. Police had arrested a campaign worker for posting an election poster on a utility pole. Angry gays blew their shrill mutual aid whistles, bounced the paddy wagon, and jeered "Cops go home, cops go home!" and "Dan White was a cop."[6]

Meanwhile, on May 1, the intensely awaited trial of Dan White had begun. Little was ordinary about this trial except the prosecution. The jury selected might have been ordinary elsewhere, but not in San Francisco: no blacks, Asians, Hispanics, or gays were seated.[7] The uninspired, pedestrian prosecution sought a first-degree murder conviction with special circumstances, which could have meant the death penalty, but it avoided issues of politics and prejudice. The defense did not deny the facts of the shootings. White had, after all, confessed within hours. Yet even the tape-recording of his emotionally strained confession was turned to his advantage. The police officer who took it, an old friend and former football coach of White's, testified to his fine character. One defense psychiatrist asserted that White suffered from depression, aggravated by his eating of junk food, including Twinkies. The defense shrewdly did not claim insanity but argued that White had been in a state of "diminished capacity" and, with a bevy of psychiatrists, portrayed him as an upright, moral citizen who had cracked under unusual pressures.[8] The strategy worked. At 5:38 p.m. on Monday, May 21, 1979, the jury, after six days of deliberation, returned a verdict of voluntary manslaughter on each count, the lightest possible finding of guilt. Maximum sentence would be seven years, eight months with probation possible in little more than five years.

WHITE NIGHT

Reaction was immediate and intense, and not only among gays.[9] TV and radio stations interrupted programs with the news. Doubtless the verdict was received with satisfaction in some quarters. It was said that some police and firemen had been wearing "Free Dan White" t-shirts. Publicly expressed views, though, ranged from incredulity to outrage. Months later even the critical *Civil Grand Jury Special Report* on the riot referred to "the astonishing result in the Dan White trial."[10] For many there was simply no doubt that a major injustice had been committed. How and by whom? That analysis awaited another day. But something had to be done, directly.

A crowd gathered at Castro and Market Streets. Up went the familiar cry: "Out of the bars and into the streets!" After some uncertainty, the growing crowd began moving down Market Street in early evening. Hand-lettered signs showed the strong feelings: "Stop Attacks on Lesbians and Gay Men"; "Gay People, Fight Back"; "He got Away with Murder"; "Avenge Harvey Milk"; and, grimly, "Manslaughter is the Man's Laughter".[11]

City Hall is roughly 1.6 miles down Market Street from the Castro. Shortly after 8 p.m., marchers and others started filling up the area on the Polk Street side of the building. At this early stage there was considerable confusion. No organization of any kind was apparent, apart from some who loudly and effectively shouted down speakers and who were politically identified as outside the gay community. There was nothing for the crowd to do. A number of speakers tried to address the constantly swelling gathering, but with only feeble bullhorns available, hardly anyone could hear them. Some were cheered, some were booed, none could lead. A more effective sound system was sent for but never arrived.

For want of a nail, the war was lost. *Had* reasonable amplification existed, *were* there an eloquent speaker who could have voiced the rage and given focus to the need to act, the riot *might* never have taken place. But there is no certainty that anyone did have a good idea for the crowd to act upon. Fitful cries of "March on Dianne's House," or "March on the Hall of Justice" met little response.

The doors of City Hall were one focus. An effort was made to break through them. Pieces of the elaborate grillwork were torn off and used to break windows. Rocks and other handy missiles also were hurled at the windows. The destruction lasted for hours.

The cross-currents within the crowd and between the crowd and the police, as the police presence grew, became intricate. "Dan White was a cop," was chanted constantly all night. Some heard police shouting "fags" and "queers." A nonviolent group of gays formed a long human chain across City Hall steps, which checked a direct assault on the building and the police defending it but did not stop rocks hurled overhead. This nonviolent group was later violently dispersed by the police. Several further speakers tried to address the crowd without effect. Supervisor Carol Ruth Silver, a popular ally of Milk and the gay community, was hit in the mouth with a rock. She was taken to the hospital and received numerous stitches. Mayor

Feinstein, inside City Hall, decided not to speak. Some in the crowd yelled, "No more bullshit," others pleaded "No more violence," but the violent bore it away. They had things to do. They set fires, uprooted trees and other park plantings, and ripped out parking meters. Tear gas was shot at one side of the crowd. Three police sweeps succeeded in rearranging but not disbanding the crowd. No one took a census of the several thousands around City Hall by 10 p.m., but the crowd was considerably larger, of different composition, and in a much angrier mood than it had been at 8 p.m. Some of the newcomers looked like ordinary rowdies and punks.

The climax at City Hall came in the final hour and a half. The San Francisco Chief of Police called for assistance from surrounding municipalities. A single police car was parked on Polk Street near the front of City Hall. Rioters bounced, smashed, and torched it. Fire trucks attempting to put out the flames were stopped by the crowd, which chanted "Dan White was a fireman!" The trucks could not get through. Missiles and insults were hurled at the police. At Polk and McAllister, rioters taunted the outnumbered police at their command post with the ultimate 1960s insult of "Oink, oink!"

The sounds of the night were memorable. To the ever-present crackle of breaking and fallen glass were added the cries and jeers of the crowd, the sirens of the police cars and fire trucks. Above all one heard the shrilling of the countless piercing whistles, the whistles carried by many gays for use in situations of danger. Close to 11 p.m. came the culminating extravaganza: the burning of nine police cars parked precariously in a row on McAllister Street, in front of the State Office Building. One by one they went, until the entire row was consumed in flames: first a huge cloud of acrid smoke, then a burst of flames, finally—bizarrely—as the heat reached a certain intensity, the siren in each car was set off, eerily wailing its own death notice until it, too, was silenced and consumed. This was White Night at its most vivid. The unforgettable scene was worthy of a film by San Francisco's Francis Ford Coppola.

Soon afterwards, the police, their numbers augmented, successfully completed their fourth sweep of the City Hall area, breaking up the crowd and dispersing it in all directions. As the heterogeneous and aroused assembly dispersed, some of its members trashed the surrounding area, looting, breaking windows, starting more fires, stoning buses and cars.

On the other hand, Castro Street itself had been quiet all night, but it was not to stay so, after the police arrived. Around 1 a.m., police cars patrolling the area increased and were saluted with jeers and bottles. More police quickly appeared. The fiercely disputed Elephant Walk Bar sweep followed. The official police version is that the bar was the haven of rock throwers, that an officer who entered was assaulted, that he retreated, returned with others, and closed the bar. Contrarily, no independent witnesses, gay or straight, saw anything thrown by patrons of the bar. The police burst in shouting "Bonzai!" and antigay obscenities, and, brutally wielding their batons, clubbed trapped and peaceful patrons, smashed windows and mirrors, and savaged the bar. A commanding officer was heard to say, "We lost the battle of City Hall. We aren't going to lose this one."[12] Other men were beaten in back alleys and doorways immediately after this raid. After several further heated confrontations between gays and police, including one with Supervisor Harry Britt, Deputy Police Chief Mullen ordered a general police withdrawal from the area. This came to be referred to as "Mullen's Retreat" by contemptuous officers.

On the morning of May 22, the city was stunned, appalled, frightened, anxious. The analyses, investigations, recriminations, Sunday morning quarterbacking, and sententious preachings began; they were to last for months.[13] But no one knew if the fury was spent. This day would have been Harvey Milk's forty-ninth birthday, and a mass public celebration on Castro Street had been planned weeks in advance. Mayor Feinstein, while beefing up the police, decided to let the event take place as planned. Scores of police were discreetly placed out of sight, while several hundred gay monitors urged calm and kept order. The mood of the gathering was apprehensive at first, but soon it was apparent that this night was different. Speakers celebrated Harvey Milk and his legacy, singers led the more than 4000 or so assembled in familiar songs. One speaker neatly summarized the attitude of many: "Yesterday we showed the world how bad we could be, and tonight we showed how nice we could be. Now it's up to the city to decide which it wants."

The immediate toll of the White Night riot was substantial. Remarkably, no shots were fired and no one was killed. Sixty demonstrators and fifty-nine policemen were treated for injuries. Twenty-six adults and two juveniles were arrested.[14] Eleven police cars were destroyed by fire and sixteen were badly damaged. Virtually every window on the Polk Street facade of City Hall was broken, and the ornate grillwork had been ripped off and mangled. City Hall damage was estimated at $60,000. A number of businesses near City Hall and the Elephant Walk Bar sustained substantial damage and, in some cases, looting.[15]

Longer-run consequences followed. Relations between police and gays grew yet more tense. Police pressure forced the mayor to remove Police Chief Gain. Long unpopular with the force for his reforming, untraditional ways, the restraint which he imposed on his men in order to contain the riot was considered insupportable.[16] The district attorney, responsible for the prosecution of the White case, was soundly thrashed in the next election. An effort, which failed in the short run, was made to eliminate the possibility of the "diminished capacity" defense. By the end of 1981, two rioters had been convicted and given suspended sentences; no police had been charged; claims against the city were still pending. The gay community, astonished, abashed, proud, ambivalent, faced the need of assessment and interpretation, for White Night was an unprecedented experience, the largest riot in known gay history.

COMMENTARY

The injustice of the jury's lenient verdict in the trial of People v. White was the ostensible cause of the riot. Normally cautious public officials, sworn defenders of legal process, were remarkably unrestrained in denouncing the verdict, both before and after the riot. Mayor Feinstein said: "As I look at the law, it was two murders." Supervisor Carol Ruth Silver, an attorney, who testified for the prosecution, commented, "I would have hung it up for murder one." State Senator Milton Marks, also an attorney, found the verdict "shocking. . . . The relatively light sentence can only fuel those who contend there are two systems of justice—one for the powerful and another for the rest of the populace."[17] Usually stolid editorialists concurred, as in the *San Francisco Examiner:* "In our view it was one of the most incredible decisions in the field of criminal law in modern history."[18] A voluntary phone-in poll to the *San Francisco Chronicle* showed that 63 percent believed the manslaughter verdict was wrong.[19] Clearly, sentiment was unusually strong, not just among gays, that the verdict was unjust.

Why, then, this unjust verdict? The system, the law, the defense, the prosecution, the jury? Each and all of these were blamed. Many who marched raged against "the system," indeed saw the verdict as confirmation that the system could not or would not mete out justice when an ex-cop killed a gay leader. Analysis does not bear out this belief. There was no *necessary* reason why White could not have been convicted of a more severe charge. No common element unites the various contingent factors which, had they been otherwise, could have led to a different verdict.

The law is more problematic. The diminished capacity defense came under fierce attack after the White verdict.[20] Yet, as conservative spokesmen happily pointed out, the controversial legal doctrine was the creation of the generally "progressive" California Supreme Court, which had been developing it gradually since 1949. It provided an intermediate position between a full-blown insanity defense and normal responsibility. Certainly the existence of such a legal possibility raises the most serious and complex questions about criminal justice, responsibility, and punishment. These cannot be decided, although they may be influenced, by this egregious single instance. The memory of this notorious case was influential when the California legislature eliminated the diminished capacity defense in 1981.

The defense was skillful, even brilliant. It got the kind of jury it wanted: white, mainly working class, socially conservative, largely female, elderly. It acknowledged the obvious facts of the case. It built up its portrait of White as an honorable, dutiful, hard-working citizen who "snapped" under intense pressure. With the use of four psychiatrists and a psychologist, the defense focused on White's state of mind and raised reasonable doubt in the jury's mind about the existence of malice.[21] The defense can hardly be blamed for having done its job well.

The prosecution was conducted by a veteran trial prosecutor. He presented a dry, meticulous recounting of the facts of the case, which were not really contested. He played the tape-recording of White's confession, which brought some of the jury to tears. He did little to contest the defense's projected image of Dan White as a hitherto responsible, upright citizen. His one psychiatric witness did not hold up well on cross-examination. His closing argument caused members of the jury to yawn and nod off. Since the prosecution was not successful, it is easy—too easy—to fault it in hindsight. Nonetheless, the principal blame for the verdict must fall here.

Much darker charges than ineptness or incompetence have been made. The most persuasive is that of Warren Hinckle that evidence of White's tough, bullying ways and consistent hostility to gays was not used because it was too explosive and would require tarring his former police colleagues with the same brush.[22] Neither the gay issue nor other political issues, which many saw as crucial to White's motivation, were raised in the trial. One cannot know if they would have made the difference, but raising them would have reduced the sense of unreality of the trial and dampened gay suspicions of a whitewash.

Finally, the jury. Dan White had grievances against both Mayor Moscone and Harvey Milk, he had strapped on his gun one morning, climbed through a window at City Hall, met with the mayor (with whom he had an appointment), fired five shots into him, reloaded his gun, crossed City Hall to the supervisors' side, called Harvey Milk into an office, and fired four shots at Milk. Does that not indicate premeditation and malice? So thought many, but not the jury. The legal definitions do not turn on common sense notions but on special, restricted concepts; about these, the defense raised "reasonable" doubt. Absent malice and premeditation, the verdict had to be voluntary manslaughter. Given the case as it was argued and the law as explained to them, their verdict, which astonished the nation, was understandable.[23]

Had a verdict of first-degree murder been returned—perhaps even second-degree—the anger, fear, and hostility directed toward "the system" in general and the police in particular would have been allayed. Instead, these feelings were strengthened, and to them was added that potent sentiment— resentment.[24] The system had protected an enemy, its integral member, who had killed the leader; the system became the enemy. There were other ways to seek justice or to express resentment at its denial.

"Avenge Harvey Milk" signs were conspicuous on the night of the riot. One sign read, "Islamic Justice—An Eye for an Eye."[25] "Vengeance means retaliation," writes Barrington Moore, Jr.

> It also means a reassertion of human dignity or worth, after injury or damage. Both are basic sentiments behind moral anger and the sense of injustice. Vengeance is a way of evening things out, and of course one that never works completely. . . . Vengeance may be the most primitive form of moral outrage. But if primitive, it is also highly contemporary.[26]

There was no way to "even things out" that White Night. Many wanted a nonviolent protest, and gay leaders and allies, themselves stunned by the verdict, tried to improvise one. But *what* could possibly have evened things out? Speech, not just amplifiers, failed.

On Black Monday, thousands had grieved. On White Monday, no one would sing "Swing Low, Sweet Chariot." On Black Monday, thousands carried candles. Trying to rekindle that spirit on White Night, Supervisor Silver sought but could not find a candle. Her Bic lighter was not the flame to light the sky that night. The marchers had marched to City Hall, site of the murders, seat of the system. No more marching would do. This was the place.

Nongay elements may well have helped promote the violence for their own political ends. Certainly in the course of the evening many joined the fray who were not gay and whose purposes, if any, were their own. Yet gays were prominent in the events all night. Violence is a substitute for action. It gave not form but outlet and focus to the rage and resentment. The SRI Report on the riot carefully notes: "The focus of the protest shifted from the verdict to City Hall and, later, to the police."[27] Just so. The sequence was neither planned nor intended, but it was sure. The verdict, which mobilized the crowd, was already beyond appeal. Massive, pompous City Hall was present, dead ahead, the very symbol of the system that had denied justice. It was protected by the same police who claimed Dan White as one of their own, the police who had harried and hounded gays for years.

Not only does vengeance not even things out, it sets off a new dynamic. The police in turn were outraged, insulted, humiliated. They saw themselves taunted and abused, abandoned or sold out or ill-led by their leaders, laughed at by the officers from outside San Francisco, their proud cars torched. They swung back on Castro Street with the "wholesale mayhem" condemned by the Civil Grand Jury.[28] The rounds of recrimination after White Night showed the same pattern: Police and pro-police elements denounced the rioting at City Hall, gays and pro-gay elements condemned the police brutality on Castro Street.

If the reaction of San Francisco's political establishment to the verdict was remarkably critical, their response to the riot was unremarkable: They deplored it. Gay reaction was more complex and revealing. Duke Smith, then political editor of the *Sentinel,* one of San Francisco's two major gay newspapers, said: "What happened last night was tragic, terrible. The overwhelming majority of the gay community was appalled by it. . . . This was a disgrace to the memory of George Moscone and Harvey Milk."[29] If so, the overwhelming majority was not talking, for such views were decidedly unrepresentative of those publicly expressed.

More typical was the "no apology" line of a number of the same figures who had tried to prevent violence the night before: Cleve Jones, Sally Gearhart, Harry Britt. Britt was conspicuous on White Night, both at City Hall and later on Castro Street. As Harvey Milk's appointed successor, his leadership was on the line in this first major crisis. Despite his misunderstood statement that "the police don't belong on the streets" on Castro and consequent citation (later dropped) for inciting a riot, he had worked hard against violence that night. Afterwards, though, he would not condemn it: "Now the society is going to have to deal with us not as nice little fairies who have hairdressing salons, but as people capable of violence."[30] Sally Gearhart, too, the prominent lesbian activist, who had pleaded with the crowd against Dan White's way Monday night, said to the peaceful gathering at the Birthday Celebration Tuesday night, "There is no way I will apologize for what happened last night but until we display our ungovernable rage at injustice, we won't get heard. Last night we got the attention we needed."[31]

This shift in stance from before to after White Night was not mere opportunism, not just generals trying to keep up with the troops. Few who witnessed the events that night were unaffected by them. Not only had the situation changed, people had changed. A new sense of limits and opportunities, of dangers and strengths, of self and community understanding, of gravity, emerged. Countless appeals to the memory of Harvey Milk were made in those days—appropriately so, for the jaunty street queen understood politics. Milk had neither advocated nor promoted violence, and as a tough streetwise leader he knew how sometimes to deflect and divert it. He also knew that people utterly incapable of violence lack self-respect and thus the respect of others, and that in confrontation the threat must exist and that an effective threat must be credible.

The riot remains ambiguous at its edges, both in its nature and its meanings. Indeed, the SRI Report and the *Civil Grand Jury Report,* which disagreed in many judgments, both concluded that the riot should *not* be called a "gay riot."[32] Much of the looting and assaulting of officers came late in the evening, after news of the events (instantly relayed by radio and TV) had drawn many nongays to the action. Some came from the adjacent, seedy Tenderloin area. Some were simply rowdy; others had their own grievances against the system and the cops. As the identities of the handful of those actually arrested that night became known, it proved difficult to raise funds for their defense because few were known to the organized gay community.

But, as we have seen, most gay leaders neither repudiated nor apologized for the riot. However ambiguous or qualified, it was absorbed into the San Francisco gay consciousness. Even as the peaceful crowd at the Birthday Celebration joined Holly Near and Meg Christian singing, "We are gentle, loving people, singing for our lives," they sang with new resonance. Yet no one bragged about the trashing of the uninsured small businesses near City Hall (if indeed gays had done it).

The riot was at once too complex and too simple. The verdict was blunt, the riot was crude but not quite indiscriminate. It was more expressive than instrumental, more symbolic than substantive. Vengeance is bastard justice, but it was sought because the justice denied was felt so keenly. With no clear focus for vengeance, the rage turned outward. The riot was a lashing out, but mainly a lashing at City Hall—the system's domed apex, the unredeemed site of the murders—and the cops, the hydra-headed, unnumbered, numberless Dan Whites. That most of the civic leaders in City Hall also deplored the verdicts and that not all the police applauded Dan White was, of course, also true.

Some who were present that night felt purged, cleansed. Some felt a new pride, a new self-respect at having stood up and fought back. A riot is frightening—to those in it, too—because it breaks limits. To many gays there present and to thousands elsewhere who identified with them, the riot said: "We can only be pushed *so* far, we will take no more, we shall stand and fight." To others, admiring or hostile, it said: "Look, they will go *that* far!" The riot both ratified and contributed to a new image of assertiveness of gays, to themselves and to others. Recognizing that many gays were by temperament and principle opposed to violence, acknowledging that some, perhaps much, of the violence that night was perpetrated by nongays, nonetheless gays saw and remembered that night as one in which they had claimed their own. The riot also confirmed what every working politician in the city knew, that San Francisco could not be governed in what was seen to be a blatantly anti-gay manner.

CONCLUSIONS

Vengeance and violence are not self-limiting. Had the gay community not exercised politically sophisticated self-discipline with over 300 of its own monitors the next night at the Castro Street Birthday Party (and had the cops not been kept out of sight), disaster would have followed. A second White Night would have been black. Nor did it end then. An intolerable level of violence against gays persists in San Francisco. Some still have scores to settle.

Stonewall, 1969; San Francisco, 1979—the comparison is as inevitable as it is instructive. The contemporary active, public movement for gay liberation dates conventionally but appropriately from the now legendary early morning of June 28, 1969, when Puerto Rican drag queens, among others, had had enough and fought back against a typical New York City police raid of the Stonewall Inn.[33] This was the gay equivalent to Rosa Parks's refusal to move to the back of the Montgomery bus. White Night was more like Watts. Gays did make notable advances in the intervening ten years. Legal disabilities, some of them, had been repealed; rights ordinances, here and there, had been enacted. Gays claimed more and had been granted more. Self and community definitions had changed. Many gays had learned that gay liberation must be the work of gays themselves.

In San Francisco, under Harvey Milk's inimitable leadership, gays had even become a (limited) power. Then the shootings, the perceived slide, the impossible verdict. The White Night riot confirmed one of the better secured of social science hypotheses: It is not the utterly downtrodden who rise up; it is those who have begun to move, those whose "rising expectations" are dashed, who revolt.[34] Stonewall was a beginning. White Night confirmed even as it advanced a history.

NOTES

1. See Randy Shilts, "The Life and Death of Harvey Milk," pp. 26-43, *Christopher Street*, March 1979, and the 1982 book by Shilts on the same subject. Shilts also shows the antic, impish, fun-loving side of Milk's nature, part of his political appeal and legacy.

2. In August 1980, it was killed, with the other ten districts, in a special election which returned the city to at-large representation.

3. Coro Foundation, *The District Handbook,* San Francisco, 1979, pp. 127, 169.

4. Across the country, I heard the news of Milk and Moscone's deaths on the car radio and shuddered to a stop. On arriving in Ithaca, New York, my host said, "So now the gays have their first martyr." Not the first, but certainly the most memorable in these times.

5. Gordon Armstrong of the Public Defender's Office, quoted by Randy Alfred, "Tenderloin Cleanup or Crystal Night?" *Berkeley Barb,* December 28, 1978.

6. See the effective chronicle of accumulating grievances during the six months following the shootings in the "No Apologies" speech of Gwen Craig, "Up Against the Wall," in the June 1979 issue of *Gayvote,* the newsletter of the Harvey Milk Gay Democratic Club. On the mini-riot, see the *San Francisco Examiner,* May 13, 1979. Ex-Supervisor Dan White was also an ex-policeman and an ex-fireman.

7. The trial abounded in ironies. Apart from defense dismissals, one gay and several blacks were dismissed by the prosecution because they opposed the death penalty. Harvey Milk had opposed the death penalty too. Dan White strongly supported it.

8. For an alternate interpretation of White, one widely believed by gays, which depicts an uptight, rigid bully with a long record of hostility to "social deviates," see the impassioned and well-argued article by Warren Hinckle, "Dan White's San Francisco, the Untold Story," *Inquiry,* October 29, 1979.

The "Twinkies defense," instantly mocked, was to become notorious in San Francisco and California.

9. Documenting a riot is no easy task. Outsiders have not seen it, eye-witnesses have seen but few of the unnumbered events, no one sees the thoughts and intentions of the participants. One recalls Tolstoy's account of the Battle of Austerlitz. The *San Francisco Chronicle* and the *San Francisco Examiner,* understandably, are not sources highly regarded by historians, but used cautiously they are helpful. Of the various post-mortem studies of the riot, that contracted by the San Francisco Police Commission and prepared by SRI International is the best. See *The May 1979 Riot in San Francisco: Police Issues,* SRI International, Menlo Park, California, 1979, 50 pp. This study was based on extensive interviews and examination of police reports, radio logs, video tapes, and so on. The judiciously compiled chronology of events (pp. 7-17) is particularly useful. It is fortunate that, despite the intense clash of views and interests in these events, "there is no significant major difference of testimony as to facts, except for the Elephant Walk Bar incident" (p. 3).

The author was himself eyewitness to events at City Hall from about 8 p.m. until the final police sweep cleared the area around 11:30 p.m. The following account is based on the above-mentioned and other cited sources and my own observations.

10. *1979-80 Civil Grand Jury Special Report,* County of San Francisco, December 3, 1979, p. 1.

11. Eyewitness account, Randy Alfred.

12. Warren Hinckle, "How the Cops Waded into Castro Street," *San Francisco Chronicle,* May 23, 1979, p. 7.

13. As examples of the latter, see Kevin Starr, "White Night," *San Francisco Examiner,* June 4, 1979 and "The Men in Blue," *San Francisco Examiner,* June 5, 1979. Starr ludicrously refers to the "self-appointed mob" which perpetrated "civil insurrection."

14. C. R. Gain, Chief of Police, S.F.P.D., *Major Incident Report, City Hall Riot 05/21/79 to 05/22/79,* San Francisco, June, 1979, p. 15 and Appendix III.

15. SRI Report, p. 12. The estimate of a "million dollar riot" was widely cited and entered popular lore. Yet the Fire Commission estimated $200,000 damage. San Francisco Fire Commission, *Report on City Hall Riot of May 21, 1979,* San Francisco, 1979, p. 3. The S.F. Police Officers' Association estimated total public and private damage at $395,902.32.

16. Much of the controversy turned on the strategy and tactics used by the police authorities on the night of the riot. Chief Gain held his responsibility to be that of safeguarding City Hall, including its irreplaceable records, and of minimizing personal injury. He further maintained that San Francisco police had a tradition of using excess force and that there were too few police present to clear the City Hall area safely before the final order. Rank and file policemen, on the other hand, saw themselves as incompetently led, left vulnerable and unprotected, humiliated and abused by the mob that night. The SRI Report and the *Civil Grand Jury Report,* in different measure, both criticize and commend the chief and the police force.

17. *San Francisco Examiner,* May 22, 1979, p. 2.

18. *San Francisco Examiner,* May 23, p. 34.

19. Of 51,776 callers. *San Francisco Chronicle,* May 24, p. 1. Such a poll does not use sampling techniques. It merely indicates the views of those who trouble to phone in and can get through.

20. See Thomas Szasz, "How Dan White Got Away With Murder, and How American Psychiatry Helped Him Do It," *Inquiry,* August 6 and 20, 1979. Szasz notes that this is not the first grievance gays have against psychiatry.

21. The defense candidly outlined its strategy after the trial. See Jim Wood, "Heavy Strategy Behind White's Light Sentence," *San Francisco Examiner,* May 23, 1979, p. 1.

22. Warren Hinckle, "Dan White's San Francisco, The Untold Story," *Inquiry,* October 29, 1979.

23. Under California law, first-degree murder requires premeditation. Without premeditation but with malice, the charge is second-degree murder. To prove malice, four elements must be shown to exist: intent to kill, knowledge that the act is unlawful, having an anti-social purpose, and an ability to "hold in mind" the first three elements at the time of the action.

Some jurors described the process of their deliberations. See Paul Shinoff and Carol Pogash, "Jurors: We Voted Our Consciences," *San Francisco Examiner,* May 22, 1979, p. 1 ff.

San Francisco Chronicle, May 23, 1979, p. 7. There is no confirmed evidence that the jurors were anti-gay, but there is evidence that some, at least, were extremely naive about the conflicts in their city. One juror said afterwards: "All we wanted to do is bring people together again." The jury was, of course, unrepresentative of the diversity of the city's population.

24. On resentment as a *moral* sentiment, see John Rawls, *A Theory of Justice,* Cambridge, Massachusetts, 1971, p. 539 ff.

25. *San Francisco Examiner,* May 22, p. 2.

26. Barrington Moore, Jr., *Injustice: The Social Bases of Obedience and Revolt,* White Plains, N.Y., 1978, p. 17.

27. SRI Report, p. 10.

28. *Civil Grand Jury Report,* p. 8. The report condemns virtually all actors that night, other than Mayor Feinstein and Supervisor Silver, in one act or another.

29. Quoted in *San Francisco Examiner,* May 22, 1979, p. 14.

30. Quoted in *San Francisco Examiner,* May 22, 1979, p. A.

31. Quoted by Robert Hollis, "Police Lie Low as Castro Party Stays Peaceful," *San Francisco Examiner,* May 23, 1979, p. 4.

32. SRI Report, p. 17. *Civil Grand Jury Report,* p. 2.

33. For an account, see Donn Teal, *The Gay Militants,* New York, 1971, pp. 17-23, and Toby Marotta, *The Politics of Homosexuality,* Boston, 1981, pp. 71-76.

34. See, for example, Ted Robert Gurr, *Why Men Rebel,* Princeton, N.J., 1970, especially Chapter 4, pp. 92-122.

• 29 •

Minority Status for Gay People
Majority Reaction and Social Context

William Paul

"It is only superficial people
who do not judge things by appearances."
—Oscar Wilde

Do Gay men and Lesbians constitute a minority group in more than just a statistical sense, or are they merely a group of individual deviants committing criminal acts (like murderers)? If injuries are disproportionately inflicted on Gay people,[1] are these justified by the strong feelings of majority people against homosexuality? Is it just for government to include Gay people under protections of civil rights laws in the face of oppression by elements of majority groups, or is this issue simply an appeal for special privileges?

Questions of this kind have seldom received adequate attention in the Gay rights debate. Individuals are, of course, ideally entitled to full civil rights whatever their group membership. Yet it is precisely lack of understanding and acceptance of Lesbians and Gay men *as a social group* that has obscured the question of minority status and recognition of social identity.

Prior to Simon and Gagnon's articulation of the sociological reality (1967), homosexual people were popularly perceived as isolated individuals. Psychiatric and moralistic perspectives both tended to intensely sexualize popular perceptions of anything labeled homosexual, with social analysis confined within restrictive notions of deviance.

As more fully elaborated in the introductory chapter for this section, there is growing awareness of a historical social reality emerging in the form of Gay and Lesbian community. Along with the burning issues of oppression and discrimination, there are more mundane tasks of accommodation required

Author's Note: This research was supported, in part, by grants from SPSSI, the Human Rights Foundation, and The Mark DeWolfe Howe Fund at Harvard University.

351

of society when confronting an emerging social group. Adaptation and cooperation are called for between groups in a pluralist social system in the daily and long-term requirements of intergroup relations.

Recognition of group identity may not necessarily confer minority status. In order to develop and assess some set of criteria for each group, it is useful to embed the discussion in the context of current social history—life as actually experienced by the group members, especially in relation to the majority and the actions of their members. Then it is also helpful to make some informed comparisons with other minority groups. Some of these groups can be viewed as somewhat analogous to Gay and Lesbian experience, and are defined as minorities given certain social conditions.

Consider a new evangelistic religious minority composed of converts from various races, cultures, and social classes and which has conflicts in values and behavior with majority values. People have not been socialized by their parents to join such a group, yet people do so, in spite of the persecution many of these groups face. Most people would agree that such a group constitutes a religious minority, deserving of the protection afforded other minorities in our legal system. This is true despite the fact that the majority finds the group's ideals and actions offensive, and that the group itself actively proselytizes for new members.

Recognition as a valid social group is the issue that underlies debate as to whether Gay people are a minority or a category of individual deviants. There is a powerful religious and political movement currently campaigning to deny such recognition and—implicitly—to repudiate homosexually oriented people as an acknowledged social entity in American society. Gay communities should not, according to this view, be defined as a constituency with legitimate group interests and concerns which they can relate to government, but rather as people displaying a kind of disorder deserving of compassion at best (Van den Haag, 1974; Cameron, 1978; McCracken, 1979).

At present, there is no universally accepted definition of what constitutes a minority (except in a statistical sense, of course). The actual process today is one of political power applied by a group that has attained enough strength to demand redress. This is not reassuring for powerless groups which are faced with a paradox: the necessity of having power in order to obtain recognition of the oppression that denies power.

Although deviance, as a field, is beyond the scope of this chapter, a number of authors long ago began to question the pariah status implied by the "deviant" label imposed on homosexuals (Becker, 1963; Schur, 1965; Simon & Gagnon, 1967). This scholarship played a positive role in the profound changes—cultural, social, and political—which emerged from the

Gay Liberation movement. Yet recognition of the Gay minority remains an issue.

Some observers have interpreted the gay movement as an attempt to falsely identify with a historical minority consciousness created by Blacks, Hispanics, Asians, Jews, and other minority groups. In contrast, some Gay civil rights activists and heterosexual supporters have contended that homosexuals are a minority group with issues identical to the movements for racial and ethnic minority civil rights. One common chant at Gay Pride Day marches, for example, is, "Gay, Straight, Black, White—Same struggle, same fight!"

However, this reasoning has elicited concern from some members of the various racial and ethnic groups:

> I am concerned lest white ethnicity join ecology and women's and gay liberation in preventing or forestalling our nation's accepting fully the truths about its racist self that the civil rights movement and the new Black affirmation have raised in the national consciousness [Jackson, 1973, p. 32].[2]

Distinctions between traditional minorities and Gay people merit serious consideration, lest the growing recognition of Gay minority status be somehow perceived as an intrusion on movements for racial and ethnic equality. Common misperceptions are formed that Gays are mostly White, affluent, and male; in fact, they are members of all races, both sexes, and all socioeconomic groups.

There are many academics who support the notion that Gays form a genuine minority. Hacker (1971), for example, concluded (as did Sagarin in the introduction) that homosexuals are indeed a minority group—largely on the basis of oppressive majority actions (denial of full social participation and civil rights on the basis of stereotyped group attributes irrelevant to the roles denied). This criterion is similar to the one I will rely on, by Wirth (quoted below).

In a sense, many Americans seem to agree. A 1977 national Harris Poll found that a majority of their respondents considered homosexuals comparable to other minorities:

> A majority of Americans feel that homosexuals suffer the greatest amount of discrimination of any group in the country today.
>
> 55 percent of the people say that homosexuals are most discriminated against, followed by Blacks, Puerto Ricans, Mexican-Americans, women and Jews, in that order. By 54 to 28 percent, people would favor a law that "outlawed discrimination against homosexuals in any job for which they are qualified" [Harris, 1977].[3]

However, these same people registered ambivalence by opposing the hiring of qualified homosexuals in certain jobs (e.g., teachers) by a 48 to 41 percent plurality.

Yet it is often asserted that discrimination against homosexuals has a rational and justifiable basis—like discrimination against murderers or spies. In particular, the belief that homosexuality is a personal disorder is often used as an argument against minority status for Gay people. Defining someone as "sick" or "handicapped" is an effective means of avoiding civil liberties questions. Leaving aside the fact that discrimination on the basis of physical handicap is now illegal in the United States, let us consider the extent to which discrimination against homosexuals constitutes irrational prejudice.

Allport (1954), an internationally respected psychologist, established the classic characteristic of prejudice—*categorical prejudgment,* or the belief that a person's status can be used to predict unfavorable personal characteristics and behavior. Another aspect of this majority reaction is *depersonalization*—the minority person is seen as less of an individual personality and more as one of "them" (Plummer, 1975). This identification as one of "them" also becomes more salient than other favorable characteristics. This reaction is often especially easy to see when a formerly invisible minority member suddenly becomes visible.

When does a minority group need recognition and civil rights protection? Many statistical minorities—people with IQs over 130, people over six feet tall, left-handed people, etc.—have managed by and large to succeed fairly well with no special protection from society. Protection as a group is needed when the discrimination of the majority becomes prejudicial and harmful to the minority. Precisely when this occurs is, of course, an empirical matter.

In this chapter, I first set out some of the important differences between Gays seen as a minority and the more familiar racial and ethnic minorities. Then I set out the similarities, and in the process document some of the prejudicial and harmful treatment received by Gays at the hands of the heterosexual majority. Final sections return to the question of the definition of a minority and address the future.

Comparisons of Gay and Lesbian communities with racial and ethnic groups are often attended by inaccurate assumptions that theirs is some special conflict over respective claims to recognition. Black and Latino people have been described, usually by White commentators, as having especially hostile anti-Gay prejudice. This is inconsistent with existing evidence. Weinberg and Williams (1974) found Black people more likely to have positive attitudes toward Gay people than Whites. The NBC voter exit polls (NBC National Poll, 1978) found Latino voters similar to the general population in support for Gay civil rights, while Black voters expressed 12 percent greater support. There are numerous examples of mutual cooperation between these communities.⁴ Yet acknowledgment of actual differences is one source of mutual understanding of minority experience.

MAJOR DIFFERENCES (WITH SOME SIMILARITIES)

To a first approximation, there are clear differences in the discrimination directed by the majority toward Lesbians and Gay men on the one hand and toward racial and ethnic minorities on the other. These differences fall into three categories: cumulative historical effects, visibility, and developmental effects. Yet lurking in each category of difference is often a subtle similarity.

Cumulative Historical Effects

Ethnic and racial groups have common bonds of culture and history transmitted over generations through social institutions affecting the family. A Black child growing up in such a family, for example, may thereby suffer social and economic disadvantages accumulated from generations of job discrimination and unequal educational opportunity. Homosexuals, on the other hand, are found in all social, racial, and ethnic groups; although the basis for anti-homosexual discrimination goes back thousands of years, it does not accumulate in families in the same way. This crucially affects the kind of discrimination homosexuals face: a White, middle-class, male homosexual has social advantages that tend to mitigate the discrimination he may experience because of his sexual orientation. Yet there are also members of ethnic and religious minorities who are homosexual; these individuals suffer a double jeopardy but may have acquired adaptive capacities allowing them to cope more effectively with majority reactions than White male homosexuals do (Hidalgo & Hidalgo-Christensen, 1976).

Visibility

The overwhelming majority of homosexuals are not visibly distinguishable from the majority population. But most Black people, for example, are Black 24 hours a day. Chester Pierce, a Black psychiatrist at Harvard, has observed that some of the most serious personal damage from racism comes from the petty indignities and aggressions inflicted on visible minority group members.⁵ Often lethal stress-related disorders and shorter lifespans are more common among Black men. Yet (as I will show below), this is not universally true even for racial minorities, and is to an extent true for contemporary homosexuals as they become more visible.

Developmental Effects

Racial minority children are identified as members of the minority from birth and may suffer the effects of racism at a very tender age. Children who will become homosexual, however, are usually not labeled "deviant" at such an early age. And some of the composite effects of the two forms of prejudice discussed above also take their toll developmentally; some Black American children, for example, suffer more brain damage from protein deficiencies, and Black, Latino, and Native American children tend to suffer greater degrees of impaired health from lack of medical services. Yet there are children who are presumed homosexual at an earlier age than many people know (see below), so even here there is a degree of similarity.

MAJOR SIMILARITIES (WITH SOME DIFFERENCES)

There are also similarities between homosexuals and the racial and ethnic groups discriminated against by the larger society. These similarities fall into four major topic areas: people who fit stereotypes, stigmatization by psychology, a distinct social and cultural life, and majority reactions. Yet in each case, often there lurks a subtle difference.

People Who Fit Stereotypes

Some homosexuals are so obviously stereotypical that they have great difficulty passing as heterosexual. Such individuals have the same difficulties as members of the most oppressed racial groups. Even as children, it is these individuals who were most likely to be labeled too "effeminate" or "tomboyish," and usually suffered considerable cruelty from other children, or even from parents.[6] (Shively and De Cecco, 1977, point out that such early discrimination results from confusing sex role with sexual orientation. Yet this fact does not diminish the effects on children.) Conversely, there are members of racial or ethnic minority groups who can pass as members of the majority as easily as most homosexuals can (the exact proportion varies from group to group). No one argues that this removes the necessity to do something about the discrimination that exists!

Some would argue that if homosexuals would only try harder, they could pass all the time. Although there are large Gay communities in some cities in which clothing styles and other group symbols make visible individuals who would otherwise not be identifiable as Gay or Lesbian, this misses the point.

For in the past, complete assimilation has not been enough in some circumstances. Prior to the Nazi era, large numbers of Jews had assimilated to the point where they no longer defined themselves as Jewish, but rather as German. Many such families had ceased to participate in Jewish religious or cultural life and were not socially visible according to stereotypes of Jewish appearance, and some held anti-Semitic beliefs similar to the majority (Sartre, 1948). Yet when the Nazi holocaust gathered its victims, all of those defined as Jewish by the majority were treated alike.

Similarly (though less severely), today large numbers of male homosexual adolescents leave home at an early age because their parents try to make them heterosexual—or even throw them out and disown them. These teens sometimes are forced to lead sexually exploited marginal lives on the streets of large cities; telling them that they are not discriminated against because they can pass as heterosexual scarcely helps solve the problem.

Stigmatization by Psychology

Isolation and self-hatred are traits shared by many homosexuals and members of racial or ethnic minorities (although clearly not their exclusive property). With homosexuals, such psychological stigmatization has often been presumed to be a symptom of pathology (see the Mental Health section), while the notion that being Black, Hispanic, or Jewish is a psychological disorder has rarely achieved popularity. Yet the "disorder" label is often applied to minorities. Family pathology is often assumed by Whites to be common in racial minority families (Rainwater & Yancey, 1967). "The father of American psychiatry," Benjamin Rush, once theorized that Blackness was a disease transmitted venereally at birth (Szasz, 1970). And during the nineteenth century a physician described a disorder causing an irrational compulsion to flee, observing that this disorder was spreading among Black slaves on southern plantations. Given the difficulties facing modern psychoanalytically based theories of homosexuality, future generations may well see current attitudes on homosexuality as equally ridiculous.

Social and Cultural Life

Although not shared by all homosexuals, there are distinctively Gay and Lesbian forms of social life and cultural expression, just as there are for racial and ethnic minorities. Distinct Gay and Lesbian communities have been described by Levine (1979a, 1979b), Wolf (1979), and Martin and Lyon (1972), among others. In San Francisco, for example, a highly visible Lesbian and Gay community exists that includes many institutions and group activities: educational, religious, social, and medical institutions; cultural institutions for poetry, theater, athletics, dance, music, and literature; professional, academic, business, and youth organizations; and community centers and social service agencies (Humphreys & Miller, 1980).[7] Although San Francisco has acquired a reputation in this respect, other cities rival or have equaled San Francisco in the diversity of their Gay institutions. These Gay social entities are recognized by the heterosexual majority as distinctive and thus qualify, by some definitions, as evidence for Gay minority status. This status should be defined, however, independent of majority approval. Remember that there are those who claim that Black social aspirations are not civil rights issues but "law and order" problems.

On the other hand, many "closet" homosexuals have only isolated and secretive sexual activity as a common bond. Yet in a sense, unconventional sexuality itself is a limited form of cultural (or countercultural) expression. Paradoxically, secretive, isolated Gay males living furtive lives tend to suffer more violence from the majority (Miller & Humphreys, 1980).

In addition, there are some homosexuals who identify themselves primarily as members of their larger majority or minority group. These people may or may not define and accept themselves as Gay. An individual Lesbian, for example, might identify herself primarily as a woman, secondarily as a feminist, then as a Puerto Rican, and finally as a self-affirmed Lesbian (Hidalgo & Hidalgo-Christensen, 1976; Ponse, 1978).

Are these people members of a homosexual minority? I argue that they are, because they must in some ways behave like members of an unpopular cultural minority. In a pluralist society especially, people have several sources of personal identity (Klapp, 1969).

Majority Reactions—Introduction

In this section and the next two, I rely on the definition of "minority" provided by Wirth (1945, p. 347):

> We may define a minority as a group of people who, because of their physical or cultural characteristics, are singled out from the others in the society in which they live for differential or unequal treatment, and who therefore regard themselves as objects of collective discrimination. The existence of a minority in a society implies the existence of a dominant group with higher social status and greater privileges. Minority status carries with it the exclusion from full participation in the life of the society.

The Nazi regime, with the acquiescence of the majority population, redefined millions of people from different groups as "deviant" and included them in a genocidal horror. Large numbers of German homosexuals, many of whom did not define themselves as "Gay," were also put into concentration camps (Hoess, 1959; Kogon, 1969; Steakley, 1975; Plant, 1977; Heger, 1980) and made to wear pink triangles, just as the Jews were forced to wear yellow stars. A report published by the Protestant churches of Austria estimated that approximately 225,000 homosexuals died in the death camps because of their sexual orientation (Steakley, 1975). No one knows the real number, and estimates vary considerably, but it is known that huge numbers simply vanished. Thousands of others were incarcerated in slave labor battalions and many were castrated (Kogon, 1969; Plant, 1977).

This is not to suggest that homosexuals as a group are precisely comparable to Jews as a people, nor that the magnitude of six million Jews was equivalent to the estimated quarter-million Gays. But for those who did die in the death camps, the consequences of Nazi classification—as an undesirable minority—were, in the crucial sense, identical.[8]

Today, assertions that Gay people only bring it on themselves by "flaunting" or disclosing their sexual orientation are contradicted by studies which demonstrate official efforts to detect and punish homosexuality (Katz, 1976; Churchill, 1967; Williams & Weinberg, 1971). Intrusions on privacy and threats of public exposure are a constant fact of life for the millions of conventional homosexuals who are forced to develop covert protective strategies in the closet (Brown, 1976). For example, until the forced disclosure of his homosexuality, James Gaylord had led a life as a popular member of his community (see the chapters on legal issues in this volume). Gaylord seemed a member of the majority until majority institutions, on the basis of revealed social stigma, decided that he was not. The case bears a close resemblance to similar events in South Africa, where apparently White citizens are sometimes discovered to be non-White, and grim consequences follow (MacCrone, 1937).

Majority Reactions—Violence

One way in which some members of a majority show their displeasure at members of a minority is with violence or aggression. In a way, this christens the members of a minority as a minority—like it or not. More sensitive, conscientious majority members simply avoid recognizing the tangible consequences of their fear and hatred. Such denial was a common reaction to the Black civil rights struggle, until vivid images of dogs attacking nonviolent marchers or Black children murdered by a bombing of their Sunday School became too much to ignore.

On June 6, 1976, Richard Heaken, a college student and gay activist, was beaten to death by a group of teenage males in front of a Gay bar in Tucson, Arizona. During the subsequent trial, the boys were described as healthy, normal specimens of American youth. In releasing the defendants without sentence or any kind of penalty, the judge described them in glowing terms as "wholesome" and complimented them on their athletic records. Journalists present reported the clear implication of positive contrast to the victim and an equally clear sense that the boys had acted as normal American youth in an understandable reaction to a homosexual (Advocate, June 30 and Nov. 17, 1976).

Only recently have dramatic incidents of anti-Gay violence begun to elicit occasional media attention. A recent widely publicized incident (New York Times, July 27, 1980) of random physical attack in New York City's Central Park resulted in five hospitalized victims, some with permanent disabilities. Media coverage and judicial proceedings on these beatings in the "Rambles" area of the park revealed that such attacks had been common for years there and that visibly Gay people were in constant potential danger in many areas of the city. Anti-Gay violence also received media attention after two Gay men were killed in a machine-gun attack on a Greenwich Village Gay bar—by a minister's son who expressed hatred of "queers" (New York Times, Nov. 19, 1980). In 1981, the New York City Council passed a resolution specifically condemning anti-Gay violence.

The visibility factor in minority status appears to be undergoing a historical change for Gay people, as larger numbers live open lives and heterosexuals learn to identify Gay cultural insignia. An informal pilot survey reported that among 50 fairly visible Gay men (mean age 34, living openly in San Francisco), 20 percent had encountered some form of anti-Gay violence.[9] These data are consistent with victimization reports compiled there by Community United Against Violence (Stingel, Note 1). The attackers are predominantly young males (aged 15-24) who usually operate in groups that outnumber victims. These groups deliberately enter areas with large Gay populations, searching for victims.[10] Data from emergency room admissions during the same period showed Gay people accounting for 72 percent of the street attack victims in an area with a heterosexual majority (Fleming, Note 2).

Lesbian women, too, share in the increased visibility. But, as would be predicted by the double-oppression theory (Martin & Lyon, 1972), violence directed against Lesbians seems to overflow and be directed at women in general. The San Francisco Women's Center in 1980 endured vandalism, arson attempts, and street attacks on women and men using the center. Victims, including many heterosexual women, were often called "dykes" by attackers. Anti-feminist epithets were also expressed, to the extent that the terms appeared to be used interchangeably. Anonymous hostile letters and phone calls followed. Finally, the center was bombed (San Francisco Examiner, Oct. 8, 1980).

The Metropolitan Community Church is a network of churches primarily serving Gays in the United States (and several foreign countries). Since 1973, 13 MCC churches have been damaged by arson attacks or fires of unknown origin—nearly 10 percent of all MCC churches. Of these, seven were totally destroyed (Los Angeles, Nashville, San Francisco, Santa Monica, Riverside, St. Petersburg, and Phoenix—Karen Davis, 1978a, 1978b). In New Orleans on June 24, 1973 (Gay Pride Day), 32 Gay people died in a fire at the Upstairs Lounge, the site of MCC services. The MCC pastor and 10 church members burned to death (Karen Davis, 1978a, 1978b). Arson was suspected, following reports of a molotov cocktail having been thrown up the stairs of the lounge.

Some social scientists find the source of such violence in homosexuality itself:

> Apart from robbery and violence, both frequent in . . . prostitution, the main
> crises arising in homosexual relationships are blackmail and homicide. . . . No
> one knows how many stabbings and murders occur in homosexual quarrels,
> but the circumstances in newspaper accounts suggest they are frequent
> [Kingsley Davis, 1976, p. 257].

Note how homosexuality is associated with prostitution; and then the cause
of anti-Gay violence is attributed to "homosexual quarrels." This is a perfect
case of blaming the victim. Ryan (1971) argued that this strategy is a classic
method used by the majority to avoid recognition of minority issues. Likewise, Shibutani and Kwan (1965) found cross-culturally a tendency for
oppressive majorities to attribute blame for majority group attacks to minority group victims, and that violence was—again, cross-culturally—a strategy used by majority group members against minority group members who
step out of their assigned role.

Progress will not be made on this issue until majority group members
come to understand how clear the issue seems to the minority. For example,
amid a recent period of intensified anti-Gay violence in San Francisco, the
mayor (Feinstein) set up an intergroup meeting to discuss the incidents.
There, a heterosexual (adult) youth leader protested such visible Gay behavior as "necking and holding hands" as "deeply offensive" to the culture
of his community. To this, Randy Alfred, a Gay journalist and sociologist, responded: "Many Gay people have a profound cultural abhorrence of
knife blades tearing into flesh. Please respect our culture" (Alfred,
1980, p. 8).

Majority Reactions—Anti-Gay Rhetoric, Fear, and Hatred

The rhetoric used by some heterosexuals to describe homosexuals, too,
is part of the way majorities define minorities. I believe that anti-Gay rhetoric
(like rhetoric directed against Blacks or Jews) has a significant effect—both
in defining the issues in the majority's terms, and in encouraging anti-Gay
violence. This rhetoric comes from hate and fear. Hate is far more than a
mere abstraction in its capacity to hurt. Some victims internalize this attack
on self-esteem and project it onto other members of their group—perhaps
the most common injury to Gay people (Hoffman, 1968; Ross, 1978; Escoffier, 1975).[11]

When this anti-Gay rhetoric becomes tough enough, it amounts to sheer
hatred, and such talk can be expected to have certain consequences. When
Anita Bryant said, "God puts homosexuals in the same category as murderers," far more was lost than her sense of proportion. In Florida, what do
folks traditionally do with murderers?

There are chilling parallels between the ways Jews and homosexuals
have been vilified in the past, and between the ways homosexuals are

vilified today and Jews were not too long ago. Few Americans are aware of the sexual themes in Nazi anti-Semitism. Bleuel (1973) documented the prewar Nazi assertions that Jewish influence was having a contaminating sexual influence on German children; they would become, according to Hitler, "the sad product of the irresistible spreading contamination of our sexual life" (Hitler, 1925/1969, p. 225). Popular culture would weaken masculine military qualities "in the morass of universally spreading enervation and effeminization." Consider Hitler's sexually lurid anti-Semitism:

> For hours on end, with Satanic joy on his face, the black-haired Jewish youth lies in wait for the unwitting girl whom he defiles with his blood, thus stealing her from her people [Hitler, 1925/1969, p. 295].

The Pollution and Contagion themes (see Chapter 4) are quite prominent here, as they were in the Nazi propaganda campaign of the 1930s, expressed by Himmler, head of the SS:

> Then he abandons the normal order of things for the perverted world of the homosexual. Such a man always drags ten others after him, otherwise he can't survive. We can't permit such a danger to the country; the homosexuals must be entirely eliminated [Kersten, 1956, p. 57].

It is instructive to compare the above rhetoric with that of Anita Bryant:

> This recruitment of children is absolutely necessary for the survival and growth of homosexuality—for since homosexuals cannot reproduce, they *must* recruit, *must* freshen their ranks [Miami Herald, Mar. 20, 1977, p. D-9].

Social "decadence" was viewed variously as the cause and outcome of this pollution and contagion. Homosexuals and Jews were both associated with the spread of venereal disease and vice. Cosmopolitan cities like Berlin were described as modern Sodoms and Gomorrahs (Bleuel, 1973, p. 31)— just as, today, "everyone knows" that prewar Berlin was decadent and ancient Rome fell because of too much license. By the mid-1930s, the rhetorical dehumanization extended far beyond metaphor. In referring to ancient Germanic executions of homosexuals by drowning, Himmler stated: "That was no punishment, merely the extinction of abnormal life" (Bleuel, 1973, p. 221). Dehumanization, indeed.

As shown in the chapter on anti-Gay arguments and themes (Chapter 4), organized campaigns of vilification against Gay people are an integral reality in this controversy. The hatreds thus engendered can have very violent consequences—as seen in the incidents documented in the previous section.

Some would assert that violence has always been present in the world and that it is impossible to attribute any specific act (such as those documented) to a specific, anti-Gay cause. Yet there have been numerous examples of violent attacks against Gay individuals and Gay groups that seem undeniably correlated with anti-Gay rhetorical campaigns. During the campaign by Bryant's followers (against the anti-discrimination measure in Dade County, Florida), there were apparently systematic violent attacks against both Gay and heterosexual civil rights workers—including beatings and fire-bombings (Miami News, Mar. 22, 1977). Data gathered by Stingel (Note 1) indicated a sharp rise in anti-Gay violence in San Francisco after the CBS special, "Gay Power, Gay Politics." And reports of anti-Gay violence increased in Key West, Florida, after Reverend Morris Wright published the following statement:

> I would get me a hundred good men, give them each a baseball bat, and have them walk down Duval Street and dare one of these freaks to stick his head over the edge of the sidewalk. That is the way it was done in Key West in the days I remember and loved. Female impersonators and queers were loaded into a deputy's automobile and shipped to the county line [New York Times, Apr. 7, 1979, p. 10].

It appears that some Americans are susceptible to this kind of incitement to violence. During 1981, amid a fundamentalist "crusade" against homosexuality in San Francisco, two ministers called for the death penalty against homosexuals as a goal of future legislatures with biblical values (Note 3). In the following two months, victim reports of anti-Gay street attacks increased by about 30 percent (see notes). Hence, when the Reverend Jerry Falwell calls on fundamentalist Christians to "Stop the Gays *dead* in their perverted tracks" (Falwell, 1980, pp. 1, 2, italics in original), it is accurate to interpret this kind of religious advocacy as escalating intergroup conflict—with a minority as the target.

LESBIANS AND GAY MEN AS MEMBERS OF A RELIGIOUS MINORITY

Religious hatred and ensuing violence against target groups are not new to American life. In their clear attempts to isolate and punish Gay people, the current religious-ideological movement, termed the "religious right," provides several compelling arguments that homosexuals are a religious minority. They comprise a religious minority group in the same sense as agnostics and atheists—people who are persecuted and denied full equality by a dominant religious group.

Religious liberty in America has been historically defined as the right *not* to believe or to practice religious precepts and restrictions on how an individual lives one's life. Hence the doctrine of separation of church and state—the idea that the state is not allowed to impose or favor dominant religious beliefs or practices. Given this historical and legal context, the following propositions, each supported by ample evidence, demonstrate the religious minority status of homosexuals: (1) They incur religiously inspired persecution, manifest in both discrimination and violence. (2) Anti-homosexual prejudice and taboo is derived from certain Judeo-Christian religious beliefs (Boswell, 1980; Bailey, 1955). This religious influence extends into psychiatry and medicine (Szasz, 1970). (3) Certain anti-homosexual laws are based on these beliefs. Anti-sodomy statutes in several states, for example, enforce particular anti-homosexual religious doctrines (e.g., "natural law"). (4) Certain courts have explicitly resorted to religious beliefs and authorities in justifying denials of equal protection to Gay and Lesbian citizens. Among several such examples, the Virginia Supreme Court quoted Leviticus (Knutson, 1980), and the Washington Supreme Court cited the Catholic Encyclopedia (Gaylord v. Tacoma; see Chapter 26). (5) These persisting hatreds and taboos tend to reflect a particular kind of very conservative or fundamentalist religious belief (Boswell, 1980), since many major religious groups currently support full equality. (6) Therefore, when government places restrictions or penalties on Gay men and Lesbians, essentially for their defiance of religious doctrines, it is favoring a particular kind of religious doctrine. (7) Survey research indicates much higher levels of opposition to homosexual orientation and equal rights among those with very conservative religious beliefs and practices (General Social Survey: Sherrill, 1977; Levitt & Klassen, 1974). (8) Therefore, in denying full equality to homosexuals, the government is favoring a certain social group composed of people with particular religious beliefs and practices.

POLITICAL MINORITY STATUS: THE RIGHT TO SOCIAL IDENTITY, COMMUNITY, AND FREE EXPRESSION OF IDEAS

Political minority status might be strictly applied only to those Lesbians and Gay men who openly affirm their identity as a social statement of values and community. Certainly those civil rights advocates who encounter suppression are a political minority, especially when such actions are imposed or condoned by government. Clearly stated anti-Gay agendas of the New Right explicitly aim at the suppression of far more than "immoral" sexual behavior—their targets are also values and ideas. The ideology of this movement calls for government action against the free expression of certain ideas and values, against the right of free association in Gay or Lesbian communities, and ultimately against the individual citizens who belong to these communities and advocate ideas defined as dangerous (see Bush & Goldstein, 1981).

Occasional dramatic events allow the issue of political liberty some public exposure. Fred Paez, a Gay civil rights activist in Houston, Texas, was shot to death by one of two police officers who knew him previously and had stopped his car. Their account was that Paez had made a sexual advance to one officer in the other's presence, and then died resisting arrest (Houston Post, June 29, 1980). Paez had been active in a citizens' group documenting police brutality and misconduct. In 1979 he had presented evidence to the U.S. Civil Rights Commission and the Justice Department (U.S. Civil Rights Commission, 1980).

In Wolf Creek, Oregon, a Gay rural collective called Creekland was fire-bombed following a period of escalating expressions of hostility from some locals. Creekland publishes *RFD,* a rural Gay periodical advocating civil rights. Foster Church, an investigative reporter, won a journalism award for his series documenting lax and hostile local law enforcement response to the bombing (Church, 1979).

DISCUSSION

Vivid incidents like these are not typical, but they are not so rare either, although seldom covered in the national media. Yet they do exert powerful intimidation on many citizens, both Gay and straight, who might otherwise openly express support for full equality. A crucial element is the widespread attempt to suppress the free expression of ideas. The more common forms of this suppression are quietly inflicted, as in the loss of employment or advancement. Yet ultimately, this process of thought control attacks the political liberty of all citizens by denying the public access to a full range of information and positions on a social issue.

Imposing limits on the free flow of ideas and facts is a fundamental threat to democratic process, even though directed at an unpopular minority. Patterns of thought control impinging on research and education have been documented by the American Sociological and Psychological Associations (see Chapter 4 on categories and themes). These reports show that heterosexual researchers have been victimized for their work in the field of sexual orientation, allowing us an academic example of a widely held maxim of democracy: An attack on the rights of any minority poses a potential threat to the political liberty of everyone.

Violent death is the final leveler of distinctions between victims who are members of officially recognized minorities and those who are not. One cannot get much more dead than someone else. Certainly I am not suggesting that the violence and extreme hatred described here is at all typical of American heterosexuals. But there is clearly a sense that—in the phrase popularized in the 1960s—if you're not part of the solution, then you're part of the problem. What many Gay people have faced is historically and tangibly comparable to the experience of other minorities in America and elsewhere. Actually, this account does not describe the problems of a minority but the problems of a majority—peculiar hatreds and fears of homosexuals by heterosexuals, termed *homophobia*.

Homosexually oriented people form a valid minority group in American society. Certainly, self-defined members of Gay communities are a minority in the same sense as members of any other cultural minority. But also those without a primary Gay social identity or with only partial affiliation to Gay communities and subcultures are a minority as a consequence of conditions imposed by majority reaction and treatment. As should be clear by now, no minority is treated in precisely the same ways by the majority as any other minority—but that in and of itself does not mean one group deserves minority status and another does not. Homosexually oriented people surely require the minimal protections that are afforded by official recognition as a minority group, with an appropriate version of civil rights legislation.

THE FUTURE:
SOCIAL CONFLICT AND IDENTITY

Many will question whether it is desirable or productive for society to have another angry and militant minority group in a social system already divided by minority groups representing race, ethnicity, gender, social class, and ideology. Current developments in pluralistic and tolerant areas like San Francisco suggest that Gay and heterosexual people can live together with common bonds formed of larger shared interests. In such future conditions, it is possible that the larger common similarities between heterosexuals and Gay men and Lesbians will emerge so as to make these group distinctions less salient. Purely in terms of minority isolation, militance, and conflict, the status of Gay people—in time—would come to resemble that of Catholics: people with a positive group identity, yet well integrated on the basis of individual characteristics shared with the majority.

This is not to suggest that homosexuals should be validated as equal citizens on the basis of perceived similarity to heterosexuals, nor that there are not some differences in lifestyle and consciousness. All indications are that Gay cultural life will continue to flourish, with or without oppression.

But this sense of shared Gay identity and community need not be ghettoized once the majority lifts the siege—both physical and psychological. Today, it is hardly feasible for Gay people to dissolve their minority identity for the convenience of a majority that continues to isolate, stigmatize, and injure people in such a way as to evoke militant group allegiance (Vida, 1978; Voeller, 1980).

Indeed, a new generation of young Gay people has emerged (without the necessity of "recruitment"). These men and women tend to have overcome most of the negative roles and stigmatized self-concepts traditionally imposed on homosexuals. They tend to consider themselves healthy, productive, and thoroughly equal to other citizens. They expect full civil liberties and equal opportunity. These expectations and aspirations have been met with recent, highly publicized backlash campaigns that seek to deny and reverse gains in equal civil rights, or impose demands and expectations that Gay people return to the closet and social invisibility.

The evidence is that such reactions—beginning with Anita Bryant in 1977—have served only to make the movement stronger and vastly larger. The national Gay community and its civil rights movement are clearly historical realities which are not about to disappear. It would be highly irresponsible, considering what has been inflicted on Gay people, to suppose (as many apparently do) that Gay people will surrender their individual and collective identity.

This historical social collision poses a clear potential for serious social conflict. The traditions of individual liberty and free expression in this country strongly indicate that no group of Americans will easily surrender liberties once achieved. The evidence derived from civil rights struggles of other minority groups suggests that they will resist tenaciously when their new hope and rising expectations are met with aggressive reactions and what are perceived as broken promises of freedom.

America currently faces a number of truly serious, primary social problems requiring immediate attention and resources. Homosexual orientation is an unnecessary source of hatred and public alarm. It is a *spurious* social problem, because it need not be a problem at all. Instead, social conflict over Gay civil rights is the problem—widespread prejudice, ignorance, religious taboo, and past avoidance of the topic are quite real sources of social conflict. Avoiding the issue or trying to ignore groups of Gay people have only served to aggravate conditions of potential social disorder.

Both in pragmatic terms and simple justice, a resolution can be reached simply by according to Gay people those civil rights a recognized minority deserves. Changing public opinion should be recognized and allowed to proceed by providing the kind of open education of an uninformed majority that would eventually encourage reconciliation through a proper recognition that heterosexuals and Gay people are far more alike than different, most of all in a shared humanity. If the majority does not wish to confront Gay people as an angry, persecuted, and rebellious minority, then it should simply cease treating them like one.

CONCLUSIONS

There are important differences between Gay people and racial or ethnic minorities:

(1) Racial and ethnic minorities in America suffer cumulative historical effects of oppression over generations.
(2) Racial and ethnic minority group members tend to be far more visible, with exceptions, and therefore more vulnerable to majorities.
(3) Racial and ethnic minority group children can suffer developmental effects of oppression from early childhood to a greater extent than homosexuals.

Because of these differences, overcoming racial and ethnic oppression is an important priority. However, there is no evidence that recognition of Gay minority status has ever detracted from the rights of other minority groups.

The above difference notwithstanding, people with a homosexual orientation do constitute a minority group, on the basis of the following criteria:

(1) Gay people who are recognized as homosexual by majority group members, voluntarily or involuntarily, are a minority quite equivalent to other minorities.
(2) Gay men and Lesbians comprise social and cultural minorities distinct from the majority communities they grew up in.
(3) Homosexuals are a minority specifically by virtue of oppression inflicted by majority groups. This has included discrimination, campaigns of hatred and vilification, and widespread physical violence inflicted on minority group members.
(4) Homosexuals comprise a religious minority.

Currently, there are majority religious and political groups actively attempting to deny Lesbians and Gay men equal protection under the law. This effort involves campaigns of intergroup hatred and vilification and efforts to pass discriminatory legislation. Gay people deserve protection from these efforts on several grounds, including the right to be free of laws based on religious dogma.

There is not enough attention by government and the mass media to specific conditions of anti-Gay oppression. Specific examples follow:

(1) Physical violence against Lesbians and Gay men is a common national problem.
(2) Organized violence has included attacks on Gay civil rights workers and institutions and the destruction of Gay churches.
(3) The beginning of anti-Gay propaganda campaigns is correlated with rising rates of anti-Gay violence, although such campaigns are not the only cause of such violence.

NOTES

1. The term "Gay" as an inclusive description for Lesbians is a matter of some debate. Many Lesbians wish to be clearly designated as such, correctly pointing out the popular tendency to equate "Gay" with "Gay male." Other Lesbians prefer to use both terms, believing "Gay" belongs historically to Lesbians as much as to Gay men. For the sake of compromise and brevity, I employ all the popular usages here. Unless specified as male, "Gay" used here, as in "Gay people," is meant to include Lesbians.

2. Actually, there has been considerable support for Gay and Lesbian civil rights efforts from various racial and ethnic political groups—the Congressional Black Caucus, for example.

3. There is no evidence that Gay people incur more discrimination than do racial or ethnic minorities. It is probably less, due to the stated differences—especially visibility.

4. Mutual cooperation between Black and Gay communities in San Francisco led to cooperative development of a community center (San Francisco Examiner, Jan. 29, 1982, p. A3). Anti-Gay violence in that city elicited a cooperative effort from Latino groups led by Centro de Cambio, working with Gay and Lesbian community groups in 1981. Many such efforts have emerged recently, usually without media coverage.

5. Personal communication, Harvard University, 1977.

6. Small children are often literally persecuted for behavior deemed inappropriate to their gender, especially boys. At UCLA, very young boys were treated with behavior modification methods for the prevention of both "gender-inappropriate" behavior and potential homosexuality, leading one 5-year-old to conclude: "I used to be a queer" (Rorvik, Ned; "The Gender Enforcers", Rolling Stone, Oct. 9, 1975, pp. 52, 67).

7. Lesbian perspectives merit much more attention than provided here. There are distinct Lesbian communities, including important segments of women's communities, which require a more comprehensive account beyond the scope of this chapter (and the knowledge of the author). Excellent accounts are provided by Martin and Lyon (1972), Vida (1978), and Ponse (1978).

8. Organized efforts in America to memorialize the holocaust have resisted acknowledgment of Nazi oppression of Gay people (Body Politic [Toronto], April 1980, p. 19).

9. McDonough, William. Anti-Gay Violence and Community Organization (unpublished), 1981, Department of Psychology, San Francisco State University, San Francisco, CA 94132. (Submitted to the Mayor's Task Force on Victimization, Office of the Mayor, San Francisco, 1982).

10. Street violence against Gay men and Lesbians is a pervasive reality of daily life in urban areas, yet often denied by agencies of social control. One example of official acknowledgment and response is San Francisco's city funding of Community United Against Violence, which also serves heterosexuals.

11. Allport (1954) called self-hatred one of the "traits of victimization" shared to varying degrees by many members of differing minority groups.

REFERENCE NOTES

1. Stingel, R. Proceedings of the Police, Fire and Public Safety Committee of the San Francisco Board of Supervisors: A presentation by Community United Against Violence, October 10, 1980.
2. Fleming, S. Proceedings of the Police, Fire and Public Safety Committee of the San Francisco Board of Supervisors: Hearings on violence against lesbians and gay men, October 10, 1980.
3. White, E. Moral war: News center exclusive report (Transcript available from KRON-TV, San Francisco), February 9, 1981.

· 30 ·

Summary and Conclusions

William Paul

The final task is to organize the information in this section into a brief list of conclusions applicable to issues regarding Gay social equality. Considering the complexity of the material covered by the four authors, this is a difficult undertaking. But on many questions, the burden of evidence is so overwhelming as to compel a strong and explicit conclusion.

This section of the book deals directly with current events, including several issues which are providing conditions for serious social conflict. It is therefore proper, once again, to ground the discussion in the social context to which the SPSSI Task Force and this book respond.

Our collaborative effort in developing this research and education Task Force was undertaken over a period of four years. During that time the intense feelings and clashing value systems that comprise the Gay rights issue have generated a process of historical conflict and change involving Gay people and their communities, and the social relevance of the research has expanded immeasurably. The conclusions and supporting evidence in this volume should ideally generate much illuminating debate while eliciting wide public exposure, as befits a major controversy concerning fundamental beliefs.

Given the recent political ascendancy of groups and ideologies which bitterly oppose Gay social equality, such ideal conditions of public dialogue are problematic at best. There is every likelihood that, amid a historical social controversy, vast numbers of citizens living in conservative areas of the country will not (for example) have free access to this information in their public libraries or schools. A rising tide of censorship campaigns nationally have selected for special wrath any source of information regarding homosexuality that does not reflect traditional taboo.

This prospect is what this section is primarily about—not simply personal liberty to pursue unconventional conduct, but freedom of ideas and beliefs. This old American idea—of individual liberty to be different and to think differently from the majority—is the essential issue, from which all other arguments about homosexuality in this section emanate. This provides the proper context for briefly presenting our conclusions. For a more detailed statement of them, and for supporting arguments, readers should of course consult the particular chapters.

Legal Issues (Stivison and Rivera)

1. The law treats Gay Americans differently, unequally, and unfairly, in comparison with its heterosexual citizens. Discrimination is widespread.

2. The state has actively elected not to protect its homosexual citizens from bigotry at the hands of other citizens, with few local exceptions.

3. Gay citizens do enjoy certain constitutional guarantees (such as freedom of association) as a result of many court decisions, but these guarantees are not nearly as often enforced or awarded as equitable treatment would require.

Minority Issues (Thomas and Paul)

1. Gay citizens will not passively accept the loss of civil rights. Gay people are no different from other American social groups in their capacity to resist restrictions on their rights and liberties.

2. Gay men and Lesbians form a legitimate minority group, especially as judged by the criteria of majority reaction and treatment, including anti-Gay violence.

3. Gay people are a religious minority, in that they dissent from a dominant religious belief system, which is an important source of discriminatory laws and oppressive majority actions.

4. However, racial and ethnic minorities differ from Gay people as a minority in several important ways.

5. Organized violence against Gay community institutions is a serious civil rights problem. Likewise, the widespread limitation on academic freedom (to pursue research relating to homosexuality) can be properly defined as thought control, transpiring in a social context of widespread ignorance about homosexual behavior and Gay people.

6. Despite these injustices, the position of Lesbians and Gay men in American society, and that society's image of them, has consistently improved in the past ten years. This is in spite of the emergence, during that same time period, of new myths and arguments designed to combat the advances.

SOME FINAL COMMENTS

Gay men and Lesbians are far too diverse a people, and the current conflict is too complex, for these four chapters to give a full account. But certain conditions are quite apparent to a number of contemporary observers. The most interesting aspect of Gay rights issues is the majority problem of persisting hatred, fear, and avoidance. Despite the deep cultural and historical roots of this taboo, American society has shown a remarkable capacity to change in response to the emergence of increasingly visible Gay and Lesbian communities. Traditionalist anti-Gay social forces accurately target this visible social participation as one of the most powerful agents of change.

Perhaps because the mystification of homosexuality has been so exotic, and the alleged dangers of Gay social equality propounded in such extravagant assertions, when confronted by ordinary Gay people other ordinary Americans begin to shed the taboo. One factor that doubtless favors the disposal of sexual mythologies is the number of heterosexual Americans who have undergone a sexual liberation of their own. This is but one facet of an expansion of pluralist diversity in American society accelerated by the 1960s, which has diversified choices in the kinds of lives one can lead.

Groups like the Moral Majority see this kind of cultural liberty as yet another enemy to be destroyed, and increasing numbers of otherwise conventional heterosexuals have perceived Gay demands for real freedom as not too different from their own. Gay social visibility makes such perceptions of basic similarity possible.

Avoidance has always been the most powerful weapon at the disposal of anti-Gay forces in the enforcement of taboo. Thus the closet served as a principal instrument of social control. The irony is that each new hate campaign launched by the radical right only seems to further dissolve their own best means of imposed conformity. After each apparent victory in overturning a local Gay rights ordinance, there remains a huge increase in public awareness that there is an important social issue involved. These battles also tend to expose the public consciousness to images of Gay men and Lesbians that are visibly compelling contradictions to the exotic stereotypes promoted by anti-Gay mythology.

This is not to underestimate the dangers posed by current efforts to attack the civil rights of Gay people. An array of explicit statements by some opponents of Gay social equality make it clear that much of their motivation is inspired not only by fear but also by sheer hatred. In terms of resources, the controversy is a vastly unequal contest, especially in the use of mass media by the New Right. Given persisting public ignorance imposed by restrictions on open education, these forces still retain sufficient power to generate fear and hatred of a kind that could have tragic historical consequences.

· VI ·

Conclusions

· 31 ·

Task Force Findings
Overview and Prospect

James D. Weinrich

It is impossible, in this brief overview, to outline all the arguments in a book as comprehensive as this one. Nor is it possible to draw up a set of conclusions that would be agreed to by every author. Each chapter has conclusions of its own, and each section's summary notes the common threads running from chapter to chapter within it. The task of this last chapter, then, is to point out the connections running between the sections.

First and foremost among these is the conclusion that much of the oldest research on homosexuality was influenced by poorly founded stereotypes and social prejudice. In some cases, "bigotry" and "taboo" are appropriate words to describe the forces encouraging such research. Whether it be the notion that homosexuals are mentally ill, hormonally abnormal, socially degenerate, or undeserving of social equality, such research had concluded that homosexuals were inferior and that the cause of that inferiority was in some sense the responsibility of the homosexuals themselves. Many parts of this book rebut these outmoded stereotypes and may thus be described as *reactive.*

A second theme connecting sections is the notion that homosexuals are rather like heterosexuals. Here, recall statements that homosexuals are as mentally healthy as heterosexuals are, that homosexual behavior is as biologically natural as heterosexual behavior is, that homosexuals of one sex are often more like heterosexuals of the same sex than like the opposite sex, and that the law should be administered in a fashion blind to sexual orientation. These arguments are in a sense *defensive,* acting to head off the stereotypical arguments rebutted by the reactive ones above.

A third set of arguments aims at a more accurate (second-order approximation) answer to the question of homosexual-heterosexual differences. These differences are not entirely denied, but are viewed as small in relation to the similarities; in some cases, they are celebrated. Fitting homosexuality and heterosexuality *together* is often an important feature here. Exemplifying this set are conclusions that homosexuals experience a coming-out pattern in stages, with consequences for other parts of homosexuals' lives; that an affirmative psychoanalytic treatment with homosexual individuals can exist alongside the psychoanalysis of heterosexuality; that homosexuality may have an adaptive function within evolutionary biology; that the lifestyles emerging among lesbians and gay men can exemplify a sense of options or freedom of choice in creating social relationships (thus providing benefits to society at large); that homosexuals are a minority similar to and different from racial or religious minorities; and that the view of oneself as a member of a minority group can catalyze reactions to an event in previously unprecedented ways. Such arguments are *affirmative,* because they move beyond the conclusion that homosexuals and heterosexuals are more alike than different, and affirm that homosexuality is good or useful in and of itself. Yet they depend on the defensive "more alike than different" conclusion, because they postulate or cite it.

The arguments spanning this book, then, reflect stages any minority goes through in its presentation to the majority: from asking for pity, to demanding equality, to valuing diversity. The arguments at each stage reject, in part, the arguments of the previous stage, even while they build on them.

Viewed in this way, the chapters in this volume speak with a remarkable unanimity. Past research on homosexuality has been plagued with many extrascientific biases against the phenomenon it claimed to study with scientific neutrality. Recent research has refuted or strongly challenged many of the social beliefs causing and reflecting this research. Present and future research should be built on a new paradigm, one that affirms the rights of people to differ and that judges those people psychologically, biologically, interpersonally, and socially as individuals, not as stereotypes representing some larger good or evil.

In particular, we conclude the following.

• Homosexuality, like heterosexuality, may accompany psychological problems but is per se unrelated to them.

• Therapy to convert homosexuals to heterosexuality, whether voluntary or not, is of dubious feasibility and is a questionable goal.

• Homophobia within the psychiatric profession has retarded acceptance of these conclusions.

• While psychoanalytic concepts show considerable promise for the understanding of homosexuality's interaction with other aspects of personality, other models (such as social psychological and developmental ones) also have much to contribute.

• Biological models involving an interaction between genetic factors (that is, predispositions) and environmental ones are promising and require further study.

• However, the simplest kinds of hormonal imbalance theories of homosexuality are all but ruled out, and homosexuality and heterosexuality are equally natural when viewed by evolutionary theory.

• Studies of gay lifestyles reveal that homosexuals and heterosexuals are more alike than different, more ordinary than extraordinary. This is true whether one looks at their patterns of loving, of parenting, or of aging.

• When average differences do exist, they are as likely to be of benefit to the rest of society as they are to be of harm; in neither case does the effect of the group have a valid consequence for discriminatory treatment of the individual. Even considering only the harms, there is no evidence that homosexuality is more harmful, as a whole, than heterosexuality is.

• In other cultures, homosexual acts are accorded widely varying treatment. But in many cultures, the homosexualities existing are integrated in positive ways into the social fabric of the society.

• Much work remains to be done in our own society to integrate homosexuality into an equitable legal framework, but this task is necessary if we wish to fulfill principles implicit in the U.S. Constitution.

• As San Francisco's "White Night" riots showed, homosexuals will continue to call these facts to the attention of the majority until appropriately recognized, or until the forces of prejudice and homophobia suppress them, at a considerable cost.

• For judging by the criteria of majority reaction and treatment, homosexuals are a minority in a sense similar to racial, ethnic, and religious minorities, although the similarity is not exact.

• In short, our society has a choice between freedom for, and repression of, its homosexual minority. It would be far better to take the former course.

THE PROSPECT FOR SOCIAL CHANGE

This last conclusion raises the question of how societies can be encouraged to change, and whether reports like the present one influence the process. This book is not the first to address homosexuality as a social issue—it is one of an unpremeditated series that stretches back to Jeremy Bentham's essay on homosexuality and the law (Bentham, 1978; written about 1785), includes Edward Carpenter's essay anticipating the majority of the conclusions of the present volume (Carpenter, 1894), and reaches up to the two scholarly volumes edited by Judd Marmor (1965, 1980a). Many of our conclusions have been stated before, and one must ask why society has not acted on many of them. Obviously, answering this would require another volume, but let's point out where such an answer would begin.

Clearly, one reason society has not changed as much as a naive reliance on logic would predict is that few people really make their decisions on the basis of facts (recall Figure 17.1 from my chapter). *How* do people reach conclusions, then, and *why* do people spend so much time arguing with facts or pseudo-facts? The latter question suggests that facts, while not decisive, influence some people some of the time; the extent to which they do should be investigated. It is much easier to found a political movement with supporters already convinced of the worthiness of one's cause and the truth of one's conclusions than to convince the skeptics. But even skeptics sometimes change their minds. Why?

The other question is how people convinced of something become convinced to begin with. In the case of homosexuality, we should ask how people holding pro- or anti-gay positions come to hold them. This suggestion echoes (yet is broader than) the statement that homosexuals should be studied less and homophobia should be studied more. Clearly, many of the attitudes common in society at large originate in simple socialization. Others may come from the larger forces studied by social psychologists, sociologists, sociobiologists, and political analysts. But many firmly held beliefs derive from personal experience, and we should also investigate how or whether people learn about homosexuality first-hand. Indeed, Gonsiorek's chapter on social psychology suggests that social stereotypes of homosexuality can *arbitrarily* influence the behavior of homosexuals, creating a false impression of the cause of the stereotype and the behavior.

In particular, how many people's personal experience of homosexuality consists of the 30-second glimpse they once got of a street transvestite, or of the time they were groped in a movie-house balcony, or of the rumors they heard about a school teacher whom they consequently never got to know? (Few people's experience of heterosexuality, in contrast, is limited to the one time they were heterosexually groped in a movie theater.) The fact that such instances may have little to do with homosexuality as we currently understand it, or have no valid consequence for a particular social policy, simply underscores the hunch: Even a simple survey asking people their first personal experience of homosexuality could shed light on the question.

Here, then, is a hypothesis for future research. To the extent that the stereotypes of homosexuals resemble those of other minorities (dangerous to children, psychologically ill, mysterious, etc.), they will be found to have either no validity whatsoever or only the self-fulfilling kind of validity discussed by Gonsiorek. To the extent that the stereotypes of homosexuals differ from those of other minorities (for example, not having children), they will be found to have only correlational validity (only some, not all, members fitting the stereotype) and may be due to inadequate contact between members of the majority and the minority. Whether this hypothesis fares well or poorly in the future, I hope it will help to organize the debate.

THE ROLE OF SCIENCE IN SOCIAL CHANGE

If so many of our conclusions have been validly reached before, why did we have to bother repeating them? There are several parts to the answer, beyond the obvious educational one that not everyone has read everything that has been written on the topic.

First, science does advance from time to time, and some theories eventually are abandoned. Carpenter (1894), for example, carefully rebutted the theory that homosexuality is a symptom of the degeneration of the nervous system, but we have not found it necessary to do so.

Second, the advance of science sometimes does provide simple explanations for phenomena that previously seemed increasingly complex and multidetermined. Scurvy was seen as a disease with multiple etiologies until the discovery that vitamin C deficiency is always the intervening variable. Likewise, there was a chance that the more precise methods of analyzing hormones worked out in the 1960s *could* have shown significant correlations with sexual orientation, even though earlier attempts failed. Indicators of investigator bias that are obvious in this case (such as the use of the language of pathology before pathology is demonstrated—see the exchange between Baker, 1972, and Kolodny, 1972) can rightly make a reader suspicious and certainly can suggest additional experiments and approaches, but they cannot of themselves divine the outcome.

Third, even the observation that there is no significant change in the information available or the conclusion reached is important. Carpenter (1894) argued against the common medical opinion of his day—that homosexuality is associated with morbid manifestations (i.e., sickness)—as follows:

It must never be forgotten that the medico-scientific enquirer is bound on the whole to meet with those cases [of homosexuality] that *are* of a morbid character, rather than with those that are healthy in their manifestation, since indeed it is the former that he lays himself out for.

This insight is so often repeated nowadays it is practically a cliché. Yet the fact that it still sometimes needs to be said is telling.

Fourth (and, I believe, most important), scientific debate takes place on many levels. As the findings pass by over the years, the overall pattern of advances and retreats becomes more important than the status of a particular allegation. Despite the current vogue among many scientists (but fewer historians of science) for the Popperian ideal of the falsifiable hypothesis, the fact is that a scientific theory is discarded not when an experiment definitively falsifies it, but when the string of false predictions of a theory's proponents becomes embarrassingly long. The existence of such a string is itself a bit of metascientific data—admittedly one difficult to apply a statistical test to, but telling nevertheless. So this book can be seen as another step in the metascientific debate, embarrassing its share of those who (say) reach the same conclusions before and after their data change.

There are, admittedly, extrascientific forces that affect the outcome of any debate and that are sometimes stronger than science. How long an embarrassing string of unconfirmed results has to be before the theory is rejected varies—no doubt with the power or arrogance of the theorizer. Studying the debate itself is one way to work out what these forces are, how they operate, and how we can influence their operation. Of course, a social issue is itself a debate, and it is in this larger battle that SPSSI is dedicated to fight.

REFERENCES

Adelman, M. A comparison of professionally employed lesbians and heterosexual women on the MMPI. *Archives of Sexual Behavior,* 1977, *6*(3), 193-201.

Akers, J. S., & Conaway, C. H. Female homosexual behavior in *Macaca mulatta. Archives of Sexual Behavior,* 1979, *8,* 63-80.

Alfred, R. On live. *San Francisco Sentinel,* December 10, 1980, p. 8.

Allport, G. W. *The nature of prejudice.* Reading, MA: Addison-Wesley, 1954.

American Psychiatric Association. *Mental disorders: Diagnostic and statistical manual.* Washington, D.C., 1965.

Arendt, H. *The origins of totalitarianism.* New York: Meridian/World, 1958.

Aronson, B. S., & Grumpelt, H. R. Homosexuality and some MMPI measures of masculinity-femininity. *Journal of Clinical Psychology,* 1961, *17,* 245-247.

Babuscio, J. *We speak for ourselves.* Philadelphia: Fortress Press, 1976.

Baker, J. Homosexuality and testosterone. *New England Journal of Medicine,* 1972, *286,* 380.

Bailey, D. S. *Homosexuality and the Western Christian tradition.* London: Longmans, 1955.

Bandura, A. *Principles of behavior modification.* New York: Holt, Rinehart & Winston, 1969.

Bane, M. J. Marital disruption and the lives of children. *Journal of Social Issues,* 1976, *32*(1), 103-117.

Barnhart, E. Friends and lovers in a lesbian counterculture community. In N. Glazer-Malbin (Ed.), *Old family/new family.* New York: Van Nostrand, 1975.

Barratt, B. B. Freud's psychology as interpretation. *Psychoanalysis and Contemporary Science,* 1976, *5,* 443-478.

Barton, A. H., & Lazarsfeld, P. F. Qualitative support of theory. In G. J. McCall & J. L. Simmons (Eds.), *Issues in participant observation.* Reading, MA: Addison-Wesley, 1969.

Bass-Hass, R. The lesbian dyad. *Journal of Sex Research,* 1968, *4*(2), 108-126.

Beck, A. T. Cognitive therapy: Nature and relation to behavior therapy. *Behavior Therapy,* 1970, *1,* 184-200.

Becker, H. Nature and consequences of black propaganda. *American Sociological Review,* 1949, *14,* 221-235.

Becker, H. *Outsiders: Studies in the sociology of deviance.* New York: Free Press, 1963. (Rev. ed., 1973.)

Becker, H. S., & Horowitz, I. L. The culture of civility. *TransAction,* April 1970, pp. 12-19.

Begelman, D. A. Ethical and legal issues of behavior modification. In M. Hersen, R. Eisler, & P. M. Miller (Eds.), *Progress in behavior modification.* New York: Academic Press, 1975.

Begelman, D. A. Homosexuality and the ethics of behavioral intervention: Paper 3. *Journal of Homosexuality,* 1977, *2,* 213-219.

Bell, A. P., & Weinberg, M. S. *Homosexualities: A study of diversity among men and women.* New York: Simon & Schuster, 1978.

Bell, A. P., Weinberg, M. S., & Hammersmith, S. K. *Sexual preference: Its development in men and women.* Bloomington: Indiana University Press, 1981.

Bem, S. L. The measurement of psychological androgyny. *Journal of Consulting and Clinical Psychology,* 1974, *42,* 155-162.

Bem, S. L. Sex-role adaptability: One consequence of psychological androgyny. *Journal of Personality and Social Psychology*, 1975, *31*, 634-643.

Bentham, J. Offences against one's self: Paederasty, Part I. *Journal of Homosexuality*, 1978, *3*, 389-405.

Berger, P. L., & Luckmann, T. *The social construction of reality*. London: Penguin, 1967.

Bergler, E. *Homosexuality: Disease or way of life?* New York: Collier, 1956.

Bergler, E. *Counterfeit sex: Homosexuality, impotence, frigidity*. New York: Grune & Stratton, 1957. (Rev. ed., 1958.)

Bernard, J. *Remarriage: A study of marriage*. New York: Russell and Russell, 1971.

Berzon, B., & Leighton, R. (Eds.). *Positively gay*. Millbrae, CA: Celestial Arts, 1979.

Bieber, I., Dain, H. J., Dince, P. R., Drellich, M. G., Grand, H. G., Gundlach, R. H., Kremer, M. W., Rifkin, A. H., Wilbur, C. B., & Bieber, T. B. *Homosexuality: A psychoanalytic study*. New York: Basic Books, 1962.

Bleuel, H. P. *Sex and society in Nazi Germany*. New York: Lippincott, 1973.

Block, J. H. Conceptions of sex role: Some cross-cultural and longitudinal perspectives. *American Psychologist*, 1973, *28*, 512-526.

Body Politic. Houston cops shoot gay activist working on anti-brutality campaign. *The Body Politic* (Toronto), September 1980, p. 16.

Boggan, E. C., Haft, M. G., Lister, C., & Rupp, J. P. *The rights of gay people*. New York: Avon, 1975.

Bohannan, P. The six stations of divorce. In P. Bohannan (Ed.), *Divorce and after*. Garden City, NY: Doubleday, 1970.

Bonnell, C. Heterosexuality: An enlightened view. *Christopher Street*, 1976, *1*(3), 59-62.

Bonnell, C. Bonnell knells: Say it loud! *Esplanade* (Boston), April 20, 1978, p. 5.

Boswell, J. *Christianity, social tolerance, and homosexuality: Gay people in Western Europe from the beginning of the Christian era to the fourteenth century*. Chicago: University of Chicago Press, 1980.

Bozett, F. Gay fathers: How and why they disclose their homosexuality to their children. *Family Relations*, 1980, *29*, 173-179.

Braaten, L., & Darling, C. Overt and covert homosexual problems among male college students. *Genetic Psychology Monographs*, 1965, *71*, 269-270.

Brandwein, R. A., Brown, C. A., & Fox, E. M. Women and children last: The situation of divorced mothers and their families. *Journal of Marriage and the Family*, 1974, *36*, 498-514.

Brown, D. G. Masculinity-femininity development in children. *Journal of Consulting Psychology*, 1957, *21*, 197-202.

Brown, D. G. Inversion and homosexuality. *American Journal of Orthopsychiatry*, 1958, *28*, 424-429.

Brown, H. *Familiar faces, hidden lives: The story of homosexual men in America today*. New York: Harcourt Brace Jovanovich, 1976.

Brown, N. O. *Love's body*. New York: Random House, 1966.

Bryant, A. The civil rights of parents: To save our children from homosexual influence. *Miami Herald*, March 20, 1977, full page ad.

BSERP. *Removing the stigma: Final report of the Board of Social and Ethical Responsibility for Psychology's Task Force on the Status of Lesbian and Gay Male Psychologists*. Washington, DC: American Psychological Association, 1979.

Bullough, V. L. Sex and the medical model. *Journal of Sex Research*, 1975, *11*, 291-303.

Bullough, V. L. *Sexual variance in society and history*. New York: John Wiley, 1976.

Bullough, V. L. *Homosexuality: A history*. New York: Meridian, 1979.

Burdick, J., & Stewart, D. Differences between "show" and "no-show" volunteers in a homosexual population. *Journal of Social Psychology*, 1974, *92*, 159-60.

Burgess, A. W., Groth, A. N., Holmstrom, L. L., & Sgroi, S. M. *Sexual assault of children and adolescents*. Lexington, MA: D. C. Heath, 1978.

Bush, L., & Goldstein, R. Gays: The New Right's first target. *San Francisco Chronicle*, "This World" (Sunday supplement), July 5, 1981, pp. 8-13.

Caldwell, M., & Peplau, L. A. Power in lesbian relationships. *Sex Roles*, in press.

California Poll, *Los Angeles Times*, June 6, 1977, Pt. 1, p. 7.

Cameron, P. A case against homosexuality. *Human Life Review,* 1978, 4(3), 17-49.

Caprio, F. S. *Female homosexuality: A modern study of lesbianism.* New York: Grove Press, 1954.

Caprio, F. S. *Female homosexuality.* New York: Citadel Press, 1967.

Cardell, M., Finn, S., & Marecek, J. Sex-role identity, sex-role behavior, and satisfaction in heterosexual, lesbian, and gay male couples. *Psychology of Women Quarterly,* in press.

Carpenter, E. *Homogenic love and its place in a free society.* London: Redundancy Press, n.d. (Originally published, Manchester: Labour Press, 1894.)

Carrier, J. Homosexual behavior in cross-cultural perspective. In J. Marmor (Ed.), *Homosexual behavior: A modern reappraisal.* New York: Basic Books, 1980.

Cass, V. C. Homosexual identity formation: A theoretical model. *Journal of Homosexuality,* 1979, 4, 219-236.

Cattell, R. B., & Morony, J. H. The use of the 16PF in distinguishing homosexuals, normals, and general criminals. *Journal of Consulting Psychology,* 1962, 26, 531-540.

Cautela, J. R. Treatment of compulsive behavior by covert sensitization. *Psychological Record,* 1966, 16, 33-41.

Cautela, J. R. Covert sensitization. *Psychological Reports,* 1967, 2, 459-468.

Chang, J. & Block, J. A study of identification in male homosexuals. *Journal of Consulting Psychology,* 1960, 24, 307-310.

Chevalier-Skolnikoff, S. Male-female, female-female, and male-male sexual behavior in the stumptail monkey, with special attention to female orgasm. *Archives of Sexual Behavior,* 1974, 3, 95-116.

Chevalier-Skolnikoff, S. Homosexual behavior in a laboratory group of stumptail monkeys *(Macaca arctoides):* Forms, contexts, and possible social functions. *Archives of Sexual Behavior,* 1976, 5, 511-527.

Church, F. Probe of firebombing stirs questioning. *Portland Oregonian,* July 22, 1979, pp. 1, B1.

Churchill, W. *Homosexual behavior among males: A cross-cultural and cross-species investigation.* New York: Hawthorn Books, 1967.

Citizens' Advisory Council on the Status of Women. Memorandum: The Equal Rights Amendment and alimony and child support laws. Washington, D.C., 1972.

Clark, D. *Loving someone gay.* Milbrae, CA: Celestial Arts, 1977.

Clarke-Stewart, A. *Child care in the family.* New York: Academic Press, 1977.

Cochran, S. D. Romantic relationships: For better or for worse. Paper presented at the annual meeting of the Western Psychological Association, San Francisco, April 1978.

Cochran, S. D., & Peplau, L. A. The interplay of autonomy and attachment in love relationships: A comparison of men and women. Paper presented at the annual meeting of the Western Psychological Association, San Diego, April 1979.

Coleman, E. Toward a new model of treatment of homosexuality: A review. *Journal of Homosexuality,* 1978, 3, 345-359.

Coleman, E. Changing approaches to the treatment of homosexuality: A review. *American Behavioral Scientist,* 1982, 25(4), 397-405.

Conover, M. R., Miller, D. E., & Hunt, G. L., Jr. Female-female pairs and other unusual reproductive associations in ring-billed and California gulls. *The Auk,* 1979, 96, 6-9.

Cory, D. W. *The lesbian in America.* New York: McFadden-Bartel, 1965.

Cotton, W. L. Social and sexual relationships of lesbians. *Journal of Sex Research,* 1975, 11(2), 139-148.

Crompton, L. Gay genocide from Leviticus to Hitler. In L. Crew (Ed.), *The gay academic.* Palm Springs, CA: ETC Publications, 1978.

Dagg, A. I., & Foster, J. B. *The giraffe: Its biology, behavior, and ecology.* New York: Van Nostrand Reinhold, 1976.

Dahlstrom W., Welsh, G., & Dahlstrom, L. *MMPI handbook, volume 1* (Rev. ed.). Minneapolis: University of Minnesota Press, 1973.

Dank, B. M. Coming out in the gay world. *Psychiatry,* 1971, 34, 180-197.

Dank, B. M. The development of a homosexual identity: Antecedents and consequents. *Dissertation Abstracts International,* 1973, 34(1), 423A-424A.

Darwin, C. R. *Charles Darwin's natural selection* (Stauffer, R.C., Ed.) Cambridge: Cambridge University Press, 1975.

Daugherty, W. E., & Janowitz, M. (Eds.). *A psychological warfare casebook.* Baltimore, MD: Operations Research Office, Johns Hopkins University Press, 1958.

Davis, Karen. Pastor? The church is on fire. *In Unity,* April 1978, pp. 8-11. (a)

Davis, Karen. What happened to the good old days? *In Unity,* June-July 1978, pp. 4-5. (b)

Davis, Kingsley. Sex behavior. In R. K. Merton & R. A. Nisbet (Eds.), *Contemporary social problems.* New York: Harcourt Brace Jovanovich, 1976.

Davison, G. C. Elimination of a sadistic fantasy by a client-controlled counterconditioning technique: A case study. *Journal of Abnormal Psychology,* 1968, *73,* 84-90.

Davison, G. C. *Presidential address to the Eighth Annual Convention of the Association for Advancement of Behavior Therapy,* Chicago, November 2, 1974.

Davison, G. C. Homosexuality: The ethical challenge. *Journal of Consulting and Clinical Psychology,* 1976, *44,* 157-162.

Davison, G. C. Homosexuality and the ethics of behavioral intervention: Paper 1. *Journal of Homosexuality,* 1977, *2,* 195-204.

Dawkins, R. *The selfish gene.* New York: Oxford University Press, 1976.

Dean, R., & Richardson, H. Analysis of MMPI profiles of 40 college-educated overt male homosexuals. *Journal of Consulting Psychology,* 1964, *28,* 483-486.

Dean, R., & Richardson, H. On MMPI high-point codes of homosexual versus heterosexual males. *Journal of Consulting Psychology,* 1966, *30,* 558-560.

De Cecco, J. P. *The psychology of learning and instruction.* Englewood Cliffs, NJ: Prentice-Hall, 1968.

Denniston, R. H. Ambisexuality in animals. In J. Marmor (Ed.), *Homosexual behavior: A modern reappraisal.* New York: Basic Books, 1980.

Derdeyn, A. P. Child custody contests in historical perspective. *American Journal of Psychiatry,* 1976, *133*(12), 1369-1376.

Doidge, W., & Holtzman, W. Implications of homosexuality among Air Force trainees. *Journal of Consulting Psychology,* 1960, *24,* 9-13.

Dollard, J. *Caste and class in a southern town.* New Haven, CT: Yale University Press, 1937. (Rev. ed., 1957.)

Douglas, M. *Purity and danger: An analysis of pollution and taboo.* New York: Praeger, 1966.

Dover, K. J. *Greek homosexuality.* Cambridge, MA: Harvard University Press, 1978.

Drever, J. *A dictionary of psychology.* Baltimore, MD: Penguin, 1964.

Duehn, W. D., & Mayadas, N. S. The use of stimulus/modeling videotapes in assertive training for homosexuals. *Journal of Homosexuality,* 1976, *1,* 373-381.

DuMas, F. *Gay is not good.* Nashville, TN: Thomas Nelson, 1980.

Durban, E. The vicious cycle of welfare: Problems of the female-headed household in New York City. In C. B. Lloyd (Ed.), *Sex, discrimination and the division of labor.* New York: Columbia University Press, 1975.

Ehrhardt, A. A., & Meyer-Bahlburg, H. F. L. Effects of prenatal sex hormones on gender-related behavior. *Science,* 1981, *211,* 1312-1318.

Eisinger, A. et al. Female homosexuality. *Nature,* 1972, *238,* 106.

Ellis, A. Are homosexuals necessarily neurotic? In D. W. Cory (Ed.), *Homosexuality: A cross-cultural approach.* New York: Julian Press, 1956.

Erikson, E. H. *Childhood and society.* New York: Norton, 1950. (Rev. ed., 1963.)

Erikson, E. H. *Identity: Youth and crisis.* New York: Norton, 1968.

Escoffier, J. Stigma, work environment, and economic discrimination against homosexuals. *Homosexual Counseling Journal,* 1975, *2*(1), 8-17.

Ettorre, E. M. *Lesbians, women and society.* London: Routledge & Kegan Paul, 1980.

Evans, R. B. Childhood parental relationships of homosexual men. *Journal of Consulting and Clinical Psychology,* 1969, *33,* 129-135.

Evans, R. B. Sixteen personality factor questionnaire scores of homosexual men. *Journal of Consulting and Clinical Psychology,* 1970, *34,* 212-215.

Evans, R. B. ACL scores of homosexual men. *Journal of Personality Assessment,* 1971, *35,* 344-349.

Fairbairn, W. R. D. *An object-relations theory of personality.* New York: Basic Books, 1954.

Falwell, J. Special call to action: Stop the gays dead in their tracks. Leaflet, mass mailing, January 14, 1980.

Farina, A., Allen, J. G., & Saul, B. The role of the stigmatized in affecting social relationships. *Journal of Personality,* 1968, *36,* 169-182.

Farrel, R. A., & Nelson, J. F. A causal model of secondary deviance: The case of homosexuality. *Sociological Quarterly,* 1976, *17,* 109-120.

Feigl, H., & Scriven, M. (Eds.) *Minnesota studies in the philosophy of science. Vol. 1: The foundations of science and the concepts of psychology and psychoanalysis.* Minneapolis: University of Minnesota Press, 1956.

Feldman, M. P., & MacCulloch, M. J. The application of anticipatory avoidance learning to the treatment of homosexuality. I. Theory, technique, and preliminary results. *Behavior Research and Therapy,* 1965, *2,* 165-183.

Feldman, M. P., & MacCulloch, M. J. *Homosexual behavior: Therapy and assessment.* New York: Pergamon, 1971.

Fenichel, O. *The psychoanalytic theory of neurosis.* New York: Norton, 1945.

Ferris, A. *Indicators of trends in the status of American women.* New York: Russell Sage, 1971.

Fisher, P. *The gay mystique: The myth and reality of male homosexuality.* New York: Stein & Day, 1972.

Fisher, S., & Greenberg, R. P. (Eds.). *The scientific evaluation of Freud's theories and therapy: A book of readings.* New York: Basic Books, 1978.

Ford, C. S., & Beach, F. A. *Patterns of sexual behavior.* New York: Harper & Row, 1951.

Fort, J., Steiner, C. M., & Conrad, F. Attitudes of mental health professionals toward homosexuality and its treatment. *Psychological Reports,* 1971, *29,* 347-350.

Frank, J. D. Treatment of homosexuals. In J. M. Livingood (Ed.), *NIMH Task Force on Homosexuality: Final report and background papers.* DHEW Publication No. (HSM) 72-9116. Rockville, MD: National Institute of Mental Health, 1972.

Freedman, M. Homosexuals may be healthier than straights. *Psychology Today,* March 1975, 1971.

Freedman, N. Homosexuals may be healthier than straights. *Psychology Today,* March 1975, *8*(10), 28-32.

Freud, A. *The ego and the mechanisms of defense.* New York: International Universities Press, 1953. (Originally published, 1936.)

Freud, S. *The interpretation of dreams. Standard edition 4,5.* London: Hogarth Press, 1953. (Originally published, 1900.)

Freud, S. *Three essays on the theory of sexuality. Standard edition 7.* London: Hogarth Press, 1953. (Originally published, 1905.)

Freud, S. *A general introduction to psychoanalysis.* New York: Pocket Books, 1971. (Originally published, 1920.)

Freud, S. *Civilization and its discontents. Standard edition 21.* London: Hogarth Press, 1961. (Originally published, 1930.)

Freud, S. Letter to an American mother. *American Journal of Psychiatry,* 1951, *107,* 252. (Originally published, 1935.)

Freund, K. Should homosexuality arouse therapeutic concern? *Journal of Homosexuality,* 1977, *2,* 235-240.

Freund, K., Langevin, R., Cibiri, S., & Zajac, Y. Heterosexual aversion in homosexual males. *British Journal of Psychiatry,* 1973, *122,* 163-169.

Friberg, R. Measures of homosexuality: Cross-validation of 2 MMPI scales and implications for usage. *Journal of Consulting Psychology,* 1967, *31,* 88-91.

Fromm, E. *The crisis of psychoanalysis: Essays on Freud, Marx, and social psychology.* New York: Holt, Rinehart & Winston, 1970.

Futuyma, D. Is there a gay gene? Does it matter? *Science for the People,* 1980, *12*(1), 10-15.

Gadpaille, W. J. *The cycles of sex.* New York: Scribners, 1975.

Gagnon, J., & Simon, W. Sexual deviance in contemporary America. *Annals of the American Academy of Political and Social Science,* 1967, *375,* 106-122.

Gagnon, J. H., & Simon, W. A conformity greater than deviance: The lesbian. In J. H. Gagnon & W. Simon (Eds.), *Sexual conduct: The social sources of human sexuality.* Chicago: Aldine, 1973.

Gallup, G. Gallup poll: Homosexuals in U.S. society. *Boston Globe,* July 18, 1977.

Garner, B., & Smith, R. W. Are there really any gay male athletes? An empirical survey. *Journal of Sex Research,* 1977, *13,* 22-34.

Gates, M. Homemakers into widows and divorcees: Can the law provide economic protection? In J. R. Chapman & M. Gates (Eds.), *Women into wives: The legal and economic impact of marriage.* Beverly Hills, CA: Sage, 1977.

Gebhard, P. H. Incidence of overt homosexuality in the United States and Western Europe. In J. M. Livingood (Ed.), *NIMH Task Force on Homosexuality: Final report and background papers.* DHEW Publication No. (HSM) 72-9116. Rockville, MD: National Institute of Mental Health, 1972.

Gebhard, P. H., & Johnson, A. B. *The Kinsey data: Marginal tabulations of the 1938-1963 interviews conducted by the Institute for Sex Research.* Philadelphia: W. B. Saunders, 1979.

Gedo, J. E. *Beyond interpretation: Toward a revised theory for psychoanalysis.* New York: International Universities Press, 1979.

Geist, V. *Mountain sheep: A study in behavior and evolution.* Chicago: University of Chicago Press, 1971.

Gibson, G. G. *By her own admission.* Garden City, NY: Doubleday, 1977.

Gill, M. M., & Holzman, P. S. (Eds.). *Psychology versus metapsychology: Psychoanalytic essays in memory of George Klein. Psychological issues monograph 36.* New York: International Universities Press, 1976.

Glueck, S., & Glueck, E. *Family environment and delinquency.* Boston: Houghton Mifflin, 1962.

Goffman, E. *Stigma: Notes on the management of spoiled identity.* Englewood Cliffs, NJ: Prentice-Hall, 1963.

Goldfoot, D. A., Westerborg-van Loon, H., Groeneveld, W., & Slob, A. K. Behavioral and physiological evidence of sexual climax in the female stump-tailed macaque *(Macaca arctoides). Science,* 1980, *208,* 1477-1479.

Goldfried, M. R., Stricker, G., & Weiner, I. *Rorschach handbook of clinical and research applications.* Englewood Cliffs, NJ: Prentice-Hall, 1971.

Goldstein, J. et al. *Beyond the best interests of the child.* New York: Free Press, 1973.

Gonsiorek, J. C. Psychological adjustment and homosexuality. *Catalog of Selected Documents in Psychology,* 1977, 7(2), 45, MS 1478. (Available from the American Psychological Association.)

Gonsiorek, J. C. What health care professionals need to know about lesbians and gay men. In M. Jospe et al. (Eds.), *Psychological factors in health care.* Lexington, MA: D. C. Heath, 1980.

Gonsiorek, J. C. Book review of Masters & Johnson, *Homosexuality in Perspective. Journal of Homosexuality,* 1981, *6*(3), in press.

Gonsiorek, J. C. (Ed.) *Homosexuality and psychotherapy: A practitioners' handbook of affirmative models.* New York: Haworth Press, 1982. (a)

Gonsiorek, J. C. Book review of Masters & Johnson, *Homosexuality in Perspective. Journal of Homosexuality,* 1981, *6*(3), 81-88.

Gonsiorek, J. C. (Ed.). Homosexuality: The end of a mental illness. *American Behavioral Scientist,* 1982, *25*(4). (b)

Goode, W. J. *Women in divorce.* New York: Free Press, 1956.

Goode, W. J., & Hatt, P. K. *Methods in social research.* New York: McGraw-Hill, 1952.

Gorer, G. *The Americans: A study in national character.* London: Cresset Press, 1948.

Gorer, G. *Sex and marriage in England today.* London: Thomas Nelson & Sons, 1971.

Green, R. Homosexuality as a mental illness. *International Journal of Psychiatry,* 1972, *10,* 77-98.

Green, R. *Sexual identity conflict in children and adults.* New York: Basic Books, 1974.

Green, R. Masculinity and femininity during boyhood: 100 families. In A. Davids (Ed.), *Abnormal personality and psychopathology,* New York: John Wiley, 1976.

Green, R. Thirty-five children raised by homosexual or transsexual parents. *American Journal of Psychiatry,* 1978, *135,* 692-697.

Green, R., & Money, J. *Transexualism and sex reassignment.* Baltimore, MD: Johns Hopkins University Press, 1969.

Greenberg, J. S. The effects of a homophile organization on the self-esteem and alienation of its members. *Journal of Homosexuality,* 1976, *1,* 313-317.

Greenson, R. R. The origin and fate of new ideas in psychoanalysis. *International Journal of Psychoanalysis,* 1969, *50,* 503-515.

Greenspan, S. I. *Intelligence and adaptation: An integration of psychoanalytic and Piagetian developmental psychology. Psychological issues monograph 47/48.* New York: International Universities Press, 1979.

Griffin, D. R. *The question of animal awareness.* New York: Rockefeller University Press, 1976.

Groth, A. N., & Birnbaum, H. J. Adult sexual orientation and attraction to underage children. *Archives of Sexual Behavior,* 1978, *7,* 175-181.

Gruen, W. Composition and some correlates of American core culture. *Psychological Reports,* 1968, *18,* 483-486.

Gundlach, R., & Reiss, B. F. Self and sexual identity in the female: A study of female homosexuals. In B. F. Reiss (Ed.), *New directions in mental health.* New York: Grune and Stratton, 1968.

Guntrip, H. J. S. *Psychoanalytic theory, therapy, and the self.* New York: Basic Books, 1971.

Habermas, J. *Knowledge and human interests.* Boston: Beacon Press, 1971.

Habermas, J. *Theory and practice.* Boston: Beacon Press, 1973.

Hacker, H. M. Homosexuals: Deviant or minority group. In E. Sagarin (Ed.), *The other minorities.* Waltham, MA: Ginn & Co., 1971.

Halleck, S. L. *The politics of therapy.* New York: Science House, 1971.

Hamilton, W. D. Altruism and related phenomena, mainly in social insects. *Annual Review of Ecology and Systematics,* 1972, *3,* 193-232.

Hammersmith, S. K., & Weinberg, M. S. Homosexual identity: Commitment, adjustment, and significant others. *Sociometry,* 1973, *36,* 56-79.

Hare, E. H. Masturbatory insanity: The history of an idea. *Journal of Mental Science,* 1962, *108,* 1-25.

Harris, L. Harris survey: On homosexual rights. *Boston Globe,* July 18, 1977.

Harry, J., & DeVall, W. B. *The social organization of gay males.* New York: Praeger, 1978.

Hartman, B. Comparison of selected experimental MMPI profiles of sexual deviates and sociopaths without sexual deviation. *Psychological Reports,* 1967, *20,* 234.

Hartmann, H. *Essays on ego psychology.* New York: International Universities Press, 1964.

Hastings, G. E., & Kunnes, R. Predicting prescription prices. *New England Journal of Medicine,* 1967, *277,* 625-628.

Hatterer, L. *Changing homosexuality in the male.* New York: McGraw-Hill, 1970.

Hechinger, G., & Hechinger, F. Homosexuality on campus. *New York Times Magazine,* March 12, 1978, pp. 15-17, 30-38.

Heger, H. *The men with the pink triangles.* Boston: Alyson, 1980.

Heilbrun, A. B. The measurement of masculine and feminine sex role identities as independent dimensions. *Journal of Consulting and Clinical Psychology,* 1976, *44,* 183-190.

Hencken, J. D. Homosexuals and heterosexuals: We are all apologists. *Anglican Theological Review,* 1977, *59,* 191-193.

Hencken, J. D., & O'Dowd, W. T. Coming out as an aspect of identity formation. *Gay Academic Union Journal: Gai Saber,* 1977, *1,* 18-22.

Henslin, J. M. Studying deviance in four settings: Research experiences with cabbies, suicides, drug users and abortionees. In J. Douglas (Ed.), *Research on deviance.* New York: Random House, 1972.

Herzog, E., & Sudia, C. D. *Boys in fatherless families.* No. (OCD) 72-33. Washington, DC: U.S. Department of Health, Education and Welfare, 1970.

Heston, L. L., & Shields, J. Homosexuality in twins: A family study and a registry study. *Archives of General Psychiatry*, 1968, *18*, 149-160.

Hetherington, E. Effects of paternal absence on sex typed behavior in Negro and White preadolescent males. *Journal of Personality and Social Psychology*, 1966, *4*, 87-91.

Hetherington, E. Effects of father absence on personality development in adolescent daughters. *Development Psychology*, 1972, *7*, 313-326.

Hetherington, E., Cox, M., & Cox, R. The aftermath of divorce. Paper presented to the American Psychological Association, Washington, D.C., 1976.

Hidalgo, H. A., & Hidalgo-Christensen, E. The Puerto Rican lesbian and the Puerto Rican community. *Journal of Homosexuality*, 1976, *2*, 109-121.

Hill, C. T., Rubin, Z., & Peplau, L. A. Breakups before marriage: The end of 103 affairs. *Journal of Social Issues*, 1976, *32*(1), 147-168.

Hitler, A. *Mein Kampf* (R. Manheim, trans.). London: Hutchinson, 1969. (Originally published in German in 1925.)

Hoeffer, B. Single mothers and their children: Challenging traditional concepts of the American family. In P. Brandt et al. (Eds.), *Current practice in pediatric nursing.* St. Louis, MO: C. V. Mosby, 1978.

Hoess, R. *Commandant of Auschwitz: The autobiography of Rudolf Hoess.* New York: World, 1959.

Hoffman, L. W., & Nye, F. I. *Working mothers.* San Francisco: Jossey-Bass, 1974.

Hoffman, M. *The gay world: Male homosexuality and the social creation of evil.* New York: Basic Books, 1968.

Holt, R. R. A review of some of Freud's biological assumptions and their influence on his theories. In N. S. Greenfield & W. C. Lewis (Eds.), *Psychoanalysis and current biological thought.* Madison: University of Wisconsin Press, 1965.

Hook, S. (Ed.). *Psychoanalysis, scientific method, and philosophy.* New York: New York University Press, 1959.

Hooker, E. A. The adjustment of the male overt homosexual. *Journal of Projective Techniques*, 1957, *21*, 17-31.

Hooker, E. The homosexual community. In J. Gagnon & W. Simon (Eds.) *Sexual deviance.* New York: Harper & Row, 1967.

Hooker, E. Homosexuality. In U.S. Task Force on Homosexuality, *Homosexuality: Final report and background papers.* Rockville, MD: National Institute of Mental Health, 1972.

Hopkins, J. The lesbian personality. *British Journal of Psychiatry*, 1969, *115*, 1433-1436.

Horstman, W. R. Homosexuality and psychopathology: A study of the MMPI responses of homosexual and heterosexual male college students. *Dissertation Abstracts International*, 1972, *33*(5), 2347B.

Hrdy, S. B. Male and female strategies of reproduction among the langurs of Abu. Unpublished Ph.D. thesis, Harvard University, 1975.

Humphreys, R. L. *Tearoom trade: Impersonal sex in public places.* Chicago: Aldine, 1970.

Humphreys, R. L. New styles in homosexual manliness. *Transaction*, 1971, *8*, 38-47.

Humphreys, L., & Miller, B. Identities in the emerging gay culture. In J. Marmor (Ed.), *Homosexual behavior: A modern reappraisal.* New York: Basic Books, 1980.

Hunt, G. L., Jr., & Hunt, M. W. Female-female pairing in western gulls *(Larus occidentalis)* in southern California. *Science*, 1977, *196*, 1466-1467.

Hunt, M. M. *The world of the formerly married.* New York: McGraw-Hill, 1966.

Hunt, M. *Sexual behavior in the 1970s.* Chicago: Playboy Press, 1974.

Hunter, N. D., & Polikoff, N. D. Custody rights of lesbian mothers: Legal theory and litigation strategy. *Buffalo Law Review*, 1976, *25*, 691-733.

Hutchinson, G. E. A speculative consideration of certain possible forms of sexual selection in man. *American Naturalist*, 1959, *93*, 81-91.

Hyde, J. S., & Rosenberg, B. G. *Half the human experience: The psychology of women.* Lexington, MA: D. C. Heath, 1976.

Jackson, A. M. To see the me in "thee." In S. TeSelle (Ed.), *The rediscovery of ethnicity.* New York: Harper & Row, 1973.

Jay, K., & Young, A. *The gay report: Lesbians and gay men speak out about sexual experiences and lifestyles.* New York: Summit Books, 1977.

Jensen, M. S. Role differentiation in female homosexual quasi-marital unions. *Journal of Marriage and the Family,* 1974, *36*(2), 360-367.

Johnsgard, K. W., & Schumacher, R. M. The experience of intimacy in group psychotherapy with male homosexuals. *Psychotherapy: Therapy, Research, and Practice,* 1970, *7,* 173-176.

Jones, R. W., & Bates, J. E. Satisfaction in male homosexual couples. *Journal of Homosexuality,* 1978, *3,* 217-224.

Kallmann, F. J. Twin and sibship study of overt male homosexuality. *American Journal of Human Genetics,* 1952, *4,* 136-146. (a)

Kallmann, F. J. Comparative twin study on the genetic aspects of male homosexuality. *Journal of Nervous and Mental Disease,* 1952, *115,* 283-298. (b)

Katchadourian, H. A., & Lunde, D. T. *Fundamentals of human sexuality.* New York: Holt, Rinehart & Winston, 1975.

Katz, J. *Gay American history: Lesbians and gay men in the U.S.A.* New York: Thomas Y. Crowell, 1976.

Kelley, K. Playboy interview: Anita Bryant. *Playboy,* May 1978, pp. 73-74, 76, 78-79, 82, 85-86, 88-90, 92-94, 96, 232, 234, 236, 238, 240-241, 244, 246, 248, 250.

Kelly, J. The aging male homosexual. *The Gerontologist,* 1977, *17,* 328-332.

Kelly, J., & Worrell, L. Parent behaviors related to masculine, feminine, and androgynous sex role orientations. *Journal of Consulting and Clinical Psychology,* 1976, *44,* 843-851.

Keniston, K., & Carnegie Council on Children. *All our children: The American family under pressure.* New York: Harcourt Brace Jovanovich, 1977.

Kenyon, F. Studies in female homosexuality: Psychological test results. *Journal of Consulting and Clinical Psychology,* 1968, *32,* 510-513.

Kernberg, O. F. *Object-relations theory and clinical psychoanalysis.* New York: Aronson, 1976.

Kersten, F. *The Kersten memoirs.* London: Hutchison, 1956.

Kinsey, A. C., Pomeroy, W. B., & Martin, C. E. *Sexual behavior in the human male.* Philadelphia: W. B. Saunders, 1948.

Kinsey, A. C., Pomeroy, W. B., Martin, C. E., & Gebhard, P. H. Concepts of normality and abnormality in sexual behavior. In P. H. Hoch & J. Zubin (Eds.), *Psychosexual development in health and disease.* New York: Grune & Stratton, 1949.

Kinsey, A. C., Pomeroy, W. B., Martin, C. E., & Gebhard, P. H. *Sexual behavior in the human female.* Philadelphia: W. B. Saunders, 1953.

Kirkpatrick, M., Smith, C., & Roy, R. Lesbian mothers and their children: A comparative survey. *American Journal of Orthopsychiatry,* 1981, *51,* 545-551.

Klapp, O. *Collective search for identity.* New York: Holt, Rinehart & Winston, 1969.

Klein, G. S. *Perception, motives, and personality.* New York: Knopf, 1970.

Klein, G. S. *Psychoanalytic theory: An exploration of essentials.* New York: International Universities Press, 1976.

Kline, P. *Fact and fantasy in Freudian theory.* London: Methuen, 1972.

Knutson, D. C. Homophobia in the American judicial system. *The Advocate* (San Mateo, CA), July 26, 1979.

Knutson, D. C. (Ed.). *Homosexuality and the law.* New York: Haworth Press, 1980.

Koch, S. Psychology and emerging conceptions of knowledge as unitary. In T. W. Wann (Ed.), *Behaviorism and phenomenology: Contrasting bases for modern psychology.* Chicago: University of Chicago Press, 1964.

Kogon, E. *The theory and practice of hell.* New York: Holt, Rinehart & Winston, 1969.

Kolodny, R. C. Homosexuality and testosterone. *New England Journal of Medicine,* 1972, *286,* 381.

Komarovsky, M. *Blue-collar marriage.* New York: Vintage Books, 1967.

Kriesberg, L. *Mothers in poverty.* Chicago: Aldine, 1970.

Kreps, J. *Sex in the marketplace: American women at work.* Baltimore, MD: Johns Hopkins University Press, 1971.

Kuhn, T. S. *The structure of scientific revolutions* (2nd ed.). Chicago: University of Chicago Press, 1970.

Lacan, J. *Ecrits.* Paris: du Seuil, 1966.

Laner, M. R. Media mating II: "Personals" advertisements of lesbian women. *Journal of Homosexuality,* 1978, *4,* 41-62.

Laner, M. R., & Kamel, G. W. L. Media mating I: Newspaper "personals" ads of homosexual men. *Journal of Homosexuality,* 1977, *3,* 149-162.

Larson, P. C. Sexual identity and self concept. *Journal of Homosexuality,* 1981, 7, in press.

Lee, J. A. *Colors of love.* Toronto: New Press, 1973.

Lee, J. A. Forbidden colors of love. *Journal of Homosexuality,* 1976, *1,* 401-418.

Leites, N. *The new ego: Pitfalls in current thinking about patients in psychoanalysis.* New York: Science House, 1971.

LeMasters, E. E. Parents without partners. In *Parents in modern America.* Homewood, IL: Dorsey Press, 1970.

Lemert, E. M. *Social pathology: A systematic approach to the theory of sociopathic behavior.* New York: McGraw-Hill, 1951.

Lerner, D. *Skyewar: Psychological warfare against Nazi Germany.* Cambridge: MIT Press, 1971.

Levine, M. The gay ghetto. Paper presented at meeting of the American Sociological Association, 1977.

Levine, M. P. Gay ghetto. In M. P. Levine (Ed.), *Gay men: The sociology of male homosexuality.* New York: Harper & Row, 1979. (a)

Levine, M. Gay ghetto. *Journal of Homosexuality,* 1979, *4,* 363-377. (b)

Levinger, C., & Moles, O. C. (Eds.). *Divorce and separation: Context, causes and consequences.* New York: Basic Books, 1979.

Levinson, D. J. et al. *The seasons of a man's life.* New York: Knopf, 1978.

Levitt, E., & Klassen, A. Public attitudes toward homosexuality: Part of the 1970 national survey by the Institute for Sex Research. *Journal of Homosexuality,* 1974, *1,* 29-40.

Lewis, K. Lesbian mother survey results. *Gay Community News,* June 9, 1977, p. 7.

Leznoff, M. & Westley, W. A. The homosexual community. In J. Gagnon & W. Simon (Eds.), *Sexual deviance.* New York: Harper & Row, 1967.

Lingle, J. H., Gera, N., Ostrom, T. M., Leippe, M. R., & Baumgardner, M. H. Thematic effects on person judgements or impression formation. *Journal of Personality and Social Psychology,* 1979, *37,* 674-688.

Lipman-Blumen, J. The implications for family structure of changing sex roles. *Social Casework,* 1976, *57,* 67-79.

Lockard, R. B. Reflections on the fall of comparative psychology: Is there a lesson for us all? *American Psychologist,* 1971, *26,* 168-179.

London, P. *The modes and morals of psychotherapy.* New York: Holt, Rinehart & Winston, 1964.

London, P. *Behavior control.* New York: Harper & Row, 1969.

Lowen, A. *Love and orgasm.* New York: Macmillan, 1965.

Lumby, M. E. Homophobia: The quest for a valid scale. *Journal of Homosexuality,* 1976, *2,* 39-47.

Lynn, D. B., & Sawrey, W. L. The effects of father-absence on Norwegian boys and girls. *Journal of Abnormal and Social Psychology,* 1959, *59,* 258-262.

MacCrone, I. D. *Race attitudes in South Africa.* London: Oxford University Press, 1937.

Macleod, M. D. (trans.). *Lucian* (Vol. 8). (Loeb Classics Ed.) Cambridge, MA: Harvard University Press, 1967.

Mager, D. Faggot father. In K. Jay & A. Young (eds.), *After you're out.* New York: Gage, 1975.

Malcolm, J. Reporter at large; work of S. Minuchin at the Philadelphia Child Guidance Clinic. *New Yorker,* May 15, 1978, 39-42+.

Mandel, J., & Hotvedt, M. Lesbians as parents. *Huisarts & Praktyk,* 1980, *4,* 31-34.

Manosevitz, M. Item analysis of the MMPI *Mf* scale using homosexual and heterosexual males. *Journal of Consulting and Clinical Psychology,* 1970, *35,* 395-399.

Manosevitz, M. Education and MMPI *Mf* scores in homosexual and heterosexual males. *Journal of Consulting and Clinical Psychology,* 1971, *36,* 395-399.

Marcuse, H. *Eros and civilization: A philosophical inquiry into Freud.* Boston: Beacon Press, 1955.

Marmor, J. (Ed.). *Sexual inversion: The multiple roots of homosexuality.* New York: Basic Books, 1965.

Marmor, J. (Ed.). *Homosexual behavior: A modern reappraisal.* New York: Basic Books, 1980. (a)

Marmor, J. Homosexuality and the issue of mental illness. In J. Marmor (Ed.), *Homosexual behavior: A modern reappraisal.* New York: Basic Books, 1980. (b)

Marshall, D. S., & Suggs, R. C. (Eds.), *Human sexual behavior.* Englewood Cliffs, NJ: Prentice-Hall, 1971.

Martin, D., & Lyon, P. *Lesbian/woman.* New York: Bantam, 1972.

Masters, W. H., & Johnson, V. E. *Human sexual inadequacy.* Boston: Little, Brown, 1970.

Masters, W. H., & Johnson, V. E. *Homosexuality in perspective.* Boston: Little, Brown, 1979.

May, E. P. Counselors', psychologists', and homosexuals' philosophies of human nature and attitudes toward homosexual behavior. *Homosexual Counseling Journal,* 1974, *1,* 3-25.

Mayerson, P., & Lief, H. I. Psychotherapy of homosexuals: A follow-up study of nineteen cases. In J. Marmor (Ed.), *Sexual inversion.* New York: Basic Books, 1965.

Mays, V. M. Making visible the invisible: Some notes on racism and women-identified relationships of Afro-American women. In S. Bennett & J. Gibbs (Eds.), *Top-ranking: A collection of articles on racism and classism in the lesbian community.* New York: February 3rd Press, 1980.

McCall, G. J., & Simmons, J. L. (Eds.). *Issues in participant observation.* Reading, MA: Addison-Wesley, 1969.

McCracken, S. Are homsexuals gay? *Commentary,* January 1979, pp.18-29.

McDermott, U., Jr. Divorce and its psychiatric sequelae in children. *Archives of General Psychiatry,* 1970, *23,* 241-247.

McDonald, G. Misrepresentation, liberalism, and heterosexual bias in introductory psychology textbooks. *Journal of Homosexuality,* 1981, *6,* 45-60.

McDonald, G. J., & Moore, R. J. Sex-role self-concepts of homosexual men, and their attitudes toward both women and male homosexuality. *Journal of Homosexuality,* 1978, *4,* 3-14.

McGuire, R. J., Carlisle, J. M., & Young, B. G. Sexual deviations as conditioned behavior: A hypothesis. *Behavior Research and Therapy,* 1965, *2,* 185-190.

Meredith, R. L., & Riester, R. W. Psychotherapy responsibility and homsexuality: Clinical examination of socially deviant behavior. *Professional Psychology,* 1980, *11*(2), 174-193.

Meyer-Holzapfel, M. Abnormal behavior in zoo animals. In M. W. Fox (Ed.), *Abnormal behavior in animals.* Philadelphia: W. B. Saunders, 1968.

Miller, A. A. Reactions of friends to divorce. In P. Bohannan (Ed.), *Divorce and after.* Garden City, NY: Doubleday, 1970.

Miller, B. Gay fathers and their children. *Family Coordinator,* 1979, *28,* 544-552.

Miller, B., & Humphreys, L. Lifestyles and violence: Homosexual victims of assault and murder. *Qualitative Sociology,* 1980, *3,* 169-185.

Miller, D. C. *Handbook of research design and social measurement.* New York: David McKay, 1964.

Miller, J. B. (Ed.). *Psychoanalysis and women.* Baltimore, MD: Penguin, 1973.

Miller, W. G. Characteristics of homosexually-involved incarcerated females. *Journal of Consulting Psychology,* 1963, *27,* 277.

Millett, K. *Sexual politics.* Garden City, NY: Doubleday, 1969.

Millham, J., San Miguel, C. L., & Kellogg, R. A factor-analytic conceptualization of attitudes toward male and female homosexuals. *Journal of Homsexuality,* 1976, *2,* 3-10.

Minnigerode, F. A. Age-status labeling in homosexual men. *Journal of Homosexuality,* 1976, *1,* 273-276.

Mitchell, D., & Wilson, W. Relationships of father absence to masculinity and popularity of delinquent boys. *Psychological Reports,* 1967, *20,* 1173-1174.

Mitchell, J. *Psychoanalysis and feminism: Freud, Reich, Laing and women.* New York: Vintage, 1974.

Mitchell, S. A. Psychodynamics, homosexuality, and the question of pathology. *Psychiatry,* 1978, *41,* 254-263.

Money, J. Pubertal hormones and homosexuality, bisexuality and heterosexuality. In J. M. Livingood (Ed.), *NIMH Task Force on Homosexuality: Final report and background papers.* DHEW Publication No.(HSM) 72-9116. Rockville, MD: National Institute of Mental Health, 1972.

Money, J. Genetic and chromosomal aspects of homosexual etiology. In J. Marmor (Ed.), *Homosexual behavior: A modern reappraisal.* New York: Basic Books, 1980.

Money, J., & Ehrhardt, A. A. *Man and woman, boy and girl.* Baltimore, MD: Johns Hopkins University Press, 1972.

Moore, J. E. Problematic sexual behavior. In C. B. Broderick & J. Bernard (Eds.), *The individual, sex, and society.* Baltimore, MD: Johns Hopkins University Press, 1969.

Moore, W. E., & Tumin, M. M. Some social functions of ignorance. In B. Rosenberg et al. (Eds.), *Mass society in crisis: Social problems and social pathology.* New York: Macmillan, 1964.

Morin, S. F. Educational programs as a means of changing attitudes toward gay people. *Homosexual Counseling Journal,* 1974, *1,* 160-165.

Morin, S. F. An annotated bibliography of research on lesbianism and male homosexuality (1967-1974). *JSAS Catalog of Selected Documents in Psychology,* 1976, *6*(15). Ms. #1191. (Available from the American Psychological Association.)

Morin, S. F. Heterosexual bias in research on lesbianism and male homosexuality. *American Psychologist,* 1977, *32,* 629-637.

Morin, S. F., & Garfinkle, E. M. Male homophobia. *Journal of Social Issues,* 1978, *34*(1), 29-47.

National News Council. Gay complaint against CBS upheld in part. *Columbia Journalism Review,* January-February 1981, pp. 76-83.

NBC National Poll. Ethnic groups split on social questions. *New York Times,* November 23, 1978, p. A-10.

Noebel, D. A. *The homosexual revolution.* Tulsa, OK: American Christian College Press, 1978.

Oberstone, A. K., & Sukoneck, H. Psychological adjustment and life style of single lesbians and single heterosexual women. *Psychology of Women Quarterly,* 1977, *1*(2), 172-188.

Ohlson, E. L., & Wilson, M. Differentiating female homosexuals from female heterosexuals using the MMPI. *Journal of Sex Research,* 1974, *10,* 308-315.

Oliver, W. H., & Mosher, D. L. Psychopathology and guilt in heterosexual and subgroups of homosexual reformatory inmates. *Journal of Abnormal Psychology,* 1968, *73,* 323-329.

Ornstein, P. H. (Ed.). *The search for the self: Selected writings of Heinz Kohut 1950-1978* (2 vols.). New York: International Universities Press, 1978.

Ovesey, L. The homosexual conflict: An adaptational analysis. In H. M. Ruitenbeek (Ed.), *The problem of homosexuality in modern society.* New York: Dutton, 1963.

Ovesey, L. Pseudohomosexuality and homosexuality in men: Psychodynamics as a guide to treatment. In J. Marmor (Ed.), *Sexual inversion.* New York: Basic Books, 1965.

Ovesey, L. *Homosexuality and pseudohomosexuality.* New York: Science House, 1969.

Pagelow, M. Lesbian mothers. Paper presented to the American Sociological Association, New York City, 1976.

Panton, J. R. A new MMPI scale for the identification of homosexuality. *Journal of Clinical Psychology,* 1960, *16,* 17-21.

Paul, W. *Religiously inspired anti-Gay violence, and incitement of intergroup conflict.* Report submitted at public hearings of the Governor's Task Force on Racial, Ethnic, and Religious Violence, Sacramento, California, October 17, 1981.

Paul, W., & Lyon, P. *The social costs of ignorance.* Final report, Education Project on Sexual Orientation, California Commission on Personal Privacy, September 1982.

Paykel, E. S., Prusoff, B. A., & Uhlenhuth, E. H. Scaling of life events. *Archives of General Psychiatry,* 1971, *25,* 340-347.

Pendergrass, V. E. Marriage counseling with lesbian couples. *Psychotherapy: Theory, Research, & Practice,* 1975, *12,* 93-96.

Peplau, L. A., Cochran, S., Rook, K., & Padesky, C. Loving women: Attachment and autonomy in lesbian relationships. *Journal of Social Issues,* 1978, *34*(3), 7-27.

Peplau, L. A., Padesky, C., & Hamilton, M. Satisfaction in lesbian relationships. Unpublished manuscript, University of California, Los Angeles, 1982.

Peplau, L. A., & Gordon, S. L. The intimate relations of lesbians and gay men. In E. R. Allgeier & N. B. McCormick (Eds.), *Gender roles and sexual behavior.* Palo Alto, CA: Mayfield, in press.

Peterfreund, E. *Information, systems, and psychoanalysis: An evolutionary biological approach to psychoanalytic theory. Psychological issues monograph 25/26.* New York: International Universities Press, 1971.

Piaget, J. *The origins of intelligence in children.* New York: International Universities Press, 1952.

Pierce, D. M. Test and non-test correlates of active and situational homosexuality. *Psychology,* 1973, *10*(4): 23-26.

Plant, R. The men with the pink triangles. *Christopher Street,* February 1977, pp.4-11.

Plummer, K. *Sexual stigma.* London: Routledge & Kegan Paul, 1975.

Pomeroy, W. *Dr. Kinsey and the Institute for Sex Research.* New York: Harper & Row, 1972.

Ponse, B. Secrecy in the lesbian world. In C. Warren (Ed.), *Sexuality: Encounters, identities, and relations.* Beverly Hills, CA: Sage, 1977.

Ponse, B. *Identities in the lesbian world: The social construction of self.* Westport, CT: Greenwood, 1978.

Ponse, B. Lesbians and their worlds. In J. Marmor (Ed.), *Homosexual behavior: A modern reappraisal.* New York: Basic Books, 1980.

Rado, S. A critical examination of the concept of bisexuality. *Psychosomatic Medicine,* 1940, *2,* 459-467.

Rado, S. An adaptational view of sexual behavior. In H. M.Ruitenbeek (Ed.), *The problem of homosexuality in modern society.* New York: Dutton, 1963.

Rainwater, L., & Yancey, W. L. *The Moynihan Report and the politics of controversy.* Cambridge: MIT Press, 1967.

Ramsey, J., Latham, J. D., & Lindquist, C. U. Long term same-sex relationships: Correlates of adjustment. Paper presented at the annual meeting of the American Psychological Association, Toronto, August, 1978.

Rangel, L. On friendship. *Journal of the American Psychoanalytic Association,* 1963, *11,* 3-54.

Raphael, S. M., & Robinson, M. K. The older lesbian: Love relationships and friendship patterns. *Alternative Lifestyles,* 1980, *3*(2), 207-230.

Rappaport, J. *Community psychology: Values, research, and action.* New York: Holt, Rinehart & Winston, 1977.

Read, K. *Other voices: The style of a male homosexual tavern.* Novato, CA: Chandler & Sharp, 1980.

Reade, B. (Ed.). *Sexual heretics: Male homosexuality in English literature from 1850 to 1900.* London: Routledge & Kegan Paul, 1970.

Rechy, J. *City of night.* New York: Grove Press, 1962.

Rechy, J. *Numbers.* New York: Grove Press, 1967.

Rechy, J. *The sexual outlaw.* New York: Grove Press, 1977.

Redlich, F. C., & Freedman, D. X. *The theory and practice of psychiatry.* New York: Basic Books, 1966.

Reich, W. The imposition of sexual morality. In L. Baxandall (Ed.), *Sex-Pol essays, 1929-1934.* New York: Vintage, 1932.

Reiss, A. J. The social integration of queers and peers. In J. Gagnon & W. Simon (Eds.) *Sexual deviance.* New York: Harper & Row, 1967.

Ricoeur, P. *Freud and philosophy: An essay on interpretation.* New Haven: Yale University Press, 1970.

Robison, J. *Attack on the family.* Fort Worth, TX: James Robison Evangelistic Association, 1980.

Roman, M., & Haddad, W. *The disposable parent: A case for joint custody.* New York: Holt, Rinehart & Winston, 1978.

Rosenwald, G. C. Personal communication. The University of Michigan (Ann Arbor), 1978.

Ross, H., & Sawhill, I. *Time of transition: The growth of families headed by women.* Washington, DC: Urban Institute, 1975.

Ross, M. W. The relationship of perceived societal hostility, conformity, and psychological adjustment in homosexual males. *Journal of Homosexuality,* 1978, *4,* 157-168.

Rowse, A. L. *Homosexuals in history.* New York: Macmillan, 1977.

Ruitenbeek, H. M. Introductory essay: Homosexuality: An evolution. In H. M. Ruitenbeek (Ed.), *Homosexuality: A changing picture.* London: Souvenir, 1973. (a)

Ruitenbeek, H. M. The myth of bisexuality. In H. M. Ruitenbeek (Ed.), *Homosexuality: A changing picture.* London: Souvenir, 1973. (b)

Ruitenbeek, H. M. (Ed.). *Homosexuality: A changing picture.* London: Souvenir, 1973. (c)

Rupp, J. C. Homosexually related deaths. In W. J. Curran, A. L. McGarry, & C. S. Petty (Eds.), *Modern legal medicine, psychiatry, and forensic science.* Philadelphia: F. A. Davis, 1980.

Ruse, M. *Sociobiology: Sense or nonsense?* Dordrecht, Netherlands: D. Reidel, 1979.

Russo, V. *Celluloid closet: Homosexuality in the movies.* New York: Harper & Row, 1981.

Ryan, W. *Blaming the victim.* New York: Pantheon, 1971.

Ryder, J. P., & Somppi, P. L. Female-female pairing in ring-billed gulls. *The Auk,* 1979, *96,* 1-5.

Saghir, M. T., & Robins, E. *Male and female homosexuality: A comprehensive investigation.* Baltimore, MD: Williams & Wilkins, 1973.

Salzman, L. "Latent" homosexuality. In J. Marmor (Ed.), *Sexual inversion.* New York: Basic Books, 1965.

San Francisco Examiner. Feminist center bombed. October 8, 1980, p. 1.

Sander, F. M. *Individual and family therapy: Toward an integration.* New York: Aronson, 1979.

Sartre, J. P. *Anti-Semite and Jew.* New York: Schocken, 1948.

Schaefer, S. Sexual and social problems of lesbians. *Journal of Sex Research,* 1976, *12,* 50-69.

Schafer, R. *A new language for psychoanalysis.* New Haven: Yale University Press, 1976.

Schafer, R. *Language and insight.* New Haven: Yale University Press, 1978.

Schur, E. M. *Crimes without victims: Deviant behavior and public policy.* Englewood Cliffs, NJ: Prentice-Hall, 1965.

Seligman, M. E. P. On the generality of the laws of learning. *Psychological Review,* 1970, *77,* 406-418.

Sherrill, K. S. *General social survey.* Chicago: National Opinion Research Center, 1974.

Shibutani, T., & Kwan, K. *Ethnic stratification.* Toronto: Macmillan, 1965.

Shively, M. G., & De Cecco, J. P. Components of sexual identity. *Journal of Homosexuality,* 1977, *3,* 41-48.

Siegelman, M. Adjustment of homosexual and heterosexual women. *British Journal of Psychiatry,* 1972, *120,* 477-481. (a)

Siegelman, M. Adjustment of male homosexuals and heterosexuals. *Archives of Sexual Behavior,* 1972, *2,* 9-25. (b)

Silverstein, C. Homosexuality and the ethics of behavioral intervention: Paper 2. *Journal of Homosexuality,* 1977, *2,* 205-211. (a)

Silverstein, C. *A family matter: A parent's guide to homosexuality.* New York: McGraw-Hill, 1977. (b)

Silverstein, C. *Man to man: Gay couples in America.* New York: William Morrow, 1981.

Simmons, J. L. *Deviants.* Berkeley, CA: Glendessary Press, 1969.

Simon, W., & Gagnon, J. Homosexuality: The formulation of a sociological perspective. *Journal of Health and Social Behavior,* 1967, *8,* 177-185.

Singer, M. I. Comparison of indicators of homosexuality on the MMPI. *Journal of Consulting and Clinical Psychology,* 1970, *34,* 15-18.

Skinner, B. F. Critique of psychoanalytic concepts and theories. In H. Feigl & M. Scriven (Eds.), *Minnesota studies in the philosophy of science. Vol. 1: The foundations of science and the concepts of psychology and psychoanalysis.* Minneapolis: University of Minnesota Press, 1956.

Smith, K. T. Homophobia: A tentative personality profile. *Psychological Reports,* 1971, *29,* 1091-1094.

Smith, L. *Killers of the dream.* New York: Norton, 1949.

Snyder, M. On the self-perpetuating nature of social stereotypes. In D. L. Hamilton (Ed.), *Cognitive processes in stereotyping and intergroup behavior.* Hillsdale, NJ: Lawrence Erlbaum, 1980.

Snyder, M., Tanke, E., & Berscheid, E. Social perception and interpersonal behavior: On the self-fulfilling nature of social stereotypes. *Journal of Personality and Social Psychology,* 1977, *35,* 656-666.

Snyder, M., & Uranowitz, S. W. Reconstructing the past: Some cognitive consequences of person perception. *Journal of Personality and Social Psychology,* 1978, *36,* 941-950.

Socarides, C. W. *The overt homosexual.* New York: Grune & Stratton, 1968.

Socarides, C. W. Homosexuality and medicine. *Journal of the American Medical Association,* 1970, *212,* 1199-1202.

Socarides, C. *Homosexuality.* New York: Aronson, 1978.

Spence, J. T., & Helmreich, R. L. *Masculinity and femininity: Their psychological dimensions, correlates, and antecedents.* Austin: University of Texas Press, 1978.

Staats, G. R. Stereotype content and social distance: Changing views of homosexuality, *Journal of Homosexuality,* 1978, *4,* 15-27.

Steakley, J. D. *The homosexual emancipation movement in Germany.* New York: Arno Press, 1975.

Stellitz, C., Jahoda, M., Deutsch, M., & Cook, S. W. *Research methods in social relations.* New York: Holt, Rinehart & Winston, 1959.

Stephens, O. *Facts in a candid world.* Stanford: Stanford University Press, 1955.

Stoller, R. *Perversion: The erotic form of hatred.* New York: Pantheon, 1975.

Stringer, P., & Grygier, T. Male homosexuality, psychiatric patient status, and psychological masculinity and femininity. *Archives of Sexual Behavior,* 1976, *5,* 15-27.

Sturgis, E. T., & Adams, H. E. The right to treatment: Issues in the treatment of homosexuality. *Journal of Consulting and Clinical Psychology,* 1978, *46,* 165-169,.

Swanson, H. D. *Human reproduction: Biology and social change.* New York: Oxford University Press, 1974.

A symposium: Should homosexuality be in the APA nomenclature? *American Journal of Psychiatry,* 1973, *130,* 1207-1216.

Szasz, T. S. *The myth of mental illness.* New York: Dell, 1961.

Szasz, T. S. *The manufacture of madness: A comparative study of the Inquisition and the mental health movement.* New York: Harper & Row, 1970.

Tanner, D. M. *The lesbian couple.* Lexington, MA: D. C. Heath, 1978.

Taylor, C. Background information on the Organization of Gay Anthropologists and Researches on Homosexuality. In K. Read, *Other voices: The style of a male homosexual tavern.* Novato, CA: Chandler & Sharp, 1980.

Taylor, G. R. Historical and mythological aspects of homosexuality. In J. Marmor (Ed.), *Sexual inversion: The multiple roots of homosexuality.* New York: Basic Books, 1965.

Thompson, C. Changing concepts of homosexuality in psychoanalysis. In H. M. Ruitenbeek (Ed.), *The problem of homosexuality in modern society.* New York: Dutton, 1963.

Thompson, N. L., McCandless, B. R., & Strickland, B. Personal adjustment of male and female homosexuals and heterosexuals. *Journal of Abnormal Psychology,* 1971, *78,* 237-240.

Toch, H. *The social psychology of social movements.* New York: Bobbs-Merrill, 1975.

Toder, N. Sexual problems of lesbians. In G. Vida (Ed.), *Our right to love: A lesbian resource book.* Englewood Cliffs, NJ: Prentice-Hall, 1978.

Toffler, A. *Future shock.* New York: Random House, 1970.

Tripp, C. A. *The homosexual matrix.* New York: McGraw-Hill, 1975.

Trivers, R. L. The evolution of reciprocal altruism. *Quarterly Review of Biology,* 1971, *46*(4), 35-57.

Trivers, R. L. Parent-offspring conflict. *American Zoologist,* 1974, *14,* 249-264.

Trivers, R. L. Sexual selection and resource-accruing abilities in *Anolis garmani. Evolution,* 1976, *30,* 253-269.

Tuller, N. R. Couples: The hidden segment of the gay world. *Journal of Homosexuality,* 1978, *3,* 331-344.

Turner, R. K., Pielmaier, H., James, S., & Orwin, A. Personality characteristics of male homo-sexuals referred for aversion therapy: A comparative study. *British Journal of Psychiatry,* 1974, *125,* 447-449.

U.S. Bureau of the Census. *Female family heads.* Current Population Reports, Series P-23, No. 50. Washington, DC: Government Printing Office, 1974.

U.S. Bureau of the Census. *A statistical portrait of women in the United States.* Current Population Reports, Special Studies, Series P-23, No. 58. Washington, DC: Government Printing Office, 1976.

U.S. Bureau of the Census. *Population characteristics.* Current Population Reports, Series P-20, No. 350. Washington, DC: Government Printing Office, 1980.

U.S. Civil Rights Commission. *Proceedings, public hearings, 1979.* Washington DC: Government Printing Office, 1980.

U.S. Department of Housing and Urban Development. *Women and housing: A report on sex discrimination in five American cities.* Washington, DC: Government Printing Office, 1976.

U.S. Department of Labor. *Handbook on women workers.* Women's Bureau, Bulletin 297. Washington, DC: Government Printing Office, 1975.

Van den Haag, E. Reflections on the issue of gay rights. *National Review,* July 19, 1974.

Vida, G. (Ed.). *Our right to love: A lesbian resource book.* Englewood Cliffs, NJ: Prentice-Hall, 1978.

Voeller, B. Society and the gay movement. In J. Marmor (Ed.), *Homosexual behavior: A modern reappraisal.* New York: Basic Books, 1980.

Voth, H. Homosexuality. *Psychiatric News,* March 17, 1971.

Wachtel, P. L. Structure or transaction? A critique of the historical and intrapsychic emphasis in psychoanalytic thought. *Psychoanalysis and Contemporary Science,* 1976, *5,* 101-136.

Wachtel, P. L. *Psychoanalysis and behavior therapy: Toward an integration.* New York: Basic Books, 1977.

Waelder, R. *Basic theory of psychoanalysis.* New York: International Universities Press, 1960.

Waldman, E., & Whitmore, R. Children of working mothers, March, 1973. *Monthly Labor Review,* 1974, *97*(5), 50-58.

Walker, P. The classification of sexual orientations such as homosexuality, or What hap-pened?—The story of a blooming, buzzing confusion. In H. T. Englehart, A. Caplan & D. Callahan (Eds.), *Homosexuality: A case study in controversy.* New York: Plenum Press, in press.

Waller, W. *The family: A dynamic interpretation.* New York: Cordon, 1938.

Wallerstein, J., & Kelly, J. The effects of parental divorce: The adolescent experience. In E. Anthony & C. Loupernick (Eds.), *The child and his family: Children at psychiatric risk.* New York: John Wiley, 1974.

Wallerstein, J., & Kelly, J. The effects of parental divorce: Experiences of the child in later latency. *American Journal of Orthopsychiatry,* 1976, *46,* 256-269.

Warren, C. A. B. *Identity and community in the gay world.* New York: John Wiley, 1974.

Warren, C. A. B. Fieldwork in the gay world: Issues in phenomenological research. *Journal of Social Issues,* 1977, *33*(4), 93-107.

Watson, A. S. The children of Armageddon: Problems of custody following divorce. *Syracuse Language Review,* 1969, *21,* 55-86.

Weeks, R., Derdeyn, A., & Langman, M. Two cases of children of homosexuals. *Child Psychia-try and Human Development,* 1975, *6,* 26-32.

Weinberg, G. *Society and the healthy homosexual.* New York: St. Martin's Press, 1972.

Weinberg, M. S., & Williams, C. J. Fieldwork among deviants: Social relations with subjects. In J. Douglas (Ed.), *Research on deviance.* New York: Random House, 1972.

Weinberg, M. S., & Williams, C. J. *Male homosexuals: Their problems and adaptations.* New York: Oxford University Press, 1974.

Weinberg, M. S., & Williams, C. J. Gay baths and the social organization of impersonal sex. *Social Problems,* 1975, *23,* 124-136.

Weinrich, J. D. Human reproductive strategy. *Dissertation Abstracts International,* 1977, *37*(10), 5339-B. (University Microfilms No. 77-8348.)

Weinrich, J. D. Psychology and sociobiology: Adaptive models of homosexuality and their social consequences. Paper presented at the annual meeting of the American Psychological Association, New York City, 1979.

Weinrich, J. D. Homosexual behavior in animals: A new review of observations from the wild, and their relationship to human sexuality. In R. Forleo & W. Pasini (Eds.), *Medical sexology: The third international congress.* Littleton, MA: PSG Publishing, 1980.

Weiss, R. S. *Marital separation.* New York: Basic Books, 1975.

Weiss, R. S. *Going it alone.* New York: Basic Books, 1979.

Westermarck, E. *The origin and development of moral ideas.* London: Macmillan, 1908.

Wheeler, W. M. An analysis of Rorschach indices of male homosexuality. *Rorschach Research Exchange Journal of Projective Techniques,* 1949, *13,* 97-126.

Wickler, W. *The sexual code.* Garden City, NY: Doubleday, 1972.

Williams, C. J., & Weinberg, M. S. *Homosexuals and the military: A study of less than honorable discharge.* New York: Harper & Row, 1971.

Wilson, E. O. *Sociobiology: The new synthesis.* Cambridge, MA: Harvard University Press, 1975. (a)

Wilson, E. O. Human decency is animal. *New York Times Magazine,* October 12, 1975, pp. 38-50. (b)

Wilson, E. O. *On human nature.* Cambridge, MA: Harvard University Press, 1978.

Wilson, M. L., & Green, R. L. Personality characteristics of female homosexuals. *Psychological Reports,* 1971, *28,* 407-412.

Winnicott, D. W. *Collected papers: Through pediatrics to psychoanalysis.* New York: Basic Books, 1958.

Winston, M. P., & Forsher, T. *Nonsupport of legitimate children by affluent fathers as a cause of poverty and welfare dependence.* Santa Monica, CA: Rand Corporation, 1971.

Wirth, L. The problem of minority groups. In R. Linton (Ed.), *The science of man in the world crisis.* New York: Columbia University Press, 1945.

Wirth, S. Coming out close to home: Principles for psychotherapy with families of lesbians and gay men. *Catalyst: A Socialist Journal of the Social Services,* 1978, *1*(3), 6-23.

Wolf, D. G. *The lesbian community.* Berkeley: University of California Press, 1979.

Wolff, P. H. *The developmental psychologies of Jean Piaget and psychoanalysis. Psychological issues monograph 5.* New York: International Universities Press, 1960.

Wolpe, J. *The practice of behavior therapy.* New York: Pergamon, 1969.

Wynn, M. *Fatherless children.* London: Michael Joseph, 1964.

Zucker, R. A., & Manosevitz, M. MMPI patterns of overt male homosexuals: Comment on Dean and Richardson's study. *Journal of Consulting Psychology,* 1966, *30,* 555-557.

NAME INDEX

Acanfora, Joseph, III, 311-313
Adelman, M., 272
Akers, J. S., 202
Allport, Gordon W., 100, 103, 117-118, 130, 354, 369
Alfred, Randy, 53, 348, 361
Amaro, Hortensia, 287, 289
Aquinas, St. Thomas, 198
Arendt, Hannah, 37
Aristotle, 194
Aronson, B. S., 75
Aumiller, Richard, 314-315

Babuscio, J., 276
Baker, Jack, 309, 381
Bailey, D. S., 364
Bancroft, J., 170, 181
Bandura, A., 93
Bane, M. J., 252, 278
Barlow, L. H., 171-172, 181
Barnhart, E., 237, 240, 247
Barratt, B. B., 124, 127, 134
Barton, A. H., 32, 53
Bass-Hass, Rita, 241, 247
Beach, Frank, 24, 300-301
Beck, A. T., 140
Becker, H., 352
Begelman, D. A., 87, 93
Bell, Alan, P., 24, 26, 85, 86, 220, 222-226, 234-236, 243-244, 246-247, 250-251
Bem, Sandra L., 59, 229
Bentham, Jeremy, 379
Berger, Peter L., 299
Bergler, E., 33, 49, 118
Bernard, J., 273
Berzon, Betty, 233
Bieber, Irving, 58, 68-69, 81-82, 92, 108, 118, 128-129, 138, 142
Birk, Lee, 171-172, 181
Bleuel, Hans P., 33, 40, 362
Block, J. H., 229
Boggan, E. Carrington, 25
Bohannan, P., 254
Bonnell, Charles, 24, 193
Boswell, John E., 23, 30, 194, 198, 199, 208, 210, 300, 364
Bozett, F., 276
Braaten, L., 76
Brandwein, R. A., 254
Bremer, J., 170, 181
Brodie, H. K. H., 171-172, 181

Brown, D. G., 228, 282
Brown, Howard, 359
Brown, N. O., 127, 147
Bryant, Anita, 29, 37, 42, 52, 198, 202, 338, 361-363, 367
BSERP, 49
Bullough, Vern L., 206, 220, 300-301
Burdick, J., 64
Burgess, A. W., 302
Burton, Peggy, 305-306
Bush, Larry, 298, 365

Caldwell, M., 242, 247
California Poll, 46, 47
Cameron, P. A., 33, 37, 42, 43, 352
Caprio, Frank S., 118, 250
Cardell, M., 238, 247
Carpenter, Edward, 379, 381
Carrier, Joseph, 30, 300-301
Cass, V. C., 227
Cattell, R. B., 67-68, 77
Cautela, J. R., 82
Chang J., 78
Chevalier-Skolnikoff, Suzanne, 202
Church, F., 365
Churchill, Wainwright, 24, 92, 193, 194, 195, 359
Citizens' Advisory Council on the Status of Women, 252
Clark, Don, 138, 276
Clarke-Stewart, A., 284
Cochran, S. D., 236, 238, 246
Coleman, Eli, 69, 70, 83, 109, 118, 149, 150
Conover, Michael R., 200
Cory, Donald Webster, 250
Cotton, Wayne L., 247
Crile, George, 53
Crompton, Louis, 30

Dagg, A. I., 194
Dahlstrom, W., 75
Dank, Barry M., 152, 221, 227
Darwin, Charles, 183, 190, 194
Daugherty, W. E., 31, 37, 53
Davis, Karen, 360
Davis, Kingsley, 361
Davison, Gerald C., 69, 83, 87, 94, 130
Dawkins, Richard, 194
Dean, Robert, 76
De Cecco, John P., 23, 51-52, 59, 227
Denniston, R. H., 200
Derdeyn, A. P., 270

SUBJECT INDEX

ABOUT THE AUTHORS

Hortensia Amaro received her Ph.D. degree in developmental psychology from the University of California, Los Angeles, where she also received her B.A. and M.A. degrees. She is currently Project Director of the Women and Alcohol Research Project at UCLA. Her thesis topic was on the psychocultural determinants of attitudes toward abortion among Mexican-American women.

Eli Coleman is Clinic Coordinator and Assistant Professor at the Program in Human Sexuality, Department of Family Practice and Community Health, Medical School, University of Minnesota. He is a Licensed Consulting Psychologist, an AASECT certified sex therapist, and member of the editorial board of the *Journal of Homosexuality*. Currently, Dr. Coleman is involved in training mental health professionals in the area of chemical dependency and sexuality.

Gerald C. Davison is Professor of Psychology and Director of Clinical Training at the University of Southern California. From 1966-1979, he was on the psychology faculty at the State University of New York at Stony Brook. Davison has published widely in the general area of behavior therapy and personality, and is co-author of *Clinical Behavior Therapy* (1976) and *Abnormal Psychology: An Experimental Clinical Approach* (Third edition, 1982). He is a Fellow of the American Psychological Association and a past president of the Association for Advancement of Behavior Therapy.

John P. De Cecco, Ph.D., is Professor of Psychology and Human Sexuality and Director of the Center for Research and Education in Sexuality (CERES) at San Francisco State University. Since 1975 he has been editor of the *Journal of Homosexuality*. He has been a member of the American Psychological Association for the last twenty years and of the Society for the Psychological Study of Social Issues for the last ten. He is currently a member of the American College of Sexologists and the International Academy of Sex Researchers. His research interests lie mainly in the normalization of sexuality, theories of sexual identity, and sexual tolerance and discrimination.

John Gagnon is Professor of Sociology and Psychology at the State University of New York at Stony Brook, where he has been on the faculty since 1968. There he has been Director of the University's Centers for Continuing Education and Curriculum Development, as well as teaching and doing research on adolescence, human sexuality, the changing character of the family and gender roles, and the use of simulations to study environmental, medical, and personal decision-making. He is working on a book on changes in the family in the U.S. since World War II, and a volume on the changes in the character of sexual life in the U.S. since the turn of the century.

Nanette K. Gartrell, M.D., is currently Assistant in Psychiatry at the Beth Israel Hospital, and Instructor in Psychiatry, Harvard Medical School, Boston, Massachusetts. She is also Chairperson of the Committee on Women of the American Psychiatric Association.

John C. Gonsiorek is Clinical Assistant Professor in the Department of Psychology and in the Program in Health Care Psychology (School of Public Health) at the University of Minnesota. He is currently in private practice as Director of Psychological Services at Twin Cities Therapy Clinic in Minneapolis. Previously he served as Clinic Director at Walk-In Counseling Center in Minneapolis, and as staff psychologist in the Department of Physical Medicine and Rehabilitation at the University of Minnesota Medical School. He received his Ph.D. in clinical psychology from the University of Minnesota in 1978. He has authored a number of works on homosexuality and other topics. He has served as a review editor for the *Journal of Homosexuality* since 1977, and recently edited *Homosexuality and Psychotherapy: A Practioner's Handbook of Affirmative Models* (Haworth Press, 1982). His other professional interests include diagnostic issues, especially in schizophrenia; community mental health; crisis intervention; professional ethics; and behavioral medicine.

Joel D. Hencken is a psychotherapist in Boston, Massachusetts, and a doctoral candidate in clinical psychology at the University of Michigan. He was Clinical Director of the Homophile Community Health Service (Boston) from 1979 to 1981, and served on the Steering Committee of the Association of Gay Psychologists from 1978 to 1980. Currently, he serves as editor of the *AGP Newsletter* and as a member of the editorial board of the *Journal of Homosexuality.* He is co-author of "Coming Out as an Aspect of Identity Formation" (*Gay Academic Union Journal: Gai Saber,* 1977). The paper upon which the present one is based was the winner of the 1980 Mark Freedman Memorial Award of the Association of Gay Psychologists.

Mary E. Hotvedt, Ph.D., is a medical anthropologist with the Department of Family and Community Medicine, University of Arizona. She has done teaching, research, and counseling in human sexuality. Her work reported in this volume came out of her postdoctoral training with the Department of Psychiatry at SUNY/Stony Brook.

John A. W. Kirsch is Associate Professor in the Department of Biology, and Associate Curator in Mammalogy at the Museum of Comparative Zoology, at Harvard University. He earned his doctorate at the University of Western Australia and subsequently spent two years in Latin America. He has written over 60 scholarly articles and reviews, a significant number of them on the biological aspects of homosexuality. As one of the handful of experts on the evolution and taxonomy of marsupials— an often overlooked group of mammals—he considers his vested interest in sexual freedom as a rather natural extension of a lifelong concern for oppressed mammals generally.

Paul C. Larson, Ph.D., is Senior Psychologist for the Extended Care Program at Dayton Veterans Administration Medical Center, and Clinical Assistant Professor at the School of Professional Psychology, Wright State University, Dayton, Ohio. He obtained his doctorate in 1977 from the University of Utah and wrote his dissertation on the subject of sexual identity and self-concept. He has been active in gay community organizations in Utah and Ohio, and served for two years on the Board of Directors of the Dayton Gay Center.

Ellen Lewin received her doctorate in anthropology from Stanford University. Before beginning research on lesbian mothers, she studied the economic dimensions of the maternal role among Latin American immigrants in San Francisco and collaborated on research concerning the professional lives of nurses. She is currently on the faculty of the Medical Anthropology Program at the University of California, San Francisco, where her teaching and research focus on women in health and healing systems, on women as mothers, and on the health implications of migration.

Terrie A. Lyons, formerly on the research staff at the University of California, San Francisco, is a clinical social worker in private practice in Oakland and San Francisco. She is currently completing her doctoral work in clinical psychology at the Wright Institute. Her interests include the separation-individuation process in nontraditional family forms and the effects of prolonged crisis on service care providers.

Jane Barclay Mandel, Ph.D., is Assistant Professor in the Department of Family Practice at the Medical College of Wisconsin, Milwaukee. She received her graduate and undergraduate education at Northwestern University, Evanston, Illinois. For the past ten years, Dr. Mandel has taught courses in behavioral science and human sexuality for medical students and medical residents. Her research on lesbian mothers and their children has made her a frequent consultant to lawyers and social service groups in determining child custody for lesbian mothers.

William Paul, Ed.D., is a lecturer in psychology at San Francisco State University. He received his doctorate at Harvard, where he served as a teaching fellow. He has also taught at Wellesley and the University of San Francisco. Having studied in Tokyo, he was a member of U.S. International and Olympic Judo teams. With a background in developing and working in community programs for inner city youth, his current interests are in educational responses to violence and intergroup conflict, which reflects his objectives in this volume and the SPSSI Task Force.

Letitia Anne Peplau is Associate Professor of Psychology at the University of California, Los Angeles. She received her doctorate in social psychology from Harvard University in 1973. Her research interests include close relationships, both heterosexual and homosexual, and the psychology of loneliness.

Richard C. Pillard is Associate Professor of Psychiatry at Boston University School of Medicine. He was co-founder of the Homophile Community Health Service in 1971 and served as its medical director. Currently, his principal interest is research in the area of sex and gender. He has also served on the American Psychiatric Association's committee for gay, lesbian, and bisexual issues.

Rhonda Rivera is Professor Law, Ohio State University School of Law, and a practicing attorney for 13 years, admitted in Michigan, Ohio, and the Federal Southern District of Ohio. Her practice areas include domestic relations, including planning for nonmarried cohabiters; her teaching areas include contracts, UCC courses, family law, and privacy. She was the 1979 Chair of Women in Legal Education (AALS), a 1980 Member of the ABA Advisory Committee, Women on Law Faculties Study, a member of the Board of Governors of the Society of American Law Teachers (1976-1979 and 1979-1982), and a participant in the 1979 Project on Humanistic Law Education. She is a member of the NLG, the ACLU, NOW, and WEAL. In 1976, she won the Uppity Woman of the Year award, and in 1977, the Susan B. Anthony award. She is a member of the Board of Directors of the Lambda Legal Defense fund.

James Eric Rodman is Associate Professor in the Department of Biology, Yale University, and is Curator of the Yale Herbarium in the Peabody Museum of Natural History. He received the Ph.D. and M.A. from Harvard University and B.S. from Michigan State University. His research interests include the taxonomy and evolution of plants and the study of chemically mediated plant-insect interactions. He has conducted fieldwork in North, Central, and South America.

David Stivison, a 1979 graduate of Harvard Law School, currently practices law in Columbus, Ohio. He is past chairman of the Committee on Delivery of Legal Services of the Columbus Bar Association and a member of the Board of the Ohio State Legal Services Association. He is a member of the Ohio State and American Bar Associations. Mr. Stivison received a B.S. degree in chemistry and a B.A. in philosophy from Ohio University in 1969. He is a member of Phi Beta Kappa.

David J. Thomas is Associate Professor of Politics and a fellow of Stevenson College, University of California, Santa Cruz. He received his B.A. from Oberlin College and his Ph.D. from Harvard. Most of his work is in the history of political thought. In 1981, he began teaching an annual seminar on gay politics.

James D. Weinrich, Ph.D., A.C.S., is on the faculty of the Department of Psychiatry and Behavioral Sciences at the Johns Hopkins School of Medicine, affiliated with its Psychohormonal Research Unit. He received his degrees from Harvard and Princeton, and has taught on Harvard's full- and part-time faculty. Much of the work he reports in this volume began while he was a junior fellow with the Society of Fellows, Harvard University. His research interests include the evolution of behavior and the application of scientific findings to social debates.